AUSTIN CLARKE
A Critical Introduction

For
John V. Kelleher
an máistir

Maurice Harmon: Publications

Sean O'Faolain; a critical introduction (University of Notre Dame 1967); updated (Wolfhound Press 1985)

Modern Irish Literature 1800-1967. A Reader's Guide (Dolmen Press 1967)

Fenians and Fenianism (Sceptre 1968)

The Celtic Master (Dolmen Press 1969)

The J.M. Synge Centenary Papers 1971 (Dolmen Press 1972)

William Carleton. Traits and Stories of the Irish Peasantry, 4 vols. (Mercier Press 1973)

The Poetry of Thomas Kinsella (Wolfhound Press 1974)

The Irish Novel in Our Time, with Patrick Rafroidi (1976)

Richard Murphy: Poet of Two Traditions (Wolfhound Press 1977)

Select Bibliography for the Study of Anglo-Irish Literature and its Backgrounds. An Irish Studies Handbook (Wolfhound Press 1977)

Irish Poetry after Yeats. Seven Poets (Wolfhound Press 1978)

Image and Illusion. Anglo-Irish Literature and its Contexts (Wolfhound Press 1979)

A Short History of Anglo-Irish Literature from its origins to the present day, with Roger McHugh (Wolfhound Press 1982)

The Irish Writer and the City (Colin Smythe 1984)

James Joyce: the Centennial Symposium, with Morris Beja *et al.* (University of Illinois Press 1986)

Editor: *Irish University Review, a Journal of Irish Studies* (Irish University Press 1970-74; IUR 1975-76; Wolfhound Press 1977-86)

AUSTIN CLARKE
1896 — 1974

A Critical Introduction

Maurice Harmon

BARNES & NOBLE BOOKS
TOTOWA · NEW JERSEY

First published 1989 by
WOLFHOUND PRESS
68 Mountjoy Square, Dublin 1.

First published in the USA 1989 by
BARNES & NOBLE BOOKS
81 Adams Drive, Totowa, New Jersey, 07512

Library of Congress Cataloguing-in-Publication Data
Harmon, Maurice.
    Austin Clarke, 1896-1974 : a critical introduction / Maurice
Harmon
        p.   cm.
    ISBN 0-389-20864-7
    1. Clarke, Austin, 1896-1974 -- Criticism and interpretation.
I. Title.
PR6005.L37Z73   1989
821'.912 -- dc19   88-32766
                                                              CIP

Cover design: Jan de Fouw
Typesetting: Wendy A. Commins.
Make-up: Paul Bray Studio.
Printed and bound by Billings & Sons Ltd., UK.

CONTENTS

Acknowledgements

Acknowledgements and thanks are due to the following publishers who gave me permission to quote from Austin Clarke's work:

Dolmen Press, Dublin for permission to quote from *Collected Poems, Collected Plays, The Impuritans, The Third Kiss, Liberty Lane*, and *The Bright Temptation*.
Allen and Unwin, London, for permission to quote from *The Singing Men at Cashel*.
Andrew Melrose, London, for permission to quote from *The Sun Dances at Easter*.
Williams and Norgate, London, for permission to quote from *First Visit to England and other memories*.
Routledge and Kegan Paul, London, for permission to quote from *Twice Round the Black Church: early memories of Ireland and England* and from *A Penny in the Clouds: more memories of Ireland and England*.

I also wish to thank the publishers who have allowed me to quote from the following works:

Patrick J. Corish, *The Irish Catholic Experience*. Dublin: Gill and Macmillan, Dublin, 1985.
Kathleen Hughes, *The Early Irish Church*. London: Methuen, 1966.
Proinsias MacCana, *Celtic Mythology*. London: Hamlyn, 1970.
Myles Dillon, *The Cycles of the Kings*. Cambridge: Cambridge University Press, 1946.
Francis J. Byrne, *Kings and High Kings*. London: B.T. Batsford, 1973.
James Carney, *Medieval Irish Lyrics*. Dublin: Dolmen, 1967.
T.W. Moody, F.X. Martin, F.J. Byrne, *New History of Ireland*, vol. III. Oxford: Oxford University Press, 1976.
Roger McHugh and Maurice Harmon, *A Short History of Anglo-Irish Literature from its origins to the present day*. Dublin: Wolfhound, 1982.
Katharine Worth, *The Irish Drama of Europe from Yeats to Beckett*. London: Athlone Press, 1978.
J.H. White, *Church and State in Modern Ireland 1923-1979*. 2nd ed. Dublin: Gill and Macmillan, 1980.
Francis MacManus, *The Yeats We Knew*. Cork: Mercier, 1965.
Próinséas Ní Chatháin and Michael Richter, *Irland und Europa. Die Kirche im Frühmittelalter*. Stuttgart: Klett-Cotta, 1984.
E. Allison Peers, *Complete Works of Saint Teresa of Jesus*. London: Sheed and Ward, 1946.
E. Allison Peers, *Complete Works of Saint John of the Cross*. London: Burns, Oates and Washbourne, 1934.
Roger McHugh and Philip Edwards, *Jonathan Swift. A Dublin Tercentenary Tribute, 1667-1967*. Dublin: Dolmen, 1967.
Eleanor Knott, *Irish Syllabic Poetry*. Dublin: Institute for Advanced Studies, 1974.
Eleanor Knott, *Irish Classical Poetry*. Dublin: Sign of the Three Candles, 1957.
Proinsias MacCana, *Literature in Ireland*. Dublin: Department of Foreign Affairs, 1980.

I am particularly grateful to Aidan and Dardis Clarke for kindly allowing me to quote from their father's published and unpublished writings.

Various friends and colleagues have helped me during the long preparation for the book and I acknowledge their help with gratitude, but they must not be held responsible for any errors or misjudgments that may be found in the book: Alan Harrison, Seán Ó Tuama, James Carney, Breandán Ó Buachalla, Dáithí Ó hÓgáin, Proinsias MacCana, Fr John J. Silke, Francis John Byrne, James McGuire, Dennis O'Driscoll, Marianne Mays, Christopher Murray, Robert Welch, Proinséas Ní Chatháin, Tomás Ó Cathasaigh.

I am grateful also to the staff of the National Library of Ireland, of the Royal Irish Academy, of the library at University College, Dublin, of Trinity College Library, and to Harry Ransom of the Humanities Research Centre, University of Texas at Austin for permission to examine and quote from their Austin Clarke manuscripts.

An tráth do mhair Fionn 's an Fhiann,
dob ansa leo sliabh na cill;
ba binn leo-san fuighle lon,
gotha na gclog leo níor bhinn.

Photo: Jack McManus, *The Irish Times*.

Introduction

(i) *Austin Clarke (1896-1974)*

As a child Austin Clarke was held aloft to see Queen Victoria on her last visit to Dublin; as a student at University College, Dublin he witnessed the Easter Rising of 1916; as a young man he went into exile as the Irish Free State emerged from the turbulence of the revolutionary period. When he returned in 1937 to live permanently at Bridge House, Templeogue, the middle-class values that would shape his country for the rest of his life were being enshrined in a new Constitution.

Victorian values together with a conservative Catholicism dominated his lower middle-class home. His mother's stern morality compelled him to weekly confession and communion, but his first confession was traumatic: he was questioned insistently, within the confessional and then inside the vestry, about masturbation, until finally, in fear and bewilderment, he admitted to a sin wholly unknown to him. Thus began his long, unhappy relationship with the Catholic Church. His mother had little sympathy for his religious anxieties which increased during adolescence and he quarrelled with her incessantly. He had throughout his growing years a haunting fear of God's punishment and a disabling sense of his own unworthiness. Religious instruction at Belvedere College did not alleviate his worries, but there were happier experiences: stories told to him by his father and elder sister, visits to the countryside, playing the violin, and some of the more comforting rituals of the Church.

When he entered University College, Dublin, his interest in literature and in the Irish language was deeply stimulated by Douglas Hyde's enthusiasm for the language and for Irish culture and by Thomas Mac-Donagh's personal interest in him. He discovered the world of the Irish Literary Revival and its mythological background, and realised he wanted to be a writer. He graduated with a first class honours BA, went on to take a first class honours MA and was then appointed lecturer in English.

But, if his academic interests were advanced at university, his emotional life became unstable. Through a combination of circumstances — the ongoing struggle between the demands of Catholicism and his own growing independence of mind and spirit, his father's unexpected death, his mother's resistance to his intellectual searches, the excitements of nationalism, his imaginative immersion in Irish mythology, and his frustrated love for Lia Cummins — Clarke experienced a nervous breakdown that required over a year's treatment in St Patrick's hospital. When he emerged he married Lia, but the marriage was brief and unconsummated. He lost his job at the university, was disheartened by AE's dislike of *The Sword of the West* (1921), and left Ireland to earn his living as a book reviewer in London.

His literary career had begun auspiciously. His first publication, *The Vengeance of Fionn* (1917), was generally well received. He met most of the literary figures of the time, often at AE's literary 'evenings', and became friendly with his contemporary, F.R. Higgins. The promise of that first publication was undermined by the loss of control in the next two long narrative poems. When he went into exile the country's future, like his own, seemed bleak. The promise and idealism of the years between 1916 and 1922 were shattered in the bitterness and division of civil war. Clarke supported the Republican cause, but the Republicans suffered defeat and in the years immediately after the civil war the new Free State Government dealt firmly with extremists. Gradually, as peace was restored and, aided by the Government's policy of encouraging native industry, a new, native middle-class began to emerge. Its values were evident in a narrow-minded policy of literary censorship. Clarke's first two novels, or prose romances, *The Bright Temptation* (1932) and *The Singing Men at Cashel* (1936), were banned. Ironically, they had been vetted under the obscenity laws in England and were found not to infringe them. Almost all of Clarke's early work was written in England, the poetry from *The Cattledrive in Connaught* (1925) to *Pilgrimage* (1929), the early plays, and the first two novels.

There can be little doubt that his years of exile were difficult in emotional and financial terms. He felt cut off from his natural sources of inspiration in Ireland. He returned frequently, to see his mother and sisters, to meet with literary friends, like F.R. Higgins, Seamus O'Sullivan, and Padraic Fallon, to attend meetings of the Irish Academy of Letters, to visit places of historical and cultural interest in the countryside, to go to the Abbey theatre. On one of these visits he had the good fortune to meet Nora Walker who agreed to share his life in England.

She was an intelligent, good-humoured, and resilient woman who gave him the love and stability he needed. He needed her support when he found himself omitted from W.B. Yeats's anthology, the *Oxford Book of Modern Verse* (1936) and when his ambitious and highly personal work, *The Singing Men at Cashel* (1936) fell apart in the final chapters. The publication of his first *Collected Poems* in the same year helped to restore his confidence. But life in England became increasingly unsatisfactory, particularly with the signs of the coming war.

But, if life in England was difficult, the years after he and Nora returned to Ireland were even worse. They had three small sons to support, were very short of money, and Clarke, who was prone to recurrent depression, had another breakdown. The war cut off his sources of income from book reviewing in England. With the help of friends he got a regular poetry programme on Irish radio and regular book reviewing with the *Irish Times*. But his work suffered. After the agonised poetry of *Night and Morning* (1938), in which he confronted the issue of intellectual freedom and clerical authority, he wrote no poetry until the Fifties. Together with the poet, Robert Farren, he founded the Lyric Theatre Company in 1944 and for the next seven years they put on verse plays at the Abbey Theatre. Their aim was to continue the tradition of poetic theatre begun by Yeats, but their work met with only moderate success.

When Austin Clarke began to write poetry again in the fifties he emerged as a different kind of poet: he wrote satirical comments on contemporary issues and autobiographical reflections. *Later Poems* (1961) brought him a wider and more appreciative audience than he had previously had. The strength and vivacity of the later poetry is all the more remarkable when one remembers that he suffered a severe heart-attack in 1956 and a slight one in 1958. As he grew older his mood lightened, his comic imagination, much in evidence in some earlier lyrics and plays, reasserted itself. He detached himself from the obsession with the problems of the Catholic conscience and wrote freely and with delight about many topics and in a variety of styles. He confronted and exorcised the trauma of mental breakdown in *Mnemosyne Lay in Dust*, published on his seventieth birthday in 1966. He and Nora were familiar figures in Dublin, notably at the various events during the commemorations for Jonathan Swift in 1967 and for J.M. Synge in 1971. Clarke was invited back to University College, Dublin by Roger McHugh to give a series of lectures. He received an honorary D Litt from Trinity College. He received a number of literary awards and was able to travel again to the continent, to England, and to America. In 1974 his second *Collected Poems* appeared and for the first time critics could assess the full range of his development as a poet. The special issue of the *Irish University*

Review, which indicated how significant his work had become, appeared just after his death. When the editor took a copy to Nora at Bridge House, the birds were singing in the tall trees, the river Dodder sparkled under the stone arches of the bridge, but the kingfisher was nowhere to be seen.

(ii) *Contexts*

Austin Clarke was born in 1896, five years after the death of Charles Stewart Parnell and at the beginning of a period of many changes in Irish life. In the thirty years after Parnell's death the country experienced many political, social and cultural changes, as it passed from colonialism to independence. In the years immediately after his death there was political division, when the unity of national purpose that he had held together weakened. Young people, who might have gone into politics, found other interests, such as the creation of a national literature, the recovery of the Irish language, and the playing of national games. Writers, like W.B. Yeats, Lady Gregory, Douglas Hyde, George Russell, and George Moore, were essentially non-political. Their energies and enthusiasm led to the creation of what was variously known as the Irish Literary Revival, the Irish Renaissance, or the Celtic Renaissance. It was a form of cultural nationalism that revived early and medieval Irish literature and mythology and built consciously on the work of scholarly predecessors in the nineteenth century. Those scholars had collected, edited, translated, and published what one might loosely call the matter of Ireland, that is, the country's heritage of legend, saga, poetry, history, and folklore. At the same time the Gaelic League, founded in 1893, wanted to restore Irish as the spoken language of the country. Douglas Hyde, one of its founders, sought, as he said, to de-Anglicise Ireland by refusing to imitate the English in their language, literature, and games. The Gaelic League was a powerful and widespread movement that attracted many followers in the younger generation; its impact lasted well into the next century, until the imposition of compulsory Irish in the educational system and its requirement as a qualification for a variety of jobs debased it. Between them, the Irish Literary Revival, the Gaelic League, and the Gaelic Athletic Association, whose members played only Irish games, advanced the idea of Ireland's recognition as a separate political and cultural entity. If the country could demonstrate its cultural identity, then it might also claim a distinctive political identity.

But more politically explicit groups also emerged, separatists like Sinn Fein and the Irish Republican Brotherhood, the former seeking by passive resistance to establish a dual monarchy; the latter seeking by armed insurrection to establish an Irish Republic. The IRB became increasingly active, attracting a large following, including some, like Padraic Pearse and Thomas MacDonagh, who were active in the Gaelic League and were teachers and poets. At the same time a smaller group of socialists, led by Jim Larkin and James Connolly, who organised the Irish Transport and General Workers Union, planned to bring about urban social revolution. Dublin had one of the worst slums in Europe in the first decade of the new century; its workers were badly paid, its death-rate higher than in any other city in Europe. Confrontation between the workers and a federation of employers took place in 1913; the strike was bitter and prolonged. The Irish Citizen Army, which was formed to protect the strikers, continued in existence after the strike was over and participated in the Easter Rising of 1916.

The Tramway Strike strengthened the feeling of revolution that was gathering. In a general and dynamic way all the movements of the time, the literary movement, the Gaelic League, the GAA, Sinn Fein, the IRB, the socialists, and other cultural nationalist groups, created a momentum that led to the Rising. The Rising itself was not popular, but the execution of its leaders, including Padraic Pearse, Thomas MacDonagh, and Joseph Mary Plunkett, stirred the people to indignation, to the kind of defiance and self-assertion that had characterised Sinn Fein. The Anglo-Irish War of 1919-21, a guerilla war, made relations between Ireland and England even more bitter. The Anglo-Irish Treaty that ended hostilities gave dominion status to the twenty-six counties of the Irish Free State. That achievement was tarnished by the brief, but divisive and disillusioning Civil War of 1922-23. This was a conflict between separatists who wanted the reality of independence and the freedom to achieve freedom and those who wanted nothing less than a full republic, in which Government deputies would not have to sign an oath of allegiance to the British Crown. The republicans were demoralised and defeated. Their political leader, Eamon de Valera, and the party which he formed, Fianna Fail, remained outside the Irish parliament until 1927, refusing to recognise its legitimacy. In 1932 Fianna Fail, with the support of the labour party, entered the Dáil, as the parliament was called, and modern Irish politics began. The first Free State government handed over office to those who had challenged the very existence of the Free State. The reverberations of the old struggle continued with the sporadic violence of the IRA but the most important development in the post-revolutionary period was the growing strength of the middle class.

Out of the disruptions of revolution had come a new society made up of a native, Catholic bourgeois class which was of predominantly peasant stock. The Catholic Church, by virtue of the fact that over ninety per cent of the southern population was Catholic, had consolidated its influence. Politically the country became isolationist and chauvinistic, seeking to protect the people in economic, intellectual and cultural terms. It supported literature and publications in the Irish language, but was suspicious of writers, particularly those writing in English, who were critical of the new society or offended its moral values. Literary censorship in 1929 restricted freedom of expression and was carried to extremes. All of Austin Clarke's fiction was banned. The Constitution of 1937 which was permeated with Catholic moral and social teaching, was characterised by a cautious qualification of virtually every freedom it granted. It mirrored the bourgeois mind of the new Ireland. In the end nationalist Ireland found its identity not in its new literature in English, nor in the Irish language, but in Catholicism. The Irish Free State embodied a conservative Catholic ethos that remained in existence at least until the time of the Second Vatican Council (1962-65).

Given such development it is hardly surprising that Irish writers lived for long periods, or permanently, outside the country, and that, if they stayed at home, experienced a sense of alienation and isolation. At the same time there were writers like Austin Clarke who were politically and socially responsive. He was sensitive to the condition of those who suffered for their political views, or from the restrictions of a middle-class society in which the socialist ideals of Connolly had little impact, or in which the religion of the majority did not always live up to the demands of charity.

The emergence of modern Ireland as a Catholic country is the result of centuries of development, whose origins lie partly in the Tridentine Reforms and more immediately in changes brought about in the organisation of the Church during the nineteenth century. After the Council of Trent religious life was founded on the catechism of the Counter-Reformation which emphasised obedience to the authority of the Church, regular sacramental practice, in particular attendance at Mass on Sundays, and a regular round of prayers and devotions, among which those to the Virgin Mary were of especial importance. In the nineteenth century as church building improved, sacraments were transferred from homes to the churches which thereby became more central to the lives of the people. Attendance at Mass increased, as did the number of Masses and the number of clergy. New devotions sprang up, such as benediction, the forty hours, the nine Fridays; devotion to the Sacred Heart spread, the cult of the Blessed Virgin increased. The parish mission, often prolonged and intensive, left behind further institutions to foster personal spirituality: 'the Sodalities of the Scapular, of the Living Rosary, of the Sacred Heart, the Confraternity of Christian Doctrine, and the Society of Vincent De Paul'.[1] Religious instruction in the National Schools became denominational.

The clergy were responsible for this devotional revolution. They were noted for their strong, childlike faith, not for their intellectual breadth. They based their sermons on the *Catechism of the Council of Trent* (1566) which in practice advocated loyalty to the Church, attendance at Mass, and devotion to Mary. John Hagan's *Compendium of Catechetical Instruction* (1911), the preacher's standby, was based on the Trent catechism. As Patrick Corish has observed in *The Irish Catholic Experience*, the sermon like the catechism 'may not have avoided the danger of a certain dichotomy between knowing the faith and living it'.[2] Seeking to explain the intellectual underpinning of traditional Irish Catholicism, he arrived at this conclusion:

> The catechetical programme of Hagan's *Compendium* set out a system of belief, based, as belief must be based, on the creeds of the church. Catholic theology was then in a defensive mood, and at times it may have suggested, and doubtless at times it did suggest, that the answer was clearer than any informed believer had any right to expect; but for the relatively uninformed believer it was clear and it was a system, and despite defects much of the central theological tradition came through. And as well as presenting a system of truths to be believed, the catechetical tradition presented clearly a set of duties to be carried out. The moral theology this rested on was based on casuistry . . . in practice moral theology was tempted towards an over-categorisation of offences, in turn tempting the less finely tuned mind to pose the moral questions in terms of 'How far can you go?' . . .[3]

Post-revolutionary Ireland was also a society which was taught a fixed system of beliefs and a definite round of religious practices. Because of the greatly increased power and influence of the Church after independence the devotional revolution continued, with an ever-widening network of Confraternities, Sodalities, devotions to the Mother of God under a variety of titles, devotions to particular saints, innumerable Catholic societies, novenas, pilgrimages, flights to Lourdes and Fatima, the erection of statues throughout the state. The Catholic Truth Society continued to produce inexpensive pamphlets for popular consumption and a number of pious magazines became widely available. The genuine theological content of all of this was mediocre, the intellectual content even worse. The Catholic Church continued to rely on controlling the laity, on discouraging intellectual debate, on protecting the people from ideas or experiences considered dangerous to their faith. Seán O'Faolain summed up the consequences in the course of a comment on the Mother and Child Scheme in 1951. 'If you shatter a man's pride — by, for example, shattering his belief that he is worthy of trust — you shatter his personality as a Christian: for as a Christian he is a whole man or he is nothing. If people are treated as children, and all that is asked of them is that they go here, go there, do this, do that, and are never left to *act* as whole Christians, why, then, you are left with children and childish morale.'[4]

These then were the major changes in Irish life during the thirty years after the death of Parnell and into the post-revolutionary period. Austin Clarke was not affected equally by all of them, but he was aware of them, all appear in his writings, all helped to shape his imagination and to determine his responses. Three are of particular significance: Catholicism, the Irish Literary Revival, and the society, already described, to which he returned in 1937, the year of the Constitution.

(iii) *Catholicism*

It is quite clear from Austin Clarke's autobiographical writings that he was affected by the post-Tridentine reforms. He was born into a family that combined the narrow conformity of Irish Catholicism with the repressive respectability of late Victorianism. His parents insisted on attendance at Sunday Mass, weekly confession and communion, and he was sent to Catholic schools, including Belvedere College where he had the same annual retreats and the same hell-fire sermons that James Joyce describes in *Portrait of the Artist as a Young Man*. Despite having given birth to twelve children his mother avoided references to physical functions, including those alluded to in prayers. Her moral delicacy communicated itself to her son who would react in shock to the grosser language of scriptural texts or to the sight of nakedness, and preferred euphemisms to plain speech in describing the more intimate anatomical areas or functions. The God of Irish Catholicism was as judgmental and terrifying as the biblical God who sent fires from Heaven on false altars. Throughout Clarke's writing the Catholic religion is associated with fear and darkness, with restriction and confinement.

As a child he found relief in visits to and holidays in the countryside. The catechism he declared later meant home and Dublin, rules and regulations.[5] The country meant freedom, discovery, storyland, adventure, although it could also be a place of deception and danger, where things were not what they seemed.[6] Of course, religion was not exclusively threatening. He enjoyed the various ceremonies and rituals of the Church. But his childish innocence was seriously disturbed by an experience to which he often returns in his writings: being questioned persistently during his first confession, in the confessional and in the vestry, about the sin of masturbation of which he had no understanding but to which, in fear and desperation, he finally admitted.

The same pattern of happy absorption in Church devotions and in sentimental religiosity together with an intense anxiety about personal unworthiness is visible in his adolescent years. He and his sisters liked to perform the ritual of visits to seven churches on Holy Thursday. His sister, Eileen, who became a nun, was a model of piety, and Clarke imitated her in her devotions.

> She read holy books before she went to sleep at night, and walked with downcast eyes through the streets, avoiding the shop windows, fingering the rosary beads in her coat-pocket. The Nine Fridays had now a special significance for her. She undertook new novenas and when the Thirty Days' Prayer was over, she began it all over again. Every new aspiration, every indulgence of which she heard, whether attached to some special devotion or gained by visiting a shrine, whether symbolized by medal or scapular, drew her. I, too, had already felt the mysterious power of those scapulars which we wore, the brown scapular of St. Francis, the red, the white, the black one for the dead, the blue for the Blessed Virgin.[7]

But his sense of sin and degradation, associated with sexuality and the physical changes of adolescence was very real. He was assailed by self-doubt as he became convinced that all his confessions were bad. He was driven into a state of unending casuistical debate within his own mind as he tried to relate his failures to remain free from sexual sins with the rules and regulations of his Church. Compulsory confession became a weekly ordeal as priests questioned him about sexual sins, warned him against them, and as the physical and emotional changes of adolescence made permanent freedom from some form of sexual failing, in thought or in deed, unavoidable; his sense of personal immorality increased. Books helped him to find a measure of independence: Arnold's *Literature and Dogma*, Renan's *Life of Jesus*, the works of Francis Newman and of Nietzsche, all writers who emphasised the importance of rational inquiry and were slow to accept orthodox views. Clarke rebelled comprehensively against the morality of his home and of his Church and tried in his writings to find imaginative forms in which to investigate and to understand the nature and the effects of this morality.

There is a clear progression from the rebellious figures of early plays, Anier in *The Son of Learning*, Attracta in *The Flame*, Sister Eucharia in the play of that title, to the examination of those made miserable by the demands of casuistical thought — Gormlai in *The Singing Men at Cashel* is the main example — to the confessional poetry of *Night and Morning*, in which the poet's own anguished response to the conflicting demands of belief and intellectual inquiry are made clear. *Night and Morning* is the turning point. Thereafter, with renewed lightness of spirit, Clarke finds release for his comic imagination in a succession of plays that touch lightly on moral matters and in his last novel, *The Sun Dances at Easter*. When he returned to poetry in 1955 the issue of the individual versus Catholicism was a central concern. The poetry moves from the commemoration of an escape from the confinements of Irish Catholicism in 'Ancient Lights' (1955) to the celebration of pagan sensuality in 'The Healing of Mis' (1970). The two Martha Blake poems exemplify the progression, the first, published in 1937, notes her happy communion with her Church, the other, published in 1963, reveals the superficiality of a life in which the religiously holy and the morally good are thought to be aspects of the same christian ideal. Since Martha Blake represents an ideal in modern Ireland, the poem is highly effective in its exposure.

(iv) *The Irish Literary Revival*

Clarke's interest in the Irish Literary Revival developed strongly at University College, Dublin, where he read the poetry of W.B. Yeats, Douglas Hyde's *Love Songs of Connacht*, and works by AE and George Moore. He went regularly to the Abbey Theatre, where he saw many of Yeats's plays and the work of other dramatists. He attended Thomas MacDonagh's lectures, subsequently published as *Literature in Ireland: Studies Irish and Anglo-Irish* (1916), met F.R. Higgins with whom he discussed poetry, including the *Love Songs of Connacht*, and began to write and, with the help of Stephen McKenna, to publish his own poetry. When *The Vengeance of Fionn* appeared in 1917, he was regarded as a significant new voice in Irish poetry and began to meet many of the literary figures associated with the Revival.

Initially he was puzzled by the poetry of the Revival. 'When I first discovered for myself the Celtic Twilight,' he recalled in 1935, 'and read the earlier poems of Yeats and others, all was entirely incomprehensible to me. I groped through lines where every accent seemed to be in the wrong place'.[8] But when he became better acquainted with English poetry, he was pleased 'to escape from the mighty law and order of English poetry into that shadowy, irresponsible world of delicate rhythm and nuance'.[9] Admiring the subtle rhythms of the Revival poetry he began to imitate its 'shadowy world of subdued speech and nuance'[10] to which AE had introduced him, advising him also to study William Larminie's use of assonance. The results are visible in some of the more musical passages of *The Vengeance of Fionn* and in the short poems of the 1916-25 period. There is a marked difference between their style and the more traditional English style of lyrics published in *New Ireland* in July and August, 1916, but not included in any collections. At the same time the melancholy mood and abstract manner of Yeats's early poetry, while expressing what Clarke called a subtle range of consciousness, was not well suited to the subject matter that Clarke explored and found in the work of his contemporaries: the wilder, more colourful life of the Irish west.

It was AE's reading of passages from Standish O'Grady's *History of Ireland* (1878 and 1880) and from his *Flight of the Eagle* (1899) that opened Clarke's eyes to O'Grady's 'power to stimulate the imagination in his descriptions of the annals and sagas'.[11] What particularly pleased Clarke in the *Flight of the Eagle* was the chapter, 'Through the Mountain Gates of Ulster', where Red Hugh O'Donnell 'sees all the heroic and mythological past in visions'.[12] The scene and the response are characteristic of what Clarke admired and imitated.

> Here lived and reigned Fuad, the far-off Milesian druid-king, till his glory faded, as all things will. The mountain was Cuculain's sign-post, when, as a little boy driven forth by the war spirits, he secretly left his home and his dear mother, seeking Emain Macha. Here the sentinels of the Red Branch from their white watch-tower, Carn Fion, scanned after the mearings of Ulster. Here Ossian's sire slew the enchanter Almain, son of Midna, who once every year, to the sound of unearthly music, consumed Tara with magic flames. On this mountain Cuculain seized the wild fairy steed, the Liath Macha, new risen from the Grey Lake, ere steed and hero in their giant wrestlings and reelings encompassed Banba, and in the quaking night the nations trembled. Here, steeped in Lough Liath's waters, Finn's golden tresses took on the hue and glitter of radiant snow. From the spilled goblet of the god sprang the hazels, whose magic clusters might assuage that hunger of the spirit which knows no other assuagement. The Faed Fia was shed around them. Here shined and trembled the wisp of druid grasses, from whose whisperings with the dawn-wind pure ears might learn

the secrets of life and death. Here beneath those hazels, their immortal green and their scarlet clusters, sprang the well of the waters of all wisdom. Three dreadful queens guarded it. Sometimes they smile seeing afar some youth wandering unconsoled o'erladen with the burthen of his thoughts, rapt with visions, tormented by the gods, a stranger in his own household, scorned by those whom he cannot scorn, outcast from the wholesome cheerful life of men.[13]

Clarke enjoys the imaginative intensity of this passage, its concentration of a vast amount of resonant material, from mythology, the Ulster cycle, and the Fenian cycle, into one ecstatic vision. O'Donnell's heightened awareness of the past is a feeling of union and communion by which he gains strength. In classical mythology the hero descends into the Underworld to find renewal so that he can fulfil his destiny. Here O'Donnell's return to his kingdom is sanctioned by a confirming vision of the mythological, heroic and romantic past. Here, the guardians of the well smile as they see him approach, because, as in a story connected with Nial of the Nine Hostages, and others, they are the triple goddesses of sovereignty who will confirm and legitimise his right to rule.

'In those early and enthusiastic days,' Clarke wrote later, 'Irish poets seemed to enjoy continuous visions of a land populated exclusively with mythological beings'.[14] They were, he observed, not exploring a borrowed mythology, as English poets were, but one which belonged to their country, survived in its oral tradition, and in the very names of its hills, rivers and plains. 'Keats went to Lemprière's *Classical Dictionary*; our poets went out of doors'.[15] His assessment of the effect on him of AE's reading is decisive: 'As I heard for the first time that Homeric roll-call of names, so long forgotten and lost in total obscurity, I was aware for the first time of an older religion than the one I had known from childhood'.[16] Before long he too would write of similar visionary experience, will describe Cuchullin wrestling with the elemental horses, will delight in the imaginative possibilities of journeys through the *fáeth fíada* into the Otherworld, will refer to the pool of wisdom and the myth of the sovereignty goddess. The Irish past becomes an obsession, an alternative religion to the restrictive religion he knew from childhood, a world to be explored, savoured, and recreated.

 . . . The discovery of our own mythology and epic stories by the poets of the Irish Literary Revival excited my imagination and I cycled with delight to many places associated with legend and enchantments — from the Glen of the Madmen in County Kerry to the Twelve Pins of Connemara and the Poisoned Glen in Donegal.

The armies of Queen Maeve on the march, the defence of Ulster by Cuchullain — all these stories from the Tain obsessed me. . . . . Equally fascinating were the tales of Fionn and his Fianna, hunting wild boar and deer through the great Munster Forest, . . . Moreover, there were the Songs and Lamentations of Oisin and his Colloquy with St. Patrick on his return, after three centuries, in Tir na nOg. These pagan figures of my childhood, and the Celtic religion, had the appeal of a lost cause. I had become aware also of that invisible Ireland into which one might at any moment step. A few minutes there could be counted as a year here and the centuries passed there as quickly. So we have the story of Oisin, who was brought by Niamh across the ocean to the Land of the Ever Young. . . .[17]

The Irish Literary Revival seized hold of Clarke's imagination and he revelled in the unimpeded perspectives of Irish mythology and story that it offered: the robustness of action and language, the romantic defiance of time, place and conventions, the magical ability to exist within both the visible and the invisible worlds. Curtailed and inhibited by Dublin, home and the catechism, he found release in the romance of landscape and of early Irish literature. 'Far and wide I wandered on to upper glens of rock and water, dreaming of the Age of Epic.'[18]

(v) *The Gaelic League*

Clarke's response to the Gaelic League was closely associated with his response to the literature of the Irish Literary Revival. He studied Irish at Belvedere College and at university, where he was instructed by Douglas Hyde, Thomas MacDonagh and George Sigerson. Hyde spoke inspiringly about the aims and ideals of the Revival. In his *Love Songs of Connacht* (1893) Clarke encountered a remarkable collection of folk poetry and song together with translations in verse and an idiomatic prose version that recaptured the simplicity, intensity and concreteness of the originals. MacDonagh laid particular stress on what he called the 'Irish Mode' in poetry, that is, the tendency to ignore strong stresses in a line of poetry, giving fairly even pronunciation to all its syllables. He argued that the Irish Mode is based on the use of assonance and internal rhyme in Gaelic prosody and spoke of the conversational tone of modern Irish poetry, what he called its 'grace of the wandering, lingering, musical voice'.[19] Sigerson's translations in *Bards of the Gael and Gall* (1897) were less effective than Hyde's; he spoiled some good attempts to write syllabic verse in the Irish manner by using a stilted English. Nevertheless, the book provides samples of Irish poetry from the early period to the eighteenth century. Its spirit may be detected in its challenging introductory sentence: 'May not a buried literature have claims upon our attention?'.[20] He compared the ingenuity that the Irish displayed in their gold and silver ornaments and the grace of form and exquisite taste of the *Book of Kells* with the 'ingenuity, grace, artistic power, delicacy, and taste' of their poetry.[21] He argued, too, as Clarke would also, that Irish poetry is not romantic but classical, not subjective but objective and restrained. 'Those who are wont to associate Irish poetry with effusiveness of thought and luxuriance of language will be surprised to find that bardic poetry was characterised by classic reserve in thought, form, and expression'.[22] Clarke's conversations with AE, Sigerson, Hyde, F.R. Higgins, and his later reading of Daniel Corkery's *Hidden Ireland* (1925), a study of Munster Gaelic poets of the eighteenth century, encouraged him to imitate the patterns of Gaelic assonance in his own poetry. It is an important issue to which he often returned.

The first extended statement about assonance comes in a note to *Pilgrimage* (1929).

> Assonance, more elaborate in Gaelic than in Spanish poetry, takes the clapper from the bell of rhyme. In simple patterns, the tonic word at the end of a line is supported by a vowel-rhyme in the middle of the next line . . .

> The natural lack of double rhymes in English leads to an avoidance of words of more than one syllable at the end of the lyric line, except in blank alternation with rhyme. A movement constant in Continental languages is absent. But by cross-rhymes or vowel-rhyming, separately, one or more of the syllables of longer words, on or off accent, the difficulty may be turned: lovely and neglected words are advanced to the tonic place and divide their echoes.[23]

His next extended statement came in 'Irish Poetry Today' (1935) where he points out that style or technique should be inseparable from the poet's own voice. Assonance, he said, should not be the enemy of rhyme.

> It helps us respect rhyme, which has been spoiled by mechanical use. By means of assonance we can gradually approach, lead up to rhyme, bring it out so clearly, so truly as the mood needs, that it becomes indeed the very *vox caelistis.*[24]

This is followed a year later by a note in *Collected Poems* (1936) which repeats the note from *Pilgrimage*, but with some changes and with examples:

> Assonance is more elaborate in Gaelic than in Spanish. In the simplest forms the tonic word at the end of the line is supported by an assonance in the middle of the next line. The use of internal pattern of assonance in English, though more limited in its possible range, changes the pivotal movement of the lyric stanza. In some forms of the early syllabic Gaelic metres only one part of a double syllable word is used in assonance, a system also found in the Spanish ballad metres, and this can be a guide to experiment in partial rhyming or assonance and muting. For example, rhyme or assonance on or off accent, stopped rhyme (e.g. *win*dow:thin; horn:*mor*ning), harmonic rhyme (e.g. hero:wind*ow*), cross-rhyme, in which the separate syllables are in assonance or rhyme. The use, therefore of polysyllabic words at the end of the lyric line makes capable a movement common in continental languages such as Italian or Spanish. These experiments were originally suggested by the submerged rhyme of Paul Fort and an early poem, *The Music-Healers*, is given as an example.[25]

Clarke had met Paul Fort in Paris. His poetry has a quiet assonantal music that Clarke liked; it is characterised by full rhyme, half rhyme, alliteration, assonance and the ability to interweave sound and theme in a long, slow-moving line. Apollinaire remarked: 'Paul Fort compose uniquement pour l'oreille'.[26]

In *Poetry in Modern Ireland* (1951) Clarke briefly reiterates what he had written in 1935 and 1936 and offers his poem, 'The Scholar' as an example.[27] The metre in the original is loose, since the only rules observed are seven syllables in each line and the rhyming disyllable at the end of the 2nd and 4th lines of each quatrain. The first two stanzas read as follows:

> Aoibhinn beatha an sgoláire
> bhíos ag déanamh a leighinn;
> is follas díbh, a dhaoine,
> gurab dó is aoibhne i nÉirinn.
>
> Gan smach ríogh ná rófhlatha
> ná tighearna dá threise;
> gan chuid cíosa ag caibidil,
> gan moichéirghe, gan meirse.

Clarke's translation, or 'free paraphrase' as he calls it[28] is as follows:

> Summer delights the scholar
> With knowledge and reason.
> Who is happy in hedgerow
> Or meadow as he is?
>
> Paying no dues to the parish,
> He argues in logic
> And has no care of cattle
> But a satchel and stick.

An idea of Clarke's freedom of paraphrase may be gained from comparing his poem with Kenneth Jackson's literal translation:

> The student's life is pleasant, carrying on his studies; it is plain to you, my friends, his is the most pleasant in Ireland.
>
> No king nor great prince nor landlord, however strong, coerces him; no taxes to the Chapter, no fines, no early rising.[29]

In the original poem one may notice that in addition to the seven syllables per line and the double-syllable rhymes on 'leighinn' and 'Éirinn' and 'threise' and 'meirse' there is considerable use of alliteration and assonance. There are the 'r' and 'c' initial letters in the second stanza, the rhymes of 'déanamh' and 'leighinn' and of 'dhaoine' and 'aoibhne' in the first stanza and similar rhymes in the second. The syllabic count in Clarke's poem is fairly regular throughout (7676). The end rhymes are not strictly maintained: in stanza one, lines two and four do not rhyme but they do in stanza two. In stanza one 'scholar' and 'reason' rhyme on and off the accented syllable and 'hedgerow' rhymes with them on its unaccented syllable and at the same time echoes back to 'knowledge' in the preceding line. Internal rhyme, or assonance, is freely used but Clarke is careful not to allow the pattern to get out of hand. In stanza one there is 'scholar' and 'knowledge', 'hedgerow' and 'meadow'. In stanza two the end-rhymes are clear, with the rhyme between 'logic' and 'stick' on and off the accent. Again the assonance is carefully worked out, the end word in one line rhyming with a middle word in the next, as in Irish prosody. In both stanzas there are examples of alliteration. Clarke has appropriated the disciplined conventions of the original and worked effectively with them. In admiration of his success in *Pilgrimage*, Padraic Colum wrote: he 'has brought into English verse a more deliberately-used and subtle assonance than has been in it hitherto . . . some of the effect of the woven vowel-sounds that are in Gaelic verse'.[30]

In his comments on Irish prosody Clarke focuses on assonantal rhyme, that is, on rhyme between a concluding syllable, the final or the penultimate syllable in a line, and a corresponding vowel sound within the following line. In practice, he imitates the larger assonantal patterns of Irish poetry by writing a number of recurrent vowel sounds within a line or within a stanza. The prosody of Irish poetry is more complicated and more varied than his descriptions indicate, involving recurrence of both consonants and vowels and a great number of metrical forms. Early Irish poetry is divided into quatrains whose lines are based on a syllable count, usually of seven or eight syllables, and rhyme is used. But, as James Carney has observed in *Medieval Irish Lyrics* (1967), what in English would be regarded as full rhyme, in Irish would often be felt to be a breach of good style.

> In Irish rhyme, the vowels generally speaking must be identical, and the rhyming consonants must be of the same quality, that is broad or slender. Furthermore, the Irish divided the consonants into six classes, and consonants, when simple, rhyme only with others from the same class.[31]

A consonant is broad when preceded by the vowels, a, o, or u and slender, when preceded by e, or i. Eleanor Knott in *Irish Syllabic Poetry* (1972) defines syllabic poetry as 'that species of versification which is characterised by regularity in the number and distribution of syllables in the stanza'.

> There is no regularity of stress, in fact, regularity of stress was probably considered as a thing to be deliberately avoided. . . . The line must consist of a certain number of syllables, and end on a stressed word of a certain syllabic length, and it is primarily by the number of syllables in the line, and by the syllabic length of the final word, that a metre is distinguished.[32]

Clarke's discussion of Irish rhyme is incomplete and he does not consider the variety of metrical forms. Rhyme in Irish may be between words at the end of lines, as in English; it may be internal, when a word or words within one line of a couplet rhymes with a word or words in the next; there may be *aicill*, or rhyme between the final word of the first line of a couplet and a word in the interior of the next, or as Clarke calls it, assonantal rhyme. Assonance, or *amus*, is simply a correspondence of vowel sounds; the consonants need not agree, and the assonating words may be of different syllabic lengths. Consonance, or *uaithne*, takes place when all the corresponding vowels are of the same quantity, when the corresponding consonants or consonant groups are of the same class, and when the final consonants are of the same class and quality.

Alliteration, or *uaim*, occurs between stressed words beginning with the same consonant or vowel.

Clarke's imitation of Irish poetry was confined to the use of assonantal patterns; the more complex groupings of consonants could not be repeated in English. In fact it is impossible to reproduce the intricacies of the sound patterns of Irish poetry in English. The main examples of his assonantal poetry are found in the poems in 'The Land of Two Mists' section of *The Cattledrive in Connaught* and in *Pilgrimage*, although he experimented with assonance from the beginning. The 'Music Healers', which he mentions, is part of the *Sword of the West*. There is a danger in imitating the larger assonantal patterns of Irish poetry, that is, in concentrating on recurrent vowel sounds, that the poetry may become monotonous or develop a jog-trot rhythm. Clarke, however, is skilful in his handling of sound and stress; he wants to modulate rhyme, to rhyme on and off the accent, as Irish poetry does, and to advance forgotten words to greater importance. His aim, in short, is not to achieve fuller rhyme or more audible stress but to reduce their effects and in this respect he imitates Irish poetry to good effect. For, as Eleanor Knott has pointed out in *Irish Classical Poetry*, Irish poetry is above all musical; it is composed for the ear, and at all periods of its history has been associated with music, the word-music of its own characteristic form and the music of an accompanying instrument.

> This delight in the music of words is what gives Irish poetry its especial aesthetic character. The balance between delight for the ear and satisfaction for the mind may in many official compositions appear to be unevenly held, but we must accept the fact that aural enjoyment was, though not the whole, an integral part of every poem. Each stanza is an aural design.[33]

The same could be said about a number of Clarke's poems; but the danger attached to achieving a mosaic of sound is that it may be deficient in sense.

Austin Clarke also imitated the accentual poetry of the seventeenth and eighteenth centuries. The sense of personal isolation and of national loss that the poets of this period often expressed sometimes suited his own feelings in post-revolutionary Ireland. He admired the devil-may-care outlook of the poets of the period, such as Eoghan Ruadh Ó Súilleabháin (1748-1784) and Brian Merriman (1749?-1803). In the *amhrán* metres of this poetry the natural stress becomes prominent and the metrical line is not confined to a strict syllabic count. Clarke's poem, 'The Straying Student', is representative of the longer line and of the assonantal pattern:

On a holy day when sails were blowing southward
A bishop sang the Mass at Inishmore

The recurrence of vowel sounds is clear: 'holy' and 'blowing', 'day' and 'sails' in line 1, 'bishop' and 'Inishmore', 'sang' and 'Mass' in line 2. He imitated or responded to various forms of modern Irish poetry, the *aisling*, eighteenth century harp songs, and folk poetry in Hyde's *Love Songs of Connacht*; the Irish poetic tradition was an influence virtually for all of his poetic career.

Initially, Clarke's use of Irish prosody is part of his programme of identification with Irish culture, with its literature and history, but it is selective and limited in range. His attempts to imitate different kinds of Irish poetry, the praise poem, the curse, the itinerary poem, or the confessional poem, are also limited. These satisfy his need to be part of a distinctive culture, to be in fact more eligible for admission to an Irish literary tradition than predecessors in the Literary Revival, or contempories, who presumed to belong to a tradition whose poetic forms, conventions, and themes they knew little about. Nevertheless, Clarke's own portrayal of Irish life at any period, in poetry, fiction, or drama, is more an expression of personal vision, a use of the past for imaginative purposes, than a realistic representation. The reality of any particular period is demonstrably different, and certainly more varied and less superficially attractive, also less reliably similar to modern Ireland than Clarke imagines. The projection of personal issues on figures in the past has little historical validity.

(vi) *The Worlds of Austin Clarke*

Austin Clarke's involvement with the Catholic revival, the Irish Literary Revival, the Irish language revival, with the general movement towards a more active and determined nationalism, means that the directions he took as a writer were determined more by external factors than by personal choice, or by choices made in response to his individual experiences. The question of the effects upon him of a puritanical upbringing, the private misery of an agonised sexual morality, did not occupy his imagination in a direct manner until 1938, when in *Night and Morning*, he faced them with courage and honesty. These issues, if present at all, are present before this date in an indirect way, in the choice of subject matter, and in a programme of stylistic artistry that became virtually an end in itself. Only gradually, in *Pilgrimage* (1929) and then explicitly in *Night and Morning* did he focus on himself. It was only much later, in *Mnemosyne Lay in Dust* (1966) that he investigated the horror of his nervous breakdown of 1919. By then he had come to understand that his experiences were not unique, that the drama of the individual conscience was the drama of the race. To have been Irish and Catholic in his time meant having experienced in some degree comparable spiritual, mental and emotional problems.

At the same time it has to be remembered that the poetry of the Revival was not characterised by psychological investigation or by exposure of individual trauma. It was a poetry of mood, a poetry removed from social and political realities, a poetry that turned with excitement to the myths of the past, a poetry that created an image of Ireland and of the Irish past that was demonstrably selective. In order to understand Austin Clarke's work it is necessary to know something of the different worlds in the Irish past from which he drew material: the three cycles of stories — the mythological, the Ulster, and the Fenian — and the Celtic-Romanesque period.

In fact it is impossible to divide early Irish narrative literature into distinct categories since all of it tends to be mythological and all of it tends to be heroic. The mythological tales deal primarily with the Celtic gods and the pagan Otherworld, with the Battle of Magh Tured which tells how the gods, known as the Tuatha De Danann, defeated the demonic forces of the Fomoiri, or Formorians, with the *Dinnschenchas*, or lore of place, and with the *Lebor Gabala*, or *Book of Invasions*, a pseudo-historical account of the arrival of peoples in Ireland. A number of literary texts are based on this material, including *Tochmharc Etaine*, which tells of Midir's love for Etain and of visits by humans to the Otherworld.

Austin Clarke makes several references to mythological tales and to mythological figures, but his most extended use of the material is found in *The Sword of the West* (1921) in which he gives a visionary account of the Battle of Magh Tured. He is particularly attracted by the concept of the Otherworld and by the *faeth fiada*. The world which is variously known as The Land of the Immortals, the Land of the Ever Young, or Moymell, is a timeless region of delight, situated on islands across the sea, under the sea, under lakes, within caves, or within so-called fairy mounds. It is a place without sickness or old age or death, where in the words of Proinsias MacCana, 'beautiful women abound and love is indulged without taint or sin, where magic vessels supply food and drink in inexhaustible plenty'.[34] There, he says, using an example that Clarke uses as the epigraph to *The Bright Temptation* (1932), as in the *Echtra Conli*, or 'The Adventure of Conle', the hero is accosted by a beautiful woman who invites him to join her in the land of eternal happiness. In *Serglige*

Con Culain, or 'The Wasting Sickness of Cu Chulain', which Clarke uses in 'The Death of Cuchullin' section of *The Sword of the West*, Cuchullin's love for the fairy-woman, Fand, arouses the jealousy of his wife, Emer, and has to be annulled. In the *Vengeance of Fionn* and in *The Sword of the West* there are references to mythological lovers, as there are in some of the short poems in the *Cattledrive in Connaught*, the first two novels, and in several of the plays, but it is used most extensively in *The Sun Dances at Easter* (1952) where the different interrelated stories move back and forth through the *fáeth fíada* and where some enjoy the magical food and drink of the Otherworld. Clarke's imaginative delight in the possibilities of romantic escape to a better land is a prominent feature throughout his earlier work; it is followed by an aesthetic pleasure in being able to transcend or disrupt with impunity the conventions of time, place or action that the Otherworld and the ability to go there allows. Even his last poem, 'The Wooing of Becfola' is a simple and pleasing story about Becfola's experiences beyond the *fáeth fíada*, in that land where the imagination is untramelled. The Irish imagination, as MacCana points out in *Celtic Mythology* (1970), in language that echoes Clarke's own comments, plays with the relativity of time and place: 'perspectives are reversed and brevity becomes length and length brevity as one crosses the tenuous border between the natural and the supernatural'.[35] There opposites combine and interchange.

By contrast Clarke's use of material from the Ulster cycle is more limited and less effective. Its most important tale, the *Táin Bó Cualnge*, or 'Cattle-raid in Cooley', deals with a cattle-raid by Maeve, Queen of Connaught, into the territory of the Ulaid, or Ulstermen, which is ruled over by Conchobar Mac Nessa and defended by Cuchullin. The story relates a long series of combats between Cuchullin and heroes from Maeve's army. Clarke may have intended to retell the whole *Tain*, but he only completed two sections in *The Sword of the West*, and one introductory story in the *Cattledrive in Connaught*, known as 'The Pillow Talk of Maeve and Ailill'. None of these emphasise the heroic qualities of the material even though the hero in heroic literature embodies virtues held in high regard by an heroic society: courage, military prowess, personal honour.

If we include King Tales within the category of heroic literature, we find several of Clarke's sources, including the *Buile Shuibhne*, on which he based his 'Frenzy of Suibhne' and his late play, *The Frenzy of Sweeny* and *Togail Bruidne Da Derga*, or 'The Destruction of Da Derga's Hostel' from which he drew the concluding section of *The Sword of the West* and which he mentions on a number of occasions. It tells of the death of Conaire Mor, the subject of Clarke's poem, 'The Lad Made King'. He remembered AE's reading of the story as told by Standish O'Grady. 'This tale starts, in its native weirdness and horror, straight from the heart of the barbaric ages. On every side it opens chasms and weird vistas of thought and feeling, which we cannot now realise or understand'.[36] There, Clarke remarked, the gods appeared for the last time, only three miles away from his home in Templeogue beside the river Dodder on which Da Derga's hostel had also been built.

The Fenian cycle, which has a lyrical romanticism that sets it apart from the Ulster cycle, is built around the figure of Fionn and his followers. The Fianna, who protected the land against actual and supernatural invaders, were bands of warriors subject only to the authority of their own leaders and standing apart from and largely independent of normal society. Living in a more anarchic world than that inhabited by the heroes of the Ulster cycle, they were outside the areas of organised society and had a closer sympathy with the supernatural world. They were in continuous, close contact with nature, but the land is not merely the familiar landscape of Ireland; it is also the domain of the Tuatha De Danann. The action of the story seems to take place in an indeterminate area that lies between the two worlds and merges in both. Their stories are therefore closer to the mythological tales of the Tuatha De Danann than to those of the Ulster, or Cuchullin, cycle. Some of their exploits are found in a work much used by Clarke: the *Silva Gadelica*, edited by Standish Hayes O'Grady, which is a compendium of Irish tales including *Acallamh na Senorach*, or 'Colloquy of the Old Men', an anthology of Fionn tradition comprising over two hundred separate tales and anecdotes interspersed with numerous lyric poems. The Colloquy is based on the idea that Oisin, Fionn's son, and Caoilte, son of Ronan, survived into the christian period, met St Patrick, and travelled about a large part of Ireland with him. A contrast of pagan and christian values is therefore central.

Clarke's debt to the Fenian cycle may be indicated in listing some of his main sources. It includes the *Altram Tige Da Medar*, 'The Fosterage of the House of the Two Vessels', which is about the clash of paganism and christianity. The same tale is Clarke's source for one of the stories in *The Sun Dances at Easter* and for the plot of his play, *The Moment Next to Nothing*. *Eachtra an Cheithearnaigh Chaoilriabhaigh*, or 'The Adventures of the Narrow-Striped Kern', tells of the coming of the god, Manannan, disguised as a poorly clad kern, to play tricks on various early sixteenth-century Irish lords. Clarke uses Manannan in an early poem, 'The Son of Lir'; in fact he is the model for several of the rogue figures in the early poems and plays, including the Prumpolaun in *The Bright Temptation*. The Prumpolaun's self-confessed model is the *bodach*, or clown figure, in *Eachtra Bhodagh a' Chóta Lachtna*, or 'The Adventures of the Churl in the Grey Coat', which is probably modelled on *Eachtra an Cheithearnaigh Chaoilriabhaigh*. *Aithed Gráinne re Diarmait*, or 'The Elopement of Grainne and Diarmuid, called *Tóraigheacht Diarmada agus Ghráinne*, or 'The Pursuit of Diarmuid and Grainne' in a modern Irish version, is the basis of Clarke's first epic narrative, *The Vengeance of Fionn*. In connection with this tale it is perhaps worth remembering that these romances have little love interest in the conventional sense. They deal with the circumstances in which the lovers find themselves, not with the psychology of their relationship or its erotic element. This seems to have suited Clarke's purposes. The story told of escape from violence and of the simple wish of the lovers to be alone and happy.[37] In general, his early work, including the *Vengeance of Fionn*, the *Sword of the West* and *The Bright Temptation*, which re-enacts the flight of Diarmuid and Grainne, is characterised by journeys whose purposes are not entirely clear: lovers escape across the Irish landscape, or into the Otherworld, they fantasise about mythological lovers, and there is a general interweaving of the real and the imaginary. But the significance of these journeys remains imprecise and superficial. Only in *The Bright Temptation* are the journeys brought under the control of the rational imagination: the figures have definable significance, however slight; there is a moral frame of reference between the monastery and the natural world; and the journeys make sense within the book's overall design. These journeys of flight and capture, of strange encounters and nightmarish events have, as later writings make clear, more personal significance than is apparent. In his accounts of flight, imprisonment and nightmare Clarke externalises his own delirious dreams in which, bereft of memory and in a frenzy to escape, he hurries through places filled with threat and peopled by lost souls. Such experiences appear loosely in the epic narratives but with more concentrated effect in *The Singing Men at Cashel*, *Night and Morning*, and *Mnemosyne Lay in Dust*. The fact that Clarke makes more use of the mythological and Fenian cycles than of the Ulster cycle is symptomatic. It is easier to be romantic and vague within the wonder and exaggeration of the two former cycles; furthermore some of the Fenian material had the advantage of contrasting paganism and christianity, an issue that was close to his heart.

When he began to look more closely into his own life and to think of ways in which he could investigate and express it, he moved with increasing confidence from the escapist world of the distant past to a world that had greater relevance to modern Ireland. This was the Celtic-Romanesque period that lasted from the coming of christianity in the fifth century to the arrival of the Normans and of the Cluniac reforms in the twelfth. It is the most important world for Clarke's historical imagination: he drew upon it extensively, in plays, fiction, and poetry, throughout most of his career because it provided satisfying imaginative parallels with his own time and with his own experience. Its discovery was a revelation:

> Having perfect faith in the Irish literary movement, as I knew it, I had set out for the south-west of Ireland. I was on the track of the lost southern mythic cycle of Curoi Mac Dara and had a notion that in Kerry some imaginative experience might aid me. But something occurred to my inner eye. I could no longer see the rugged landscape of Ferguson and Herbert Trench, another landscape, a mediaeval landscape, was everywhere I looked. I could not understand this intrusiveness until, suddenly, in Clare, turning the corner of a market place, I saw Scattery across an inlet of the Shannon. I scarcely saw either the island or its monastic tower owing to the silver blaze of water and sun. But I saw because of that light and in their own newness the jewelled reliquaries, the bell shrines, the chalices, and guessed at all the elaborate exactness of a lost art.[38]

Clarke's portrayal of this medieval world is selective and sometimes inaccurate. His use of history tends to be sketchy, but he is intent on describing a world that is similar to his own and yet significantly different. It is similar in that both are christian, in both there is a strong element of asceticism that reveals itself not only in habits of self-mortification and self-denial, but in a form of moral instruction in which the pleasures of this world, including in particular those of the body, are denounced and the pleasures of the next life are enthusiastically upheld. What he experienced in his own life could be mirrored in the medieval past, as, for example, in the experiences of the boy, Aidan, in *The Bright Temptation*, who is the product of a strict moral training, is subjected to terrifying forms of rebuke for a dimly understood breach of morality, and has to struggle hard to find life and love, in unashamed delight, with the visionary Ethna. The novel is an allegory of that progress from repression to freedom that occurs often in Clarke's work. That he was able to project it in the distant past instead of in terms of his immediate surroundings was an advantage.

But the two periods are also dissimilar in that the Irish Church was in some respects independent of Roman control, had superb achievements in scholarship and art, in metal ornaments, high crosses, illuminated manuscripts, whereas the modern post-Tridentine Irish Church was controlled by the Papacy and neither the clergy nor the people were distinguished for their intellectual independence or their artistic achievements. As Margaret Stokes pointed out in *Early Christian Architecture in Ireland* (1878) Irish teachers in the eighth to tenth centuries were noted for their independent outlook, their learning, their philosophical speculation, and their freedom of will. They were also noted for their fearless denunciation of sin and their courageous faith.[39] Irish thinking, as Kathleen Hughes has written in *The Church in Early Irish Society* (1966) expected diversity rather than uniformity.[40] Even if one might point to the literary success of the Revival between 1890 and 1920, or thereabouts, postrevolutionary Ireland had not projected itself in intellectual or imaginative terms and in Clarke's view there had been a decline since 1916. He thinks of the medieval period in idealised terms, imagining an integrated culture where men of letters and crafts, poets, scholars, monks, were respected. And the evidence was abundant: the great sculptured crosses at Monasterboice and Clonmacnoise, the illuminated works, such as the *Book of Kells* or the *Book of Durrow*, the metalwork, such as the Tara Brooch or the Ardagh Chalice, monastic cities which were renowned centres of learning. Kathleen Hughes has given a graphic account of these:

> . . . Relics were enshrined, not in simple cases but with a variety of techniques, the metal cast or beaten, overlaid with a filigree of twisted gold thread, inlaid with enamel, inset with precious stones. The texture was varied, the patterns intricate and delicate. A church might be small and dark, but its altar must have gleamed with reliquary, hanging bowl, chalice, or book-cover. In stone-work the contrast between the simplicity of the early crosses, incised or dressed slabs of stone, and the elaborate beauty of the later, freestanding crosses with their panels of ornament, vividly illustrates the transition from an apostolic and ascetic to an established church.[41]

Clarke knew that the Irish Church became wealthy and powerful, although he made little use of this in his work. Too great a vine, he declares in a later poem, 'The Loss of Strength', can sour the best of clay. That is, a Church grown rich and powerful feeds off the people and this is a reversal of its true function, which is to feed its flock. The metaphor works for the early Irish Church and for the modern Irish Church. His picture of the Celtic-Romanesque takes in the period as a whole; he characterises it in general terms, in terms of its morality, its independence, its scholarship and crafts. He does not distinguish between its different periods. The general picture, however, is more varied and more changeable. The ascetic revival of the eighth century was neither comprehensive nor permanent. Clergy often lived with their wives and it is unlikely that they were continent. Clarke gives the impression that women were always excluded. In fact abbots were often married and were succeeded by their sons. Kathleen Hughes observes: 'Married clergy, lay abbots, some succeeding their fathers in ecclesiastical appointments, offices held in plurality, all characteristics considered as abuses of the Viking age, were in fact, all present in the Irish Church before the Viking raids began'.[42] The Church increased in material wealth and in political power during the ninth and tenth centuries. Cormac Mac Cuilleanain, for example, whom Clarke admired, was a foremost scholar, but he also plundered monasteries. As a king-bishop it must have been very difficult for him to keep spiritual and secular interests apart. Clarke's portrayal of Cormac's life in *The Singing Men at Cashel* is not really a portrait of the man and his age; its description of the political struggles is defective.

Eventually conflict developed between the Irish Church and Rome over such matters as the dating of Easter – the issue in Clarke's play, *Black Fast* – the tonsure, marriage and baptismal vows, and the rites of episcopal confirmation. Rome also disapproved of the organisation of the Irish Church along tribal lines, an issue that was resolved in the early twelfth century when the Church was reorganised into dioceses as a result of the reforms introduced by Malachy of Armagh and Bernard of Clairvaux. Clarke's historical authority, G.T. Stokes, declared: 'St Malachy was the person who finally reduced Ireland beneath the supremacy of Rome and introduced complete Roman discipline'.[43] At Armagh, he said, Malachy 'had thoroughly broken the old clan or tribal system connected with the See'.[44] Given Clarke's sensitivity to Roman control in his own time, it is understandable that he should regard the arrival of the Cistercians in the first part of the twelfth century as important historically as the arrival of the Normans in 1169. But Stokes's nineteenth-century, Protestant interpretation of the Church in the pre-Norman period is simplistic. Twentieth-century scholars, like Kathleen K. Hughes, John Ryan, and Patrick J. Corish, have shown that the historical background is extremely complex and that the Church was fundamentally in harmony with Rome. In a recent essay Patrick J. Corish points to the basic fact that the authority of a church is linked to the quality of its witness which is seen in the cumulative witness of its holy dead. 'Rome,' he says, 'was the chief witness to the faith for the churches of the Western patriarchate ... and the highest praise that could be given to another church was to compare the witness of its saints to the witness of the saints of Rome'.[45] In short, accounts of conflict between the early Irish Church and Rome in Stokes, and in Clarke, are exaggerated.

The medieval Church permeates Clarke's work more comprehensively and with greater personal relevance than any other world that fed his imagination. Furthermore, it was largely free from the kind of romantic distortions and exaggerations that marred his treatment of the others, particularly in the epic narratives. It is true that the title poem, 'Pilgrimage', is an idealised picture. Equally it could be said that the portrait of the ascetic in 'Celibacy' is a caricature. Nevertheless in other poems in that collection, Clarke finally comes close to what most concerned him: the casuistical mentality which he finds in certain historical figures who suffer from the same kind of mental uncertainty that Clarke himself had been educated into and which was the consequence of the modern Church's insistence on rules and regulations, rather than on christianity's generosity of spirit. *The Singing Men at Cashel* is a compelling, even forbidding, and objective account of a moral universe, unyielding and implacable, in which the sensitive Gormlai, honest and intelligent about herself, is reduced to a traumatic state of labyrinthine sophistry. No other work in Clarke's entire output holds the mirror of the past up to modern Irish Catholicism with such force and accuracy. The majority of Clarke's plays are set in the medieval period and although none have the psychological complexity or intellectual depth of *The Singing Men at Cashel*, some have considerable power and relevance, including *The Son of Learning*, *The Flame*, and *As the Crow Flies*.

Two christian worlds coexist in Clarke's work. In the medieval one he includes the schoolmen, or scholastics, both European and Irish, who exemplify what he admires: the power of reason, the freedom that men once had, before the Council of Trent, to participate in what he calls in *Night and Morning*, 'the holy rage of argument', the debates and discussions by which they argued their way towards God. But there is one other religion which is found in his final poems, a religion of pagan sensuality, of joyful sexuality, of uninhibited delight in the physical.

(vii) *The New Generation*

When Austin Clarke died in 1974, a new generation of Irish writers had emerged, whose lives had been shaped by forces of the post-war world and by the opening up of Ireland to outside influences, both intellectual and economic. Unlike their predecessors in Clarke's generation, they had not been greatly attracted by his shining word — 'Nationalism'.[46] Their most vivid memories were not of republican guerillas, but of wartorn Europe, Hiroshima, and the futile heroisms of a number of limited wars from Cyprus to Vietnam. Within their lifetimes leadership passed from the hands of those who had participated in the birth of the state and who reflected the antagonisms and aspirations of the revolutionary period. Their vision of Ireland was embodied in the commercial revolution of the First Economic Programme in 1958, in the promotion of industrial and economic growth, in participation in the United Nations, in joining the European Economic Community. Much of this came too late to be a significant influence on Clarke's later development, but materialism and the moral dilemmas it posed are reflected in his poetry. He was encouraged by the interest shown in his work by the younger poets, Thomas Kinsella, John Montague, and Richard Murphy. His own poetry after 1955 responded directly to contemporary life, to its politics, its social inequalities. He voices the spiritual dilemma of one excessively hedged about by a dogmatic and authoritarian church. He speaks out against the insensitivity of a state that cares too little about the poor, the unemployed, unmarried mothers, and children in need. He condemns profiteering. He laments the loss of spiritual strength in both the Catholic and Protestant Church. He articulates alternatives: a more desirable vision of life, sometimes with examples from the past; a vision of a more tolerant, less repressive society, more compassionate towards the poor, more just in its treatment of all the people, more accepting of human feelings, more respectful of the mind. At the same time the work becomes more personal, particularly in the long autobiographical poems, 'The Loss of Strength', 'The Hippophagi'; more confident, in *Flight to Africa*, more intense in *Mnemosyne Lay in Dust*; and more relaxed in the final collections: *A Sermon on Swift*, *Orphide*, and *Tiresias*. Clarke's work divides loosely between the more romantic earlier period and the more realistic later period, which we may date from 1955, when he published *Ancient Lights* after a 'silence' of seventeen years. Parts I and II of this book are divided in accordance with these two major divisions in his work, with the chapters on the novels and on the plays included in Part I.

This book, as its title indicates, is introductory. It tries to provide a critical basis for the study of Clarke's work. Because his work has not received much critical attention, it has been necessary to explain allusions, to describe sources, and to attempt to puzzle out the meaning of 'difficult' passages. Much fruitful work remains to be done; there are issues still to be examined, and much that needs further investigation. While some attempt is made here to relate Clarke to the Irish Literary Revival and to the cultural contexts of his time, other significant relationships are not examined, such as his connection with the English poetic tradition, with the modern movement in poetry, with W.B. Yeats, with Thomas Kinsella, with James Joyce. But if this book stimulates others to read Austin Clarke with greater understanding and appreciation it will have served its purpose.

PART I

REMEMBERING
OUR INNOCENCE

Chapter 1: Short Poems 1916-1925

When Austin Clarke visited W.B. Yeats at Ballinamantane House in 1918, the older poet advised him to study certain English poets in order to discipline his imagination, and spoke of his desire to see the emergence in Ireland of a school of neo-Catholic poets.[1] But this advice did not appeal to Clarke who had studied English, French, Belgian and American poets, but was more interested in Irish poetry, its forms and prosody. He certainly did not want to become a Catholic poet, since he associated that religion with repression and trauma. Ten years later he would begin to investigate the subject of the Catholic conscience but when he wandered through the woods at Coole Park and had his meeting with Yeats, he was in search of freedom, freedom to explore Irish culture, to learn the language, to accustom himself to the life style and the speech of those who lived in the west. For him, as for many others at that time, the west retained elements of traditional life and had an attractive easy-going atmosphere that was far removed from the values and the restrictions of urban, Catholic Dublin. His rejection of Yeats's advice is made in response to the poetry and to the behaviour of poets who enjoyed a life of personal freedom.

> How could we learn to write the traditional songs of repentance before we had known those 'merry sins' of which Synge had spoken. I thought of the extravagant Gaelic poetry of the eighteenth century. Once more the strapping heroine of 'The Midnight Court' was railing against aged bridegrooms, denouncing the celibacy of the clergy. . . . Once more the Mangaire Sugach was reeling from another parish with a satire on his tongue, and in a distant tavern, O'Tuomey was filling his till with the fine words of his fellow craftsmen.[2]

Four years later he associates the ballad dancers of Rome and the learned goliards with 'MacConglinne who had cured a possessed king by the devilment of his own songs', with the Mangaire Sugach 'who had been driven from every parish', with 'Blind Raftery, the last of them, singing of a woman, the star of knowledge, whom he could not see'.[3] In three letters to the *Irish Statesman*, Clarke and F.R. Higgins argued for objectivity in Irish literature, for a reliance on Gaelic craft, and for the 'fine generosity, lavish colour and concrete imagery' of 'The Destruction of Da Derga's Hostel' and the poetry of Eoghan Ruadh Ó Súilleabháin'.[4] In a review of F.R. Higgins, *The Dark Breed*, he identified the 'wilder, sterner' achievements of his contemporaries, who had what he called 'a joy in the coloured, vigorous patterns of western life'.[5] The short poems of the 1916-1925 period show the appeal of this colourful life to Clarke also.

A spirit of comic irreverence permeates his early career. It is expressed in the short poems, particularly in the figure of Manannan Mac Lir, in the figure of Anier MacConglinne in his first play, *The Son of Learning* (1927), and in the figure of the Prumpolaun in his first novel, *The Bright Temptation* (1929). Indeed, the comic spirit is present in much of Clarke's work, but because his literary career has never been fully investigated, he has been identified with the poetry of guilt, sexual repression and social satire. But the work of his comic imagination is also important, both for its own sake and for the sake of a more complete and more balanced assessment of his career. The absence of comedy at certain stages of his career or in particular works, such as *The Singing Men at Cashel* (1936), *Night and Morning* (1938), the poems and satires (1955-1960), or *Mnemosyne Lay in Dust* (1966), is in itself significant in terms of the issues they explore and of the society that makes comedy inappropriate.

While some of the short poems respond to the colourful aspects of western life, the ballad singers, the fishermen, the storytellers, the excitement of pubs and fairs, Clarke's approach is not just that of cultural pilgrim or observer. He uses types of Irish poems as models, the praise poem, the blessing, the curse, the itinerary poem, entering into the culture by imitating its poetic forms and conventions, and by using some of its linguistic idiom and turns of speech. Situated in specific places, the poems record what happens to Clarke on his journeys through the west. His essays, written at the same time and subsequently absorbed into *A Penny in the Clouds* (1968), provide a context for the poems. Focussing on colourful figures and on lively experience, Clarke creates a relaxed and stimulating world in which he can forget personal care. His myth of the west is a form of escape.

Were I in Clare of the ships
Drinking with fishermen, I would not care
Not I, not I, until the vat ran dry,[6]

The poems give a dramatic sense of actual life and lay claim to it. Initially, as may be seen in poems like 'Blessing', or 'The Curse', they are too restricted and compact to give adequate expression to the freedom they advocate. Others, and in particular the itinerary poems, have a more appropriate shape and style. They celebrate freedom. The individual stanzas in 'The Itinerary of Ua Cleirigh', that is, of Clarke, are declarations of memorable experience — 'I know an isle', 'I prayed on Croagh Patrick', 'I saw from Galway', and so on. All bear witness to direct, uncomplicated involvement. The poem, a combination of literary autobiography and invention, recovers and recreates examples of satisfying experience and animates the countryside with the vividness of its witness.

I saw from Galway
A Spanish ship flaming
Beyond the phantom isles of Arran;
Grey stone for hedges
Has bound the green county
Around branchy Coole of the manor,
Where I halted with Yeats
To share the wise salmon
He grassed from the Lake of Jewels;
I dipped in his plate
Without praise, without wine,
Though he asked me to come to his Castle.

The perspective is both realistic and imaginary as it turns the visible towards the invisible. The Spanish ship that flames in the sunlight reminds us of Galway's trading history with Spain but also of the Armada, some of whose ships foundered along the western coast. The Aran islands appear and disappear in the distance, like phantom isles. In the meeting with Yeats reality and myth are side by side: the salmon might be Fionn's salmon of knowledge, its source the lake in which AE seemed to detect the jewels of the Tuatha De Danann. Unable to resist a jibe, Clarke contrasts the meagre fare with the lordly invitation. The whole stanza turns reality towards fancy with a light playfulness that matches the persona of the speaker.

The final stanza reiterates Clarke's feeling of an imaginative pilgrimage through a landscape made exciting by the conjunction of the actual and the supernatural.

By the holy well
And the honey house
Of stone, I read the Gospel
Until a bird called me
Over bright water
That was sapping the green miles of barley:
And when the chill rain
Was setting at night,
I met the great horsemen with plunder
And among black hills
I feasted with them,
In the royal house of Curoi Mac Dara.

Once again the two worlds conjoin: the remnants of a former era, present in the holy well and the beehive hut, evoke a simple response; the bird evokes the blackbird that Fionn heard, and in these linkages between landscape, history and mythology, Clarke imagines an encounter with Curoi Mac Dara who is associated with Cahirconree, Co Kerry.

Similarly, at the end of 'The Pedlar', another itinerary poem, based on Padraic O'Conaire's account of his travels with a donkey in *An Crann Géagach*, the journey is an occasion for wonder – 'How can I deny that enchantment?' – and ends in history and mythology with reference to Tara and 'a queen that had been married', who could be Deirdre or Gormlai, perhaps even the goddess of sovereignty.

A spirit of histrionic entertainment grows through the poems in the 'Induction' section. The title poem invokes the figure of Manannan Mac Lir. It is spoken by Anier MacConglinne, the hero of *The Son of Learning*, who identifies with Manannan, 'the patron saint/Of merry rogues and fiddlers'.[7] That mood is present in more subdued form in 'Secrecy' and 'Silver and Gold' which contrast romantic and realistic love, artifice and actuality.

'Secrecy', an *aisling* or vision poem, addresses the *spéar bhean*, the 'woman of brightness' or 'Sun woman', in a style whose intricate use of imagery, syntax, assonance and alliteration, mimics the vivid colours and labyrinthine designs of the *Book of Kells*.

Had we been only lovers from a book
That holy men who had a hand in heaven
Illuminated: in a yellow wood,
Where crimson beast and bird are clawed with gold
And, wound in branches, hunt or hawk themselves,
Sun-woman, I would hide you as the ring
Of his own shining fetters that the snake,
Who is the wood itself, can never find.

Such a well-wrought context would be ideal, a preferred haven for the lovers. But they are not lovers in a holy book. Clarke's delight in this ingenious use of language is also evident in 'Silver and Gold', a poem of more sustained artifice, in which the speaker plays the part of experienced amorist who regards love as a game. He contrasts romantic with realistic love, the one intense and single-minded, the other detached and complex:

> Hammer the gold and silver into steel:
> I have another metal that rings clear
> To mind; the coining air knows, and I know,
> That harp, thrown high, will turn a lucky head
> And they that love once never have been loved.
> She glittered in me as the twilight star
> That like a patient crane haunts one bright pool
> When sedge is bare. Now that we are awake,
> Come with me, golden head, for every wood
> Thickens again and the first callow light
> Flutters around the hedges; we shall hear
> The birds begin as sweetly as the chinking
> Of few pence in my pocket. When the tides
> Of sun are full and the salmon come up from
> The south, Love, we shall hurry where the waves
> Carry the heavy light into the shore
> And see the marrying wings, for all the day
> They are more silver than the lifting oar,
> But in the evening they are gold again.

The speaker's confidence appears in his command to the damascene workers and in the controlled artifice of his language and syntax. The attempt to enshrine precious metals in a permanent form goes against the knowledge he has gained from nature itself. Love, like the game of pitch and toss, depends on luck. The turn of the penny, made equivalent to the turning of the woman's head, introduces a value that is at once more common and less precious. 'They that love once,' he declares, 'never have been loved'. That assertion is modulated by the pointed simplicity of the next statement, a memory of past, single-minded love. But the remaining lines in their deliberate, drugged romanticism tempts the woman, his 'golden head', to go with him, an invitation whose value is measured by the sound of money 'chinking' in his pocket. In the further enticements in which the language again plays on traditional images of 'sun', 'salmon', 'south', and 'stars', silver and gold are associated with oars and wings, with time and change. Love itself, although the woman is not meant to understand this, is also transient.[8]

The six poems in 'The Land of Two Mists' section, another Irish name for the Otherworld, have a narrative base and three are dramatic monologues but they are generally more subjective than those in the 'Induction' section and more accommodating of mystery. In 'The Son of Lir' Mannanan exacts the tribute of adulation for his performances.

> Last night in the house of Red Hugh
> I tumbled, I juggled, I danced.

He delights in his feats of entertainment and in his freedom of movement. 'I will do what I will as my mind is pleasing'. He proclaims his delight in his freedom — 'I ran', 'I came', 'I heard', and so on — and his delight in nature — 'the bird-lakes of the morning', 'the golden sedge of corn'. In its mode of emphatic saying the poem is close to the itinerary poems in 'Induction', but 'The Lad Made King', another first person monologue, is a different kind of itinerary poem. It has the topographical identifications of the itinerary poem — the glen of the blindmen (Glendallan, Co Sligo), the road from Midluachra that ran northwards from Tara to Ailech, the road from Fieries in Co Kerry — and an apparent equivalence of manner.

> In the glen of the blindmen
> I was alone for a night,
> With a stone in the flighty boughs
> I gathered a bite;
> On the road from Midluachra
> I will come to an empty house
> Where a fire is, . . .

Despite these declarations about apparently real experience, 'The Lad Made King' is about mythology. The speaker is Conaire Mor who became King of Ireland and then lost everything in the breaking of taboos before his death at Da Derga's Hostel. The 'mists' of the title refers to the mists of illusion that appeared over the approaches to Tara when the land seemed to be full of armed men and bad omens, and when Tara itself appeared to be on fire. The poem touches upon the realities of its source but like the source evokes an incomprehensible and threatening Otherworld. Its central issue is Conaire's loss of freedom once he has been crowned king. Where Mannanan moved freely on his circuit of kingdoms Conaire begins in freedom but ends in the confining responsibilities of kingship, 'snared' and 'hurried into Tara'. He laments the freedom of hurlers playing in the small fields where he once 'ran with the birdflocks'. The repeated references to birds reminds us of his kinship with birds and that he was forbidden to kill them.[9]

That vestiges of Irish mythology may be detected in the landscape, place-names and folklore of Ireland is fundamental to Clarke's approach. 'The Lad Made King' establishes a mysterious dual perspective in which the ordinary is resonant with suggestions of the unreal. 'The House in the West' and 'The Musician's Wife' are also written in this spirit. The former, drawing upon Jeremiah Curtin's observations on the presence of the goddess, Mor, in the landscape and the beliefs of Kerry.[10] describes everyday life but shows the vestigial presence of Mor, whose house, Tighe Mhoire, or 'great house', is mentioned in the opening line. The way in which reality and the supernatural exist in this poem is too simple to be fully effective, but 'The Musician's Wife', combining reflection and narrative, offers better evidence of what Clarke wants to do.

Its plot entangles its main figures, making them into emblems, or 'shadows', of the unhappiness that affects them. Craftine's wife eloped but is haunted by the thought of her husband's sadness. Her lover in turn is lured by fairy women. While such details are present, they are turned in upon themselves and subordinated to the predominant mood of sadness. The narrative impulse of the romance is restrained, stilled in the movement of the lines, which reflects the wife's realisation of sorrow.

> They hurry, forever
> Where forests are felled
> By lake-water, they
> Have no rest from the fluting
> And though they are shadows,
> He dreams of strange beauty
> And she weeps to herself
> As they fade in the dew.

Such poems have a vague narrative impulse but weave the threads of the story into a static tapestry of sound and syntax. Where the itinerary poems are extravert, these are preoccupied with mood. Their allegorical potential is explicit in 'The Lost Heifer' which, as its title indicates, is about Ireland.

> When the black herds of the rain were grazing
> In the gap of the pure cold wind
> And the watery hazes of the hazel
> Brought her into my mind,
> I thought of the last honey by the water
> That no hive can find.

Brightness was drenching through the branches
When she wandered again,
Turning the silver out of dark grasses
Where the skylark had lain,
And her voice coming softly over the meadow
Was the mist becoming rain.

Written, as Clarke says, when the country's ideals had been obscured during the civil war, the poem creates a delicate feeling of loss in its pattern of sounds and the suggestive radiance of its imagery. The speaker reflects nostalgically on a better past and there is an implicit contrast with the present. After the poignant reference to the unattainable ideal — 'the last honey' that no bees can find — the imagery of radiance, silver and voice set against the previous images of rain and cold is particularly effective. That the poem turns back upon itself, when the mist becoming rain suggests the harsher black herds of the rain in the first line, appropriately denies the potential freedoms conveyed in the second stanza and finalises the pervasive elegiac atmosphere.

There are echoes of Francis Ledwidge's poem, 'Thomas MacDonagh', the executed leader of the Easter Rising, who had been Clarke's teacher at the university and had encouraged his interest in poetry: 'lain' and 'rain' in the second stanza repeat the same rhymes in the first stanza of Ledwidge's poem.

He shall not hear the bittern cry
In the wild sky, where he is lain,
Nor voices of the sweeter birds
Above the wailing of the rain.

The imagery from nature, together with the use of assonance further identifies the two poems within a particular tradition. In the final stanza Ledwidge also uses the image of 'the Dark Cow', representing Ireland, to suggest a better future for the country.

But when the Dark Cow leaves the moor,
And pastures poor with greedy weeds,
Perhaps he'll hear her low at morn
Lifting her horn in pleasant meads.

Ledwidge writes an elegy for a lost patriot whose cause lives on, Clarke writes an elegy for a lost ideal.

Clarke favours the single-sentence stanza in all the short poems of this period, even grouping some under the titles 'Three Sentences' and 'Six Sentences', but in itself this does not account for the achieved stillness of poems like 'The Lost Heifer' or 'The Musician's Wife', nor for their

unique moods. The first stanza of 'The House in the West' illustrates
the style of many of these poems.

> Where low rains are heavier
> Than the sail in haze
> And the cold sea is spread
> On the soil to raise harvest,
> Black calves are bred to reign over
> The fair and behind their green tether,
> In a bare land that halves every cloud,
> There is a great house.

This eight line stanza is composed of one run-on sentence, with no end-
stopped lines and no internal interruptions. But the possibilities for a
fast pace that this structure provides are denied by the use of patterns
of Irish prosody, by the uneven length of the lines, and by the virtual
absence of end-rhyme. For example, the 'ai' sound links words across
the whole stanza from 'Rains', 'sail' and 'haze' at the beginning to 'bare'
and 'great' at the end. In addition there is the internal assonance, visible
in 'sail . . . haze', 'sail . . . raise', or 'Black calves' and 'land . . . halves',
and the combination of masculine and feminine rhyme in the last two
lines. The effect of all of this is to slow the pace of the lines by bringing
individual words into prominence and by marking out their tonal relationships. The dominance of monosyllabic words contributes also to the
slow motion effect. Even the acceptance implicit in the last two lines,
in keeping with Clarke's general attitude towards mythology at this
time, dismisses any notion of an alternative response. When he wrote of
some of Herbert Trench's poems as poetry 'gazing into its own reflection',[11] he might have been describing his own work. While the next
collection, *Pilgrimage* (1929) continues to use the style of these particular
poems in 'The Land of Two Mists', they do not have the same effect.
Poetry gazing into its own reflection comes very close to describing 'The
Musician's Wife' and its associated poems.

But the outstanding poem of the 1916-25 period is 'The Frenzy of
Suibhne', which has the emphatic listing of places and experiences
already encountered, the self-dramatisation, the selective use of a literary
source, but uses natural imagery to convey psychological states. It transforms the episodic *Buile Shuibhne*[12] into a compressed, impressionistic
and bizarre portrait of madness. All its material is absorbed into its drama
of the mind, including the descriptions of landscape which become
metaphors for mental and psychological instability. Clarke omits all
references to the Battle of Magh Rath and the pursuit by Suibhne's
foster brother, plays down the topographical features and concentrates

on the main figure, on his subjective, anguished, confession.

> Run, run to the sailmaker —
> While I pluck the torn white hedges
> Of sea to crown my head —
> And tell him to bind hard the canvas
> For the waves are unhorsed to-night;
> I cracked a thought between my nails
> That they will light a candle
> When I swim from the loud grass
> To the holy house of Kieran.

The opening command, apparently sensible, becomes part of a deranged perception of reality: the 'crown' is appropriate but 'hedges of the sea' indicates sensory distortion; 'waves are unhorsed' carries this ambivalence forward, since the metaphor is both accurate and hallucinatory. The demented 'I cracked a thought' leads unexpectedly to the wish for peace in the monastery at Clonmacnoise, 'the holy house' of St Kieran. After the turbulence of 'torn', 'unhorsed' and 'cracked' the images of lighted candle, holiness and arrival have a calming effect. The stanza anticipates the overall direction of the poem. Its swift pace through one long, run-on sentence that sweeps along the parenthesis in its course, is characteristic of the entire poem, in which stanzas and lines are unpredictably uneven in length.

Initially no explanation is provided as to the cause of Sweeny's condition. In the urgent opening the poem plunges into the phantasmagoric, surreal world of a mind under stress and then maintains its eerie ambivalence: the storm is 'masted' in the oakwood and the marine imagery continues. Manannan, son of the sea-god, 'splashes by', not as prankster but as a figure in a developing sequence of frightening figures. Sweeny appreciates the sensual beauty and fruitfulness of his natural surroundings and has an objective understanding of his own appearance — 'the wild-eyed man of the water/. . . feathered like a hawk to the foot'. His hypersensitive reaction animates the landscape in bizarre perceptions of shadows cropping, sloe-bushes running, boulders crossing, and the terrifying figure of the one-eyed Swineherd. These images lead to the curse of the Furies, who are bound to the rafters, dripping blood and cursing.[13] This apocalyptic passage is part of an extended sequence of foreboding and hallucination. In this atmosphere Sweeny frees the horses and reacts violently to the news of his wife's remarriage.

I fought them with talons, I ran
On the oak-wood — O Horsemen,
Dark Horsemen, I tell ye
That Sweeny is dead!

The sexual betrayal is the single, most powerful cause of his madness —
for his frenzy, his alteration into a bird, his flight through the forest.
Immediately the poem registers the sensory distortion and psychological
division. Voices, both real and imaginary, again torment him and Sweeny
is driven again into violent reaction.

Stark in the rushlight
Of the lake-water,
I heard the heads talking
As they dripped on the stake:
Who runs with the grey moon
When ravens are asleep?
It is Sweeny, Little Sweeny
Looking for his mind.
When dogheads were barking in the wood,
I broke the horns of a goathead
For I heard them on the water
Call: *Sweeny, Little Sweeny*
Is looking for his mind.
But Robbers, dark Robbers, I tell ye
That Sweeny is dead!

The tone of suffering and of alienation grows. For the sake of alliteration
and of assonance Clarke alters the mill-hag to the hag of the haggard
and the pool of Dun Sobairce to the pool of Achill. At the same time
he indulges his fondness for punning in the 'hag'/'haggard' rhyme and in
the reference to Achill Sound as the 'dark pool that has no sound'; and,
more subtly, an *aicill* cannot exist without sound. He condenses the
incident in which Muirgeal, wife of Moling's swine-herd, puts milk in
cow-dung and adds the incidents of the hundred men fleeing from the
sight of him and the digging up of the royal cup and collar. The poem
ends in a combination of apocalyptic vision, despair about identity, and
a final longing for sanctuary. Midna, in this final stanza, was a musician
whose reed-playing put hearers to sleep. He also caused Tara to be burnt
by his fiery breath.[14] The Ridge of Judgment is the Rath of the Synod
at Tara and may refer to the final judgment. Like Conaire Mor, Sweeny
has a vision of the destruction of Tara and of signs in the sky. He remains
nameless and an outcast. In the original story Suibhne received the

sacraments of the Church and died in Moling's church. Clarke's Sweeny simply wishes to rest with the hermit culdees with the blessing of St Kieran whose monastery is across the river from Snámh Dá Éan.

> I have heard the little music
> Of Midna, I have seen
> Tara in flame and a blooded moon
> Behind the Ridge of Judgment . . .
> But how can they find my name
> Though they are crying like gulls
> That search for the sea?
> Nine years I hurried from mankind
> And yet, O Christ, if I could sail
> To the Island of the Culdees,
> I would sleep, sleep awhile
> By the blessing of the holy Kieran.

In this summarising stanza Clarke concludes his poignant portrait of a man outcast from society and the church and makes his sexual loss into the fundamental cause of his mental breakdown. There can be no doubt that Sweeny expresses much of Clarke's anguish and sense of loss of identity during the time of his own mental collapse to which he returns in *Mnemosyne Lay in Dust* (1966).

On the whole Clarke's short poems in this period are not personal. Some speak of disappointed love: a sorrow to be forgotten, a scandal to be endured, an emotional crisis brought on by one 'who crazed' his heart, a sexual betrayal. The theme of romantic loss and haunting recurs in seven of the twelve poems in 'Induction', and it could be said that by adopting the persona of pilgrim to the west and the manner of Manannan, Clarke creates a satisfying alternative for himself. But the poems grouped under 'Six Sentences', also written in the early 'twenties, are more personal and in their reaction to contemporary events, the civil war in particular, represent a side of Clarke's work that becomes dominant much later. The two stanzas on the Republican figures, Liam Mellows and Rory O'Connor, both executed without trial, engage directly with that event. The one on Mellows balances anger with qualified tribute, but the one on O'Connor is explicit and satirical.

> They are the spit of virtue now,
> Prating of law and honour
> But we remember how they shot
> Rory O'Connor.

Two other personal poems, 'No Recompense' and 'Tales of Ireland', are reflective and self-critical. The former, since it is included in *Night and Morning* (1938) may be considered in that context. 'Tales of Ireland' is a farewell to the writing of long narrative poems based mainly on Irish sources which also occupied Clarke during this 1916-1925 period.

Chapter 2: Epic Narratives 1916-1925

I

It is easy to understand why Clarke was attracted to the romance of Diarmuid and Grainne which he first read as a schoolboy and which first made him aware of a Gaelic background. The flight of young lovers across the countryside is a story of rebellion against duty and of a quest for happiness and independence. It takes place in an attractive, timeless world in which reality mingles effortlessly with the supernatural. In *The Vengeance of Fionn* Clarke creates a romantic ideal in which Grainne personifies beauty, freedom and sexual passion. To travel imaginatively with Diarmuid and Grainne is to cast aside the moral imperatives of society and to enter a region of delight. The original narrative, within the frame-story of the elopement and the pursuit, is full of episodic adventures. It emphasises the delights of love, but stresses also the virtues of protective companionship, Diarmuid's bravery and fighting skills, and his special relationship with Aongus, the God of Love. In the original, Fionn's pursuit is always a threat to the enjoyment of love, but in Clarke's version it is not an immediate threat. The conditions and the circumstances in which the lovers find themselves seem to be congenial, but, strangely, they become poignantly aware of sorrow.

Clarke divides the poem into seven parts. In Part I Fionn accepts the invitation from Diarmuid and Grainne to visit them; in Part II he and Diarmuid confront each other on Beann Gulbain; in Part III Grainne awaits the outcome. In Part IV she remembers her seduction of Diarmuid at Tara; in Part V, which is still in the past, Fionn discovers she has betrayed him by eloping with Diarmuid and in Part VI the lovers are in the countryside. In Part VII Diarmuid is dead, killed on Beann Gulbain. The contrast between the present and the past is therefore central. The first three sections and the last take place in the present, long after the passionate incidents of the elopement, after years of marriage, and after age has taken its toll on all three figures. The other three are set in the past. Clarke's real interest is revealed in the fact that Parts IV and VI which relate Grainne's youthful seduction of Diarmuid and their idyllic flight through the countryside, are by far the longest. He is clearly more interested in the lovers than in the marvels, or the adventures, or the military exploits, or Fionn's threatening pursuit.

Individual sections are also built upon contrasts: the tension between reconciliation and enmity in Part I, the differences between Fionn and Diarmuid in Part II, the one, old and treacherous, the other, younger and more open. Contrasts of youth and age recur in Fionn's memories of his own earlier heroism and of Grainne's beauty, in Grainne's memories of her youth which contrast with her haglike appearance at the end of the poem. Her recreated youth appears more ideal when set against these indications of what age has done to her. Diarmuid faces death in defiance of what time does to youth and love. Fionn rages impotently against age. Grainne's memories of beauty in Part IV transcend the effects of time in its imaginative vitality but at the same time confirms them. Such broad and simple contrasts help to bind the different parts of the poem together and to bring realism to the characterisation and to the plot. They also support Clarke's introductory note. 'The poem,' he says, 'begins in the middle age of Diarmuid and Grainne, and changes rapidly, visionally, to their youth and love — so that the reader has an awareness of the past — ideal in itself, yet further idealised by memory in the present'.

> . . . . dazzling her memory rose and wrought
> Her to its likeness that was as a flame
> Burning the toppled years and all her thought
> Shook in passionate pulses and voices sprang
> Around her like storm-exulting birds that sang
> And rose and dropt in fire and rose again
> Singing in the brightness, in the flame:
> 'O it is Grainne the golden, the beautiful
> Who has not passed, who has not died
> Though the flowers die. The years are light
> Shining around her'.

The lilting refrain 'O Grainne the golden, the beautiful', the incantatory rhythms and repetitions prepare for her proud appearance at Tara. She exults in her youth and beauty, asserts her right to choose freely. 'Oh all the night', she sang 'is mad/With music. . . . Am I not glad?/And beautiful? And young? . . .' By threatening to go to Fionn's bed, she rouses

Diarmuid to her own pitch of sexual desire and they leave Tara on a wave of passionate resolve.

The account of the lovers is momentarily interrupted by a turbulent account of Fionn's sexual rage. Even Grainne's discarded bridal dress disturbs him. But moving from the mainly iambic pentameter and regular rhyme scheme used in the announcement of the arrival of the dawn, Clarke uses a shorter iambic line to describe Grainne in the rush-strewn sheiling. This is the wood in Connaught, known as Doire dha Bhoth, where the lovers first took refuge. Diarmuid cut a clearing with seven doors and made a bed of rushes and birch-tips for Grainne. Clarke omits the rest of the incident in which Fionn and his men surround the lovers, Aongus saves Grainne, and Diarmuid leaps over the heads of the besiegers. The description of Grainne seems to have been one of Clarke's favourite passages. Its musical, figurative language creates a harmonious relationship between her and the natural surroundings.

> Flower-quiet in the rush-strewn sheiling
> At the dawntime Grainne lay,
> While beneath the birch-topped roof the sunlight
> Groped upon its way
> And stooped above her sleeping white body
> With a wasp-yellow ray.
>
> The hot breath of the day awoke her,
> And wearied of its heat
> She wandered out by noisy elms
> On the cool mossy peat,
> Where the shadowed leaves like pecking linnets
> Nodded around her feet.
> She leaned and saw in pale-grey waters,
> By twisted hazel boughs,
> Her lips like heavy drooping poppies
> In a rich redness drowse,
> Then swallow-lightly touched the ripples
> Until her wet lips were
> Burning as ripened rowan berries
> Through the white winter air.
>
> Lazily she lingered
> Gazing so,
> As the slender osiers
> Where the waters flow,
> As green twigs of sally
> Swaying to and fro.

Sleepy moths fluttered
In her dark eyes,
And her lips grew quieter
Than lullabies.
Swaying with the reedgrass
Over the stream
Lazily she lingered
Cradling a dream.

The narcissistic, ethereal nature of the portrait makes Grainne remote. The landscape itself becomes less congenial and we hear that 'a sorrow hid/One from the other'. The source or cause of this sorrow is unclear but its presence becomes increasingly real. 'O Grainne, Grainne,' Diarmuid cries, 'wild Love/Of my heart, we two are free, are free', but seeing that she is silent and unresponsive, he laments to himself:

'O Heart, it is too late
Since her white hand pulled open the little gate
Of silence. All the sweet strangeness of her
Has gone from me and I am like the air
Remembering dead wings. O bitterest love
Brooding on its own love. But O that we
Had seen and loved like Lovers long ago;
Self-found, each in the other's mystery.'

Despite the sexual intensity of their elopement, their love is not fulfilled. Grainne's 'silence' puts her at a distance and he is left to brood bitterly on love and to come to the conclusion that only in myth or legend can lovers find an exclusive, all satisfying love. 'It is,' he cries, 'too late. I know her utterly'. At the same time he yearns for the ideal and his heart cries 'Is it too late, too late?'. The tension between the ideal and the real, the supernatural and the natural, is reiterated in his contrast between those in the Land of the Ever-Young, who have gone beyond mortal longing, and those in the real world. Yet, he concludes, 'to be/Piteously human is sweetest'.

The whole section alternates between his realisation that the love he seeks is unattainable and his longing for it. It is expressed in the language of desire and of loss. Once again he declares

'Grainne, my Grainne . . . We are free,
Alone in green twilight glades. O, Come to me
Like night. Thy love has waked in me love beyond love . . .'

Once again she fails to respond: 'Grainne, the wild, the beautiful, fled'. She gazes across a beautiful landscape; she dances 'delicately, lightly', her singing is 'Joyous'. Yet when Diarmuid hurries to her, calling 'Come, O Grainne, come to me!', she fades away through the pines and he hears her voice saying 'O Sorrow, Sorrow, Sorrow'. In the concluding lines he again seeks, repeatedly inviting her to come to him and this time is successful.

> She slowly rose and came with night to him.
> Strangely they paused, gazing, they two alone
> 'Diarmuid'
>   'O Grainne'
> — and their voices were one.

They mime a drama of desire and withdrawal, in which she both causes his advances and deflects them. The unity of voices at the end of the poem, which signals a unity of response, concludes their mating ritual.

There is little in *The Vengeance of Fionn* to suggest that Clarke is deficient in narrative skills. The best sections are descriptive but there is enough evidence in Parts I and II to show his narrative ability. At an important level his story of Diarmuid and Grainne lacks psychological depth. After the celebration of Grainne's sexuality and strength of will and after the dramatic force of their flight, their failure to find happiness is disappointing. But it is also significant. Throughout the poetry of this period, in the short poems and in the longer narratives, love as Clarke sees it, is inseparable from sorrow. This is not simply a Yeatsian or Pre-Raphaelite mood, although it owes something to them. It expresses personal experience. The beloved may be imagined as the embodiment of loveliness and the object of intense, idealising desire, but the quest to win her love always leads to sorrow. Nowhere in Clarke's early work do we find a celebration of love's physical consummation. It is the harmonious voices that we hear at the end of Diarmuid and Grainne's radical rejection of duty and loyalty. If we inquire further, we find figures on whom time's passage has been severe. Only in legend or in the Otherworld can lovers be totally happy, unaffected by the processes of time and change, untouched by moral anxieties.

There are, as one might expect in an early, long poem written in five or six weeks, failures in language: a straining for effect, a blurring through exaggeration, a false dramatisation, some examples of unnatural dialogue, and at times the diction is mannered and archaic, with echoes of Elizabethan dramatists or nineteenth century British poets. Clarke mentioned Herbert Trench's *Deirdre Wedded* (1901) as an immediate stimulus, praising its 'mad discordancy like fifes, drums, brasses', its epic strength which he compares to Ferguson at his best, and its fusion of Deirdre's 'wild loveliness' with the Irish landscape.[1] There is some truth in these observations, although Trench's narrative is dull and his descriptions are heavy. There is a resemblance between Trench's development of incident after Deirdre persuades Naoise to take her away and Clarke's account of the elopement of Diarmuid and Grainne; there is a parallel between Trench's account of an old king's betrayal at a wedding-feast and Clarke's, and between their respective versions of the pursuit and the freedom of the lovers. Both writers compress the action, disrupt the chronology, and make use of dramatic voices. On the whole *The Vengeance of Fionn* is successful, as reviewers recognised.[2] But the reception given to the *Fires of Baal* (1921), which he had finished in May, 1917, was rightly less favourable.[3]

Dealing with events immediately preceding the death of Moses, when his followers turned to worship the fertility god Baal, and combining the sermonic manner of Deuteronomy with the sensuality of the *Song of Songs*, the *Fires of Baal* presents Moses as a moral leader but makes him into a remote and inhuman figure. It provides Clarke with an opportunity to write of sensual and sensuous matters — fruit, concubines, sexuality, exotic places, pagan architecture, pagan gods and goddesses. But it is essentially static: in the first part Moses addresses the Israelites and turns the leadership over to Josue; in the second he climbs Mount Abarim, meditates on the sinful ways of his people and sees the fertile lands of Canaan in the distance before they are obscured by the fires of the Baal worshippers. The poem also lacks syntactical control. Excessively long and poorly organised sentences impede the sense as well as the narrative. One sentence runs to fifty-four lines, another to forty-seven, some are over thirty, many are over ten. Their subjects are often widely separated from their verbs and the lines are burdened with descriptive adjectives.

Clarke modelled his poem on Laurence Binyon's *Death of Adam* but Binyon's poem has a better narrative momentum and the style is clear and orderly. But the resemblances between the two poems is merely general. Both have biblical themes and in both the hero goes out to die, one seeing 'the gates of Paradise' from a mountain-top, the other seeing the Promised Land. Clarke is also influenced by Henry O'Brien's *Round Towers*, in which he read about the cult of Baal, and of course he is influenced by Book I of *Paradise Lost*. He tries to emulate Milton's remote grandeur, his use of epic similes and the catalogue of gods and cities. But none of this was successful.

When he turned to material from the *Táin* one might have expected him to do better, but *The Sword of the West* (1921) is the worst of these early epic narratives and this time the critics were blunt in their comments.[4]

II

The Sword of the West has two main sections: 'Concobar' (1918), which deals with incidents prior to the birth of Cuchullin, and 'The Death of Cuchullin' (1920-21), which deals with incidents prior to his death. 'Concobar' has six parts: Part I describes Concobar's kingdom, Part II the disappearance of his sister, Dectora; in Part III an unarmed stranger is sent to find her; in Part IV her husband, Sualtem, believes she is dead; in Part V the stranger relates his vision of the demi-gods, in Part VI he says that Dectora told him she will return and that she is pregnant with the son of the god, Lugh. That son will be Cuchullin. The central weakness of *The Sword of the West* may be observed in this summary. A potentially interesting plot is established with the disappearance of the king's sister. It is suspected that Maeve's forces may have abducted her. But that interest is deflected in the account of the stranger's search for her, in his account of his vision of the demi-gods and of the Battle of Moytura, and in the reports of Dectora's wanderings with the god, Lugh.

'The Death of Cuchullin' has four parts: Part I describes the disarray of Maeve's forces; in Part II an unidentified 'I' figure laments his loss of love; in Part III, by far the longest, voices compete for Cuchullin's attention during his sickness; in Part IV Conall Cearnach rides to help Cuchullin but encounters omens of disaster. Cuchullin's defeat is obscured by an over-elaborate recreation of the drama of the rival voices that try to claim his attention, some to lure him back to battle, some to lull him into domestic peace. They include the voices of Emer, his wife, of Niav, his mistress, of Calitin's daughters — the Furies — and of other phantoms. In an obscure sense the scene is about madness, about a man distracted from reality and destined to go out again, and for the last time, to fight. He moves in dreams of battle, saying 'They bred a fire into my bone/ That will not let me rest'. In the final ride by Conall Cearnach to his support the news of Cuchullin's death is predicted in successive omens: voices warn him, Emain Macha burns, dead riders pass by, three red phantoms precede them, as they do in the story of the destruction of Da Derga's hostel; they encounter the phantom Herdsman, the Washer at the Ford, both borrowed from Samuel Ferguson's epic, *Congal*, and hear that Cuchullin is dead.

The absence of a controlled narrative is largely responsible for the failure of this poem. Not that Clarke is unable to tell a story or to describe incident, but that he is constantly drawn away from the story by material that he finds attractive. Part I of 'Concobar', for example, has an appropriate amplitude of manner and of imaginative scale for an introductory section. It moves easily from a static description of the kingdom to functional summaries of events, such as the birth of Macha's twins, the curse of Dana, the debility of the Ulstermen and the plot by which Fergus was relieved of his throne and came thereby to be on Maeve's side during the *Táin*. The style of the poem, however, detracts from the pace required in a long narrative poem; it is often excessively wordy, whole passages have a loose syntactical structure, and there is a fatal tendency to make use of nameless voices to create atmosphere or to prepare a scene. The style is not altogether bad. Some passages have an attractive simplicity and clarity, others are vivid and immediate.

Apart from the inadequacies of style is the problem of Clarke's sense of what is significant. His subjective, romantic response to mythology affects his portrayal of characters who wander in the countryside, recall lovers in romance, speak in awe of kings, or are excited by a vision of demi-gods. Even his main characters are remote figures, lacking in imaginative sympathy. Clarke's subjectivity includes a metaphorical use of two kinds of landscape, the one composed of the wilder regions of mountains, cataracts, storms, red sunsets and mythological beings, the other composed of pastoral peace, domestic crafts, sunlight, a place 'without care', 'without grief'.

Landscape is also part of the world of love. When Dectora is about to leave home, her attendants remind her how Aongus, god of Love, sorrowed for his beloved in the woods and how they flew together by 'lake and hazelwood as sad white swans'; they go on to speak of other figures in romance — Etain, Eochaid Baun and Midir, even Deirdre. Dectora and Lugh become part of the world of romance and romantic landscape, but love once again is an unattainable ideal and connected with sorrow. 'O', Lugh says, 'sing the loss,/For it is beautiful, of love'. The theme of the sorrow of love is also found in Part II of 'The Death of Cuchullin', in a passage that remained unchanged, except for the addition of a few lines at the end, through the revisions of *Collected Poems* (1936) and *Collected Poems* (1974). The language is incantatory and intense, although the identity of the speaker, a lonely wanderer, whose 'sad mind' is filled with 'strange kingdoms' and whose unhappiness is reflected in the 'sorrow of the glen', is not clear. He is a connoisseur of sorrow.

> O Love there is no beauty,
> No sorrowful beauty, but I have seen;
> There is no island that has gathered sound
> Into dim stone from wave-reeded waters
> But we have known.

but that memory is accompanied by the fear that he may lose her

> Heart of my sorrowful heart,
> Beauty fades out from sleepy pool to pool
> And there is a crying of wings about me
> And a crying in me lest I lose you.

Just as the woman is seen within a shaping landscape of beauty, the speaker is related to a landscape of loss which prepares for his sense of lost community and of isolating love.

> I have no clan but her;
> Being a dream, though the fierce incense burn,
> Love, love me, as no woman ever loved
> With intellect tense and more passionate
> Than the heart, for when the hunger of ourselves
> Is over, there is no joy but in the mind.

By the end of the passage he has become resigned to loss, resigned also to seek refuge in song.

Another of the distracting elements is Clarke's fascination with mythological material. He finds the stranger's vision of the Tuatha de Danann and the Fomorians intrinsically interesting and writes about it well, whereas it is a deflection from the search for Dectora. Clarke's appreciation is evident in the following passage which begins with Goibniu's sight of Ruadan during the Battle of Moytura.

>   Far off like torches
> He saw the eye of Ruadan; a spear
> Pierced deeply through his jagged breasting wolf-skins
> And tore the tender pap. Backward he staggered,
> Fearfully swaying like a charioteer
> Drunken with speed between the plunging stallions
> And roar of earth, then forging his great arm
> He grasped his sword and with a heaving groan
> Cleft the great Fomor through the groin.
>   Out of the night
> Came Brife, the mother of fierce Ruadan,
> And crouching like a she-wolf from the woods
> Above her dead she raised so shrill a cry
> Into the night that distant warriors hushed
> Their swords and looked on one another, aged
> With fear; and Goibniu by a flooded river
> Washing the heavy blood stained rich in moonlight,
> From his deep wounds, trembled.

In the light of its many defects — structural, stylistic and psychological

— it is not surprising that Clarke tried to have the book suppressed. When he revised it for *Collected Poems* (1936), he omitted two thirds and drastically pruned the rest.[5]

Four years after the publication of *The Sword of the West* he published *The Cattledrive in Connaught* in which the title poem is much different. The language is precise, the characterisation is realistic, and the narrative is controlled. The poem deals with the incident of the pillow talk between Maeve and Ailill. She is tormented by the thought that her husband may excel her in possessions, he is concerned to keep their quarrel within manageable limits. In a series of rhetorical questions that begins the poem we hear the voice of a real woman whose assertions of superiority undermine themselves with the doubts of the interrogative mood, the 'have I nots' of a troubled mind: 'Have I not filled/The west with lowing herds, have I not fleeced/The hills. . . .'

Maeve boasts of her possessions and of her lineage in what is a well-realised portrait, quite different from those of the ethereal Grainne and Dectora. Here the setting is real, not idealised, and a real person moves within it — vain, boastful, aggressive, wilful. Her rhetorical flight breaks against Ailill's stubborn, terse denials, but these drive her into an immediate display of wealth. The whole incident is extravagantly humorous, an outrageous reversal of the conventional roles of King and Queen, here mocked and made absurd in this elaborate domestic battle over what each owns. The quarrelling voices are like figures in a play; they have the timbre and thrust of real people, with the force of personality behind them. In Section II Clarke uses several voices in dialogue. He has discovered how to make the narrative bear different voices, how to keep description subordinate and how to project character through distinctive, defining voices. The pace of the narrative is energetic; it has an inner vibrancy that impels it forward.

It could be said that in this relatively short narrative poem, of eighteen pages, Clarke finds a different voice, one that speaks the language of everyday speech and exists in vigorous contact with reality. It has a zest for life, for action, for sex, for humour and never loses contact with the physical. This realism and openness, including its joyous sexuality, are another version of Clarke's escape from and rejection of the puritan catholicism of his background, another version of a preferred world in which his imagination delights. In language, tone and subject matter this narrative avoids the issue of mental conflict that is central to his next two collections.

Chapter 3: *Pilgrimage* (1929)

Pilgrimage continues what had been started in the short poems of the 1916-25 period, particularly in so far as the use of Irish poetic forms and prosody is concerned. Clarke has a clearer sense of what he wants to achieve in subject matter and style and of the differences which he wants to create between his poetry and that of his predecessors in the Irish Literary Revival. More than any other single collection before 1955, *Pilgrimage* demonstrates his independence of the dominant concerns and style of the Revival. He wants above all to express what he calls 'the drama of racial conscience', by writing of those stricken by the conflict between sexual desire and clerical teaching,[1] and he wants to break away from the subjective, romantic poetry of the Revival. The poems in this collection give substance to these aims and to his memorable discovery of the Celtic-Romanesque world. Five of its poems are set in that period: 'Pilgrimage', 'Celibacy', 'The Confession of Queen Gormlai', 'The Scholar', and 'The Cardplayer'.[2] It provides imaginative parallels for his own time. So, also, did the period of the Anglo-Norman and Gaelic lordships, whose cultural rise and decline he regarded as similar to the cultural flowering of the 1890-1916 period and its decline after the Easter Rising. Five poems — 'The Young Woman of Beare', 'South Westerly Gale',[3] 'The Marriage Night', 'Planter's Daughter', and 'Aisling' — have associations with the fifteenth, sixteenth and seventeenth centuries, that is, with the period of the Anglo-Norman earls, the Gaelic resurgence, the defeat at Kinsale, and its dismal aftermath.

'Pilgrimage' is an imagined journey to places and scenes that represent highlights and characteristics of the Celtic-Romanesque period. It combines simplicity of diction with an elevated, formal style. Its introductory temporal clause, providing both setting and time, is followed by a sentence in which even the rain is absorbed into the delicate simile of the books; the enjambement, the "w" alliteration and the consonance of "n" sounds round out the propitious natural signs.

> There by dim wells the women tied
> A wish on thorn, while rainfall
> Was quiet as the turning of books
> In the holy schools at dawn.

These lines illustrate the syntactical fluidity and control that Clarke sought; the words at the end of the first and third lines rhyme with a word, or words, within lines two and three and four ('tied' with 'while' and 'quiet'; 'books' with 'schools'); at the same time the second and fourth lines have end-rhyme, on and off the accent ('rainfall' and 'dawn'). But it is the effects of the speaking voice crossing from one line to the next that is basic, moving in a single, uninterrupted movement from 'There' to 'thorn'. Then, in a perfect example of Clarke's mastery of style, there is another single movement from 'while' to the end of the stanza. In these two movements we hear and perceive the patterned sounds of vowels and consonants and have the pleasing sense that the idea is present in the music of the lines, not so much because the simile is arresting and exact, but because what it says is heard in the manner of its saying. The absorption of lines into the fluid syntactical movement characterises the whole poem and is central to its impact and its distinction. The first stanza is composed of three such movements.

The reverence of women, foreshadowed in the second meaning of 'beaded plains', which refers to light seen through dry-stone walls and to rosary beads, is the first act in a poem that reveres the spiritual and artistic achievements of an era. The poem moves from the simplicity of that faith in holy wells, in which pagan custom is absorbed into christian practice, to the splendour of Clonmacnoise and Cashel, to the final picture of penitential people and pilgrims from Croagh Patrick being reproved and blessed by a saint, to the boat of the poem's pilgrims 'kneeling' over the waves, retaining, as it were, an attitude appropriate to the pilgrimage. In that circular progress from the simple, more primitive setting of Aranmore to the sophisticated culture of the mainland, and back to the 'barren isle' where ascetic Culdees pray, no gesture or note has displaced the dominant attitude of reverence. The art work of 'the holy schools', the activities of those whose lives are acts of honour to God, and the lives of simple people are all part of the medieval christian setting. Arrival, observation and departure form the overall structure of the poem and a similar pattern is present in some of its stanzas.

Although there is considerable evidence for the importance of Clonmacnoise and Cashel as centres of learning and of artistic achievement,[4]

Clarke's poem is neither factual nor documentary; it gives an impression of their significance through its harmonious tribute of sound, imagery, and rhythm. In its initial imagery of the rain's decrease the stanza about Clonmacnoise delicately prepares for the illuminating insight about to be experienced in 'that blessed place' in which 'hail and honey meet', where, in other words, a life of austerity issues in a nourishing sweetness.

> O Clonmacnoise was crossed
> With light: those cloistered scholars
> Whose knowledge of the gospel
> Is cast as metal in pure voices,
> Were all rejoicing daily,
> And cunning hands with cold and jewels
> Brought chalices to flame.

The familiar Clarkean apostrophe anticipates the exclamatory tone used to describe the miraculous blend of cross with light towards which it directs our attention. That sign of God's approval confirms the pilgrims' identification of the place as 'blessed'. The harmonies of sound, a delicate tracery of vowels and consonants, are themselves analogues for the intellectual and spiritual refinements of the scholars. The 'c' sounds link with one another throughout; a sequence of 'o' sounds continues the tone of wonder heard in the apostrophe; the connecting sounds of 'Clonmacnoise', 'cloister', 'voices' and 'rejoicing' express the happy fulfilment of the scholars. Clarke praised F.R. Higgins's poem, 'Heresy', for 'lines which bring us the loveliness of medieval Celtic art' and in a review of Aodh De Blacam's *Gaelic Literature Surveyed* spoke of the 'intricacy of metres and verbal music . . . comparable with the exquisite metalwork and the illuminated pen-work of ecclesiastical art'.[5] A similar observation could be made about his own lines.[6] These are the singing men of Clonmacnoise: the very sounds of their voices reflect the dedication and completeness of their lives. Their 'rejoicing' is proof of the value of what they do; the image of metal, known for its fusibility, suggests the harmony that exists between what they do and what they are. Their ability to create richly ornamented and beautiful chalices is a further sign of their combination of spirituality and artistic skill.

The movement of stanza three is also of arrival, at Cashel: the sight of the buildings, the sounds heard as the visitors approach and then their entry to where they can see the carvings. What they are about to experience is first indicated in the placing of the word 'Loud', which is followed by the less emphatic reference to the architectural outline of the buildings on the Rock, in which the 'towers' are prominent, as it rises above the 'grassland' of the plain. The effects are subdued and aural:

the 'chanting' of the canonical 'hours', the sounds of 'a fasting crowd at prayer', a choir singing, and then as 'we' pass, the sight of the saints in the stained glass, the anagram illuminating the meaning, and the characteristic 'dragons' of Celtic design over the 'arch'. 'White' is the traditional colour for religious in medieval Ireland; it also indicates the vestments worn on a joyful occasion, when 'rejoicing' is appropriate. The stanza avoids being too specific. Cormac MacCarthy's chapel has two towers and there is a round tower close by. The chapel's doorways have carved tympana, but not of dragons. The south door has a grotesque beast with a trefoil tail; the north door has a centaur shooting with bow and arrow at a great trefoil-tailed lion that has struck down two smaller beasts.

> Loud above the grassland,
> In Cashel of the towers,
> We heard with the yellow candles
> The chanting of the hours,
> White clergy saying High Mass,
> A fasting crowd at prayer,
> A choir that sang before them;
> And in the stained glass the holy day
> Was sainted as we passed
> Beyond that chancel where the dragons
> Are carved upon the arch.

The rhythm of the lines change, in lines 4-7, from the onward syntactical flow of the first stanza. These form a series of appositions within the single, run-on sentence, slowing the pace to allow each observed detail to play a full part: the chanting, the saying of Mass, the praying, the choir. The image of saints in stained glass seems to crown the sequence and leads to the triumphant 'arch' of dragons. This method varies again in stanza four, which is also about Cashel, where the first three lines are more fragmented; lines two and three divide internally. But then the stanza concludes with one ongoing wave that leads to the magnificent affirmation of the final couplet.

> Treasured with chasuble,
> Sun-braided, rich cloak'd wine-cup,
> We saw, there, iron handbells,
> Great annals in the shrine
> A high-king bore to battle:
> Where, from the branch of Adam,
> The noble forms of language —

> Brighter than green or blue enamels
> Burned in white bronze — embodied
> The wings and fiery animals
> Which veil the chair of God.

The stanza focusses on beautiful objects: a sun-braided chalice, a 'rich cloak'd wine-cup', handbells used by clergy,[7] great annals that a high-king carried into battle to ensure God's protection. The picture is again generalised, the objects representative of wealth, artistry, and spiruality. Clarke evokes events and customs that are emblematic, and not verifiable. There is no record of annals being carried into battle and no evidence that a high-king of Cashel ever did so. Annals are not sacred texts, would not have been carried in a shrine, and would have no special protective powers. The northern O'Donnells did carry the *Cathach* ('the Battler') into battle, but it is a book of the Psalms and could be expected to attract supernatural power and to enlist it in aid of those who carried the shrine. Clarke probably realised this but was guided by the fact that the chief line of assonance in the stanza is a short 'a': 'Chasuble', 'handbells', 'annals', 'battle', 'branch', 'Adam', 'language', 'enamels', 'animals'. Therefore 'annals', a fairly impressive-sounding word, fitted the sound pattern satisfactorily.

He ascribes activities and attitudes to Cashel in a symbolic way, making it a focal point for the whole period. Politically establishing a high-kingship there in the preceding line, he then affirms its artistic, spiritual and political achievements in the art work of the illuminated manuscripts; they 'veil the chair of God' by bringing reverence, beauty and mystery to God at the centre. Just as the sumptuous ornaments in the opening lines, the handbells that call men to worship, the annals that protect kings, were all part of a religious faith, so the books, and in particular the illuminated manuscripts, are signs of an integrated christian culture in which God is the focus and the source of human activity.

The syntactical movement of the stanza leads towards this affirmation with considerable potential of meaning. There seems to be a reference to Cormac Mac Cuilleanain's *Glossary*, an etymological dictionary that begins with the word 'Adam' to whom it traces Cormac's ancestry. There is the possibility that Clarke is confusing the annals and *Lebor Gabála* which also begins with Creation and Adam, but in neither is there a description of God on His throne, surrounded by fiery angels, and neither is noted for its noble forms of language. In addition, there may be an association with the genealogy of Christ in the *Book of Kells* which ends with a reference to Adam as the son of the Lord: '*Adam qui fuit Domini*'. The lines refer to illuminated manuscripts, to their vivid colours, their famous drawings of animals and humans, and their religious orientation. Clarke wants to associate Cashel, as a focal point of his portrait of medieval christian Ireland, with the medieval illustrations of the *Majestas Domini*. He selects two representative colours from the illuminated manuscripts, emphasising their brilliance, intensity and translucent glaze. The script of the *Book of Kells*, both literally and figuratively, embodies 'fiery animals': the bizarre drawings of birds, beasts and humans within, between and around the lines, enmeshed with 'the noble forms of language'. In general they are symbols of christian belief.

The concluding lines recall the original sources of the *Majestas Domini*: Ezekiel's vision of a great cloud filled with fire and in the heart of the fire, four living figures, human in shape but with characteristics of the lion, the ox, and the eagle, and above them a figure enthroned and the vision in the Apocalypse of a figure enthroned in Heaven, four living figures around it with the characteristics of a man, a lion, an ox, and an eagle, crying unceasingly 'Holy, holy, holy is the Lord God, the Almighty who ever was, and is and is still to come'.[8] These four figures became identified with the four Evangelists and are present in many medieval manuscripts, including the *Book of Kells*. In Clarke's evocation the 'shrine' at Cashel has a comparable significance and symbolises a comparable integration of the artistic and the spiritual. The 'wings and fiery animals' suggest portrayals of Christ between the four 'beasts' of the Evangelists that figuratively 'veil the chair of God'. In a corresponding manner the scholars, monks and people of Cashel, representing an entire culture, reflect and celebrate the centrality of God. The poem rises to this moment of identification, in itself a corresponding act of imaginative faith, and in its concluding two stanzas moves away from this vision, but without forgetting it.

The poem smoothly incorporates the harsher aspects of medieval christianity in stanza five's references to 'wild confession' . . . 'Black congregations' and the crowd wailing on the 'holy mountain', which seems to be Croagh Patrick. The final stanza quietly contrasts the wine merchants and the ascetic Culdees as the pilgrim ship departs. The communal personae have witnessed an idealised, selective version of medieval christianity: 'we came' . . . 'We heard' . . . 'we passed' . . . 'We saw, there' . . . Other aspects, including what Robin Flower called 'unlovely asceticism'[9] are the subject of 'Celibacy' and of the two longer confessional poems that follow it.

The setting is strikingly different from those in 'Pilgrimage', being composed of nettle, straw, flagstone, cold water, a bare island, thistle, and reed, all penitential images that reflect Clarke's avoidance of traditional religious images of English poetry – thorn, rose, lily, poignard.[10] The persona is also quite different from those in 'Pilgrimage'. Here the first person narrator, an ascetic, confesses to the sexual temptation that afflicts him. The tone of the poem seriously reflects his predicament but with a suggestion of mockery in some of its exaggerated language.

> Bedraggled in the briar
> And grey fire of the nettle,
> Three nights, I fell, I groaned
> On the flagstone of help
> To pluck her from my body;
> For servant ribbed with hunger
> May climb his rungs to God.

The language of the poem is cold and attenuated; it is also, despite its subject of temptation by a persistent, beautiful woman, almost without sensuality. Later in this collection, in 'Aisling' Clarke personifies the visionary woman in the conventional physical detail of the genre; here the description is restrained. The ascetic imagines her in images that correspond to his own emaciated, mortified body. Like the barren setting, the biblical allusions — to plucking out what offends, Jacob's ladder, wrestling with an angel, and John the Baptist — are correlatives for his condition. Even his sexual phantasies lack substance.

> On pale knees in the dawn,
> Parting the straw that wrapped me,
> She sank until I saw
> The bright roots of her scalp.
> She pulled me down to sleep,
> But I fled as the Baptist
> To thistle and to reed.

Determined abnegation and the pain of the conflict between asceticism and sexuality are the components of the man's life. 'Celibacy' has the same elements of alliteration, assonance, run-on lines and syntactical control found in 'Pilgrimage', but for different purposes. By shortening the line to two stresses Clarke provides a tighter frame for the ascetic's life. The use of the shorter line, appropriate for this brief confessional declaration, this self-dramatisation, is less effective when used for the longer, more expansive narratives of Gormlai and the Young Woman of Beare. It becomes clear in *Pilgrimage* that Clarke no longer celebrates the 'merry sins'. 'Celibacy' shrinks from them, 'Pilgrimage' ignored them, and Gormlai and the Young Woman of Beare, while confessing sins of the flesh, do so in an ambivalent manner. The style of *Pilgrimage*, whether in the longer three-stressed or the two-stressed line tends to be restrained and formal. It inhibits the free expression of sexuality. While

Clarke may not want to celebrate sin, he does want to respond openly and realistically to the subject of sexuality, to take away the mystery that poets have, he thinks, woven around women. Detecting a fear of women in many periods, the medieval, the time of the aisling poems, the Irish Literary Revival, and the modern, he was determined to face up to this fear.[11]

The story of Queen Gormlai is found in several texts, in the Annals, in O'Curry, in Douglas Hyde, in Sigerson[12] and, because a number of poems have been attributed to her, she has been of interest to Celtic scholars.[13] Briefly her story is as follows: she was the daughter of Flann Sinna, king of Ireland, and was married first to Cormac of Cashel, the king-bishop of Munster. He however renounced the marriage. Her father then arranged for her to marry Cearbhall, king of Leinster. Cearbhall and her father made war upon Munster, killed and beheaded Cormac at the Battle of Belamoon. Cearbhall was wounded, Gormlai nursed him but when she regretted the killing and mutilation of Cormac, Cearbhall kicked her in front of her servants. She left him and after his death married Nial Glundubh. This seems to have been a love-match. Nial became king of Ireland and was killed fighting the Danes near Dublin. Sometime earlier their son had been drowned. In her last years, according to tradition, Gormlai lived in poverty, no longer beautiful or powerful, becoming a *caillech*. She is supposed to have written a number of poems lamenting Nial's death, the death of their son, and her own miserable circumstances. In fact these poems belong to a later period and may have been influenced by the earlier poem, 'The Old Woman of Beare'. In some accounts of her life she sought refuge in a hovel and once, imagining that she saw Nial and stretching out her hand to detain him, she fell across a stake supporting the bed and was pierced through the heart. The impression given sometimes is that her death was a punishment for her life of 'pleasure' with three husbands.

Gormlai is of particular interest to Clarke because hers was a conscience wounded by others.[14] Her 'Confession' is an appeal for understanding. She contrasts her present poverty with the wealth that she once had and remembers her beauty and innocence. The poem is modelled upon 'Poems attributed to Gormlaith' which Osborn Bergin discussed in *Miscellany Presented to Kuno Meyer* (1912).[15] There Gormlai also laments her age, loss of beauty and wealth. Clarke writes a similar disciplined, classical poem. While Gormlai remembers her elegance and life of ease at Cashel, she recalls her bewilderment at Cormac's celibacy.

> Cormac bared
> Himself upon the flagstone
> And was alone in prayer.

All night he turned to God
Because the body dies;
But had it been immodest
For him to rest beside me?

Nothing that she has read tells her

                 goodness can insult
The mind, that meeting looks
Are bright adultery.

One of the highlights of the poem is her account, inaccurate but dramatic, of Cormac's death, which is reminiscent of the murder of Thomas Beckett.

He cropped the greener land
To Cashel top. He took
The bishop in his chapel
And wrung the holy mass-book.
But Cormac, in the fury,
Stumbled from crook to handbell —
And by the axe-red tonsure,
At his own font, he fell.

When Nial rescues her, the poem expresses their love in imagery of natural beauty. Then they 'repented/With penance on bare feet'. Drawing a lesson from her experience, Gormlai declares that all sex is sinful: 'Yearly parents/Your pleasures are unchaste'. Seeing her present abandonment as a form of punishment she concludes that even wedded sex is wrong. Even Cormac sought harsh forms of penance, 'wore the shirt/ Of fire, the shoes of stone'; but she is 'impure with love'. Her confession concludes with her defence of her third marriage. Then the poem reminds us, as it did in the first stanza, that she speaks as the wretched, forsaken creature on the 'wild' bed, she who was once beautiful and desired by men. Her confession is framed between the italicised descriptions of the first and the last stanzas of the 'hovel' and 'that wild bed', where 'Her flesh became a dagger', both emaciated and wounded by the prick of conscience. The 'stake' of the wild bed recalls the stake to which heretics were tied and burnt; in Gormlai's case the torment is of the mind, as she tries to understand and explain her story.

Gormlai confesses but is ambivalent about her sins. A similar ambivalence pervades 'The Young Woman of Beare' which is based on the old Irish poem, 'The Old Woman of Beare', but with significant changes of emphasis. In the early Irish poem the old woman laments her lost youth; in Clarke's poem the young woman laments her inability to become old and thereby gain freedom from the tormenting conflict between desire and church teaching. The real subject of the old Irish poem, as Proinsias MacCana has pointed out, 'is the incompatability between Christianity and the world of pagan belief'.[16] The real subject of Clarke's poem is the conflict between christianity and individual desire, treated in a careful balance between joyful revelations of sensual pleasure and fearful admonitions against sins of the flesh.

The conflict between soul and body is implicit in the first stanza between references to people going to evening Devotions and those going to visit the Young Woman, between the house of God and her house, a contrast that recurs. The people hurry to the church in the first stanza and return in the last with the result that her narrative of sinful pleasures parallels their religious devotions. Soul and body are thus constantly related. The poem alternates between the two: sections that describe her sexual progress and sections in which she warns women against sexual sin. Once again, as in Gormlai's confession, the conflict is stated between pleasures of the body (sex, clothes, material possessions, social and political power) and the spiritual claims of the Church which condemn unlawful sex and material wealth.

The first stanza in its sound pattern of 'walled' . . . 'hall' . . . 'low fires' . . . 'nightfall' creates a feeling of illicit enclosure that contrasts with the open activities of the praying people. Countering them also are the references to horsemen galloping and the vigorous rhyme of 'roused' and 'house'.

> Through lane or black archway,
> The praying people hurry,
> When shadows have been walled,
> At market hall and gate,
> By low fires after nightfall;
> The bright sodalities
> Are bannered in the churches;
> But I am only roused
> By horsemen of de Burgo
> That gallop to my house.

In the second stanza the hush of stanza one is replaced by gold, sunlight, delight in clothes, in the excitement of 'bad thoughts', sexual desire and self-indulgence. The concluding enigmatic couplet raises the problem: the secret eye of sexual pleasure whose 'opening' is ambiguous in being both a release and a realisation. The 'secret eye' that she pleases includes what the eye can see under closed lids, in fantasy, and what it sees when conscience asserts itself. The erotic meanings prepare for the more open assertions of sexuality in the following stanza. The Last 'Judgment' is also ambiguous in the context, since it involves a final awakening to the reality of sin and that reality contrasts with the 'dream'. The Young Woman is not simply an advocate of sexual permissiveness. When we look closely at the images with which she describes her sensual nature the manner undermines the means. There is an over-ripe, decadent quality about the imagery so that the final couplet is less an unexpected reversal, a going against the grain of her portrait, than a confirmation of things implicit in these images. She relates the joys of the flesh but sees them *sub specie aeternitatis*. Her confession both discloses and judges.

The self-portrait is at times triumphant and defiant: 'I am the bright temptation' . . . 'I triumph in a dream' and at times subdued: 'I am the dark temptation'. References to the Ormonds and Desmonds place the poem in the fifteenth and sixteenth centuries, specifically in 1462 when the fortunes of the Ormonds declined after the Battle of Pilltown and in 1584-85 when the 'President of Munster', Sir John Perrot, put down the Desmond rebellion and confiscated their lands. The woman's self-centred hedonism is indifferent to political collapse or the sufferings of war. She is equally defiant of women's scorn, since she knows her power over their husbands.

Even though she associates herself with Anglo-Norman lords, the portrait is not confined to a particular historical context. Fundamentally, the young woman is the voice of desire, the spirit of sensual delights. The Old Woman of Beare also had political associations; she was the 'caillech Bhéire Buí', a goddess of sovereignty, associated with the kings of Corco Loígde in West Munster who had been defeated by the Eoganachta. Francis John Byrne has pointed out that she appears in the genealogical tradition as the foster-mother of Corc Duibne, ancestor of the Corcu Duibne of the Kerry peninsulas and that in 'The Lament of the Old Woman of Beare' a 'subtle use is made of two landscapes which form the basic imagery of the poem: that of the lonely island of Beare in the south-west and that of the prosperous plain of Femen around Cashel in the territory of the Múscraige'.[17] Her succession of lovers relates to her role as goddess of sovereignty. In the old Irish poem these political lovers are submerged in her mythical status. Clarke's Young Woman of Beare resembles her in that her political connections are present, indeed more explicit, and in that her symbolic role also transcends them. In her case unchanging youth is not a sign of marriage to a rightful king; she is not the goddess of sovereignty but the goddess of desire:

It is my grief that time
Cannot appease my hunger;
I flourish where desire is
And still, still I am young.

Through her sexuality is given a voice, triumphant, defiant, glorying in her power over men, but not freed from the nagging sense of moral responsibility. Her triumphs are always in a 'dream'. The high point of her declaration of such power comes in stanza seven:

See! See, as from a lathe
My polished body turning!
He bares me at the waist .
And now blue clothes uncurl
Upon white haunch. I let
The last bright stitch fall down
For him as I lean back,
Straining with longer arms
Above my head to snap
The silver knots of sleep.

The poem has moved seductively from half-dream to this actualisation, this revelation of a Venus in a whirl of blue and white, a perverse Madonna of the bed. The tone of urgency and passion is the climax of the poem's progression in sensuality.

The concluding stanza of the first section asserts the counter-claim of the clergy; the woman's argument is that she and her lover can enjoy 'what is allowed in marriage', but the metaphor of the coin devalues her claim. 'The jingle of that coin' she says, 'Is still the same, though stolen'. But the following five lines submit that it is unthrifty to spend the coin of sexual pleasure in a manner that brings 'shame', 'ill' and 'repentance', when through marriage they 'might pinch and save/Themselves in lawful pleasure'. The line carries a double meaning of physical relationships and of the metaphor of storing up treasure in Heaven. The stanza works strongly against the section which it brings to an end, since it admits so readily, even lamely, that illicit sex is sinful and pays bad dividends.

The transition to the note of warning follows logically from that admission. Her history becomes an *exemplum*, a parable of loss and degradation, a downward progress from 'idle thoughts', courting, straying from the path of virtue into 'common ways'. The diction becomes appropriately colloquial: she 'got a bad name' and was 'blamed'. The account now is not sensual, nor is it a defiant demonstration of her power. She tells her story, or *uirsgéal*,[18] in a straightforward manner, bluntly illustrating her 'common ways'. But, as in the case of Gormlai, the narrative contains a defence; she is more victim than conscious perpetrator; her sinful ways began when she was too innocent to realise the consequences; then she was blinded by desire and sensuality; then her joy was greater than her fear of scandal or condemnation. This note of troubled defensiveness occurs in both poems: the sinful predicament in which Gormlai and the Young Woman find themselves is not freely chosen. They are victims of decisions made by others, victims of their own human nature, victims of an over-rigorous, male-dominated church.

The third section continues the warning to women:

> Women, obey the mission —
> Be modest in your clothes.

She returns to her present condition. Condemned to recurrent periods of youth and so to unceasing desire, she hungers for sex. The Young Woman confesses to a condition that is inescapable and recurrent, committing her to inevitable conflict with the church and with society. Whereas Oisin in the Land of Youth, and similar figures, could return with enticing accounts of everlasting youth and pleasure free from moral censure, her state of permanent youthfulness is a curse — 'still, still I am young'. She is frightened by the prayers of the 'black friars'. She continues her story of success with men, with a Flemish merchant in Limerick, with horsemen at the Curragh, with chapmen in the Pale. She is at the centre of political power and sees Sir John Perrot's scorched earth policy in Munster. She identifies herself again as the 'dark temptation', condemned by clergy who try to 'save' all those she has 'corrupted'.

> I fear, lost and too late
> The prelates of the Church.

The duality of her self-portrait remains: she is both bright and dark, attractive but sinful, desired but to be shunned, lawful in marriage but unlawful outside it. The paradox cannot be resolved; her state of conflict remains, she is what she is. She belongs to the condition of the ever young, but in the mortal world whose moral imperatives she understands exactly. At its best her portrait expresses the christian dilemma in which the individual's attempts to follow the teachings of Christ are thwarted by flawed human nature. Hers is a portrait that comes alive in the ebb and flow of her thoughts. Gormlai is a more remote figure, caught in a more marmoreal style.

Of the poems that remain in *Pilgrimage*, two may be regarded as vision poems. 'Aisling' is an imitation of the Irish *aisling* poem with its stressed metre and conventional 'plot': the sad poet meets the beautiful woman, he describes her beauty in decorative detail and asks her who she is; she identifies herself and he is left in dejection. The genre, in Clarke's view, was another example of the fear of women. By identifying the beautiful woman as an abstraction for Ireland, poets, he argued, could transcend their fear and escape from moral censure. They could indulge their mental images of feminine beauty and write 'glowing studies in the nude, voluptuous with colour and sound' without endangering their consciences. [19] In the conventional list of identifying questions Clarke includes 'I asked her was she the Geraldine', that is, the 'Fair Geraldine', daughter of Gerald Fitzgerald, whose beauty Henry Howard, earl of Surrey extolled in a series of songs and sonnets first printed in Tottel's *Miscellany* (1557). She is also the subject of a poem reputedly by Domhnall na Buile which is called 'The Geraldine's Daughter' and may be read in *The Poets and Poetry of Munster* (1850). [20]

'The Marriage Night' may also be regarded as a vision poem, since it creates an imaginary wedding between a beautiful woman and the great earls, Hugh O'Neill and Red Hugh O'Donnell.

> All saw in that cathedral
> The great Earls kneel with her;
> The open book was carried,
> They got up at the gospel.
> In joy the clergy prayed,
> The white-clad acolytes
> Were chaining, and unchaining,
> Fire-hearted frankincense.

The wedding takes place in the years of Irish unity and hope prior to the Battle of Kinsale which signalled the end of the Norman and Gaelic lordships and the possibility of an independent aristocratic kingdom for Ireland.

The two poems are carefully related: 'The Marriage Night' gathers into itself the power and splendour of the period prior to Kinsale when papal blessings and Spanish aid seemed to present the possibility of success for the Catholic, counter-reformation forces in Ireland. The poem might be read as an Irish answer to Spenser's *Epithalamium*, written to celebrate his wedding to Elizabeth Boyle in Christ Church, Cork. Clarke's attitude to a marriage service that blessed the union of the political and religious forces of the time resembles his treatment of the Irish monastic world in 'Pilgrimage'. 'Aisling' is heavy with the disruption and disillusion that fell upon the land after the calamity of Kinsale. Then the great earls went down in defeat and into exile, the Gaelic civilization collapsed and the old order that had a favoured place for the poet disappeared for ever. No amount of hope in help from abroad could dispel the sense of defeat. Clarke's identification in 'Aisling' of post civil war Ireland with post Kinsale Ireland is significant, as is the sarcastic note in the final stanza that in modern Ireland the poet can expect nothing from the state except neglect.

In both poems Clarke touches upon one of the central myths of early Irish literature: the marriage of the king with the goddess of the land. Behind most of the ancient stories, of Deirdre, of Maeve, of Niamh, of the Hag of Beare, lies the primitive ritual in which the new king had to lie with the earth mother in order to guarantee fertility for his reign. That union is essential to the woman if she is not to be old and barren like the Hag of Beare. The *aisling* poems of the seventeenth and eighteenth centuries retain this old belief in a subliminal manner. 'The Wedding Night' harkens back to it in that its best mode of illustration is an imaginary wedding between the unnamed bride and the princes of the North. This poem also has some of the conventions of the *aisling*: the visionary woman riding down to Kinsale, who is praised in the 'holy courts of Europe', is the 'wonder of our days' and represents the forces of the Counter Reformation which supported the Irish struggle against the first Elizabeth. In defeat she has to lie beside 'heretics', just as the woman of the *aisling* has to lie with foreigners.

The myth of the sovereign goddess is also present in 'Wandering Men' (1932) which Clarke included with the *Pilgrimage* poems in *Collected Poems* (1936).[21] It too is a vision poem in which the pagan aspects of a christian saint are revealed. Brigid of Kildare is a blend of christian saint and pagan goddess, or triple goddess. In Irish mythology, according to Cormac's *Glossary*, she is the daughter of the Dagda, patroness of poetry, whose sisters were Brigid, goddess of healing, and Brigid, goddess of smithcraft. In old Irish her name means 'the exalted one'. Whitley Stokes says that 'her breath revives the dead, a house in which she is staying flames up to heaven . . . a fiery pillar rises over her head'.[22] Ale is also associated with her as it is with the goddess of sovereignty. In a footnote Clarke identifies her as 'goddess of Fire and Poetic Inspiration'.[23]

The movement of the poem is from a perception of her as abbess of her convent at Kildare to a vision of her mythological nature. The men, called 'clergy' in the manuscript, stumble upon her convent; the associations are of night, entrapment, an unknown path and the religious connotations of bare knee, prayer, canticles and the flame round the convent. Her vestigial associations emerge; her austere habit disguises her role as fire-goddess — 'the flaming of her forehead'. In stanza three the food seems to be from Eden and she pours ale. The high point of these growing indications of her pagan status is reached in stanza four:

And all that night I was aware
Of shapes no priest can see,
The centaur at a house of prayer,
The sceptred strangers from the East.
Confined in dreams we saw again
How Brigid, while her women slept
Around her, templed by the flame,
Sat in a carven chair.

The vision now recorded by a first person narrator is essentially pagan and mythic, beyond the power of 'priest', but incorporating figures close to or attendant upon religious experience. 'The centaur at the house of prayer' refers to the figure in Cormac's chapel at Cashel. 'The sceptred strangers from the East' refers to the three wise men who journeyed to Bethlehem; they are represented on the Cross of Flann at Clonmacnoise. Brigid's appearance in the 'carven chair' and 'templed by a flame' recalls her former role as goddess of pagan worship. In the last stanza the men who have strayed upon this unknown path return to the visible world, but echoes of the pagan past remain in the 'oaks' and 'sun-circle'. They praise 'that sky-woman', the *spéir-bhean* of the *aisling*, the woman whom Cormac Mac Cuilleanain called, 'goddess of poets'. 'Wandering Men' is a parable for the imagination's ability to discover the unknown within the known, the mythical within the christian, the past within the present. It is analogous with many similar experiences in Clarke's work, including his creative engagement in these poems with a world he had discovered and made his own.

Pilgrimage shows Clarke's determination to rely on native forms and native prosody and to illustrate the drama of racial conscience through examples from the past. Its success made him confident that he and his contemporaries could bring about a renewal in Irish poetry by expressing their 'casuistic mentality', 'the drama of conscience and of inner conflict',[24] which he felt had become intensified in their time. He pointed in evidence to episcopal pastorals against immodesty in female dress and to the censorship of books.[25] It was a subject that had been ignored by the poets of the Irish Literary Revival, whose recovery of mythology and folklore, 'did not extend to the imaginative literature and hagiology of mediaeval Ireland'.[26] They did not deal with the issue of Catholic guilt. His generation, he believed, could escape the dominance of English tradition, the 'mental discomfort' and 'lingual maladjustment' it caused, by basing their work on native forms and by expressing their 'scholastic mentality'.[27] There were neglected areas of Irish poetry to be explored: a school of rich sensuous poetry, Norman Gaelic love poetry and religious poetry, which he particularly advocated. 'Reviving it,' he argued, 'reviving for ourselves its formal diction, we forget the abasement of religious imagination today. We are in a world of art in which emotion is pure, choice and disciplined'.[28] The emphasis is on an art that is classical and formal and he objects to religious art that fails to acknowledge the dignity and independence of the individual. He went on in this essay to recall the 'delicate and rare' style of sixteenth- and seventeenth-century Irish religious poetry, the confessional form, and mediaeval forms that expressed 'the natural man'.[29] He found fault with the Revival poets because they tried to become part of an Irish tradition without taking the trouble to learn the language. He criticised his contemporary, Lyle Donaghy, because it 'never occurred to him to learn Irish and study the literature before he started claiming to be in the tradition'.[30] Two years later, in 1941, in a review of M.J. MacManus's *Rackrent Hall*, he said again that Irish poets should learn from native forms: 'the witty, graceful verses to be found in the collection of mediaeval Gaelic poems recently published by the Rev Lambert McKenna, the mock heroic manner of Donnchadh Ruadh, Mrs Costello's Gaelic collection of homely and humorous folk-verse . . .'[31]

Clarke's positive, crusading outlook in 1932, 1935, 1939, and 1941, was determined by his belief that Irish poetry had deteriorated since 1916 and had lost some of the independence that it had achieved during the Irish Literary Revival. Its poetry, Clarke argued, was 'well in advance of contemporary English poetry both in its technique and its subtle range of consciousness'.[32] It was a poetry that had escaped 'from the mighty law and order of English poetry into the shadowy, irresponsible world of delicate rhythm and nuance'.[33] The Easter Rising swept away a new school of poets — Thomas MacDonagh, Padraic Pearse, Joseph Mary Plunkett. Furthermore, W.B. Yeats had returned, in Clarke's view, to the main sources of English Literature, or, as he wrote to Seamus O'Sullivan: 'Yeats, in transforming himself into a world poet, has left the Irish Revival baby on the doorstep, and the question is what are we to do with it?'[34] Clarke's answer is found in *Pilgrimage*, in its use of native forms, in its emphasis on spiritual crisis. It is found in the prose romances, in many of his plays, and in the anguished engagement with the conflict between personal freedom and church regulations in *Night and Morning*.

Chapter 4: *Night and Morning* (1938)

The poems in *Night and Morning* are scholastic in that they deal with the conflict of reason and faith which was central to the philosophical and theological debates of the medieval schoolmen from Eriugena in the ninth century to Aquinas in the thirteenth. At the heart of the conflict between the individual and the Church is the ancient struggle between reason and faith, that is, between the need for intellectual freedom on the part of the individual and the insistence on faith as a higher authority on the part of the Church. The conflict, in other words, resembles the issue at the heart of the struggle in the middle ages, prior to the Council of Trent, when the scholastics were trying to harmonise the philosophy of Aristotle with the teachings of the Church fathers. The degree of independence given to or argued for on behalf of private judgment varied from the early period to the later as did the degree of authority granted to or demanded by the Church. That Clarke is aware of this philosophical and theological framework is clear: it is specifically drawn in 'No Recompense', is referred to in 'Night and Morning' and is part of each poem that draws attention to the conflict between 'thought' and 'belief'. There is an ongoing, general contrast between pre-Council of Trent Europe and twentieth-century Ireland.

In reality, as the poems make clear, the issue was more particular and more complex: before the individual reaches the age of reason he inherits the burdens of mortality and of his own sinful nature; he is the heir to sin and bears responsibility for Christ's suffering and death; he is responsible for his own salvation. But he is inherently hampered: he cannot fight evil successfully on his own; he has to avail of God's help, has to avail of the redemption earned on his behalf through Christ's death and resurrection. When he tries to act in accordance with what he believes,

77

he is liable to come into conflict with the laws of the Church; when he tries to act in accordance with his instincts, particularly his sexual feelings, he is also liable to come into conflict with clerical prohibitions.[1] Despite his sinful nature, he is entrusted with a soul which he is required to keep free of grave sin in order to gain the rewards of everlasting life after death. To fail at the point of death, the moment towards which he is inexorably propelled by virtue of his mortality, is to ensure eternal damnation. His mortality is a constant reminder of the possibility, even the likelihood, that at the moment of death he may be judged and cast, like Lucifer, into the darkness of oblivion.

In *Night and Morning* Clarke confronts the dilemma of the man caught in the insoluble conflict of reason and faith, not through the persona of the monk, the scholar or the 'loose' woman, but in his own educated, scholastic voice; not through mythological landscapes but in a twentieth-century, Catholic setting, with a few historical parallels. He portrays the conflict in varying degrees of protest and detachment, grief and anger, submission and fear. But the overall mood is confessional and contrite. Even the apparently most assertive poems, 'Night and Morning' and 'Tenebrae' have a reflective, penitential manner. They acquire their authority from their ability to present both sides of the conflict. Their references to religious ceremonies and imagery strengthen the position of the persona as a voice from within the Church, speaking with knowledge and from experience. That sense of authority is also present in the opening lines: 'I know the injured pride of sleep' and 'This is the hour that we must mourn'. In both the speaker is part of a congregation, at Mass in the first poem and at the office of tenebrae in the second. In one he acknowledges responsibility for Christ's suffering and death, in the other he recognises the mood of mourning that the Church expresses during Holy Week. In each he is a divided being: his instinctive need is to participate, to be one with the communion of the faithful, to assent to the mystery being enacted at Mass, to merge with the mood of lament at tenebrae; he is however separated from those around him by his inability to give mental allegiance, by his realisation that the price paid for obedience is his independence of mind. His knowledge of the Church's history of opposition to independent philosophical and theological inquiry, with which he identifies, prevents him from yielding readily to the Church's insistence on faith.

'Night and Morning' begins with an acknowledgement of guilt: Christ's death — 'the miserable act of centuries' — was an atonement for the sins of mankind; each sinner contributes to that agony. At the same time, Clarke uses these incidents of Christ's passion to represent personal nightmare, mockery and betrayal:

> I know the injured pride of sleep,
> The strippers at the mocking-post,
> The insult in the house of Caesar
> And every moment that can hold
> In brief the miserable act
> Of centuries. Thought can but share
> Belief — and the tormented soul,
> Changing confession to despair,
> Must wear a borrowed robe.

The ignominy of Christ is also Clarke's. The 'pride' refers to human dignity, Christ's which was derided, Clarke's which is endangered by the gulf between 'thought' and 'belief' and by the Church's denial of intellectual freedom. He can 'know' the significance of Christ's agony, but unless he can believe it as an act of redemption he cannot share in its benefits. Therefore Christ's agony is his, it heightens his sense of isolation. The more clearly and intensely he apprehends Christ's suffering, the more he himself suffers from the knowledge that he is not a beneficiary of the rewards of that suffering.

The confessional mode, which in itself is an act of faith in God's mercy, gives way to despair, that is, to a loss of confidence in God. The persona can only dissemble. Stripped of his individual identity, he can like Christ, wear a borrowed robe, can pretend to participate in what he cannot believe. At best 'thought can but share belief'.

The second stanza is an elaboration of the consequences. If he cannot share in the effects of Christ's atonement, then the sacraments fail. The sacrifice of the Mass does not involve him, and like the madmen in 'Summer Lightning' he is 'one in whom God's likeness died'. The passing of time is a reminder of his mortality and of the inevitable approach of the Judgment Day.

> Morning has moved the dreadful candle,
> Appointed shadows cross the nave;
> Unlocked by the secular hand,
> The very elements remain
> Appearances upon the altar.
> Adoring priest has turned his back
> Of gold upon the congregation.
> All saints have had their day at last,
> But thought still lives in pain.

He cannot believe in the miracle of the transubstantiation by which the 'elements' of bread and wine are changed into the body and blood of Christ and feels excluded by the priest. Ironically, his exclusion takes place on the Feast of All Saints, when the Church commemorates all its martyrs and saints. He identifies instead with the scholastics who suffered for their allegiance to the freedom of the mind and who are the subject of the next two stanzas. Clarke links his own isolation with those whose intellectual efforts 'perished', that is, had to yield to the Church's authority. He equates their attempts to 'elevate' the soul through reason with the priest's elevation of the ciborium at Mass. The schoolmen tried to transform words into living substance, a miracle comparable to the priest's re-enactment at Mass.

> How many councils and decrees
> Have perished in the simple prayer
> That gave obedience to the knee;
> Trampling of rostrum, feathering
> Of pens at cock-rise, sum of reason
> To elevate a common soul:
> Forgotten as the minds that bled
> For us, the miracle that raised
> A language from the dead.

Clarke is also referring to the scholastics' rejuvenation of Latin. 'Even when it was dead,' he wrote, it 'came to life as the language of the soul'.[2] They too, like Christ, sought to bring men to God and suffered. On this day Clarke commemorates these forgotten saints and martyrs of the mind.

He also commemorates a period when God's humanity was passionately and proudly realised through argument and when the interrelationship of heaven and earth was convincingly demonstrated.

> O when all Europe was astir
> With echo of learned controversy,
> The voice of logic led the choir.
> Such quality was in all being,
> The forks of heaven and this earth
> Had met, town-walled, in mortal view
> And in the pride that we ignore,
> The holy rage of argument,
> God was made man once more.

In referring to the forks of heaven and earth Clarke may be thinking of some medieval cities in which the church stood at the intersection of two main streets; the inspiration for this plan was the Heavenly Jerusalem where God was the centre.

'Night and Morning' recalls an ideal. 'Tenebrae' is more realistic. The occasion is Holy Week, during which the Church remembers Christ's suffering and death and prepares for His resurrection. In the churches, religious statues, images and the crucifix are covered with purple cloths to represent Christ in the tomb. A triangular candelabra has its candles extinguished one by one during the Tenebrae service to recall Christ's desertion by his Apostles in the Garden of Gethsemane. The last candle is taken behind the altar as a sign of His burial; its reappearance on Easter Saturday signifies His resurrection. It is a time to mourn.

> This is the hour that we must mourn
> With tallows on the black triangle,
> Night has a napkin deep in fold
> To keep the cup; yet who dare pray
> If all in reason should be lost,
> The agony of man betrayed
> At every station of the cross?

It is a solemn occasion, but the questioning self, once more isolated by thought, asks if this mourning is for the betrayal of man, not God. Who dare pray, Clarke asks dramatically, if man's intellect excludes him from that salvation which Christ's suffering and death were meant to achieve? To be human is to be an involuntary victim: mortal, subject to despair, bereft of innocence.

> O when the forehead is too young,
> Those centuries of mortal anguish,
> Dabbed by a consecrated thumb
> That crumbles into dust, will bring
> Despair with all that we can know;
> And there is nothing left to sing,
> Remembering our innocence.

The 'despair' induced by the knowledge of human frailty limits the poet's imaginative freedom. There is nothing left to sing when the horror appears to be inescapable. There is nothing left to sing when one has been expelled from the Eden of childhood by the Church's harsh decrees. Even the priest's thumb, as it marks the sign of mortality on the child's forehead, becomes the victim of the message.

The dilemma experienced in the conflicting demands of reason and feeling is dramatised in stanza three.

> I hammer on that common door,
> Too frantic in my superstition,
> Transfix with nails that I have broken,
> The angry notice of the mind.
> Close as the thought that suffers him,

> The habit every man in time
> Must wear beneath his ironed shirt.

'Hammer', 'frantic', 'transfix', 'angry', the words capture his state, as does the dramatic transformation by which the nails used by Luther to fix his theses to the cathedral door become Clarke's finger nails broken in a desperation that is both intellectual defiance and emotional need. The opposition continues in the last three lines: the habit of obedience is as binding as the habit of independent thought that causes pain and that persists. Every man in time, that is, every mortal being comes, in time, to death and judgment. Mortality itself is a habit, an inescapable context of existence. Ash Wednesday bears witness to this message. Man's 'ironed shirt' is made of all these restraints, of social life, of time, of thought, of feeling.

All four stanzas juxtapose reason and mortality, as Clarke assesses the consequences of intellectual defiance and disbelief. For no matter how 'frantic' his 'superstition', his wish to belong to the Church, to share in Christ's redemption, the price paid is one he is unable to pay by virtue of his given nature. The 'despair' brought 'with all that we can know' refers not just to the limits of human inquiry, but to the certainty that what we know is that we are mortal and that by knowing, by seeking knowledge, we are excluded.

But Clarke is not cowed by that knowledge. An 'open mind disturbs the soul'; that cannot be denied. But, associating soul and sun, or a church that favours faith over reason, that in both approval and mockery 'makes a show/Of half the world', he refuses to be defeated by the knowledge of death and the fear of everlasting exclusion.

> An open mind disturbs the soul,
> And in disdain I turn my back
> Upon the sun that makes a show
> Of half the world, yet still deny
> The pain that lives within the past,
> The flame sinking upon the spike,
> Darkness that man must dread at last.

Significantly the last candle does not promise resurrection for the speaker; it is 'sinking'. The final image is of 'darkness' and 'dread'.

In the concluding stanza Clarke reverses the order of the opposition of faith versus reason that he presents in stanza one. In both the opposition turns on the central 'yet'. Stanza one says 'we must mourn', because we are guilty of Christ's agony and death and we are mortal and must be prepared for death and the afterlife. But it counters that general call of Holy Week with the idea that it is man who is betrayed, not Christ.

That idea is explained in stanza two. Its effects are highlighted in stanza three. Its independence is stressed in stanza four, where the opposition presented by 'yet' is modified to mean at the same time. The position held by the argumentative self, while intellectually strong is at the same time emotionally vulnerable; the strain of the opposition shows throughout the poem, and particularly in stanza three where the desperate responses reveal the attraction of succumbing to the 'common' appeal. Even more clearly, in stanza four, Clarke describes an independence that is in danger of being frightened by the very forces it wants to, and has to, deny: the 'pain', the 'flame', the 'darkness', the 'dread'.

Of the remaining ten poems in *Night and Morning* five — 'No Recompense', 'Repentance', 'Mortal Pride', 'Summer Lightning' and 'The Jewels' — may be said to exist within the shadow of the dreaded darkness and five — 'Martha Blake', 'The Lucky Coin', 'Penal Law', 'Her Voice Could Not Be Softer' and 'The Straying Student' — to view it with more detachment.

'No Recompense' taken from its earlier position in *Collected Poems* (1936) and revised slightly to emphasise the disruptive effect of sexual sin, 'the anger of vein', identifies Clarke with the medieval scholastics. When the 'schoolmen' are told to 'forget' their efforts to reconcile Aristotle — whose categories are referred to in 'sweet divisions', 'quality' and 'number', a subdivision of the category of quality — and the Scriptures, that is, to harmonise reason and faith, Clarke is signifying his own failure to achieve a similar equality. His resolute pursuit of truth fails to relieve him of his fear of God's judgment. No earthly recognition can compensate for the loss of Heaven.

> Quality, number and the sweet divisions
> Of reason may forget their schoolmen now,
> And door-chill, body's heat, anger of vein,
> Bring madness in our sleep. I have endured
> The enmity of my own mind that feared
> No argument; but O when truth itself
> Can hold a despairing tongue, what recompense
> To find my name in any mortal mouth?

'Repentance', which is more explicitly penitential, also links problems of conscience with sexual sin and openly advocates submission, not independence. At one time, Clarke could find 'all knowledge' in Connaught but his experience of God's forgiveness for sexual sin — 'I felt/Repentance gushing from the rock'[3] — has led to his present contrition. The language of submission is explicitly fearful:

> Could I unbutton mad thought, quick-save
> My skin, if I were caught at last
> Without my soul and dragged to torment,
> Ear-drumming in that dreadful place
> Where the sun hides in the waters?

'Caught', 'dragged', 'torment', 'Ear-drumming', 'dreadful' — these words emphasise terror at the thought of damnation. Through a complex web of ambivalence and paradox, 'Mortal Pride' expresses a similar loss of certainty in one's own independence. The pain of that state is developed in 'Summer Lightning' which deals with the price paid when 'reason fails at midnight' and brilliantly uses the effects of the storm on mental patients[4] to illustrate their pitiful condition:

> I pity, in their pride
> And agony of wrong, the men
> In whom God's likeness died.

The problems of *Night and Morning* are quietly restated in 'The Jewels', the final poem. Once again Clarke expresses the view that we are victims: 'The crumbling centuries are thrust/In hands that are too frail for them'. He is loyal to 'truth' but riven by fear. There was a time when he could belong to the communion of the faithful; now, because of intellectual independence, he is excluded.

> The misery of common faith
> Was ours before the age of reason.
> Hurrying years cannot mistake
> The smile for the decaying teeth,
> The last confusion of our senses.
> But O to think, when I was younger
> And could not tell the difference,
> God lay upon this tongue.

Clarke's lament for a lost innocence, the lost security of being part of the communion of the faithful, before the age of rational doubt entered his life, is as genuine as his more spirited defiance in 'Night and Morning'. Despite their narrow ideological range, the lyrics are subtly varied in response, ranging from despair in 'Repentance' to the stark revelations of the consequences of the failure of nerve in 'Summer Lightning' and the calm weighing up of pros and cons in 'The Jewels'. Of the five poems that are more detached, four may be dealt with briefly; the other, 'The Straying Student' requires a more extended treatment.

Martha Blake in the poem of that title finds fulfilment within the church, unlike the 'I' persona in 'Night and Morning', 'Tenebrae' and the so-called darker poems. She has a simple, unquestioning faith, 'does not see through any saint' and participates happily, almost erotically, in the 'miracle' of the Mass. Three stanzas out of eight bear witness to her joyous absorption in the 'Presence'; the climactic sixth enacts a drama of love and fulfilment. In an ironic perspective Clarke notes how unaware she is of the questions that torment him:

> The flame in heart is never grieved
> That pride and intellect
> Were cast below, when God revealed
> A heaven for this earth.

'The Lucky Coin' contrasts post-revolutionary Irish life with the nineteenth century, specifically with Catholic Emancipation which ended the Penal Laws, with Daniel O'Connell, the Liberator, and with Nephin, the *venusberg* of the *Love Songs of Connacht*.

> Lovers forgot on the mountain-side
> The stern law of the clergy

The coin of the title is defined by the activities associated with it. In the past it 'glittered', providing excitement and causing people to forget grief in song. The imagery of the 'fairground' includes gaiety, love-making, political freedom and the ability to behave freely, without clerical interference and without any sense of guilt. The coin of sensual pleasure and personal freedom however has been lost. Despite the 'rising' of 1916 Irishmen have not been truly liberated:

> . . . when our dread of the unseen
> Has rifled hold and corner,
> How shall we praise the men that freed us
> From everything but thought.

'Penal Law', which once formed the last stanza of 'The Envy of Poor Lovers' comments sarcastically on official attempts, such as the Censorship Act of 1929, to suppress instinct:

> Burn Ovid with the rest. Lovers will find
> A hedge-school for themselves and learn by heart
> All that the clergy banish from the mind,
> When hands are joined and head bows in the dark.

The title of this poem is taken from the laws which were enacted against Irish Catholics in the eighteenth century. Censorship now, Clarke argues, is also harsh but, like the penal laws, will fail. Denied education by law, the Catholics founded 'hedge-schools'. Denied freedom to love, the Irish discover secret places to meet. Forbidden to learn about love, they will learn it 'by heart', that is, instinctively, naturally. The clergy banish love but lovers become its devotees, finding a religion of love, with hands joined and heads bowed. The attitudes of prayer are appropriated to describe the lovers. The contrast, once again, is between heart and mind, between clerical rules and natural feeling. Clarke invites censors to do their damnedest: 'Burn Ovid with the rest'. Love cannot be legislated out of existence and in 'Her Voice Could Not Be Softer' he gently shows the grief that stern laws may cause.

'The Straying Student', positioned at the centre of the book, is a vision poem that adapts the conventions of the *aisling* for the purposes of the moral imagination. The setting is described in the opening stanza: an Aran island scene, a *Missa cantata* celebrated by a bishop on an important religious occasion, the custom of segregating the sexes within the church, and then the 'spiritual disruption', as Clarke called it, introduced by 'But' in the other half of the stanza, as the 'I' figure hears and sees the woman calling him away. The associations are not only with the *aisling* poems of the seventeenth or eighteenth centuries, but with mythological tales in which women figures arrive on the shores of Ireland and lure men away to the Invisible World. As in those tales of enticement there is a confrontation between two systems, two ideologies.

> On a holy day when sails were blowing southward,
> A bishop sang the Mass at Inishmore,
> Men took one side, their wives were on the other
> But I heard the woman coming from the shore:
> And wild in despair my parents cried aloud
> For they saw the vision draw me to the doorway.

The beauty of sound, over-abundant in the manner of the *aisling* in decline, is deliberately unresolved in the interrupted rhyme of 'shore' with 'doorway', 'to prevent too much sweetness'. In the case of 'shore' and 'doorway' Clarke wanted to introduce some Wagnerian discord, to link back through the recurrence of 'o' sounds in the stanza and to point forward to the 'o' sounds in the next stanza, 'to suggest', as he said, 'the continuity of action'. A 'closed rhyme would not echo the sense of spiritual disruption'. He explained

> I think that if one is trying to express a drama of inner conflict in lyric form, the outward form of sound should echo that conflict and that one can use effects similar to sharps, flats and unresolved intervals in music.[5]

In other words, his use of Gaelic prosody, at its best, is inseparable from the meaning and not just a matter of technical ingenuity.

Stanzas two and three describe the woman's attributes, connecting her with the Renaissance, the Revival of Learning, and sexual liberation. She is the bright temptation of the *Pilgrimage* poems, Gormlai, the Young Woman of Beare, all the visionary women of Irish tradition, but fused with the glories of the Renaissance, both secular and spiritual:

> Long had she lived in Rome when Popes were bad,
> The wealth of every age she makes her own,
> Yet smiled on me in eager admiration,
> And for a summer taught me all I know,
> Banishing shame with her great laugh that rang
> As if a pillar caught it back alone.
>
> I learned the prouder counsel of her throat,
> My mind was growing bold as light in Greece;
> And when in sleep her stirring limbs were shown,
> I blessed the noonday rock that knew no tree:
> And for an hour the mountain was her throne,
> Although her eyes were bright with mockery.

Just as the Young Woman of Beare was associated with English power in Ireland, so she is associated with the corrupt papacy of the late fifteenth century and with wealth. She is the dark temptation. She teaches him 'all I know', releases him from feelings of sexual guilt and shame, 'with her great laugh'.

Stanza three extends his education to intellectual and artistic knowledge; the emphasis is on the 'light' of philosophy, the illumination of the 'mind'. The sexual associations of 'throat', 'stirring limbs' reinforce the discovery of a self-reliant mind, whereas in 'No Recompense' the loss of the 'sweet divisions of reason' resulted in the separation of one from the other. In stanza four the references to Salamanca identifies the student as an Irish seminarist who went to the College of St Patrick in Salamanca, as was the custom in the seventeenth and eighteenth centuries. As John J. Silke has pointed out,

> Salamanca was the most outstanding of the Iberian colleges. Nurse of bishops, provincials, theologians, martyrs, and in great number, missionaries, it sent home in the space of a hundred years some five hundred priests to Ireland, England, and Scotland.[6]

The enthusiastic tone continues from 'taught me all I know/Banishing shame', through 'I learned', 'I blessed', 'I wrote', 'I might read' and 'I know', all positive achievements in an expanding educational process. The euphemistic explanation for his departure from the seminary is joyfully countered with the emphatic assertions and the touch of mystical selection in 'She laid her hand at darkfall on my page' and in the broadening of his education beyond the seminary curriculum. That curriculum included rhetoric, philosophy and theology; the horarium at *El Real Colegio de los Nobles Irlandeses* was rigorous, even ascetic. The stanza, by contrast, has an indefined generosity of reference:

> She laid her hand at darkfall on my page
> That I might read the heavens in a glance
> And I knew every star the Moors have named.

Moorish astronomers, who had developed their own star catalogue and predicted the positions of planetary bodies in *The Alphonsine Tables*, were responsible for the rebirth of astronomy; they are invoked here to suggest the expansion of the student's intellectual and imaginative horizons.

Like others in *Night and Morning*, this poem delineates a process of discovery and loss, potential and disappointment, hope and despair, light and darkness. The result of his experiences is that 'Awake or in my sleep, I have no peace now'. He has doubt: within the portrayal of the visionary woman are some warning signs: the despairing cries of his parents, the seduction of stanza two, the fact that the encounter is temporary — 'for a summer', 'for an hour'. If 'the noonday rock that knew no tree' may be 'blessed' for being exposed and unashamed, it may also be harsh and without shelter. If the woman is enthroned on the mountain, accepting the reverence of the student, her eyes, as he notes, are ominously 'bright with mockery'. The opposition initiated in the opening stanza between the setting and the woman, between its religious and social orthodoxies and the disruptive call that the student follows is developed further in these ambivalences. These signs become more insistent and more real in stanza four, with his fear that 'she may deceive' him, may leave him to his fate, to carry the coffin of mortality. What she embodies, for all its sensual and intellectual worth, may not be enough to save him in the restrictive, church-dominated country in which he resides:

> And yet I tremble lest she may deceive me
> And leave me in this land, where every woman's son
> Must carry his own coffin and believe,
> In dread, all that the clergy teach the young.

The poem seems to introduce a release of musical energy into the collection, but its assonantal and rhyming melodies are used in the service of an illusion, to depict the visionary woman and what she represents, not in the service of the reality in which the student has to exist. Clarke interrupts the harmonies when describing those circumstances.

'The Straying Student' is cleverly handled. It outlines in attractive and melodious terms the expansion of the Renaissance period, its independence from ecclesiastical despotism, its restoration of confidence in human faculties through the rediscovery of the classical past, and its comprehensive movement of the European intellect and will towards self-emancipation and towards the reassertion of the natural rights of the reason and the senses. These are all present in the alluring and exciting encounter of the student with the symbolic woman. Just as the Renaissance itself marked man's endeavour to reconstitute himself as a free being and not as the thrall of theological despotism, so Clarke's poem marks his own belief in an analogous liberation of the self from the clerical obscurantism that marked the Irish church in his time and that had obscured and distorted his own development. But it seems to be more than a particular allegory. Its splendid and sonorous depiction of Renaissance achievements serves as a foil for the deprivations of the present, with its imagery of death and dread.

The poem sweeps to its conclusion, gaining momentum from the very first stanza, buoyed up by sound and syntax. Clarke has learned to handle the long assonantal line. That momentum only suffers a set-back in stanza five where appropriately the pattern of sound is also interrupted and where, awakening from the heady experience, the student assesses the reality of his life. While he can recall and celebrate the past, he quails before the pressures within his own society.

Almost every poem in *Night and Morning* has this duality: the recognition of a way of life, or a time, in which the individual enjoyed freedom, whether intellectual, or sexual or both, but the realisation also of present circumstances hostile to that freedom. Both explicitly and implicitly the poems are confessional, acts of contrition for sins committed, for liberties taken. They seek forgiveness and in their abasement of the mind and the imagination deny those values, those needs of the spirit, that Clarke held dear.

Night and Morning may be classified as a book of religious lyrics; its ancestry may be the Irish religious poems of the sixteenth and seventeenth centuries and the religious poems of the Belgian Renaissance of the late nineteenth century, as Clarke said,[7] but the poems in *Night and Morning* represent a one-sided, stunted Christianity. The God they invoke is judgmental, a remote Old Testament figure from the Douai bible of Clarke's childhood who thrusts sinners into everlasting flames and into the wastes of exterior darkness. He is not the God of Love. There is little trust in His mercy but much fear of His punishment. The love that is missing in the relationship between the individual and God, in Clarke's perception of that relationship, deprives him also of human, sexual love and of self-esteem. His barrenness of spirit is almost total. Only in the past can sexuality be imagined as a natural part of life. Only in the past can reason be enthroned as a human right. Only in the past can the interconnection of heaven and earth be credibly realised. Clearly Clarke's immediate concern is the Jansenistic church and the primitive society of his own time of which Inishmore is an example. The poems are attempts to externalise his own values, to clarify his own position; they create situations that expose and objectify the issues. While it would be unwise to identify the 'I' persona too closely with the poet, it seems clear that the book as a whole speaks of personal trauma. The poems issue from pain. Stated bluntly, they define Clarke as a heretic within the Church, alienated by its inhuman clericalism, vulnerable to its authoritarian voice.

In the middle ages the Church saw reason as the handmaid of faith. But this view was not accepted throughout the medieval period. Eriugena, for one, did not believe in it because to him philosophy and theology are in implicit unity and speculative reason is the supreme arbiter. Later, in the work of Albert and Aquinas, the rights of reason are fully established and acknowledged.

For Clarke the holy rage of argument was a lost ideal. His own strugggle for intellectual independence was fraught with risks. If one cannot believe in Christ's triumph over darkness, sin and death and feels excluded from the process of redemption, then the imagination is endangered. It has to seek alternative sources of faith, or has to search for resources within the self. Abelard could declare: 'A doctrine is believed not because God has said it, but because we are convinced by reason that it is so' and 'Doubt is the road to inquiry, and by inquiry we perceive the truth'. Such sentiments were seldom heard in Clarke's time. *Night and Morning* speaks with integrity and power, in a compact, declarative style, from deep within Clarke's experience. It objectifies what is central to his life, confronting what has been implicit in previous work, particularly in his first two novels and in his plays, but it is unique in the first period of his career.

Chapter 5: Three Prose Romances

When Clarke began to write fiction, the Irish novel was mainly realistic. In reaction to the subjective, romantic literature of the Irish Literary Revival, the new generation of novelists, Sean O'Faolain, Frank O'Connor, Liam O'Flaherty, Kate O'Brien, were intent upon examining Irish life and character as objectively as they could.[1] Their mood of critical investigation resulted from the disillusion brought into their lives by the Civil War and by their realisation of the actual circumstances of life in a small, independent country of limited resources. While there is a degree of romance in their early work, such as O'Faolain's *Midsummer Night's Madness* (1932), or *A Nest of Simple Folk* (1934), in Frank O'Connor's *The Saint and Mary Kate* (1932) or *Guests of the Nation* (1931), or in Liam O'Flaherty's *Spring Sowing* (1924) or *The Martyr* (1935), the bulk of Irish fiction in the first two decades of independence was devoted to analysing the emerging middle-class of the towns and the rural society. The exceptions are few: Jack B. Yeats's dreamy reminiscences in *Sligo* (1930), *Sailing, Sailing Swiftly* (1933), or *The Amaranthers* (1936), or, later, after Clarke's first two novels had already appeared, Flann O'Brien's *At Swim Two Birds* (1939), which is innovative in form and ironic in manner. It may have encouraged Clarke in his third novel to fuse separate narratives, but that, as they both knew, was common in early Irish literature, as for example, 'The Colloquy of the Old Men'. The antecedents of *The Bright Temptation* (1932) may be found in James Stephens's *The Crock of Gold* (1912) and *The Demi-Gods* (1914), in their blend of realism and fantasy, in their liberated, fanciful journeys through a landscape in which the human and the supernatural move together and converse. *The Crock of Gold* interweaves its story of the leprechauns with the allegorical story of Caitilin's involvement first with Pan and then with Oengus Og. Stephens's later fiction, *Irish Fairy Tales* (1920), *Deirdre* (1923) and *In the Land of Youth* (1924) have a more restrained manner in handling familiar legendary material, but they demonstrate that it can be done without the breathless enthusiasm of O'Grady. Stephens's sources are also Clarke's: the innumerable versions of saga and legend found in the poetry and fiction of the Revival, of which Yeats's *Wanderings of Oisin* is but one example.

Despite Clarke's hope of creating a new kind of literature, objective, classical, and based on a first-hand knowledge of Irish literature, a hope that affected his poems and plays significantly, *The Bright Temptation*, which is immature in form and substance, is romantic in theme, setting, and use of allusion. *The Singing Men at Cashel* is more substantial. Examining the psychology of a personality under stress, it deploys incident and character in an illuminating and controlled manner. Its structural collapse at the end affects its ultimate success, but it is an outstanding contribution to the issue of ecclesiastical and/or social pressure on personal freedom that other writers were handling at the same time: Kate O'Brien in *The Ante-Room* (1934), Francis Hackett in *The Green Lion* (1936), Sean O'Faolain in *A Purse of Coppers* (1937). Clarke's romances do not describe the conditions of Irish society directly. Indirectly, he uses medieval life to show the ways in which one may suffer at the hands of an unenlightened church. One reason why Irish fiction, with the exception of Samuel Beckett and Flann O'Brien, is not experimental and did not follow up on the innovations of James Joyce, is that novelists are preoccupied with trying to understand Irish life as it emerged about them out of the confusions of the revolutionary period. Because of the changed circumstances, including the social shrinkage that had taken place with the virtual disappearance of an upper-class, the novel in its traditional, socially representative form did not flourish. 'We had all been dazed,' Clarke wrote, 'and afflicted by the internecine struggle'.[2]

Clarke's fiction enables him to examine in more expanded form the issues that concern him in his poetry and plays. *The Bright Temptation* is an allegory of what adolescent development should be like, were it not distorted by an excessive emphasis on sexual morality. In an oblique manner it pursues the incident of Clarke's first confession and his subsequent religious training that eventually turned him against religion. In the manuscript of *Twice Round the Black Church*, he wrote 'As I grew older the mental strain of prayer began to afflict me and despite myself I began to hate it.' *The Singing Men at Cashel* adjusts the imaginative focus to illuminate the mental stress of Gormlai, whose natural innocence is disturbed by a rigorous system of moral values. *The Sun Dances at Easter* moves beyond such issues. It is a true romance and celebrates the goodness of human nature, of existence, of love, and of the imagination.

All three novels belong to the genre of the romance which by its very nature is well suited to handle their theme of the struggle between individual freedom and moral constraints. Since the romance is not primarily interested in man as a social being, in rendering reality in comprehensive detail, or in examining the complexity of human nature, characters can be moved away from society, allowed to wander through the countryside, even to move beyond the veil of invisibility into the Otherworld, and be made representative of particular qualities. Place, too, can be symbolic rather than actual and the plot may plunge towards nightmare or melodrama without any loss of fictive integrity. The romance tends to be allegorical and it is clear that in Clarke's mind the moral universe of medieval, christian Ireland, in which all three works are set, mirrors in all its essential elements the moral climate of modern Ireland. We read them in a spirit that allows for the conventions of the romance and in the knowledge that like medieval Irish romances they often relate the immediate story to its romance or mythological antecedents. The past, as so often in Austin Clarke, provides a moral counterforce to the life-denying moral constraints that threaten his characters.

The story of *The Bright Temptation* (1932), Austin Clarke's first novel, is simple. Aidan, a young student at the monastery of Cluanmore, falls into the river Shannon, is swept downstream, captured by three fierce warriors, escapes with the help of a beautiful girl, Ethna, and wanders with her across Ireland. During this idyllic journey they fall in love, but Aidan is captured by the monstrous Prumpolaun, who takes him to Glen Bolcan, where the madmen of Ireland gather. He escapes, is rebuked by the ascetic monk, Bec-mac-De for his 'sinful' behaviour with Ethna, hurries back to the sanctuary of Cluanmore only to find it being pillaged by the Danes. He flees once again in search of Ethna whom he finds in the little wood of Monarua, where they first met.

There are two major aspects to the novel — a lyrical, romantic central narrative about young love and, infringing on that, incidents and figures that threaten to destroy love altogether or to distort it into something shameful. Some of these are risks that must be endured or overcome, obstacles in the realms of church and society. Others, such as the Prumpolaun, Glen Bolcan, and the destruction of Cluanmore, have more profound implications. Love must be shown to be superior in value to the moral teachings of the Church. The conflict between restrictive ecclesiastical laws and the emotional needs of Aidan and Ethna constitute the novel's fundamental life. Its account of the revelation of love counters the Church's teachings on human sexuality. Love's gentle realisation in the realm of nature demonstrates the validity of the relationship between

Aidan and Ethna. The overcoming of obstacles, whether in the form of inner fears or external forces, contributes to that demonstration and it is significant that Aidan's ultimate ability to love, freely and without fear, has to be earned through the traumatic experience with the Prumpolaun, the horror vision of Glen Bolcan, and the degradation of Cluanmore. Only then can he return to the wood of Monarua to consummate his love for Ethna, the spirit of life and joy. The identity of the supernatural agent who calls Aidan initially away from Cluanmore and brings the lovers together is not made clear. It is Oengus, god of love and happiness, who has a similar function in *The Sun Dances at Easter*.

For Aidan, Cluanmore, one of the great monasteries of Celtic-Romanesque Ireland, with its great cathedral, round tower, seven churches, high cross and monastic cells, is a haven of sanctity and learning. His adventures outside the monastery are an education in values that are alien to those practised there. They include his first intimation of sexual attraction, his encounter with the three champions who sweep him 'into a bardic world of fear and violence',[3] and, above all, his gradual realisation of the delights of love with Ethna, the 'bright being', the 'sky-maiden' or *spéir-bhean* of vision poetry.

> Was she not one of those self-delighting creatures of whom the wandering scholars were to dream, so that, failing in all their examinations, they would forget the doctrine of the Fall, and search for that Eden which poetry alone remembers?[4]

Ethna tells Aidan the story of Diarmuid and Grainne, including the incident at Doire-da-Bhoth which is again only told in part. Aidan's learning lacks this imaginative ingredient. In the monasteries tradition is recorded and stored. In Ethna's case it is alive and life-enhancing. Her awareness of figures in romance is instinctive; her emotional life is stimulated by them in the same way as Aidan's spiritual life is shaped by Church laws and the lives of the saints. In the pastoral world he discovers personal freedom and happiness. In place of the stern male teachers of Cluanmore, he is taught by the spirit of life who moves lightly and freely with him through the countryside. The movement of this section of the novel is a gradual, indirect unfolding of the subtle and unselfconscious response of the young couple to each other.

There are two major instances of this growth: their night spent under the cromlech and their night in the cave. The cromlech, which they imagine was once slept in by Diarmuid and Grainne, looms out of the countryside like a temple, bathed in golden sunlight. Its two-part division resembles two monastic cells. It therefore combines the religious and the pagan, both Cluanmore and the stone-beds of Diarmuid and Grainne.

Aidan, however, is unable to participate in the make-believe that Ethna creates, because his mind is troubled by 'uneasiness and strange fear'. Stern, reproachful faces from Cluanmore appear to him once more. Indeed, both of them are afraid that it is 'wrong' for them to be there. 'The shadow of conscience,' Clarke explains, 'that darkens Ireland at night, filling the young with trouble, with torment, was cast between them'. The episode in the cave marks the triumph of love over fear and inhibition. The intricate nurturing and growth of the fire is an emblem of its progress.

> Their heads were together, so eager they were, as she uncurled little shavings with the knife from a core of soft wood. Delicately, with skilful fingers, she set those little springes in which the spark might be caught and nourished. Lightly, she prepared the tiny paths along which the first fledgling of flame would flutter. Eagerly, with bated breath, they watched, as the first spark leaped, and afraid of existence was gone. Quickly, lightly, she worked, and at last the tinder yielded. On her own sweet breath she reared that weakling, and soon it was strong. Together they led the flame, enticing it along every splinter, anxious when it feared to jump. But soon it could venture by itself, and when they heard the first crackle, saw the pleasant curl of smoke, they turned to each other with joyful faces.

'Delicately', 'Lightly', 'Eagerly', 'Quickly' — the progress is an analogy for the movement of feeling. They can no longer deny their mutual attraction.

> Enspelled by each other they hovered; they gazed with a stead-fastness that fulfilled itself and yet was daring. Softly, softly, the discovery of their own presences by that fire drew them towards one another, so that every moment might have been the next and the moment after, the one before.

They discover 'the joy of the human senses' and are 'lost in the imagination which poetry alone remembers, for it is in joy that we discover ourselves'. Simultaneously, they declare their love and lie together under Aidan's cloak. But his happiness is undermined by his awareness of the 'evil' of desire from which he feels only Ethna can save him.

That assumption is correct, but it cannot be proven until he has faced the 'evil' in its most frightening manifestations. Next day, entering more fully into the enjoyment of love, they decide to cling together without clothes. When Ethna appears naked before him, Aidan, whose knowledge of the human form has been gained only from illuminated manuscripts, sees how beautiful she is. But their consummation of love must be deferred. At this point the novel's counter-movement takes over. Once again Aidan encounters strange dark men with cruel faces who accuse him of sin and thrust him out of the glen.

> Aidan ran blindly forward along the road, his whole body throbbing with shame and confusion. He could still hear those voices, their strange tone of accusation, still see eyes reproaching, glaring at him. His happiness had been shattered by some terrible evil.

His capture by the Prumpolaun follows at once. The Prumpolaun externalises Aidan's fears and by bringing him to Glen Bolcan provides images of the consequences of sinful behaviour. His physical grossness, gluttony, bizarre behaviour and enforced companionship contrast with the beauty, sensuality, and imaginative delight Aidan has experienced with Ethna.

The fact that he is also a comic monster, mad in his humour, makes the episode grotesquely funny. The humour derives in part from the Prumpolaun's comic view of himself and of his predicament as a messenger who forgets the message, and of his resemblance to his literary ancestor, the Bodach a' Chota Lachtna in *Silva Gadelica*. In Glen Bolcan Aidan reaches the lowest point of this journey through terror and hallucination. The style shifts from the outrageous good humour of the journey with the Prumpolaun, an episode that is too prolonged, to a taut apprehension of the unearthly and the unnatural: frightening fowl-creatures with 'grey, dead faces' in the crab-trees, loud shrieks from the valley, like 'the cry of a lost soul that demons have seized and borne away', demoniacal laughter from the hidden dykes, whose 'starts' and 'shakes of merriment were more horrible than the shriek he had heard across the river', and a circling multitude — in Clarke's recurrent metaphor — who despair of Christ's aid: 'He never died for us, I tell you. He never died for us. He gave His body, but not His mind. It was never broken. He did not die for us, who are lost, . . . lost! . . .'[5] They walk in nightmare, the pupils of their eyes dilated with terror, each 'sunk in an awful loneliness of his own', each in personal torment. On being told that he is in Glen Bolcan, to which all the madmen of Ireland are drawn, driven there in particular by the 'sin' of masturbation, Aidan is even more terrified.[6]

> Tempted by ignorance, driven by the moral rigour which forbids passion in Ireland, they succumb to the solitary sin, ever with insane hands that they cannot keep from themselves, wasting their pale watery substance. Through the brakes went tortured things that had been men or women, crazied by scruples of conscience, by injustice, scandal or wrong, flying in fear of themselves, in fear of the rushing force that was once their minds. . . . the cries of beings

that swarmed and twisted in its depths. Multitudes of faces were lifted there in agony, bodies writhed among the rocks, more horrible than their own viscera. Existence, when it breaks, becomes the instrument of its own torture, for the mind is fitted to suffer pain which it can no longer comprehend.

From this 'pit of lost humanity', where he sees 'in simulacra the tortures of the damned, the pains which all who die in mortal sin must endure throughout eternity', Aidan recoils in terror; he loses consciousness and awakes in the presence of Bec-mac-De, a mock-heroic saint, a 'chastiser of unchastity', who compels Aidan to acknowledge that his relationship with Ethna was evil and to return to the sanctity of Cluanmore.[7] Bec-mac-De's outlook is uncompromising: the joys of the world are brief, its vanities frail compared with the bliss of eternity. To die in a state of mortal sin is to be plunged into the fire of hell for all eternity.

Cluanmore, however, has become a place of outrage and blasphemy where Aidan's trust is shattered in a succession of incidents: the sight of the obscene figure of Sile na gCioch on the wall of the church, the sight of the naked woman being worshipped on the altar, and the desecration by the Danes.[8] He flees in terror, longs for life and for Ethna, its personification. 'He had escaped from death, he was safe and all his life was before him'. For a brief period he had been untrue to his newly discovered belief. Faced with the weight of clerical argument, backed up as it was by examples from the lives of the saints, he had submitted and had sought refuge in the monastery. But throughout that return Ethna's face haunted him. Throughout the novel's counter-movement he had held on to the determination to find her again.

On his way he visits the bardic college at Luachra and longs to enter more fully into poetic knowledge,

> longed to study the divisions of poetic knowledge, commit its commentaries to heart, and learn the Thousand Tales of Ireland. All night in his sleep he seemed to hear music that freed him from the shadowy fears of his early education.[9]

Strengthened by this experience, Aidan hurries to Ethna who had first shown him 'that fairer world of which he had known nothing'. When they meet 'the fears, the doubts which had tormented Aidan's mind vanished as though they had never existed'.

Aidan's experiences with Ethna resemble those of Oisin with Niamh in the Land of Youth, to which Clarke draws attention in the epigraph which is taken from *Echtra Condla Caín*, 'The Adventures of Connla the Comely'. *The Bright Temptation* has the organisational pattern of the *eachtra* — a series of incidents, often of the marvellous kind, which involves the hero. Like Niamh, Ethna is a creature of the timeless, place-less country of the imagination, where the identifying marks are few and often idealised. Like Oisin, Aidan goes into the land of youth, returns to the reality of Cluanmore and, unlike Oisin, escapes from the conse-quences of his return and finds his golden-haired girl again.

Like *The Vengeance of Fionn*, *The Bright Temptation* is a partial re-enactment of the romance of Diarmuid and Grainne. It resembles that epic narrative, the poems in 'The Land of Two Mists' and in *Pilgrimage* in its uncritical delight in landscape and in mythological stories. The journey of Aidan and Ethna parallels the flight of Diarmuid and Grainne and is essentially timeless. The quality of timelessness is increased by the ways in which the narrative moves from its own figures and incidents to figures and events in earlier stories. Ethna, as storyteller, refers to previous examples:

> . . . I could tell you of the courtship of Emer, or Lasara who fell in love and followed the track of great wheels far along a mountain road, and of Liadain who came south in the spring to meet Cur-rither, of Etain, too, Fionnuala and Fedelma.

For her, as for Clarke, past and present coalesce. She identifies with Deirdre with whom Clarke also compares her. He, too, invokes former models of romance, as when he compares Ethna with Etain:

> . . . it might have been the gold, silver-rimmed basin in which Etain, long ago, had washed herself, knowing that Midhir was watching from his saddle. Not more gracefully could Etain have dipped into her jewelled basin than Ethna as she wet her fingers in that pool.

and he adds: 'Only by stories and lovely example can the young find themselves . . .'

The editorialising nature of this remark is a characteristic of Clarke's approach in the first two prose romances. He likes to emphasise that the moral drama he writes about in medieval Ireland is relevant to his own time, that it is not only in the Celtic-Romanesque period that people suffered from ecclesiastical puritanism. When, for example, Aidan and Ethna become afraid that they may commit sin, Clarke writes that the shadow of conscience that darkens Ireland at night, filling the young with trouble, with torment, was cast between them. And when Aidan discovers the married couple in bed, Clarke moralises as follows:

> . . . Moral training in Ireland is severe and lasts until marriage. Even in childhood we are taught by the pious clergy to battle

against bad thoughts, so that we may preserve our holy purity. In youth we learn the dangers of idle talk, the temptations of self-sin, the need of avoiding stories that incite passion. For passion in Ireland is denounced as evil and obscene. Women are the snares set for us by the Devil. Even to think of a woman's body with pleasure is a mortal sin.

In the opposition between conformity and individuality that is the recurrent subject of these works, the role of women is important. On the one hand they represent the spirit of life, including imagination and sensuality. On the other they represent evil in that they may tempt men to commit sin. So powerful is evil in Clarke's moral universe at this time that good holds a precarious position. Goodness in the sense of sympathetic understanding, imaginative freedom and the absence of a life-denying sexual puritanism is embodied in Ethna. But goodness associated with asceticism can be mocked, as it is in the descriptions of the monks at Cluanmore or in the portrait of the absurdly authoritarian Bec-mac-De. Evil is ever-present, erupting from within the self, distorting the mind with images of guilt, terrifying it with visions of damnation.

In some respects *The Bright Temptation* is an apprentice work, derivative in material drawn from the mythological and Ulster cycles, careless about chronology,[10] and not well disciplined in its handling of incidents and characters. There are Joycean influences in the account of Ethna and Joycean echoes in the style of the narrative when Aidan journeys back to Ethna. She, like the girl on the beach in *Portrait of the Artist*, embodies the spirit of life. The novel is highly romantic in its account of young love and in its creation of contrasting figures and opposing values. Nevertheless, despite these weaknesses, it is an attractive work in which Clarke works out some of the basic issues that he has to face. *The Singing Men at Cashel* shows him in better control of his material, working out the conflict between conformity and individuality in a sustained, objective manner. His second novel combines a high degree of sympathetic understanding of Gormlai's crisis of conscience with an objective deployment of incidents.

The Singing Men at Cashel (1936) is a romantic tragedy about Gormlai, but the central issue is the conflict of mind and body which she experiences in her first two marriages and not the happiness which she enjoys in the third. The novel also has a comic subplot in which this conflict is expressed through the story of Anier Mac Conglinne.

Initially, Gormlai finds Cormac's scholarly interests and natural courtesy attractive, just as her intellectual refinement and chastity appeal to him. And they are similar in their sexual inexperience. Cormac, who left the monastery of Dysart to assume the kingship of Cashel, has married from a sense of duty. While he has read about sexual passion, he is surprised on his wedding night by the 'vindictive fury of mortal passion' and has to struggle hard to overcome it. Gormlai, whose imagination has been shaped by christian and poetic influences, is even more ignorant. 'What,' she asks herself, 'was all her knowledge of poetry and story to her? There were secret Latin books which the clergy possessed in their schools, but no lay person could be permitted to read them, much less a woman. She must be instructed by her husband — and at the thought a mood of rebellion rose in her mind'.

Clarke creates a sympathetic portrait of a young woman shaped by a romantic response to poetry and christianity. As her story begins she has a unified personality, is happy in her enjoyment of poetry and contented in her religious experiences. During the marriage ceremony she 'felt the divinity that issued from Heaven. A great ray was descending and her soul was strengthened by it'. It is the disruption of this life and its consequences for her personality that the novel describes, first of all in her gradual realisation of the presence of evil in the world, then in her shocked reaction to Carroll's sexual aggressiveness.

Her innocence is shown in her meeting with Nial at the Well of Nemna on her 'last morning of dreams'. Her mind, as yet untroubled by intimations of evil, delights in the beauties of nature which she associates happily with 'the delicate, involved designs of poetry'. The natural harmony of the setting and the similarity of their imaginative delight in early Irish literature are presented in a fluid style that contrasts with the stiff and formal account of Gormlai's wedding and the emphatic account of Cormac's struggle against lust. But her innocence is disturbed by what happens at the monastery of Glenalua. Once again, seeing Cormac in conversation with the monks, she notices his ecclesiastical affinities. Once again, knowing that her presence is tolerated only because she is Cormac's wife, she reflects unhappily on the inferior state of women.

> Men lived here all their lives far from women and banished them even from their thoughts, as though they were harmful. . . . Informing its daily life and practice, the male ceremonies of religion, was that law which divided man from woman. The King of the Sky remained a celibate when He was on earth and gave His example to men. She was joyless as she brooded there in the sunlight.

But it is her disturbing encounter with the lustful hermit, Malachi, in the wilderness outside the monastery, that foreshadows what she has yet to realise. The force against which Cormac struggled on his marriage night is manifest in Malachi, with his 'terrible eyes glittering . . . thorn-patched rags and twisted pelts... human only to the waist.... She could not see the coils but among the tatters that hung around the stranger's waist, a snake had raised its head, as if about to strike'.[11] Even though she does not understand she knows that she has seen 'the evil that is hidden in the very midst of life'.[12]

These intimations of evil alternate with Gormlai's memories of the past, but Cashel brings an even greater challenge to her romantic and cherished response to secular poetry. At first she feels contented there, relishing its intellectual activities. Cormac, the chief scholar of Ireland, has assembled jurists, historians, and poets 'to collect and set down the entire system of ancient law and jurisprudence'. 'Those voices, as in a chant, held her imagination so that she seemed aware of shining intelligences that move forever in a world of ideas'. But while she learns from them that there are moral truths among much that appears fantastic and irrelevant in pagan literature, it is their post-Revelation sense of superiority that disturbs her. Even Cormac, she discovers, when responding to the assertion that the 'impious stories of the past' should be abolished, is condescending in their defence.

> He had agreed that such tales might cause harm to simple minds. But the stories themselves should be set down in writing by scholars ... There was much merit in the stories, much of historical interest, though the good were mixed with folly and the delusions of paganism. But scholars had carefully excised from these stories all that enshrined the false doctrines of the past. ... He agreed, however, with his guest that the subject of poetry in a Christian age should be religion.

Such a view is anathema to Gormlai who longs to revive 'the great Tailteann Fair at which the poets, musicians and craftsmen of Ireland gathered in old time'. Marriage means that she must sacrifice this imaginative world and since Cormac fails to appreciate how deeply these matters affect her, their marriage comes under strain.

> She must forget the secret happiness of her thoughts when she was single. Less than a year ago she could go to the college at Brecan, sit in the place of honour above the students, hear the storytelling and the poems. Her young imagination adventured then into ever new regions of delight or discovery. She was lost in a world of loveliness and joy, so that her heart praised all woods and waters, companioning shore and shade. Those poems brought to her mind companies of men and women, delighting in each other's voices and looks, happy, innocent. Bran sailed the streams of Ocean until he came to the Island of Promise. Had not Niav ridden

over the wavetops that she might bring the poet, Oisín, to a hidden land?

Cashel's renowned learning and scholarship are not adequate alternatives to this world of wonder. Gormlai no longer delights in its intellectual activities. 'The historic facts, the inquiries into spiritual states made her uneasy'; 'the secret world of poetry which she guarded in her imagination dwindled before syllogisms and the truths of Revelation'.

Her happiness is also undermined by the feeling that her marriage is somehow flawed. Cormac has not consummated it; he wants, he tells her, 'to transcend the physical . . . the nastiness of the instincts' so that they can live together like saints, whose examples he provides. Gormlai shrinks from this proposal, feeling depressed and humiliated by it, without knowing why, but knowing that her inability to support Cormac in his plan is a form of deception.

> Night and day she would have to conceal from him her real self. The mystery of marriage had become even deeper, the shadow of some unknown evil remained between them.

She is determined to understand this mystery. Every night she searches secretly among ecclesiastical tracts, all written by men.

> Searching among those moral treatises, she felt indeed that she was craving for a knowledge forbidden to women. She fought the unreasonable fear, for it was no sinful curiosity that impelled her, but a need of mind that she must obey whatever the cost. Even as a girl she had felt that clear urgency of mind, had rebelled secretly at her convent when the Abbess reproved her and sent word to the Rí. She thought of those pious virgins, in their cells there, following the example of St Ita, living in simple faith, untouched by the toil of intellect. But was not intellect the highest work of the Creator? Even as a youngster she had despised those recluses, their ignorance, their docile obedience, and she had felt proud of her own mind.

It is a central element of her character that Gormlai, unlike the unquestioning saints, should rebel against the unjust views of women that she encounters in the ecclesiastical writings. 'Woman was denounced by the Early Fathers, arraigned as a temptress, the bringer of evil and disease. She read with growing indignation and horror.' It is typical of Clarke that he should emphasise her intellectual curiosity and pride. Marriage, she discovers, is indeed regarded as an inferior state, as Cormac had told her. But Gormlai is not content with these views, despite the authority of their sources. Indignation, horror and intellectual determination drive her onward. Nothing that she reads makes the meaning of marriage clear. But the search breaks her. Her frustration grows to a 'torment of doubt and suspicion' until within her subconsciousness a debased self comes into being, whose nightmares disturb her.

Both Cormac and Gormlai are propelled into sophistry, in which the mind debates with itself, Gormlai because of her doubts about marriage, Cormac because he partly yielded to the excuse that to look with lust on his wife is not sinful. He struggles with determination against that temptation and subdues his flesh by flagellation. She fails to resolve her mental division and is subjected to a nightmare of anxiety and guilt. The isolation that she has felt in her search for knowledge manifests itself in incidents of radical rejection. In the image of a priest disfigured by leprosy and offering her communion the sources of grace are defiled to mirror her subconscious sense of being tarnished. The grief of an afflicted people, whose homes and lands have been destroyed, reflects her state of despair in which she cannot remember what has happened. The image of herself as a penitent rejected in horror by shining souls on the heavenly mountain externalises her feelings of sin and degradation. In the final judgmental scene her life is spread out in the Book of Life; she is accused of sexual sin, of multiple marriages, of adultery, of rebellion against women's subservient role and sees herself clinging to the Tarpeian rock which falls with her into the bloody abyss. Her mind has been invaded by doubt, her sense of herself, of her own integrity and worth, have been seriously undermined, as she has become increasingly aware of an as yet uncomprehended evil.

Her innocence has been betrayed. She looks at the landscape of Munster, remembering that poets used to say that within the visible landscape was a lovely, timeless land, but as a result of her mental agitation those 'lovely imaginings of the past, the beliefs that ennoble life were all gone'. But where, she wonders, remembering her nightmares, 'was that grim world of sin and retribution that hid behind the mystery of sleep . . . ?' The answer is seen in the bleeding figure of Cormac. Then 'everything was clear — utterly clear'. At the moment when he had committed himself to the spiritual life, when he had decided to take Holy Orders and assume the hereditary bishopric of Cashel, Cormac had again been afflicted with sexual desire for his wife. Knowing that to yield would destroy his spiritual mission, he has resorted to self-flagellation. The sight of him abased before the altar, his back lacerated, his voice raised in anguish, crystallises for Gormlai the degrading view of women that she has found in books, the 'grim denunciations', the offensive terms; she sees that his scheme of dissolution and sublimation is a judgment on marriage, on her as a woman, and she finds it intolerable. His bloodied back bears witness to that ugly, life-denying asceticism that has denounced women and sexuality through the ages. She remembers stories of enclosed anchorites, of saints who slept by open graves or beside corpses, of others who tortured themselves and fasted in atonement for the sins of the wicked.

The knowledge that Gormlai has sought among the secret books becomes hers in her marriage to Carroll of Leinster: 'all the degradation that belongs to night'. This marriage is in stark contrast with her marriage to Cormac and the world of Naas is quite different from that at Cashel. Carroll is warlike and proud. His harsh and turbulent court reflects his personality just as Cashel reflected Cormac's. If Gormlai rebelled against Cormac's proposed annulment of their marriage, she reacts even more strongly against Carroll's physicality. Now she understands why Cormac subjected his senses and is contrite that she looked with contempt on his bloodied back.

Her revulsion against her husband's crude physicality is externalised in the frightening figure of the Great Kneewoman, midwife and *caillech*, who corresponds to her first intimation of evil in the figure of Malachi. The Great Kneewoman represents another area of experience of which Gormlai is ignorant — the physical side of marriage as experienced by women, including conception, birth, contraception, the menstrual cycle, sexual fears and anxieties. Gormlai shuns the implications of the Great Kneewoman's remarks and questions, but her inner division is clearly seen in the conflicting voices of her Guardian Angel, Caol, and Iafer Niger, the Devil. Caol urges obedience to her marriage vows, Iafer urges the appeal of the poetic imagination and the memory of Cormac's chastity. Her meeting with Nial Glundubh at Cnocbeg, a place hallowed for both of them by its associations with Fionn and the Fianna, reveals that there is an alternative. The meeting is prepared in their common memories of the past.

> There was no hill or wood in all the land which had not been remembered in poetry. Had not those great teachers of the past taught that matter was holy as the mind, that hill and wood were an external manifestation of the immortal regions? The faith of Fintan and of Amergin was stealing into her imagination once more and she forgot the misery, the tormenting doubts that darkened it. She was among the proud, she did not fear the exhilaration which had returned so strangely to her this night.

When she and Nial embrace, she realises the 'essential goodness' of man, prior to the lessons of Revelation. Nial confesses his love for her and she feels that the 'enchantment' of their story resembles 'some impossible story that belonged to the past'.

Her struggle with her conscience intensifies after this meeting. In desperation she goes to the monastery at Dysert where Cormac had sought advice before taking his momentous decision to renounce his marriage. The consequences of the two visits are different. Cormac was confirmed in his decision, Gormlai is faced with an inflexible orthodoxy. To refuse Carroll his 'rights', she is told, is to commit mortal sin. To shrink from him in disgust is sinful. It is her responsibility to save Carroll from the sin of adultery which he might commit if she refuses to have sexual intercourse with him. She could then be responsible for his damnation. These 'grim facts' reduce Gormlai to despair. Her mind is as distraught now as it was when she searched in desperation through 'the forbidden books' at Cashel. Once again she has come up against the insensitivity and obduracy of a male dominated church.

The failure of her visit to Dysert increases her inability to take responsibility for her own actions. Once again she questions her motives and, despite her resentment at Benignus's harsh logic, refuses to blame him. She admits the selfish nature of her desire to be released from her marriage. Self-accusation gives way to a protest that the monk could 'never understand all that she had suffered, all the loss of the early delicacy of her mind'. That protest, in turn, gives way to an expression of hope that her imaginative development may be over and that she may be 'facing a deeper, a moral and spiritual development'. In the midst of her mental distress, however, is the memory of the night she and Nial met when 'she had known that all was different, that they were on the verge of some imaginative reality in which her heart still believed, that they had not been driven together by a common sensuality'.

Even that memory cannot prevent the neurotic flounderings of her thoughts: she must not destroy Nial by making them both sinful fugitives; Benignus was right to suspect her motives; she does not love Nial; she must obey her husband; Nial must forget her, she must forget him. 'The thought of sacrificing their love, of destroying the purity, the instant emotion which united her self to him, sustained her in a fury of desperation and despair'. These pages mark the climax of the novel's investigation of Gormlai's divided, scholastic, casuistical mind. Her decision to obey Carroll is not final, but it marks the conclusion of the novel's real theme. Significantly, at this point, its approach and structure change and the novel loses direction and power.

When Gormlai arrives back at Naas war has broken out between Carroll and Cormac and her father is in alliance with her husband. There are only six chapters left. Chapter ten of Book II moves to the limited perspective of Ceallachán a hundred years later as he tries to record Gormlai's story by means of an historical tract and a court romance. Cormac's death is not described directly but indirectly through Ceall-achán's moralising reaction. The romance of Gormlai and Nial is also told indirectly. Gormlai's life with Nial, which might have been the subject of Book III is briefly summarised and we are told that she revived the Aonach Tailteann.

> She had aided the revival of secular art and poetry. She had estab-
> lished new poetic colleges and endeavoured to give influence to
> those orders which had been deprived of their educational power
> long ago, by the ecclesiastical decree at Drumceat.
>   Ceallachán read with disapproval. . . He was aware that a literary
> and poetic revival was taking place throughout Ireland. He had
> heard at Devenish that once more the pagan imagination of the
> past was astir in the minds of men, that the poets in their dark
> cells were conjuring up deceitful visions of immortal beings.

At this point Ceallachán's work is disturbed by the passing of the thrice-married Kermala, another example in his eyes of an evil woman, whose life is then summarised. Chapter eleven returns to the main narrative: Cormac's death and mutilation makes Gormlai decide to leave Carroll. In one violent speech she flings her resentment in his face.

> You believe you are great and powerful, but the shame of what
> you have done will not escape the pens that you despise; all noble
> minds will remember and despise you. You have slain the greatest
> scholar of this century in an unjust quarrel, and if there was any-
> thing worse that could be done, it was done that day. Your hire-
> lings and servants dishonoured his poor remains, not even death
> was sacred to those barbaric men. Therefore, Carroll Mac Muinenan,
> Ri of Leinster, you are nothing to me, nothing to me.

Chapter twelve deals in a comic manner with the contention between the poets of Ulster and Munster[13] and this leads to the foolish wager by Anier Mac Conglinne that he will prove that the Cave of Demons at Lough Derg does not exist. At the very end of this chapter we hear that Gormlai has fled from Carroll.

  Book III has only three chapters. The first deals with Anier's arrival at St Patrick's Purgatory on Lough Derg, the third briefly describes Gorm-lai's wedding to Nial, the second relates Anier's nightmarish descent into the Cave of Demons where his alienated soul tries to escape from his body. His soul, made horrible by his sinfulness, is the 'dreadful watcher', the unseen spirit waiting to seize him; it wants to destroy itself forever and is beyond repentance. In the abyss he hears 'the pitiable shrieks of the lost souls'. Under the strain he loses consciousness and sees devils coming to take his body. In a furious chase through the blankness they try to capture him and he falls headlong into nothingness, just as Gormlai in her nightmare fell into the gulf. When he awakens he is back in the monastery, experiencing a renewal of the senses and an intense appreciation of the beauty of life.

It is clear that the last six chapters interrupt the narrative and the finely realised sequence of events that had characterised most of the novel up to then. It is also clear that Clarke did not want to describe the third marriage, nor did he want to deal directly with Gormlai's recovery of imaginative faith. His deepest concern is with her loss of innocence and its replacement by mental anguish: 'that other self which had only appeared since she came to Cashel — a darker self that she scarcely recognised, and yet could not deny, a self troubled by intimations and a guilt of which she herself was innocent'.

To bring out the full weight of that conflict the novel carefully establishes the moral universe in which she lives. The moral order that determines her life is visible in the mental conflict it causes, but it is also present in the controlling tone and perspective of the narrator. There are many examples of his moral outlook. For example, he approves of Cormac's success in conquering lust on his wedding night and strongly disapproves of the unfortunate Malachi. In his view man is stained by original sin and is vulnerable to temptation, especially when young and innocent. He knows that rational man aspires to the prelapsarian state of 'innocence and reason' but believes that he is by nature 'unhealthy' and moves 'in a twilight of sinful impulses'. He approves of Cormac's plan to sublimate sexuality in marriage, writes sympathetically of his shamed reaction to Gormlai's nakedness, and speaks eloquently, with many examples of the rewards of sexual abstinence. When Gormlai reads the condemnations of multiple marriages, he merely records what she finds:

> 'If there are two Christs there may be two husbands or two wives. If there is but one Christ, one Head of the Church, there is but one flesh, a second is repelled. But if He forbids a second, what is to be said of third marriages?'

Throughout, the novel balances Gormlai's struggle against such rigorous morality with references to another source of imaginative strength. If the novel is an elegy for lost innocence and a protest against a crude, distorted asceticism, it also affirms the enduring validity of the imagination. The meetings with Nial at the Well of Nemna, and at Cnocbeg, together with Gormlai's memories and her eventual marriage to Nial,

confirm the truths of the pre-Revelation world, that Eden to which Gormlai must return. The novel affirms man's 'essential goodness', despite
the Church's emphasis on fallen man, on the ever-present force of evil,
and in the face of the emotive language with which the narrator asserts
Iafer Niger's corruption of the innocent. Eriugena's theory that all men
return to God is dismissed as intellectual pride. The mind, in this view,
must be humbled before man can fully enter the spiritual life; only supernatural grace can help man to prevail against evil. Gormlai's mind is
assailed by this view but in the end she finds imaginative redemption outside of the narrow morality that surrounds her. 'In our exalted moods
we discover imaginatively in ourselves an essential goodness and it is
only by the insistent lessons of Revelation that we succeed in remembering our fallen state'. So the narrator comments when Gormlai and
Nial find happiness at Cnocbeg.

Although *The Singing Men at Cashel* is a flawed work, it is written
with a high degree of intelligence and detachment. Each chapter advances
and illuminates the set of related issues that form its structural and
imaginative life: the tensions between reason and instinct, clerical teaching and individual freedom of conscience, an ugly sexual puritanism and
a natural sensuality. It is a scholar's novel, filled with knowledge of Irish
literature, history and hagiography, but it also explores, more fully, more
deeply, and more successfully than any other single work in Clarke's
career, issues and experiences that are central to his work. In the succeeding novel, *The Sun Dances at Easter*, its moral emphasis and formal
structure have been replaced by an ingenious and amusing interweaving
of three narratives. *The Singing Men at Cashel* was much less successful
in making the story of Anier Mac Conglinne intersect significantly with
the story of Gormlai. The two narratives are only moderately successful
as parallel and mutually illuminating versions of the one theme. *The Sun
Dances at Easter* outlines parables of existence within contrasting fictions
whose combined effect is to collapse the tension of the personal choice
into a variety of comic alternatives. Clarke's concern is not to berate the
church for insensitivity or for moral heavy-handedness but to create a
playful fiction about man's capacity for error and to celebrate it.

The Sun Dances at Easter (1952), written 1946-48, is made up of a
number of separate, interrelated narratives. The main story concerns
the pilgrimage undertaken by Orla to the holy well of St Naal in the
belief that she will thereby be enabled to conceive. On the way she
meets Enda, a handsome clerical student, who tells her two stories, one
about Eithne and Ceasan in the time of St Patrick and one about Congal
More, king of Ireland in the early eighth century. Both are based on Irish
tales. 'The House of the Two Methers', or *Altram Tige Da Medar*, tells

how Eithne, the beautiful daughter of Manannan and foster child of Oengus, passed from the Land of Youth into the real world where she met the monk, Ceasan, and became a christian. Enda's second story, which he calls 'The Only Jealousy of Congal More', is based on the story known as 'The Adventure of the Skin-Clad Cleric', or *Eachtra Chléirigh na gCroiceann*, which tells how Oengus came to Congal's court disguised as a fat cleric to prove to the king that his boast of his wife's chastity is premature.[14] He transforms Congal into a goat for a while so that he can witness his wife's infidelity. Even the main story has its unusual occurrences: Orla and Enda are led beyond the *fáeth fíada* and enter a building that resembles the House of the Two Methers in Enda's first story. There they are served the magical food that had been left for Eithne and Ceasan in his second story!

The interweaving of narratives has the effect of dissolving the real world. Characters cross from one world of experience to another, back and forth through the *fáeth fíada*. The disruption of modern fictive conventions has the effect of subverting the attempts of Church and State to maintain order. Congal More's transmogrification into a he-goat, in imitation of Apuleius, is but one example of human rebellion against social norms. Orla, Enda and Ceasan also deviate from the laws that should bind them: Orla by being attracted to the handsome Enda and by yielding to the possibility of sexual adventure at the holy well; Enda by being drawn to the beautiful Orla; and Ceasan by yielding to the pagan beauty of Eithne.

Reality itself becomes unreliable when humanity is shown to exist where 'everything is next to nothing', where existence is fraught with uncertainty and trembles on the brink of the supernatural. 'Were there many worlds, each with its own order of beings, known in dream or delirium by the different races of men?', Ceasan asks, as he sees the immortal Eithne shimmering on the banks of the Boyne. The mystery of existence is depicted in the story of Eithne and Ceasan which deals with the conflict between paganism and christianity. In the original, Manannan tells Oengus about the one omnipotent god who made the world, about the fall of the angels and the creation of man. St Patrick baptizes Eithne and saves her from Oengus. In Clarke's story Eithne is both a temptation and a challenge to the young hermit, Ceasan. She responds eagerly to his accounts of christianity, but he is immodestly attracted by her ethereal beauty.

The changes in their relationship are rendered in three separate incidents. In the first, Ceasan is drawn towards the paradise beyond the Boyne while Eithne cries out against it. He had tried not to believe in the Tuatha De Danann, but 'reason was failing him and ancient superstitions were beating through his veins. He could struggle no longer, yet Eithne was resisting their power, and her body was rigid with suffering'. Her anguish makes him recognise the 'menace that had almost drawn the soul from his body'. On the second occasion when Eithne speaks across the river and is disappearing from sight, Ceasan advises her to tell Oengus that another religion has come into being. 'We, too, are immortal, though we must choke into another world, though our remains stink in earth through slow rottenness'. As his language suggests, his faith in his own religion has been shaken. He opposes Oengus with christianity but yields to the power he represents. The final act in this spiritual drama comes when Ceasan leads Eithne to the Boyne to baptize her, thereby saving her from Oengus, as St Patrick did in the original story.

> He laid his hand gently on the crown of her head and the light of her coming grace suddenly shone around her so that she did not seem mortal. Her flesh was glorified, her smile so joyful that he closed his eyes from such a wonder and began to pronounce the words of the ancient rite. But scarcely had he uttered a syllable when the chill of horror held him. His fingers touched nothing and he knew that he was alone. He sprang back and stared at the spot where Eithne had been, stared at the rushing waters, and, then from the cliff-wood, came, in echo, his own cry of disbelief.

In this ending Clarke reverses the conclusion of the original in which it is Oengus who cries out in anguish when he loses Eithne through baptism. There the pagan god is defeated by christianity, here he triumphs over it.

Mystery is increased by such ironies. Orla, for example, goes on pilgrimage to St Naal's well whose fertility rituals are survivals of pagan customs. Oengus, putting more trust in the natural than the spiritual, sends Orla to participate in its bacchanalian customs. She goes to the well, falls in love with Enda and he with her; her pilgrimage, as Oengus had promised, is successful, but is her baby boy (who resembles both Enda and her husband, Flann) the result of the practices at the well, the result of the night she spent in the hut with Enda, or the result of her marriage to Flann? When Flann, in his search for Orla, was misled in the mist by Oengus, did he meet Orla beyond the *fáeth fíada*? Whom did Orla meet there, Enda or Flann? Mystery also attends 'The Only Jealousy of Congal More'. Since he has been punished for suspecting his wife's virtue, the king knows he must not yield to jealousy again. Nevertheless, during his existence as a goat, he saw his wife, Fial Fairbrow, with her lover in the hunting lodge. But was that real or imagined?

Story-telling has several purposes: it can cause distraction to what is actually happening, it can embody moral issues, it can delight with illusion, it can do all these things, and others, at the same time. The mood may vary from one story to the next. The tone of the Eithne-Ceasan story is subdued, its mood elegiac, its ending a cry of loss. The mood of the Congal More story is broadly comic. The king's animal nature, when he has a goatish form, counters the absurd attempts by the Archbishop and himself to hide sexuality completely in the kingdom. In one view his goatish self symbolises his secret lust, in another it celebrates his liberation from feelings of guilt. In contrast with the restrained romance of Eithne and Ceasan and the decorous romance of Enda and Orla the parable of Congal More highlights the delights of the senses. Not only does it deride the morality of king and Church but it replaces the complacent ethics of the court with sensory gratification. In his goatish paradise Congal discovers the elemental delights of grass. 'He could walk on his food all day, sleep in it all night and when the sun came up, reach out and take his breakfast in bed'.

The comic spirit of the novel as a whole is embodied in Oengus. The imagery of dancing scraps of clothes, of birds, of fantastic agility, are all associated with him, as are the sounds of music and the feeling of gaiety he causes. In Enda's first story he is a power more compelling than christianity, in the second he turns up at Tara as an irreverent monk and once again his tattered garments and agility convey his humorous, irreverent spirit. This time his power is manifested in the transformation of Congal. In both cases what he signifies is release from a too earnest morality that characterises both Ceasan and Congal. Orla, too, discovers through Oengus a more enjoyable love than she has at home. The new Flann, changed into a more lovable shape, is also it seems more fertile.

Such connections and correspondences between the three stories add to the novel's spirit of lightness and whimsicality. The story of Orla and Enda resembles that of Eithne and Ceasan, since both deal with a clerical student and a beautiful woman and the food that they eat is the same. The salmon that Ceasan catches reminds us of the trout that leaps in the holy well; both have magical associations. Orla's pilgrimage resembles Ceasan's response to the Tuatha De Danann and Congal's animality is another version of this. The presence of Oengus in all the stories guarantees that man's so-called lower instincts will not be ignored.

There are lessons to be drawn between the stories. Orla wonders about the potential meanings of Enda's first story. Is it a parable about his own loss of faith? It raises questions about paradise by juxtaposing the pagan and the christian. By conveying the attraction of love and beauty it qualifies the austerity that denies sensual delights. Orla feels grateful for her own joyous certainty, unaware that its source is pagan. Nor does she consider the effects of her love on Enda whose faith she wants to restore. Our confidence in her virtue is gently undermined more than once: she entertains the thought that Enda might give her the child she wants and she lies with him in the hut. The novel's treatment of such incidents is amused and tolerant. Ceasan's life of solitude and prayer is disturbed, Congal More's self-esteem is comically shaken, and Orla's girlish innocence is tested, not spoiled. Human nature is attractively flawed and vulnerable.

The stories mesh and mirror one another in an ingenious, comic and mutually enriching manner so that the sum of their interrelationships makes each more entertaining than it would be in isolation. Just as Congal More's young wife, Fial Fairbrow, is attracted by a young man at the court so Orla is attracted by Enda, and Ceasan by Eithne. Just as Congal More succumbed to lust so Orla is ready to yield to her pursuer at the well. Enda's story about Ceasan may be a sympathetic reflection of his own difficulties of belief and Ceasan's attraction for Eithne is paralleled in Enda's love for Orla. In turn Orla sees Enda as another Diarmuid whose love spot made him irresistible to women. Disguises are endemic: people are hidden by mists induced by Oengus who himself goes in disguise. Orla goes in disguise on her pilgrimage, so does Fial Fairbrow to the hunting-lodge. Congal More is disguised as a goat. But in that state he sees the naked girl and enjoys her beauty without lust or prurience, despite his bestial shape. Orla sees Enda's naked body in the light from a passing flight of angels and feels guilty. So, ironically, does Congal More when he remembers his human morality. Enda rescues Orla from sexual assault at the very moment when she intends to be caught. Similarly, Ceasan loses Eithne back to Oengus at the very moment when he was to have gained her for christianity. Flann, a would-be rescuer, set out after Orla, but Oengus keeps them apart so it is Enda, Flann's double, who rescues her. If the mortal world is hedged about by moral prohibitions, the timeless world of Oengus into which Orla and Enda stray and to which Eithne returns is without prohibitions. What Orla and Enda do there no mortal will ever know.

Ultimately the book offers versions of existence, parables of ways by which men live or might live. There is Ceasan's way of prayer and sublimation with the hope of salvation hereafter. There is Eithne's natural paradise from which Oengus, the embodiment of an irrepressible and healthy comic spirit, comes. The appetite for living that he exemplifies stands as a counter force to the restrictive life style of Ceasan. Eithne's shining beauty and the music that signifies the presence of Oengus evoke the timeless happiness of their paradise. Orla and Enda experience its magic and Ceasan feels its attraction. Its potency, most vividly rendered in the exuberant Oengus, is a counter force to a restrictive and humourless christianity. There human worries and doubts do not exist. The moral problems that torment humans have no place. The issues of the novel are not new in Clarke's work but the self-delighting ingenuity and the lightness of emphasis are. It is the last of his novels, more akin in spirit and tone to his Pierrot comedies than to the rigorous morality of *The Singing Men at Cashel* or the anguish of *Night and Morning*. Oengus's dancing rags represent a joyousness of spirit that is far removed from the threatening morality of Malachi's sign of the serpent.

Chapter 6: Plays

The Irish dramatic movement, which was an important element in the Irish Literary Revival, had two innovative aims: the authentic artistic use of Irish material and the restoration of poetic and imaginative drama to the stage at a time when commercial theatre was dominant. In 1898, two years after the birth of Austin Clarke, Lady Gregory, Edward Martyn and W.B. Yeats announced the formation of the Irish Literary Theatre and declared their intention of producing 'Celtic and Irish plays' and of developing 'a Celtic and Irish school of dramatic literature'. The terminology, 'Celtic' and 'Irish' is inexact, but it is clear that they are thinking in terms of Irish literature and traditional sources. Surprisingly, the movement was moderately successful in its first three seasons and was at least taken seriously. Above all it showed that it might be possible to create an Irish theatre based on Irish materials, both legendary and contemporary. There were, however, difficulties inherent in the divergent motives and abilities of the dramatists. Edward Martyn and George Moore wanted to write a modern type of Irish play. Yeats, as he explained in *Samhain* (1901), wanted 'to get our Heroic Age into verse and to solve some problems of the speaking of verse to musical notes'; both he and Lady Gregory wanted 'peasant plays' in English.[1]

The Irish National Theatre was formed in 1903, with Yeats as president, and Maud Gonne, AE, and Douglas Hyde, as vice-presidents. The plays that they put on in 1903 determined the future development of the theatre: they combined the verse-play and the heroic play, represented by Yeats's *The Hour-Glass* and *The King's Threshold*, and the 'peasant play', represented by Lady Gregory's *Twenty-Five*, J.M. Synge's *In the Shadow of the Glen*, and Padraic Colum's *Broken Soil*, later called *The Fiddler's House*. Buoyed up by the arrival of Synge, whom

114

he defended from attack, Yeats now began to define what he wanted for the theatre: plays of intellectual excitement, where language was supreme, with simple, restrained acting, scenery, and costume. In 1904 he began to discuss such matters as the necessity for proper voice-production, the dramatic possibilities of using choruses and interspersed lyrics in the manner of Greek and Elizabethan dramatists, and the effect, never clearly defined, of speaking dramatic verse on a planned series of musical notes.

In 1904 the new company acquired and reconstructed the buildings which since then have housed the Abbey Theatre and for the next five years had considerable success, with masterpieces by Synge, *Riders to the Sea* (1904), *The Playboy of the Western World* (1907), two successful comedies by Lady Gregory, *The Rising of the Moon* (1907) and *The Workhouse Ward* (1907), and work by new dramatists: Padraic Colum, George Fitzmaurice, Lennox Robinson, Lord Dunsany, and others. The death of Synge in 1909 deprived the young theatre of its only dramatic genius and marked the virtual disappearance of the heroic play and of the imaginative 'peasant play'. From now on plays of a naturalistic kind would dominate. There was, in fact, little public demand for verse plays and this was true elsewhere as well. Yeats turned more and more to a private kind of theatre, of limited popular appeal, but in which he could continue to experiment. The success of his work has been discussed by Katherine Worth in *The Irish Drama of Europe from Yeats to Beckett* (1978), in which she argues that Yeats anticipated 'all that is most original in the European theatre'.

> All the resources of the theatre — scene, colour, music, dance and movement — had to be brought into play: only a synthesis of the arts, supporting and high-lighting the words, drawing attention to their value by allowing spaces between them, stretches of silence, unanswered questions, could hope to render anything like the complexity of the mind's processes, its intuitions and fine shades of feeling, the whole undertow of the stream of consciousness.[2]

Ironically, in view of his excited response and the long-lasting impact of the experience, the Abbey Theatre was going through one of its periodical lean periods when Austin Clarke began to attend. In the seven years after the death of Synge, Yeats contributed only one new play, *The Green Helmet* (1910), although his plays continued to be performed. Lady Gregory contributed about eight new plays, none of which are among her best. There were, however, new plays by the emergent and increasingly dominant realist school — Padraic Colum, Lennox Robinson, T.C. Murray, and St John Ervine. Clarke records his first visit to the theatre in terms of shock, illumination and lasting appreciation. Yeats's plays 'were a deeply imaginative experience',[3] but it was a play by Gerhardt Hauptmann that he best remembered. *Hannele*, an experiment in expressionism, had the kind of theme that had a personal interest for Clarke and the play's theatrical conventions were ones that he would use. 'Reality and hallucination,' he said, 'mingled in the strange scenes; sacred and profane figures dissolved into one another . . . I realized instinctively that the play was a protest against the oppression of the young and that insidious sense of spiritual guilt which is instilled by custom into the adolescent mind'.[4] *Hannele* is full of visions and apparitions — of a little girl's father, her dead mother, angels, Jesus. This visionary world overlaps the real world of the almshouse and of the girl's sickness, at times suffusing it with light and beauty, at times invading it with fear and terror. The child has an intense fear of sin and of her father, wants to escape into the Otherworld, and to be released from physical pain and mental distress.

It is difficult to assess Clarke's understanding of Yeats's experiments, but when he and Robert Farren founded the Lyric Theatre Company their aim was to revive the tradition of verse-drama that Yeats had initiated at the Abbey. Like him they were both interested in how verse-drama should be spoken. Clarke had been a judge at the Oxford Festival of Spoken Poetry and had been co-founder, with Farren, of the Dublin Verse-Speaking Society which trained actors and radio broadcasters to foster the recitation of rhythmic speech. Members of the Society gave regular broadcasts of dramatic and choral poetry on Radio Eireann and presented festivals of verse-speaking at the Peacock Theatre in Dublin. In 1944 when the Lyric Theatre had been formed the company hired the Abbey Theatre for performances of verse-drama on Sunday nights. This arrangement lasted until the theatre burnt down in 1951. The complete list of stage performances indicate the directions of Clarke's dramatic interests.[5] It includes most of Clarke's own plays written before 1951 and plays by W.B. Yeats, George Fitzmaurice, Donagh MacDonagh, Padraic Colum, and Gordon Bottomley. Clarke admired Bottomley. In a review he wrote of his *Lyric Plays* (1932), he praised his ability to create a poetic world rapidly and by means as simple as 'the folk music ritual of balladry'; he also singled out the 'sound texture' of the poetry.[6] In the same year, in a review of S.F. Lysaght's verse play, *The Immortal Jew*, he noted that verse drama 'is no longer sensitive: technically it has remained completely static'.[7] In fact, there were very few verse dramatists. In 1935, reviewing Yeats's *Collected Plays*, Clarke praises his 'remarkable and sustained attempt to revive poetic drama'.[8] Clarke, however, is not an analytical critic; his remarks tend to focus on general aspects of a writer's work rather than investigating structural or organisational details. Thus, although he admired Archibald MacLeish's *Panic*, an expressionistic play in verse, for its use of two stage levels, an upper and a lower, what he particularly comments on is the attempts 'to solve the problem of contemporary speech rhythm in stage verse'.[9] The question of adapting the rhythms and stresses of the poetic line for the stage always concerned him. In reviewing Gordon Bottomley's *Choric Plays* (1939) he pointed out that 'the dramatic element in his choric dramas is inseparable from his poetry. . . . Here is a pure form which, for all its dramatic action, would defeat the ordinary producer who still believes that a verse-play must be turned into a prose play in a few quick rehearsals before it can be put on the stage, a little haranguing and elocution being thrown in to pacify the unfortunate author'.[10] In the same year in a review of T.S. Eliot's *The Family Reunion* (1939) Clarke questions the point of having characters speak of trivial matters 'in half a pentameter or a couple of anaepests'.[11] Verse or rhythm, he declares, 'is caused by a heightening of emotion and is, in effect, the expression of a high tension. If the subject does not require that heightened emotion, then rhythmic speech in itself sounds false'. His note to his own *Collected Plays* (1963) asserts his position.

> All these plays are metrical because stage speech only resembles natural speech and goes more easily, being set to definite patterns. The accented syllables are never separated by more than three unaccented syllables, but when the rhythm takes control, the secondary stresses point the way, paragraphically, line beyond line.[12]

Roger McHugh makes the point that Clarke's plays are narrow in range of subject matter, being confined to the drama of conscience, medieval and modern, but that they have varying poetic techniques: flexible blank verse, couplets of four or five stresses, straight rhyme or rhyme modified by end and internal assonance, interspersed lyrics or lyrics spoken to music. He also praises Clarke's sense of humour· he 'can be serious, ironic, gay, witty and humorous by turns'.[13] Initially Clarke's plays were reactions to the over-reverent manner in which the Abbey players performed Yeats's plays. He wanted more zest, more liveliness, qualities he admired in Bottomley and MacLeish. It is the comic side of his temperament that appears most successfully. McHugh's statement about the need for contemporary performances of Clarke's plays, if we are to judge their effectiveness as plays, also affects their consideration in this chapter.

Austin Clarke's plays are of two kinds: those written in a spirit of entertainment and comedy and those written to explore the effects of moral crises on individual consciences. The comedies, which are dramatically the more successful of the two kinds, represent a side of Clarke's personality that appears only occasionally in the early and late poems and more explicitly in *The Sun Dances at Easter*. The other plays take up those moral issues that are also found in *The Singing Men at Cashel* and *Night and Morning*. They examine in particular the ways in which man's awareness of evil may impinge upon his consciousness.

The comedies include *The Son of Learning* (1927), *Black Fast* (1942), three plays in the *commedia dell'arte* manner — *The Kiss* (1942), *The Second Kiss* (1946), and *The Third Kiss* (1976) — and, less successfully, *The Viscount of Blarney* (1944), *The Plot Succeeds* (1950), *The Visitation* (1974), *Liberty Lane* (1978), and two adaptations from Cervantes.

The Son of Learning is based on *Aislinge Meic Conglinne*, 'The Vision of MacConglinne', an irreverent attack on the Church, on ecclesiastical scholarship, and on clerical contempt for the poet.[14] Clarke shortens the narrative, highlights the conflict between the poet and the Church, introduces the figure of Ligach, who is betrothed to Cathal, King of Munster, and gives histrionic life to MacConglinne. In the original Anier is rewarded for curing Cathal of the hunger-demon that has possessed him. In Clarke's play he is treated with cruel injustice.

The first scene, within a lively and ironic contrast of quarrelling beggars, praying monks and a howling demon, gives the necessary information about the king's affliction and introduces the figure of MacConglinne, poet and satirist, rogue and scholar, 'A wicked unbeliever/A great deceiver'. His appearance, Clarke tells us, suggests the wandering scholars of medieval Europe, but with a racial or bardic touch. Anier, whose songs have the folksy realism of Clarke's early poems about rural Ireland, lives by his wits and adopts a variety of roles to suit his audience, including that of the visionary poet when he discovers Ligach, disguised as a pilgrim:

> Are you
> Etain, who washes in a basin of gold
> With carven birds or that horsewoman, Niav
> Taking the fences of the sea? Are you
> The wife of the musician, Craftine,
> Who was unhappy when the holeheaded flute
> Began to play . . .

He becomes master of the revels when the beggars dance gleefully around him but his irreverence angers the Abbot whose indignant assertion of authority is unconsciously self-deflating:

Am I not a bishop? Have I not
A mitre, a golden crozier, a red carbuncle
On my finger? Have I not secular power?
Am I not a prince in my own right?

In Act II Anier's poems about food excite the King to a crescendo
of greedy anticipation. Borrowing the royal collar of gold so that he may
have supreme authority and binding Cathal in a high chair, Anier becomes
a lord of misrule, consuming food and drink and praising both lavishly
in order to lure the demon from the King's stomach. Utterly bewildered,
Cathal tries to pray but can only manage a comic 'act of nutrition':
'Through my dumpling. Through my dumpling. Through my most suety
dumpling'.

In Act III Anier uses Ligach to help him to entice the demon. He
gabbles in broken Latin, leaps backward as the demon emerges and the
stage is plunged in darkness. When light returns the King rewards the
Abbot who sanctimoniously declares that prayers and fasting have
effected the cure. As the chorus of beggars drily observe: 'There's but
one party wins — respect and power'. Anier is reported, without regret,
to have been carried off by the demon. But the King's golden collar is
also missing. The poet, it seems, has wisely rewarded himself.

The compactness of *The Son of Learning* shows Clarke's ability to
shape the original story for his own dramatic purposes. He was helped
by the affinity between the comedy of the medieval comedy and his
own satirical intentions, but the changes he makes are dramatically effective. The plot is swiftly advanced and executed in a lively, economic
manner. He provides good material in particular for the actor playing
Anier, leaving room for improvisation, verbal display and role-playing.
At the same time the parts of Ligach, the Abbot and the King are substantial, while the background figures of beggars, monks, soldiers, the
Old Blind Man and the Amadán, provide colourful, realistic life. Despite
the dangers involved, the exorcism is treated as high comedy with the
ravenous King tormented by the nearness of food and the cunning poet
playing his part with relish. Its climax is rendered as comic melodrama
with thunder, wild music, a blaze of light, and sudden darkness. Anier's
mistreatment is Clarke's opinion of what the poet may expect from
authority, in church and state.

Black Fast also aims its comedy at the Church. It is based on Bede's
account in his *Ecclesiastical History* of the quarrel between King Oswy
and Queen Eanfled as to the correct dating of Easter. 'The confusion,'
Bede wrote, 'was so great that Easter was kept twice in one year, so that
when the King had ended Lent and was keeping Easter, the Queen and
her attendants were still fasting and keeping Palm Sunday'. Most of the

play is derived from George T. Stokes's account of the Paschal Controversy in *Ireland and the Celtic Church*.[15] Clarke transfers Bede's setting to Ireland, changing names of people and places accordingly, mocks scholastic pedantry and its reliance on authorities, mocks the sanctity of the clerical disputants by exposing their enormous pride in their own knowledge and power, and pokes fun at male-female disputes in the disagreement between the King and the Queen. Unlike the sources in which the dispute is resolved, Clarke creates a cyclical plot, farcical in nature, in which the disputants, both secular and ecclesiastical, remain as fiercely and foolishly opposed at the end of the play as they were at the beginning.

The play begins in a lightly comic row between servants as to whether it is the season of Lent or not, moves quickly to a brief repetition of the same disagreement between Connal More of Ulster and his wife, Blanaid, and then to the learned dispute between rival ecclesiastics. Cummian, from the North, in confrontation with Romanus, from the South, issues a solemn challenge:

slowly

> Let two books, one of the older order, another of the new, be cast into the fire and let us see which of them will escape the flame.

He pauses but there is silence. He continues with a smile

> Or, if you have no books, let two monks, one of yours and another of mine, be shut up in the same house. Then let the house be set on fire and we shall see which of them will escape the flame.

The Munster monks look at one another anxiously

An Ulster Monk

O Father, let me go into the flame
Again to see the terrors of the past,
The trumpet-scattered armies of Canaan,
The brasses of the Moloch . . .

Another

No, it is

My turn.

Another

No mine!

Cummian

in a firm but kindly tone

Be patient

addressing his opponent

If

You fear the flame,

impressively

then, let us go to the grave of a deceased monk and raise him up to life and he will tell us which order we ought to observe in the celebration of Easter.

Romanus politely declines these challenges, admitting adroitly that Cummian's holiness is such that he could 'rock' a local hillside with his staff, if he wished. Instead Romanus invites Connal More to sit in judgment on a debate between the two sides. Flattered, Connal agrees and Cummian appoints Cogitosus to present the Northern view; Romanus speaks for the South. Cogitosus appeals to Irish tradition, to Patrick, Brigid and the sanctity of the early Irish church. Romanus takes a larger perspective. He speaks of the universal church and emphasises how out of step the Northern church is with what 'all men practise now', in Rome, in Gaul, in Greece, in Antioch, in Carthage, and so on. His narration of personal experience is intended to impress the Northerners and to undermine their trust in the 'nettled hermits' of Cummian's ecclesiastical lineage:

Your nettled hermits
Assume, no doubt, that God Almighty rests
On the Old Law. Borrow these eyes that saw
Last year the wonders of the New. Beyond
The Isle of Golden John, our pilgrim ship
Was stopped by darkness on Good Friday. All
Could see the alp that opens into flame
At the Third Hour. Believe me, I have sponged
From this poor body, this passing dust, the pock
Of cinders flying from the lower regions
Where the lost souls are tortured.

But his reply to Blanaid's awestruck question — 'And you saw/The wonders of the Holy Land, too?' — is unconsciously comic. At the annual fair in Jerusalem, he says:

> Those streets are never staled with donkey dung
> Or camel drench, for when the fair is over —
> A sudden clap of cloud comes down to cleanse
> The cobbles. I sheltered from that miracle, . . .

Even Connal More loses his detachment and asks — 'And did you see Mount Olivet?'. Romanus outlines the experience impressively: we climbed, we saw, we stood:

>   We climbed
> The rocky pathway to the last basilica
> Of all. We saw the sacred circle of air
> No roofing stone can vault. We stood in fear
> And trembling there . . .

and then challenges his audience

>   But who will dare
> To contradict what is decreed by councils,
> Deny what is believed by all the faithful
> From Palestine to Rome?

   The argument then turns to the question of the dating of Easter. But the disputants grow excited as to what method of computation is correct, until Connal More insists on a final summing up by both sides. Cogitosus describes the saintly death of Columcille and asks rhetorically if such a man could not calculate the 'true date of the Resurrection'. Romanus allows that Columcille may have lived in truth according to the limited knowledge available to him. The Ulster monks feel insulted and walk out. In a final incident the dishes set for a feast dramatically disappear, thereby seeming to confirm Romanus's view that this is a fast day. But then it is discovered that they have appeared on the monks' table, thereby seeming to confirm that it is a feast day. Romanus, however, says this is an evil sign, Blanaid agrees, Connal disagrees, so nothing has been resolved and chaos returns.

   Black Fast is unified by the single topic of its controversy and, despite the historical remoteness of its subject matter, by the perceptions of human nature. The variety and humour of its action throughout is well-paced, from the initial disagreements among servants to the learned dispute between clerics, to the ludicrous miracle of the floating dishes. The style moves from the blunter encounter between the servants to the the formal arguments, where Clarke might easily have become entangled in Bede's detailed account of the different methods of dating Easter.

Even in the necessarily more elevated style of the clerical debate he is able to express individual psychology, contrasting attitudes, and to puncture ecclesiastical pomposity.

Clarke's mastery of comedy is however exemplified more clearly in the trilogy of the Pierrot-Pierrette plays. These are light and inventive treatments of protean changes of character and of lightning transitions in place and time. They show to best advantage the playful mode that Clarke employs in other plays also, including *The Viscount of Blarney*, *Liberty Lane*, and *The Plot Succeeds*. But the Pierrot plays form a group in themselves. Their setting is pastoral: a wood near Clonsilla, an open space outside Dublin; the characters are from the *commedia dell'-arte*: Pierrot, Pierrette, Columbine, Harlequin; the theme is love; the method is openly theatrical. The characters are themselves actors in a play that they readily discuss with the audience, like their predecessors in *commedia dell'arte*. Sometimes they follow a script, sometimes improvise, playing variations on a theme, ingeniously making up situations and dialogue. It is as though they are in love with make-believe, with the possibilities of the play as a vehicle for their theatrical talents and are involved in emotional situations whose ramifications and developments are predictable. Their lines are, as it were, written in the human heart. In a happy conspiracy between actors and audience each knows what is likely to happen and this familiarity creates a mood of expectancy in which the truths of human behaviour are once again revealed. Happiness is assured, the comic tone will not be broken no matter what momentary setbacks occur. An imaginative world is created in which disappointments and evils may be acknowledged, but in which nothing prevails against the cleansing comic spirit.

The plays have only a marginal social significance; they take place outside the city, apart from its political and social concerns. Their verisimilitude is mainly psychological and the feelings they express are cocooned in self-evident illusion. Pierrot, for example, who is 'young and ingenuous', has no occupation. When Uirgeall asks him what he does for a living, he replies, 'Nothing much, I fear, delight/In momentary fancies, dress in white'. Uirgeall herself represents 'light' and 'innocence'; she is also the ideal Columbine. The style of the plays is suitably light, playful in rhythm and rhyme. So, when Pierrot enters, carrying a basket, he says:

to audience

> What's in the basket?
> That is your question and before you ask it,
> I'll answer everything. But let me take
> My luncheon out.

Suiting rhythmic action to word

> First, an old-fashioned cake.
> What are the specks? You've guessed it — caraway.
> Some muscatels,
>   a cake knife,
>   corkscrew, —
>   — Pray
> Excuse the tissue paper and twine —
> Together with a bottle of light wine.
> For when I drink, I love to see the grape.
> A napkin —
>   I can wrap it round the nape.
> Two little glasses, one inside the other
> For company.
>   You ask why do I bother?
> Well, anything can happen in a wood
> Like this.

Uirgeall appears from behind a tree, but is unseen by Pierrot

In *The Kiss* Clarke reworks the legend of the loathly hag. Uirgeall, whose name means 'very bright', is a *caillech* trapped in a condition of age from which she can be rescued by a young man's first, innocent kiss. Pierrot's reaction to her request for a kiss is balanced between alarm at the thought of having to kiss one so ugly and honest refusal to go back on his promise to help her. His references to Horatio, Scaevola and Theseus provide a mock-heroic framework for his ordeal, as do his comparisons between Uirgeall's instantaneous transformation into Columbine and Ovid's metamorphoses. Her identification with the ideal woman of Yeats's poetry keeps the theme of imaginary love, despite Pierrot's suggestion that they should enjoy the pleasures of love in a more realistic way. Uirgeall, however, prefers her ethereal existence knowing that 'mortal longings are the deathward flight/Of midges towards the dusk'. For a moment she is tempted; together they outline a domestic idyll and consider the possibility of marriage. Uirgeall's reluctance to enter the condition of mortality — 'Must I weep . . . weep . . . come to earth?' — yields to the fact that she loves him and will therefore choose 'All the responsibilities of life'. But voices call her away. She returns Pierrot's kiss and disappears. Pierrot's sorrow is brief and histrionic. The play has entertained the theme of ideal love: Pierrot imagines an ideal companion for his picnic, is confronted with the hag, agrees to her request and gives her back her youth and beauty so that she becomes his ideal. Ultimately the ideal endures by remaining free of mortality and Pierrot continues to enjoy his illusions.

The Second Kiss also deals with illusion and reality, lightly touching upon fears that have a psychological reality, playfully juxtaposing the ideal and the real, the Columbine of Pierrot's fantasy and the Pierrette of actuality. The conjunction of the real and the ideal, the present and the past serves to reveal the complexity of human relationships. The playful shadow-dance of Pierrot and Pierrette, domestic lovers, recently wed, turns to misunderstanding and tears; the ideal Columbine brings back memories of destruction, of plays, of happiness. Columbine is, as it were, Pierrette before marriage; to bring Columbine into marriage is to introduce her to the tears of the everyday. Harlequin is Pierrot's fears externalised: the fear, in particular, of losing Pierrette. He seems threatening, even devilish, but ambiguously says it is all in play; nevertheless, he tells Pierrot that Columbine-Pierrette is his. So the play, in its cyclical progress, turns back to the beginning: the quarrel of the lovers is over and they can again play with their shadows, forgetting what those shadows may suggest. The device of the play within the play relates the external to the internal, showing, lightly and amusingly, fears hidden in the human heart.

In *The Third Kiss* Pierrot and Pierrette play the parts of respectable people in a realistic Abbey theatre play of 1913 — 'unhappy/Tormented by conscience'. The theme is expressed in Pierrette's question: 'Why is the world mysterious with evil?'. Harlequin is again her would-be seducer. He is an 'air-demon', reputed to have been a 'mediaeval/Vice in Cathedral plays'. He is the first sign of evil. 'Offstage', he says, the 'human mind is quite obscene'. In their abstract roles Pierrot and Pierrette can remember a happy holiday they shared; in their realistic roles, as Peter and Pauline, such carefree days are unachievable. They remember the childhood game of running three times round the Black Church and remember that one child saw a small black cat which Pauline thinks 'really was the Devil'. When they play the game again, as required in the play, Pauline sees a gentleman in an opera cloak, with 'a devil mask'. Evil is present each time. But evil is ambiguous: the distinction between good and evil is not clear. Fr Doyle, Pierrette's confessor, ought to represent good, yet he is tormented by sexual temptation. Scene II has the same pattern of repetition in which the present re-enacts the past, making the adult experience into a confirmation of childhood's intuitive perception of the presence of evil. When Peter and Pauline walk in the wood, Pauline remembers being there before as a girl and being frightened. Now when they kiss thunder sounds and rain falls, as though in rebuke. When they run for shelter Pauline sees 'Something hideous'. When, in a lightning change of scene, Pauline relates to Fr Doyle her sight of the naked man in the wood she realises 'in horror' that it was Fr Doyle. Scene IV returns to the end of Scene I, when Pauline finishes the third circuit of the Black Church. She explains to Peter: she saw the Evil One 'in a nightmare/Or trance', saw also the evil figure in the wood and now thinks she sees the man in the raincoat. All these manifestations, whether real or imagined, from the present or the past, are signs of what the mind contains. Harlequin appears again, as voyeur, watching Pierrot and Pierrette undress, but also to express the dramatist's farewell to *commedia dell'arte*. 'We are', he says, 'international types. . . . The centuries have made us artful'. His wickedness, he says, 'is really not in earnest/Or is it?'

The Third Kiss is a little masterpiece, light and delicate in touch, precise in its indications of evil within quick, spontaneous action and dialogue and within lightning temporal and spatial transitions. *The Second Kiss*, by contrast, is less successful, drawn into memories of the past and into references to government and politics. The three Pierrot-Pierrette plays have however an irrepressible sense of comedy and with some other comedies form an important part of Clarke's work, a counter-presence to the more sombre side of his imagination.

The other comedies however are less successful. *The Viscount of Blarney*, which is based on the loosely structured story 'Cauth Morrisey Looking for Service' in Patrick Kennedy's *Legendary Fictions of the Irish Celts*[16] presents a succession of manifestations of evil. All the figures that appear to the defenceless Cauth in the form of a cyclorama — the Pooka, the evil-minded Fostermother whose thoughts run on unwanted pregnancies and infanticides, the eighteenth-century gallant who tells her that the Viscount of Blarney wants to marry her, the frightening night-hag or knee-woman with her mysterious bag — are all part of a psychological drama, each evocative of Cauth's fear, each connected with female sexuality. What they represent or suggest is made more visible in the figure of the Viscount, who is the Devil in disguise. The play's structure depends on the quickly-changing episodic appearances of these dream-figures. A similar weakness is found in *The Plot Succeeds*, which is based on *Compert Mongain ocus Serc Duibe Lacha do Mongán*, 'The Conception of Mongan and His Love for Dubh Lacha'.[17] The play is hampered by the complexities of the original in which Mongan, King of Ulster and son of Manannan, exercises his magical powers. The story requires impersonations and disguises. At best the play is a comedy built upon deceptions but it is made sluggish by the need to explain the changes of identity and by a plot that never becomes significant, despite its farcical conclusion. The play lacks the pace to make the plot-complications entertaining. *Liberty Lane: a ballad play of Dublin* is based on F.R. Higgins's play, a *Deuce of Jacks* (1935). Clarke takes the central device of the mock wake and a gathering of mourners who have been lured to the bedside to avail of the drink which is freely available. He delights in the bizarre comedy, infuses it with fast-moving action, with exuberance, with the language of Dublinese. It is a ballad play that combines narrative, song, dance, and bawdy entertainment within a form that breaks through the conventions of the realistic play into a condition of gaiety, mischief, and abandonment. His adaptations from Cervantes, *The Student from Salamanca* and *The Silent Lover*, bawdy situation comedies about wives deceiving their husbands, merrily delight in the confusions and panic that ensue. These plays mock at solemnity and pomposity.

Clarke's graver plays include *The Flame*, *Sister Eucharia*, *As the Crow Flies*, and several less successful ones: *The Plot is Ready*, *The Moment Next to Nothing*, two plays in manuscript, 'St Patrick's Purgatory' and 'The Frenzy of Suibhne', and an adaptation from Cervantes.

In *The Flame* and *Sister Eucharia* Clarke moves from the high comedy and anarchic individualism of Anier's confrontation with clerical authority to an examination of rebellion within the controlled world of the convent. The conflict is between the order and decorum of a community's rules of personal behaviour and the claims of imagination and feeling. The formalism of the plays' structure and language, the use of choric voices, and the orderly movements of the nuns express a way of life in which individuality is subsumed by the communal and the impersonal.

The conflict between the secular and the ecclesiastical develops with dramatic force in *The Flame* which introduces the issue of Attracta's vain and defiant growing of her hair, develops her conflict with authority to a climactic confrontation with the Abbess and turns swiftly to its resolution. When Attracta confesses that she has let her hair grow, the nameless 'Nun' is horrified and the 'sudden harsh clangour of handbells' stresses the enormity of the deed and 'the distorted imagination' of the novice. The Abbess forces her to a fuller confession of her visions of a secular world of strong men and their female companions. When Attracta refuses to obey her command to kneel down to have her hair cut, handbells again sound loudly, Attracta struggles and screams, the flame begins to sink 'to an angry glow and the stage fills with shadows'. While the nuns pray in distress against the evil spirits that, as they think, hide the flame, Attracta sees Absalom removed from the tree by mourning nuns and attended by repentant clergy. Her personal symbol of life and beauty receives the understanding she is denied. But her prayer to St Brigid — 'Hide me with pity/Hide me with your blue mantle . . .' — seems to be answered when the flame disappears and Brigid's blue mantle seems to fill the stage, 'enfolding and wrapping her until there is complete darkness'. The nuns discover they have forgotten to fill the lamp with oil but that its spark has, as they quickly declare, been miraculously maintained. The Abbess, reminding them that their faith has been weak, refills the lamp and, as the play ends, the flame rises again.

In *Sister Eucharia* convent decorum has been disturbed by the religious intensity of Sister Eucharia who wants to die so that she can go to Heaven. She is strengthened in her resolve by a vision of souls in Purgatory who are joyful in their pain. When Eucharia moves in a trance-like manner towards the chapel, the convent bell sounds in awesome accompaniment. When news is brought that she has died in the chapel, Reverend Mother quickly interprets this as a sign: 'God has at last granted to our order/A saint'. Even the admission of the timid lay Sister, that it was she who rang the bell, does not deter the nuns from seeing this too as evidence of God's purpose, although it introduces an ambivalent element into the play's conclusion.

Anier's confrontation with the Church is high-spirited and self-reliant and the Abbot is shown to be vain, opportunistic and unjust, but the conflict between the individual and the institution in these two plays, while less exuberant, is more intense. The confrontation is violent in Attracta's case; the climax is nightmarish, as though she were possessed by the devil who must be exorcised. The Abbess moves resolutely to excise the sign of Attracta's vanity. In so far as the images of Attracta's imagination belong to early Irish culture it could be argued that Clarke is defending his own imaginative preferences and showing how traumatic it is to have them curtailed. The descent of Brigid's mantle may be said to sanction both his and Attracta's imaginative needs, since Brigid is also goddess of imaginative fire. They both triumph over clerical disapproval and aridity. Similarly, in *Sister Eucharia*, the young nun's passionate longing for death, so excessive in the eyes of the community, is confirmed in her vision of souls and her calm fulfilment in death. Neither the Abbess in *The Flame* nor the Reverend Mother in *Sister Eucharia* can control such transcendent imaginative power.

The contrast in style between *The Son of Learning* and the other two plays is considerable. One of the most effective devices in *The Flame* is the use of movement to convey spiritual states. The nuns move in a drilled and disciplined manner whereas Attracta moves erratically, clearly out of step with the others, particularly during the confrontation scene when she darts in desperation from one nun to another in search of aid. That visual contrast is present also in the heavily hooded and veiled appearances of the nuns and the exposed head of Attracta whose hair shines with a 'bright, metallic halo'. Attracta's singing tones when she relates her secular vision of men and women, 'O I could be happy in/ A house where armies have been kept, . . .', and when she orders the nuns away in a strange, possessed voice contrast with the monotonous undifferentiated voices of the community. 'Harsh exorcising bells' accentuate the climactic moment in which the Abbess cuts Attracta's hair. The flame itself functions as a symbol of the dedicated lives of the nuns, the focus of their existence and its controlling power. At the same time it is shown to represent more, to be open to and approving of the fire of imagination and of life for which Attracta yearns. The dramatic intensity of the play and its tightly controlled progression make it one of Clarke's best plays. Despite the extreme heightening of tension in the climax, indeed because of it, the suffering of the young nun is presented with sympathy and understanding.

In *Sister Eucharia* the agitation of the community is conveyed in the broken sentences of their exchanges and in their choric comments that express their fears and apprehensions. While the alternation of voices between groups, or between individuals and groups, creates atmosphere, provides information and advances the action, the device is over-used. Even Eucharia's dialogue with the dead souls, for example, is reflective in manner. But the over-long expository build-up of apprehension and anxiety makes the actual climax seem relatively slight and disappointing.

Clarke's first three plays are also part of his plan to change the mood of modern Irish literature. The irreverent gusto of *The Son of Learning* expresses his reaction to the more muted verse drama that he had seen at the Abbey Theatre. He found the greater boldness he wanted in Anier's story. This merry satire suited Clarke's purposes. His portrayal of King, Blind Man and Fool creates a comic contrast with W.B. Yeats's portrayal of the same figures in *On Baile's Strand*. His hilarious depiction of royalty at the mercy of a greedy demon subverts Yeats's usual account of kingship. His rogue poet contrasts to similar effect with the noble Seanchan of *The King's Threshold*, fasting to uphold the position of poets. All belong to a less reverent approach to Irish mythological figures and to a different kind of theatre. In their focus on issues that affect the Catholic conscience, *The Flame* and *Sister Eucharia* also belong to Clarke's attempt to broaden the range of Irish literature and to bring it closer to modern experience. The traumatic nature of the clash between a sensitive individual and an inflexible authoritarian figure, rendered with almost melodramatic intensity in *The Flame*, is modulated in *Sister Eucharia* through the sympathetic presence of the Reverend Mother. In each case clerical disapproval, which Anier rejected, causes mental and emotional distress. The direction of Clarke's plays at this time is from the extrovert to the subjective, from comic independence to anxiety and trauma. *As the Crow Flies* illustrates this tendency quite clearly. The problematical power of evil, which was an issue in some of the comedies, impinges here more intently on Clarke's imagination.

He borrowed the plot of *As the Crow Flies* from 'The Adventures of Léithin' and its folklore version, 'The Comparison as to Age between the Four Elders; namely, the Crow of Achill, the Great Eagle of Leac na bhfaol, the Blind Trout of Assaroe, and the Hag of Beare', which he found in Douglas Hyde's *Legends of Saints and Sinners*.[18] In this story when monks from Clonmacnoise shelter in a cave from a storm they overhear a conversation between the Eagle, Léithin, and the Crow, who has taken refuge in the Eagle's nest. The Crow asks if the Eagle remembers a storm as bad. Prompted by the Crow, the Eagle asks a number of creatures, known for their longevity: the Stag of Ben Bulben, the Black-bird, the Salmon of Assaroe who warns her that she has left an evil bird, the Crow of Death, sheltering in her nest with her young. To this simple linear narrative Clarke brings a suggestive psychological dimension.

As the Crow Flies effectively uses the techniques of the radio play — the sounds of voices, the noises of oars, of storm, of wind and wave, of people moving about — and is careful to identify speakers; it quickly establishes the occasion: the monks, the storm, the voices above the cave, the question of the presence of evil. The Eagle's quest for knowledge is in fact cyclical; what Fintan, the Salmon of Assaroe — in the original blinded by the Crow — tells her is ironically already present in her nest; her young are already endangered by the dissembling, ancient Crow who is synonymous with death, cruelty and betrayal. Evil, in other words, as the Pierrot-Pierrette comedies also revealed, is part of nature, part of us. Fintan, the supreme authority in matters of tradition because he has lived so long, has witnessed all the invasions of Ireland and spent long periods in the shapes of a salmon, an eagle, and a hawk. Therefore, the Eagle's flight towards Fintan is, as it were, an encounter with successive metamorphoses of the one figure who contains their combined wisdom. In fact, the truth that he holds is known to all men subliminally. Some-times imaged in dreams, it lies below the level of consciousness.

The clever Crow, once she has ingratiated herself into the Eagle's nest, initiates the Eagle's quest with vivid accounts of a comparable storm she once witnessed. The language of her account is lively, full of concrete detail, and rhymed, as when she describes the Hag of Beare changing from age to youth:

> Every two-hundredth year
> In storm, she casts another skin.
> I saw her do it as I came in,
> Step out of it on younger toes,
> Quickly as someone changing clothes;
> And brighter than a brand-new pin,
> She shone from nape to slender shin,
> Naked and shameless as a sin.

As intended, the Eagle is caught up in the question of whether this is the worst storm ever. Her conversations with the Stag and the Blackbird limns a chronology of Irish history. The Stag recalls the pursuit of Diarmuid and Grainne and the days of the Fianna, but the Blackbird, blind to reality, still urges Patrick, three centuries later, to listen to her wonderful song. In an intervening scene the monks puzzle over the significance of these voices and Aengus, the youngest, prays that he may not 'dream of evils that afflict/The young' and that he may be saved from 'the dreadful voice beneath the waters'. The original story relates a frightening saga of the Crow's cruelty, from her taking of Nuadha's hand at the Battle of Moytura, to her ripping off of Cuchullin's eyelashes and his blinding, to her habit of creeping guilefully into nests and killing the young. In Clarke's version the Salmon's memory also contains intimations of elemental 'horrors that shrieked/Before creation':

> There the sightless
> And deafened creatures grope to life
> With deathly gulp: the giant claw
> Searching the forest of the fronds.
> In pulps of sperm, the shapeless maw
> Swam slowly past me and mute monsters
> Uncoupled one another's armour
> Though they were blind.

and goes on to articulate a despairing view of man: all creatures are at the mercy of disease, violent attack and the irrational. Fintan's madness has resulted from his realisation that 'the forethought of defilement' makes it impossible for him to believe in the christian message of love. 'I cry to God,' he says, 'To pity my madness'. Despite his years of waiting and praying, he has been left in ignorance. His mind is burdened with memories of 'chronicles of war, greed, slaughter/Unchanging misery of mankind'. When in the final scene the monks see the Eagle dashing herself in despair against the cliff, Aengus says that now she knows 'the ancient thought that men endure at night'.

Despite its linear structure the play's unity is assured by the single-mindedness of the Eagle's mission and the growing certainty of its outcome. The tragedy is inevitable and we wait in apprehension for the conclusion. But perhaps the play's most successful quality is its ability to convey its intimations of things hidden in the depths of the mind. The Salmon sunk beneath the Falls of Assaroe is a symbol of man's submerged terrors.

The rest of these plays are flawed. Although *The Plot is Ready* is a drama of conscience based on the semi-historical tale, 'The Death of Muircertach Mac Erca', and uses hallucination to express the King's hidden guilt, it is weak in characterisation, slow in development and written in a language that is often obscure.[19] Muriadach's dream-scene in which he is threatened with damnation and urged to abandon his pagan mistress is not strong enough to motivate his delirious exit from the house and his fall into the grave that monks have prepared for him. The Abbot's casuistical interpretations are also dramatically ineffective. *The Moment Next to Nothing*, which could be interpreted as, in part, a response to W.B. Yeats's play *Where There is Nothing*, is, like *The Sun Dances at Easter*, based on *Altram Tige da Medar*.[20] The plot, however, is inherently static and the characterisation of Ceasan and Eithne too one-dimensional; the language in many places lacks dramatic tension. 'St Patrick's Purgatory' is also set in Ireland at the time of St Patrick. It is freely adapted from Calderon's *El Purgatorio de San Patricio* which Denis Florence MacCarthy translated in 1887. Its conflict between paganism and christianity is resolved in a general movement of the plot towards Lough Derg where several characters descend into the Cave of Demons and emerge repentant. The play suffers from its melodramatic elements — spirits, horrific incidents, wild swings of feeling, lurid contrasts and grim denunciations — and from its poor characterisation. Clarke improves upon the original by speeding up the action, reducing the melodrama, curtailing the long speeches and eliminating many of the naïve beliefs, but the play still relies too much on a judgmental view of humanity, which is perhaps more in tune with seventeenth-century Spanish morality than with twentieth-century taste. The other play manuscript, 'The Frenzy of Suibhne: A Lyrical Play', like the work on which it is based, is essentially a series of encounters with different figures, Colgan, Eorann, the Madman of Britain, the mill-hag, to which Clarke adds a number of hallucinatory figures, Sheela-na-Gig, the Decapitated Heads, and Emer, thereby increasing its episodic and digressive qualities. Apart from its stylistic features, the play has little to recommend it, although it is written in the vigorous, dense style of the later poetry. Clarke's version of Hawthorne in *The Impuritans* emphasises Young

Goodman Brown's delight in sensuality, thereby altering the original in which the young Puritan does not recover from his discovery of the pervasive presence of evil. It is however a slight play.

Austin Clarke's dramatic career begins with the histrionic gusto of Anier MacConglinne whose affinities with Manannan, the Prumpolaun and the protean Oengus are apparent. The Pierrot-Pierrette plays also show Clarke's enjoyment of comic material — the pantomime, pretence, romantic comedy. But his more solemn plays, with the exception of *The Flame* and *As the Crow Flies*, are less successful. Weaknesses appear: poor characterisation, inadequate plot, slack dialogue. But perhaps the more fundamental problem lies with the use of hallucination. This can bring an effective non-realistic dimension to the plays, as in *As the Crow Flies* or *The Viscount of Blarney*, where it stands for psychological experiences. But there is a tendency to use it as a convenient device, rather than to make it imaginatively functional. It then ceases to have an impressive, abnormal or eerie effect.

Clarke's plays are usually dramas of the mind. He is not interested in the portrayal of character for its own sake, or in character development, or even in conflict between characters. He is interested in situations that contain emotional states: Attracta in forceful conflict with the nunnery, Ceasan torn between the attractions of paganism and christianity, Muriadach tormented by guilt. These situations include encounters with different figures, real or imaginary, which advance our understanding of the character's emotional, or mental, state. The play's structure, as a result, is often linear, not organic, a succession of incidents whose only link is their impact on the consciousness of the focal character: the flight of the Eagle in *As the Crow Flies*, Suibhne's dialogues, Cauth Morrisey's cyclorama, Pierrot's relationships.

The modern theatre with its revolving stage and sophisticated use of lighting is ideally suited to the creation of situations in which the quick-moving action of the mind, including the rapid transitions of the dream state, can be revealed. Just as dreams can be powerfully evocative of emotions, so the theatre can effectively register, through movement, gesture, language, sound effects, lighting, and so on, the drama of the mind. Irrational or inexplicable psychological experience can be vividly, and profoundly, conveyed. While Clarke understood the technical possibilities of the theatre quite well and often used them successfully, particularly in the comedies, he did not use them as effectively for the other plays. Despite his concern with the hidden and darker recesses of the mind, he rarely succeeded in making them of compelling interest in his plays. That is partly the result of their brevity of form. They simply lack the range for a major investigation of emotional or moral crises. The few that have sufficient length, *The Moment Next to Nothing* or *The Plot Succeeds*, have insufficient psychological or imaginative energy to be successful.

There is, one might suggest, a tension in Clarke's plays between the comic and the grave. The former is self-delighting and objective, the latter is timid and subjective. While his imagination could delight in the world beyond the *fáeth fíada*, his christian imagination, fed on images and accounts of the damned, could not withstand the pressure of guilt and fear. Eucharia can be strengthened by her contact with voices from Purgatory, but Ceasan is weary of the uncertainty that attends the christian life. Muriadach is driven crazy by his tormenting guilt, Cauth is haunted by degrading views of sexual sin. The Pierrot plays always have Harlequin, a comic devil, even though the balance between good and evil always tips in favour of the good. Horror lies in wait, evil is everywhere, as Aengus knows in *As the Crow Flies*. Man is a sinful creature, prone to error. The comedies present the human predicament in entertaining shapes, but the other plays can at best assert man's independence or evoke the pervasive presence of evil; they cannot give it the sustained treatment it requires.

Chapter 7: Conclusion

Although Austin Clarke wanted to celebrate the merry sins, he was by temperament and training not well suited to the task. The combination of Victorian prudery and jansenistic Catholicism that shaped his growing years made him reticent about earthy matters. It is true that he spoke out strongly at times against moral censure and bemoaned its stifling effects on human nature, but he found it hard to deal with it directly in his imaginative writings. Only in his later poetry did he find the freedom to treat sexual experience realistically. At the same time, his early work is an attempt to oppose excessive restrictions on human behaviour. Both the short poems and the epic narratives advocate a life of freedom and pleasure, freedom to enjoy the carefree life of the west, freedom to participate imaginatively in the romance of Diarmuid and Grainne, or the heroic world of the early Irish sagas. Diarmuid and Grainne offer one kind of delight — a journey of love and sexual awakening through a timeless landscape. In *The Bright Temptation* that journey becomes an allegory of joyous sexual discovery. The *Fires of Baal* relishes the heady excitement of a sensual culture. *The Sword of the West*, while seriously impaired by Clarke's mental breakdown, evokes the romance of landscape and the allurements of mythological beings. The *Cattledrive in Connaught* marks a return to the realism that characterised the first play.

The confessional narratives in *Pilgrimage* provide opportunities for the relation of merry sins, but they are restrained by the ambivalences of the casuistical mind. The concept of the divided being is at the heart of *The Singing Men at Cashel* and *Night and Morning*. The casuistry that could be explored objectively in historical figures, both in poetry and prose, is the subject of intense personal investigation in *Night and Morning*. The conflicts between the individual and society, or between the individual and the Church, that have been inherent in all the previous work, including the first three plays, are now at the centre of a life for which they are the key issues. Since Clarke finds no comfort in religion, he has had hitherto to seek elsewhere for imaginative faith. The romance of landscape and of the mythological past gives way to the romance of the medieval period where, because of parallels with his own time, he could move closer to the issues that are now at the centre of his life and are the key issues. In such previous works alternative worlds could be imagined in which characters could exist in relative freedom, but there is no such escape in *Night and Morning*. Gormlai's breakdown follows upon a logical setting forth of the components of her conflict, but in *Night and Morning* there is a reduced and concentrated portrayal of the individual whose intellectual needs drive him in search of truth outside of the Church but whose emotional needs direct him to return to the communion of the faithful.

Clarke's poetry in *Night and Morning* no longer concerns itself with the harmonies of language; nor does it appeal to authority, since the only acceptable authority is the Church itself. This volume portrays unaccommodated man, apart from the support of society, or Church, or mythology. Not since Sweeny, who was similarly bereft, has Clarke revealed the experience of mental anguish, its desperation and its hopelessness, in such uncompromising terms. Mental breakdown is seen in Cuchullin, in Sweeny, in Gormlai, in the nightmares of Aidan and Anier, in the stress of Sr Attracta, but *Night and Morning*, specifically 'Summer Lightning', deals with the condition of men in whom God's likeness has died. They are in despair, excluded from the communion of the faithful, abandoned for all eternity. The horror of that position assails the mind; and the pride of intellect that sustains the individual also leads him with inexorable logic towards damnation.

Night and Morning bears witness to the strain of this condition. Its portrait is not of the divided woman, or the afflicted ascetic, or the student who strayed and now fears what may happen, but of the self under the threat of intellectual and imaginative extinction. The west is now a place where the merry sins were once enjoyed, the past is that of the medieval schoolmen, when logic could bring a man to God, or the time of the *Love Songs of Connacht*, when people were emancipated from the restrictions of ecclesiastical rules. Burn Ovid as well, Clarke declares, in magnificent contempt for laws that try to repress instinct, and 'The Straying Student' asserts the values by which a man might live.

At the basis of Clarke's faith is a belief in the essential goodness of man. The novels take up this issue. Their theme of innocence and guilt parallels the directions taken in the poetry from the romance of *The*

Vengeance of Fionn, to the existential strain of *Night and Morning*, to the lighter mood of the comedies. In *The Bright Temptation* Aidan finds Ethna, whereas in 'The Straying Student' the student is left in dread of what life may do to him, but he has seen the light.

The two sides of Clarke's temperament, the realistic and the romantic, did not exist on equal terms. One side advocated a realistic interpretation of and response to experience; the result is evident in *The Son of Learning*, in the exuberant persona of Manannan, in the realistic elements in the epic narratives, and in the realism of some of the short poems, in *Black Fast*, *As the Crow Flies*, and *The Viscount of Blarney*. But the romantic side was stronger, as is evident in *The Vengeance of Fionn*, the poems in 'The Land of Two Mists', *Pilgrimage*, and *The Flame*, *Sister Eucharia* and the Pierrot plays. The treatment of love throughout the early phase of his career is strongly romantic and idealistic. It is a poetry of loss rather than of passion, of disappointed love rather than of fulfilment. The love story of Aidan and Ethna, for example, is childlike. That between Gormlai and Nial has a similar innocence. While it is clear that they consummate their love, the novel avoids that side of their relationship as decisively as *The Vengeance of Fionn* avoided the physical union of Diarmuid and Grainne. The poet could express Fionn's jealous rage and Grainne's passion but the natural outcome of the emotional intensity between her and Diarmuid is shunned. The novelist could portray Gormlai's perception of sexual evil in Malachi and of frightening physicality in the Great Kneewoman, but not her happiness with Nial. In *The Bright Temptation* the language of censure and of accusation is more vibrant than the language of love. In *The Singing Men at Cashel* the language of Gormlai's struggle against male dominance is more credible than the language of her response to Nial.

Strength comes from the past, but also from within the individual. Much of Clarke's early work remembers the more innocent former days, in the distant past, in the medieval period, in childhood, but *Night and Morning* turns inward, to the realities of personal life. The consequences are found in the plays written between 1938 and 1955 and in *The Sun Dances at Easter*, in their affirmations of the transcending power of the imagination, their demonstrations that love, laughter, and make-believe can prevail against evil. But nothing in the work of this period accounts for the growth and vitality of Clarke's poetry after 1955.

PART II

NOTHING LEFT TO SING?

Ancient Lights

The two upper storeys of this building have been taken down, but the rights to light enjoyed thereby have not been abandoned and are reserved pending rebuilding. Particulars from the owners.

(Notice displayed at School Lane East)

Chapter 8: Poems and Satires (1955-1962)

i *Short Poems*

Austin Clarke wrote two types of poetry in the nineteen-fifties, short poems, often satirical, seldom personal, in which he voiced his observations on contemporary Ireland, and long poems, one in each collection, in which he explored in greater range and detail the circumstances and directions of his own life, both in relation to the contemporary scene and in relation to the personal and historical past. The three collections, each subtitled 'poems and satires', are *Ancient Lights* (1955), *Too Great a Vine* (1957), and *The Horse-Eaters* (1960). Many of the short poems concern themselves with instances of clerical influence or of social injustice. The effect is paradigmatic and accumulative. Individual poems do not in themselves amount to a major statement about Irish life but together they identify and address significant moral and social issues. They show Clarke in the process of pinpointing what he finds objectionable. As he discovers his voice he finds his subjects and as he finds his subjects he discovers ways of expressing how he feels and what he thinks of them. Identification and development go together. At the heart of his emerging vision is a contrast between past and present, between former periods of greater individual freedom and self-reliance and the present; between the outlawed Catholic Church of the Penal era that was close to the needs of the people and the clericalist, wealthy Church of the present; between the joyous, unashamed expression of love in the *Love Songs of Connacht* and the furtive, guilty expression of love, both inside and outside marriage, in his own time; between the idealism and courage embodied in the 1916 Rising and the apathy and materialism of the present. In a historical sense the short poems are markers in the social and spiritual map of the modern Irish state, each an illustration of social injustice and ecclesiastical oppression. The subject has a natural attraction for Clarke. He knows what it is to feel guilty and afraid, to be alienated from Church and society. Because he has experienced pain he is able to identify with the socially disadvantaged and with those who experience spiritual suffering. The autobiographical poems, each a case history of one person, represent many. The individual experience is that of the race. This realisation, in itself a liberating discovery, gives Clarke's poems their power and resonance. It gives him strength and determination to persist with his identification of public wrongs and with his exploration of his own experience. His vision of Irish life has its roots in his own life; he knows from personal experience what the local and the topical represent, what they stand for in terms of human hurt, what they reveal in terms of the public good. Therefore he can make the state of Irish life and of his own life a reflection of the major subject of his final phase.

The style of the poems, of the short commentaries and of the longer personal narratives, registers the perceptions and values of a personality grounded in the actual and the immediate. Its distinguishing feature is a realism untouched by the blandishments of the mystical or the romantic. Its historical and mythological allusions are present on a realistic level. What happened in the past, what happened in myth are examples of what may happen. Clarke signals his position in the legal term, the claim to light, in the title *Ancient Lights*. This becomes a metaphor for that resistance to clerical and social restrictions that motivates him; it justifies all those references to the past, whether personal, historical, or mythological that help to clarify the way things are in the present. The title poem triumphantly identifies a particular moment, the time, the place, and the nature of Clarke's own liberation from an oppressive Church, in which his defiance of authority and his assertion of self-reliance were sanctioned in the world of nature. The first poem in the collection, 'Celebrations', identifies the subject matter of the three collections: 'Prosperity of church and state'.

The title is ironic: this is not a matter for celebration. Hence the defiant, rhetorical question of the opening lines:

> Who dare complain or be ashamed
> Of liberties our arms have taken?

which echo the opening lines of two well-known, non-ironical nationalistic songs — 'Who Fears to speak of Ninety-Eight?' and 'Who Fears to speak of Easter Week?'. The assumption that no one dares is in itself indicative of complacency and moral inertia. The ironical beginning establishes the controlling tone and introduces the poem's ambivalent method. 'Liberties' refers both to the freedom won in the Easter Rising and those subsequently lost through the emergence of a middle-class Catholic state.

> For every spike upon that gateway,
> We have uncrowned the past:
> And open hearts are celebrating
> Prosperity of church and state
> In the shade of Dublin Castle.

The past has been 'uncrowned': Ireland has removed the British Crown whose administrative centre was Dublin Castle, now a 'shade' because British power has passed away but also because Irish power is not unlike British power in its operation; rebel heads are no longer displayed on spikes over the gateway to Dublin Castle. The phrase 'open hearts' refers to the openness of the celebrations and to the 'open' gullibility of those who do not have reservations about them. 'Open hearts' also refers to the banners of the Sacred Heart on display. In Clarke's view a prosperous state may lack social justice, may not cherish all the children of the nation equally, and a prosperous church is likely to be an uncaring church and therefore not cause for celebration.

Stanza two maintains the contradiction between appearance and reality, developing the paradoxical relationship between freedom and the dual power of Church and state. A sarcastic tone connects the 'So many flagpoles' clause with the 'God only knows' conclusion.

> So many flagpoles can be seen now
> Freeing the crowd, while crisscross keys,
> On yellow-and-white above the green,
> Treble the wards of nation,
> God only knows what treasury
> Uncrams to keep each city borough
> And thoroughfare in grace.

The Irish and papal flags, with the Church's on top, are displayed in such abundance that Clarke wonders sceptically at the unnatural union of 'treasury' and 'grace', about the quality of the 'Freeing'. The idea of excessive control is present in 'wards', meaning political divisions, rooms in an asylum, and wards of state, as though the 'nation' is being controlled and managed. This is not freedom.

Stanza three begins in a tone of sarcastic injunction.

> Let ageing politicians pray
> Again, hoardings recount our faith,
> The blindfold woman in a rage
> Condemns her own for treason:
> No steeple topped the scale that Monday,
> Rebel souls had lost their savings
> And looters braved the street.

Those who participated in the Easter Rising are now 'ageing politicians', no longer prepared to risk all for an ideal. 'Hoardings recount our faith': in the new Ireland faith in money has replaced religious belief. The hoardings are the places where religious posters are displayed during the celebrations and also financial savings. The figure of Justice over the gateway of Dublin Castle, angered by such developments, now condemns her own people for 'treason'. In the past it was British Justice that condemned Irish rebels for treason. Now the treason, more reprehensible, is against the ideals of those who successfully and bravely replaced British rule by Irish rule. 'Rebel souls' risked everything and even 'looters braved the street'. In 1916 the scales held by the figure of Justice were not tipped in favour of clerical interests, now the Church's influence is dominant and men, the new traitors, no longer dare to complain. The uncrowning includes the removal of the rebel spirit that was seen in 1798 and again in 1916.

In its style of internal complexity, well-wrought ironies and ambiguities, 'Celebrations' expresses Clarke's reaction to the way in which the state operates in relation to the Church. 'Mother and Child' focuses on the event that most clearly demonstrated ecclesiastical interference in politics. In 1950 the Coalition Government decided to introduce legislation that would provide free medical services for mothers and children. The Catholic Hierarchy objected on the grounds that the proposed legislation would give undue rights to the state to interfere in the private morality of the people. The bishops maintained that the rearing of children belonged to parents, not the state, that the state should provide for those unable to provide for themselves and did not have the right to impose a state medical service on everyone.[1] The man at the centre of the controversy was Dr Noel Browne, Minister for Health, whose publication of the correspondence between the bishops, the Taoiseach, and himself revealed the pressures exerted by the Church in private on the elected representatives of the people. Clarke condemns the subservience of the politicians and the lack of compassion in the episcopal response. His poem bristles with images of thoughtless servility, from the suggestion of automatic response in 'Obedient keys' and 'old dispensaries' to the image of politicians on their knees. It is a 'pity' they are so craven and that their acquiescence makes them also so uncaring. Two short sentences sums up the conflict and 'mitred' combines the sign and the sound of episcopal disapproval.

> Obedient keys rattled in locks,
> Bottles in old dispensaries
> Were shaken and the ballot boxes
> Hid politicians on their knees
> When pity showed us what we are.
> 'Why should we care,' votes cried, 'for child
> Or mother? Common help is harmful
> And state-control must starve the soul.'
> One doctor spoke out. Bishops mitred.

Ironically in the following hear, 1953, the Fianna Fail Government passed an amended Health Act that met with the approval of the Hierarchy. Clarke's poem, written in the year in which the Catholic Church celebrated its Marian Year, expresses his disgust with the hypocritical contradiction between that commemoration and the lack of concern for mothers and children demonstrated by the Church's opposition to the Noel Browne scheme.

> We profit from God's love and pity,
> Sampling the world with good example.
> Before you damp it with your spit,
> Respect our newest postage stamp.

The contradiction devalues the moral message, as Clarke succinctly shows in the conjunction of 'spit' and 'Respect'.

Although he can be blunt, Clarke's point of view is compassionate. 'Fashion' lightly mocks clerical warnings on the so-called immodesty of female dress; 'Marriage' shows the injustice of the Church's teaching on contraception; the rhythm method of birth control, based on the woman's fertility cycle, is not only unreliable, resulting in more children than parents can easily afford, but subverts the grace of the marriage-sacrament.

> But shall the sweet promise of the sacrament
> Gladden the heart, if mortals calculate
> Their pleasures by the calendar?

Clarke uses a lightly mocking tone — 'Parents are sinful now . . . Aye, there's the rub!' — to illuminate a serious subject. The metaphor of the calendar by which parents 'calculate/Their pleasures' carries over easily to the partly comic but pathetic conclusion.

> Night school
> Of love where all, who learn to cheat, grow pale
> With guilty hope at every change of moon!

The romantic image of the moon is associated with anxious calculation. The 'sweet promise of the sacrament' suffers a similar debasement.

'Offerings' links our ability to remember the dead with the amount of money they leave for Masses to be said for their souls. 'Bequests' derides the greed of 'religious institutions' who wrest money from the dying.

> When money burns in the last breath
> Of frightened age, such bells are set
> In air, their tongues will stick at nothing
> Until religious institutions
> Have storied every contribution.

The church bells are put to perverted use. Beginning with a sequence of harsh monosyllables — 'burns', 'breath', 'bells' — and the coarsely aggressive 'will stick at nothing', these lines result in the deliberate loss of linguistic energy in the mock solemnity of the last two lines, the movement of sound itself being an illustration of rapacity leading to satisfaction.

Ecclesiastical greed and clericalism are recurrent themes in these poems. Freedom from clerical control is the theme of a number of poems, such as 'An Early Start' and 'The Blackbird of Derrycairn', reprinted from *As the Crow Flies*. Two, 'The Vanishing Irish' and 'The Envy of Poor Lovers', are of particular interest. The former combines the title of a controversial sociological book on Ireland, a collection of essays called *The Vanishing Irish* (1954), with a poem ascribed to Raftery, called 'Brighdín Bhéusaidh', collected and edited by Douglas Hyde as the fifth chapter of his *Songs of Connacht*. The book, written in response to the serious decline in Irish population in the Fifties, argued that a low marriage rate and emigration were leading to the virtual disappearance of the race. Much emphasis was placed on the effects of clerical prohibitions on men and women. Even emigration was seen as the result not only of unemployment but of a pervasive jansenistic clerical influence. Raftery's poem is an account of a young man's love for a girl whom he is determined to bring back from the Underworld. Clarke's poem celebrates the power of love, making Raftery's poem into an example of the ability to enjoy love despite poverty. The young man owned nothing yet poured out his love for the girl and declared his determination to face the gods in order to bring her back. Clarke expands Raftery's three stress line into a long line of irregular and varied stresses in order to convey the wild exuberance that characterises his image of the nameless lover. Raftery begins as follows:

> Phósfainn Bríghdín Bhéusaidh
> Gan cóta bróig ná léine,
> A stóir mo chroidhe dá mb'fhéidir liom,
>   Do throisgfinn duit naoi dtráth.
> Gan bhiadh gan deoch gan aon chuid
> As oileán i Loch Éirne,
> D'fhonn mé, a's tú bheith i n-éinfheacht
>   Go réidhfimis ár gcás.

Hyde's translation, while not literal, captures the spirit of the original and tries to illustrate the operation of Irish prosody.

> SHOELESS, shirtless, GRIEVING,
> FOODLESS, too, my BREEDYEEN,
> SURELY I'd not LEAVE YOU;
>   Nine MEALS I'd fast for you.
> Upon Loch Erne's ISLANDS,
> No food nor drink BESIDE ME,
> But hoping I might FIND YOU,
>   My CHILDEEN, to be true.[2]

Clarke's poem, which is not a translation, communicates the spirit of passion transcending poverty. His references to 'long and short' and to the 'mighty mortar' are sexual in connotation, emphasising the explosive power of love that in this case:

> . . . sent a young fellow, with shirt-tails flying the flag
> Of his country, in search of bare toes and a shawl as bedraggled.
> But how could he marry? His only belongings were longings,
> Hugs, squeezes, kisses, a hundred thousand strong.

Both the boy and the girl are poor. His national flag is his shirt-tails and she goes shawled and barefoot. The extravagant 'hundred thousand strong', in keeping with the exaggerated manner of the poem, echoes the Irish greeting, *céad míle fáilte*. The daring visit to the Underworld becomes a comment on the restrictions that attend love in Modern Ireland, where 'silence' prevails and 'telltale' is 'frowned on'. 'Somewhere,' Clarke muses, 'the last of our love-songs found a refuge' and imagines that the classical Underworld would be suitable, because it is 'Free from our burden of bad thoughts'. Ireland has become so puritanical that songs of love have almost vanished, victims also of a jansenistic church. 'The Envy of Poor Lovers' is a picture of poor lovers in modern Ireland. They have lost the joyous freedom of Raftery's poem, being haunted by fear of what society and the Church thinks of them.

> Pity poor lovers who may not do what they please
> With their kisses under a hedge, before a raindrop
> Unhouses it; and astir from wretched centuries,
> Bramble and briar remind them of the saints.

Clarke is sympathetic: the lovers are 'children', their love is conducted in 'ignorance'; illegitimate babies, the result of their 'folly', are snatched away and put into orphanages paid for by the state and run by nuns; for them, 'it seems, the sacraments have failed'. Conscious of 'blame' and 'shame', the lovers express their love in 'dread . . . of Ireland keeping company with them'.

Just as the Noel Browne affair illustrated the Church's political influence, so the fire at an orphanage for girls run by Poor Clare nuns in Co Cavan, in which thirty-five girls and one adult were killed, illustrated the Church's lack of true compassion. 'Three Poems about Children' is an angry response to a remark made by Dr Lyons, Bishop of Kilmore, when he spoke of the dead: 'Dear little angels, now before God in Heaven, they were taken away before the gold of their innocence had been tarnished by the soil of the world'.[3] It was this heartless transformation of a human tragedy into a spiritual triumph that angered Clarke. His feelings are audible in the assertive diction, the uncomplicated syntax, and the alliterative and consonantal recurrences of the short, four-stressed lines. The Bishop minimised the horror that the girls had experienced. Once again the Church fails to show sympathy for those who had suffered. Once again Clarke uses the contrast of the Penal Church.

> Better the book against the rock,
> The misery of roofless faith,
> Than all this mockery of time,
> Eternalising of mute souls.

The 'misery' of the Penal Church is preferable to the casuistry that turns burnt children into 'mute souls', the dear little angels of the Bishop's address. The idea of a church grown materialistic — 'offerings increase, increase' — and uncaring is contained in the next five lines: the 'ancient arms' of mother church 'bring no peace'. Illegitimate babies — 'unforgiven' — are taken from their mothers — 'Redeem' and 'charity' are used ironically — and placed in orphanages. Such hardship causes Clarke to cry out:

> O, then, at the very font of grace
> Pity, pity — the dumb must cry.
> Their tiny tears are in the walls
> We build.

The inability to feel for these children, to be as heartless as Cromwell, 'unropes the bell', that is, stifles pity and subverts the Church's mission of love. The Church fails to cherish her children, puts them into institutions, the 'walls' of the poem, and then even when they die horribly fails to mourn them properly.

The second poem, adopting the Catholic teaching of the time, that unbaptised children go to Limbo after death and are not saved, protests at a response that similarly denies these children the benefit of love. They are, in Clarke's words, 'Unfathered in our thought', that is, removed by the bishop's reasoning from the natural human response to their deaths 'Before they can share the sky/With us'. Clarke's metaphor for the human experience is appealingly natural, involving the enjoyment of life, the participation in the normal experience of existence, with the idea of 'salvation' ('to share the sky'). He goes on to admit, reasonably, that one may accept the mystery of existence and the doctrine of the resurrection — 'Obscurity of being/And clay rejoice' — but not the heartlessness of a response that denies the reality of death. His metaphor of the flowers withering singly during Benediction of the Blessed Sacrament tellingly illustrates the individuality of each death which the Bishop's remark so cruelly denied.

> flowers
> That wither in the heat
> Of benediction, one
> By one, are thrown away.

The third poem, closely allied in its reasoning to the second, also objects to an unthinking reliance on faith; both 'martyr' and 'heretic' have been burnt; 'trust in Providence' can prevent us from asking questions and deprive us of the so-called 'vain expense' of feeling. Therefore, Clarke concludes, with a question that seems to accept such reasoning, why should we allow 'pity' to 'uncage', to expose what happened in the fire; why should we question the comforting notion of the transformation of children into angels? It sets 'no churchbell tolling', because it removes the need for grief. Clarke, as it were, appeals for acceptance of the Bishop's spurious argument and urges his mind to deny what his heart feels.

> Leap, mind, in consolation
> For heart can only lodge
> Itself, plucked out by logic.

'Cast-iron step and rail' refer to a fire-escape. The idea that its presence would only have prolonged the suffering of the children adds to the inhuman cruelty of the argument. Had the children lived, according to the Bishop, they would only have suffered more, have had to endure what he called the soil of the world. That vision of existence runs directly against Clarke's earlier reference to sharing the sky. The final couplet, with its macabre rhyme, sums up the Bishop's argument but in a manner that rejects it.

> Those children, charred in Cavan,
> Passed straight through Hell to Heaven.

'Three Poems about Children' is a powerful, public statement, rigorously argued. It affirms Clarke's belief in the validity of 'enquiry', that the individual must exercise independent judgment and not allow himself to be persuaded by clerical opinion when this denies the reality of human suffering. The idea of a Church grown inordinately powerful and remote is still more evident in *Too Great A Vine*.

> Too great a vine, they say, can sour
> The best of clay.

In christian art the vine is a symbol of Christ and just as a vine can by excessive growth sour the clay that supports it so the Irish Church by an excessive spread of influence has sapped the morale of the people. In poem after poem, in 'Irish Mother', 'The Choice', 'War Propaganda', 'Pilgrimage', 'Marian Chimes', 'St Christopher', Clarke criticises the damaging results of clerical power. The effects reach into many areas of human activity: into the mother's moralistic response to her son's sexuality ('Irish Mother'), the medical profession ('The Choice'), the promise of rewards in the next life ('War Propaganda'), the exploitation of invalids ('Pilgrimage'), the mechanical prayer-wheel ('Marian Chimes'), and the question in 'St Christopher' that ends the book. The fable in the latter resembles the metaphor of the over-grown vine. Here the christ-bearer collapses under the weight of a child that has become a giant.

> Fabulist, can an ill state
> Like ours, carry so great
> A Church upon its back?

The question of the Church's prosperity is crucial. In these five poems at the end of *Too Great A Vine* Clarke uses a style of pointed verbal attack but in two preceding poems, 'Miss Marnell' and 'Local Complainer', he uses a different style and a different approach. The line is dense with detail, the rhythm varied to reflect the movement of thought and perception, the sentence sometimes short to focus on a specific point but often fragmented and running on to form a unit of observation. Furthermore, he writes about ecclesiastical wealth from the point of view of a Protestant.

In 'Miss Marnell', a portrait of a charitable woman, details lead to the conclusion that her zeal is extreme. The poem contrasts her poverty with the amount of money she gives to the Church and its structure develops in accordance with the progressive discoveries of its Protestant narrators: first a few introductory remarks about the woman's social decline, then their benevolence, her hunger and their pity. The poem's characteristic method emerges after Miss Marnell's mental collapse.

> Every room surprised:
> Wardrobes of bombazine, silk dresses, stank:
> Cobwebby shrouds, pantries, cupboard, bone-bare.

Nevertheless, 'she had prospering money in the bank' and spent generously in support of the Church. The detailed account is both fascinating and repulsive, combining images of decrepitude and decay with information about good works. 'Her withered hand was busy doing good' or 'False teeth got little acid from her food:/But scribble helped to keep much mortar wet/For convent, college, . . .'. Hers is an obsessive response. Appeals to her charity 'made her madder'. The 'faded notes of thanksgiving,/All signed — "Yours Gratefully, In Jesus Christ" ', are the ultimate irony.

The poem is an example of a method Clarke often uses again. Its alternation between the personal and the impersonal, that is, between the evidence of the woman's impoverishment and crazed isolation and the evidence of the causes she espouses, creates a memorable portrait. Clarke's imaginative construction of a life out of mundane, naturalistic details is an example of his capacity to feel for the needy and particularly for those who have been affected by the rapacity of the Church. Miss Marnell dies but the Church thrives, the one a direct result of the other. 'The figure on her cross-cheque' is the sign of her crucifixion. She dies to save the Church. Christian apologists could argue that she is saintlike in her generosity and self-denial, that her miserable way of living is a sign of a life dedicated to Christ. But Clarke's language and the details that shape his poem run counter to that interpretation and in doing so provide an alternative view at a time when self-denial, even of an extreme kind, was not always discouraged.

The accumulative method is also present in 'Local Complainer' which deals with something that Clarke also describes in *Twice Round the Black Church*: the large number of 'open-air statues' being erected, including a gigantic one of the Virgin on the North Wall, paid for by Dublin dockers. In a note to the poem he refers to a newspaper report that both Catholics and Protestants subscribed and makes a general comment:

> As the result of wide organizing, religious statues have been erected in many towns and villages, by the roadside, on hilltops, outside factories, quarries and mines, and in the poorer districts of Dublin. Most of these are painted plaster casts, supplied by enterprising firms. They may prove our public piety, but certainly display our total lack of artistic taste.[4]

In his poem the details work towards an ironical contrast between public piety and economic decline. 'They lead so reverent a high-life', Clarke declares, tongue-in-cheek in his role of Protestant observer, that 'No Protestant can call it a sin'. The erection of statues is made with such pious intentions by Catholics that their Protestant fellow-countrymen cannot condemn them. But they can point to the imbalance between sentimentality and practicality, when so much money is spent on statues and so little in the service of the economy. The opening sentence draws attention to this.

> Their new Madonna at the quay-side,
> Without a vessel in the tide-way,

'Cut, dressed and chiselled' in the 'best Italian marble', the cost is 'eight hundred pounds'. Clarke's precise accountancy, an exactness in language and in tone, demonstrates that values are one-sided. The next lines parade officials of Church and state past the social and economic realities: the 'derelicts of mill and warehouse/That bulge with emptiness'. The poem builds a succession of empty manifestations of piety. The Protestant narrators, in a communal voice, speak of 'their statue' and of 'Our chequebooks', since they too contribute, even though the 'Decalogue' forbids the worship of statues. The 'loyalist' resembles the Jesuit.

> The loyalist become Loyola,
> Each week another Fontenoy won.

These mocking metaphors emphasise the absurdity of what is being described. Even the Protestants are drawn into the irrational behaviour. The references to Loyola and Fontenoy, the one a Knight of the Blessed Virgin who founded the Jesuit order to help oppose the Protestant reformers, the other an epic battle that became a model for military theorists, give the affair a mock-heroic, ironic quality. The expenditure of human resources in Ireland is by contrast ridiculous and of questionable moral value. It is made more absurd by the evidence that Protestants are so bewildered by what is happening that they too are involved. As the narrators say: 'We scarcely know ourselves on Sunday'.

By 1960 Clarke's attack on the Church is less intense. *The Horse-Eaters* has a handful of relevant poems, including 'Intercessors', an amusing sonnet about the newly acquired freedom of clergy to shop, visit hotels, and enter cinemas, and 'Irish American Dignitary', a satirical portrait of a visit by Dr Cushing, then Bishop of Boston. In any case *The Horse-Eaters* is a slim collection of twelve poems in which the title poem is much the longest and most important. Even the political or social satire in this collection is confined to two poems: 'Christmas Eve', an ironic description of police dispersal of a crowd, and 'Knacker Rhymes', an angry protest at the ill-treatment of horses that is closely allied thematically with the title poem. Although *Ancient Lights* has one political poem, 'Inscription for a Headstone', which points out that James Larkin's social ideas have been adopted by the Church in order not to be left behind, Clarke's social satires are mainly found in *Too Great A Vine*, which has a group of five: 'Abbey Theatre Fire', 'Wolfe Tone', 'The Trial of Robert Emmet', 'Past and Present', and 'Nelson's Pillar, Dublin'. The continuity of mood in this collection is explained by their being written in two weeks, except for 'Marian Chimes' and 'The Trial of Robert Emmet'.

In the social satires former patriots and the eighteenth century stand for qualities that are absent in the Fifties. Wolfe Tone loved Ireland, although he never experienced the religious deprivations of the Penal Laws, since he was a Protestant, or as Clarke writes in his fierce, metaphorical manner:

> He called a conquered land his own
> Although he never bowed at Mass
> Behind locked door or knelt on grass.

The 'But' in line four introduces the fact, amazing in this context, that Ireland disowns him. The rhyming of 'own' and 'disown' emphasises this injustice and ingratitude. For, as Clarke adds in a homely metaphor, man needs to have heroes like Tone. Tone's memorial statue however was only erected recently even though the money for it had been collected in 1898 and the space reserved. 'What can we do,' Clarke asks, adopting a position of helplessness as a means of protest, 'but rattle his chains'. To 'rattle his chains' refers literally to the chains that mark off the space set aside for the statue but also to the manacles that Ireland has placed on Tone, refusing to honour him because he was a Protestant and committed suicide ('cut veins'); one can also rattle them in protest, since as Clarke drily concludes 'We cannot blow his statue up'. There is a slight emphasis on 'his', since other statues were blown up, including the fine Gough memorial in Phoenix Park.

'Past and Present' contrasts the respect for education in the past, when Ireland was poor and education denied, with the contemporary concern for fashion, for the superficial rather than the substantial, for style rather than knowledge. 'Our anguish was in vain', Clarke laments: the miseries endured have not brought improved values in the present. The independence that sent people abroad to seek education has been lost; now that 'lashings' of money are dominant, freedom of speech is curtailed: 'a word can give offence'. Clarke's advice to 'put by our history books', that is, to abandon independence of thought, and to 'gape' without questioning, is of course sarcastic. Nelson on his pillar, his eye turned heavenward, serves as an image for a time in which people are content to expect rewards in the next life.

Clarke's most effective satire is contained in 'The Trial of Robert Emmet' which refers to a proposal to re-enact his trial as a play in Green Street Court House. Clarke sarcastically urges the public to:

> See British greed and tyranny defied
> Once more by that freethinker in the dock
> And sigh because his epitaph remains
> Unwritten.

The language is double-edged: 'freethinker' is an objectionable term for Catholics, but for Clarke it is a term for independence of mind; 'sigh' expresses regret that Ireland has not gained independence, and therefore Emmet's epitaph cannot yet be written, but 'sigh' also expresses Clarke's judgment on the complacency of those who attend the play but do not see that 'British greed and tyranny' has been replaced by Irish greed and tyranny. The theatre-goers can smugly applaud Emmet's defiance without seeing the re-enactment, outside the courthouse-theatre, of social injustices comparable to those Emmet sought to change. They may applaud his rebellion for the duration of the play, 'by the clock', and then drive home in security and comfort, ignoring the social inequalities implicit in 'our dirtiest lanes'. Their pious display of badges and medals is unrelated to any awareness of social injustice. Clarke scorns their indifference. Adopting a brusque manner — 'Sentence the lot and hurry them away,/ The court must now be cleared, . . . No need of drop-scene . . . Forget the cells . . . See . . . sigh . . . cheer' — he attributes a form of rough justice to the law and goes on to mimic an attitude of public blindness to the rights of 'miscreants'. The poem proceeds by a series of commands; its authoritarian tone both imitates and derides.

Clarke's satirical poems are a form of personal purgation, an emission of anger, an expression of compassion. Together with the autobiographical poems they help to free his imagination from emotional restrictions, from the trapped feeling that is so starkly reflected in 'Return from England' and within the tight syntactical structure and the compression of many of the satires. If his mind, as he says in 'Respectable People' is 'too horrible with life', it is made so by what he sees about him and by an inner world of which he is not yet ready to speak openly. 'Return from England' concludes *Ancient Lights*; it is one of the very few personal poems among the short poems in these three collections. It expresses the paradox that in England Clarke longed for Ireland but in Ireland dreams of England. In England he had to endure a frustrating cycle of physical need and wanted to escape to Ireland. In Ireland, where his mind is free, he is surrounded by tales of wrong and made wakeful by the miseries of others.

> Though every office stair
> I climbed there, left me poorer,
> Night after night, my wants
> Toil down each step in selfsame
> Dream; night after night, enduring
> Such failure, I cast away
> My body, on fire to reach
> Mail-boat or train-from-Euston,
> Catch up at last with smoke.
> But mind, pretending pity,
> Unslaves me in like haste,
> Only to take me closer,
> With some new tale of wrong here,
> Holy retreat of tongue.
> When I had brought my wife
> And children, wave over wave,
> From exile, could I have known
> That I would sleep in England
> Still, lie awake at home?

It is a poem locked within paradox, equating Clarke's physical deprivation in England with his mental anguish in Ireland. What seems to promise release produces even harsher bondage. The rigidly balanced ironies embody a feeling of entrapment that is close to despair.

The 'I' persona appears twice in *Ancient Lights*: in the joyous release of the title poem and in this tightly-wound self-portrait. The book moves from an objective description of the unacceptable celebrations of 'Celebrations' to this bleak portrayal of the poet. There is throughout the book little to celebrate. The title poem is a release from the enslavement, both mental and moral, that other poems portray and from the grimly restrictive emotional state of 'Return from England'. *Too Great A Vine*, on the other hand, begins with the personal 'Usufruct' and concludes with the satirical 'St Christopher', the one a wry account of the conditions under which Clarke lives in his home, the other a rhetorical question about the fate of a society that has to support an oppressive Church. Of the personal poems in *The Horse-Eaters* 'Menai Strait' is an oblique, cryptic poem about separation, 'Early Unfinished Sketch' is the first erotic poem of the period, and 'The Flock at Dawn' is its first descriptive, autobiographical narrative. Before examining the three long personal poems at the centre of these collections, it is worth examining 'Usufruct'.

Like 'Return from England', 'Usufruct' is about self and circumstance. The title is a legal term meaning the right of temporary possession. It defines the conditions under which Bridge House, Templeogue was bought in his mother's name with only a life interest in it for him. After his death it would be given to a religious order.[5] 'This house,' Clarke declares in the opening line, 'cannot be handed down'. 'I live here, thinking, ready to flit/From Templeogue, but not at ease'. Occupation includes 'thinking', alertness, and unease. Images of process and of erosion, in the river and in the traffic, indicate how Clarke perceives his situation. The 'midge' is both an image of vulnerability and luck, of participation and survival.

> I hear the flood unclay the trees,
> Road-stream of traffic. So does the midge,
> With myriads below the bridge,
> Having his own enormous day,
> Unswallowed.

It is particularly ironic in the light of Clarke's anticlericalism that he should find himself in temporary possession of a house that will become yet another clerical possession. It is indicative of his growing lightness of mood that he is able to write with understanding and with humour of his mother's legal arrangement. 'What could she do, if such in faith/ Be second nature?' Being what she was, her choice was natural. The 'in faith' colloquially acknowledges her religious belief. It is not much consolation that she hopes to aid him 'by-and-by,/Somewhere beyond the threatening sky'. As other poems make clear, Clarke is not impressed with that kind of reasoning and the echoes of Yeats's 'Wild Old Wicked Man' and 'No Second Troy' give his mockery more flavour. His references to the kingfisher, a bird much admired by Clarke, shown here as beautiful and secretive, a source of beauty but 'too seldom seen' because he is wary, are used to rebuke his own rashness. 'Flash/Of inspiration makes thought rash', as indeed it does in this book in which the satire is sharper and more explicit than in either of the other two collections.

ii *Long Autobiographical Poems*

The special flavour of the longer autobiographical poems comes from Clarke's determination to record what happened to him in his life, to identify events that were significant. He is not a maker of myths, nor is he greatly interested in creating a personal version of Irish tradition. He looks into his own life and sees there a mirror of his time. Without these autobiographical poems our knowledge of what it was like to grow up in his Ireland would be less. In them the past is recreated, our understanding of it and of Clarke is deepened. The poems stand out in their poetic contexts, they subsume the material and the issues in the short poems that cluster about them. They do not reverberate with linguistic play and tension like some of the shorter, related poems. Nor have they the conversational ease of others, but they are formidable in their investigations of the past, in their recreation of a man's life, in their handling of specifics, and each has lines and stanzas that are as memorable for their vigour and clarity, their linguistic energy, their exact rhythms, as lines and stanzas in the shorter poems.

'Ancient Lights' begins the series with its manifesto of personal and poetic deliverance. It has a couple of stanzas that create problems of interpretation but it is carefully structured and developed; it moves confidently from its depiction of entrapment and fear to its celebration of freedom. 'The Loss of Strength' is more ambitious, not only because of its length — seventeen twelve-line stanzas — but for its reflective, autobiographical manner. The revelations of an individual mind, which draws upon its own resources, expressing its own ideas, engages the imagination and the intellect in a different way from the short satires. The process of self-definition requires a subtler movement of the mind. 'The Loss of Strength', which seems at first to be difficult to comprehend, because of its allusions and occasional syntactical density, is remarkably vibrant in rhythm. Its manner is confident, the details controlled, the atmosphere relaxed. While the pervasive theme is as indicated in the title, the actual emotions which are expressed are many and varied, such as nostalgia for lost freedom of movement, pride in his former questing nature, criticism of contemporary developments that inhibit the individual, respect for certain periods in the past, a recognition that history itself is subject to the same processes of change and loss that he has seen in his own lifetime, and a determination to persevere as a poet, despite the various losses that have affected him. Clarke's consciousness is at the poem's centre; the substance of the poem is determined by what exists in and emerges from the narrator, whose memory one might say is a specifically Irish memory. Understandably, 'The Hippophagi' is the hardest to penetrate, because so much of its material is drawn from Clarke's own life. We cannot often go outside the life to verify or explain what is being said. At the same time the language sometimes suggests meaning by creating an atmosphere or by a series of allusions intended to give merely a notional outline of a range of similar experiences. Childhood awareness is often unclear, more sensory, and imaginative, or imagined than rational. Clarke's purpose is to recapture the child's imperfect understanding of incidents that may be important, but lie below the level of conscious thought. Language may therefore be used to suggest what the mind barely understands. Clarke was a complex, sensitive, brooding man, inclined to be morose, known to be gentle, inclined to be quarrelsome, known to be humorous. The total portrait is complex. When he moves close in upon himself, as he does in 'The Hippophagi', the result is almost inevitably 'difficult'. He does not smooth away the rough, the muddled, or the unpleasant. When he finished this poem and was commissioned to prepare a poem for public delivery at a poetry festival, his mood lightens and we have the wholly enjoyable *Forget-Me-Not*, in which memory runs lightly over some of the same material as in 'The Hippophagi'. This suggests not just that the recognition of a new poetic stature brought out a lighter side but that the actual writing of 'The Hippophagi' helped to purge material that had lodged in his psyche; the writing is a release, a way of distancing the older self from material that the younger self had found unpleasant, and from material in the public arena to which Clarke reacted angrily; it confirmed his sense of Ireland in the Fifties as a place of cruelty. 'Knacker Rhymes' denounces that Ireland just as 'Three Poems about Children' denounces ecclesiastical casuistry. Both were written from a sense of hurt. So is 'The Hippophagi': 'be my hurt./Rhyme is no comforter'. This time the hurt goes even deeper and releases decades of pain. Once again the self is victim, misled, unprepared for life's realities: 'I was immortal,/Yea, so important that monks pursued me'.

The first three stanzas in 'Ancient Lights' provide a setting from which Clarke has to find release. From the beginning he indicates the direction the poem will take: even in boyhood when he 'knew the next world better' than this world, he countered the spiritual with the physical, the knowledge of heaven with the discoveries of earth. His 'missions' are not spiritual but physical, directed towards places in which he could find 'what man has made'. The list of places, all close to Clarke's boyhood home, is the beginning of a firm anchoring of experience in reality that characterises all the important events of the poem. But stanza one, in keeping with another feature of this poem, its compact drama of perception, also includes the nightmare of childhood, contrasting now, not the spiritual with the physical, but the physical with the supernatural, darkness with light, night with day, fear with the courage of his 'missions':

> But darkness
> Was roomed with fears. Sleep, stripped by woes

No matter how adventurous he was by day, he was beset by fears at night. The source of nightmare, realised in images of galvanic action, are external, induced by others. He is a victim: 'stripped by woes/I had been taught'. The experience is rendered in violent language — 'stripped', 'beat', 'leaped', 'Lied' — and of rapid propulsion into nothingness, the void already featured in his work. The movement of the stanza parallels the conflict between the positive, chosen direction of his daytime quests and the negative, imposed violation of his nightmares.

> When all of us wore smaller shoes
> And knew the next world better than
> The knots we broke, I used to hurry
> On missions of my own to Capel
> Street, Bolton Street and Granby Row
> To see what man has made. But darkness
> Was roomed with fears. Sleep, stripped by woes
> I had been taught, beat door, leaped landing,
> Lied down the bannisters of naught.

Propulsion gives way to compulsion in stanza two. The vague terrors of stanza one are replaced by those associated with religion: the reluctant walk towards the church, the distorted visual images of penance, candles, shrines, stained-glass that reflect not love but fear, the priest's hand on the shutter, and the insistent questioning about sexuality.

> Being sent to penance, come Saturday,
> I shuffled slower than my sins should.
> My fears were candle-spiked at side-shrines,
> Rays lengthened them in stained-glass. Confided

Tonight again, my grief bowed down,
Heard hand on shutter-knob. Did I
Take pleasure, when alone — how much —
In a bad thought, immodest look
Or worse, unnecessary touch?

The emphasis in stanza three is also on confinement, misunderstanding, secrecy, confusion, guilt, and an increasing fear. Even religious ornaments are associated again with violence and damnation. The figure of Christ crucified, that ought to be a sign of hope is transformed into a sign of fear and loss:

. . . shuddered past the crucifix,
The feet so hammered, daubed-on blood-drip,
Black with lip-scrimmage of the damned.

Stanza four, at the centre of the eight stanzas, describes a turning point: 'Once as I crept . . ./Beside myself'. The release from terror comes in the movement of birds, in 'An evening lesson' to be 'read'. The imagery of flight — 'flutter', 'Atwirl' — replaces the imagery of fear. The cage-bird that has been confined is destroyed by sparrows. 'The moral' is, indeed, 'inescapable' in its personal application to a boy who has been closeted and restricted. The sparrows make bits of the cage-bird. 'O', Clarke, the ex-violinist exclaims, depicting the sounds of its plucking apart, 'The pizzicato of its wires!'

In stanza five the movement of the poem pauses to allow him to reflect on the significance of that lesson in nature. 'Goodness of air,' he concludes, 'can be proverbial'. For an even greater lesson is also to be read:

Goodness of air can be proverbial:
That day, by the kerb at Rutland Square,
A bronze bird fabled out of trees,
Mailing the spearheads of the railings,
Sparrow at nails. I hailed the skies
To save the tiny dropper, found
Appetite gone. A child of clay
Had blustered it away. Pity
Could raise some littleness from dust.

A moment of fabulous truth in a real place. The imagery associated with the bird, a hawk, in the manuscript, is of an armoured knight: 'Mailing', 'spearheads', 'railings', 'nails', and of metallic force. The railings and spearheads refer to the railings around the Black Church in Rutland

Square. The bronze bird clutches a sparrow in its claws. Clarke cries out and frightens the bird who drops the sparrow, its 'appetite'. 'A child of clay', that is, the poet — the manuscript reads 'poor child of Mary' — has saved the sparrow. 'Pity/Could raise some littleness from dust.' The lesson is not of the inability of the cage-bird to defend itself against sparrows, but of the ability of an insignificant human being to rescue a sparrow from the awesome bird. The effect of the metallic imagery, including the sound effects, is to highlight the contrast between bird and man, thereby emphasising the achievement of the man.

The poem then poses a question: after the liberation of the evening lesson, can religion bring about change? The answer comes in the form of an inner dialogue. He is urged to dismiss rational inquiry, to follow the example of his namesake, Saint Augustine, not that of Martin Luther. The former stands for acceptance of faith, for obedience, the latter for intellectual independence. Clarke's response is to reject that advice and to reject as well, or to include in that, 'Nights jakes', the world of closets and confinement, of darkness and fear laid down in the first three stanzas. 'No, let me abandon . . .', he says in a defiant assertion of freedom. It is also a moment of affirmation in the name of poetry: its rights to light have not been abandoned. 'Poetry burns at a different stake', not the stake of persecution, of martyrdom, of acceptance of suffering, but the fire of the imagination pursued in freedom.

The imagery of the fire is resumed in the last two stanzas which re-create a natural baptism with the cleansing power of rainwater that sweeps away the old fears and timidities. The movement begins with the verbal quickening of 'Still, still I remember'. A place previously associated with fear is transformed in the beneficent and awe-inspiring 'downpour':

> There, walled by heresy, my fears
> Were solved. I had absolved myself:
> Feast-day effulgence, as though I gained
> For life a plenary indulgence.

Light floods into the poem like the lights in a church on the feast-day and like a flood of a life-time's absolution from sin and its associated guilts and fears.

The final stanza is a celebration of his new state, of his release from the bondage of terror and darkness, including those described in 'Tenebrae' and associated poems in *Night and Morning*, in its images of dawn-like emergence, of upward flight, of joyous musical sounds, of a liberating flood. The linguistic energies orchestrate the sense of joyful release, with its accompanying sense of forgiveness, of a secular baptism, of a freeing movement. The apparently grandiloquent final lines suggest something affecting the whole country and thereby magnifies the effect, but more particularly it refers to the 'shores' or conduits along the streets through whose 'gratings' the water roars in flood.

> The sun came out, new smoke flew up,
> The gutters of the Black Church rang
> With services. Waste water mocked
> The ballcocks: down-pipes sparrowing,
> And all around the spires of Dublin
> Such swallowing in the air, such cowling
> To keep high offices pure: I heard
> From shore to shore, the iron gratings
> Take half our heavens with a roar.

Whereas 'Ancient Lights' signalled renewal, 'The Loss of Strength', written after a severe heart attack, broods over the consequences and merges personal diminishment with national loss. It is composed of statements about personal loss and considerations of other losses, in history, religion, politics, language, and culture. It operates through patterns of contrast within its general theme of change; these are presented in extended contrasts between stanzas and in contrasts within stanzas. The theme may be the changes that the loss of strength impose, but the poem's flexibility of organisation is one sign of Clarke's liveliness of mind. A similar flexibility attends the poem's changing moods and rhythms.

Clarke's poetry in this book is both public and private. 'The Loss of Strength' combines the two. It begins in a first-person narrative, placing the self in a highly metaphorical natural setting that is replete with lessons of liberation and of loss, and includes the creatively playful interaction between the poet and nature. The movement of the lines, their own liveliness and verbal energy, attest to the presence in the poet of qualities that survive physical loss. His skills are a sign of his mental, emotional and imaginative life. His range of movement has been restricted, but his memory is unimpaired.

> Farm-brooks that come down to Rathfarnham
> By grange-wall, tree-stop, from the hills,
> Might never have heard the rustle in barn dance,
> The sluicing, bolting, of their flour-mills,
> Nor have been of use in the steady reel
> On step-boards of the iron wheel-rim,
> For Dublin crowds them in: they wheeze now
> Beneath new pavements, name old laneways,

> Discharge, excrete, their centuries,
> Man-trapped in concrete, deeper drainage.
> Yet, littling by itself, I found one
> That had never run to town.

The stanza introduces the theme of loss, of movement, of freedom, their replacement by controls, their desecration, and concludes with the consolatory delights of the little stream that has escaped. The first stanza is made up of one twelve-line run-on sentence. Clarke varies the rhythm from the uninterrupted flow of lines 1, 3, 5 and 6 to the fragmented 2 and 4; thereafter the interrupted movement mimics the water's freedom being restricted as the streams descend from the Dublin hills into the spreading suburbs of Rathfarnham. The control is also evident in the play of meanings: the allusions to barn-dance carried over in 'reel' and 'step-board', while the primary reference is to water wheels turning with the flow of water onto their wooden steps. The brooks are crowded-in, as crowds at a dance impinge on the dancing space; their music, both of the water flowing and of the dance, has been changed to a 'wheeze'; whereas in the past the streams gave pleasure, their function now is practical: they are 'Man-trapped in concrete', they 'Discharge, excrete'. The whole stanza is a metaphor for loss, descending from the relative free movement of the opening lines to the impeded ugliness of lines 9-10, to the lighter diction of lines 11-12.

Stanza two, also descriptive, focuses on this little, pleasure-giving stream.

> No artificial fly or wet-hook
> Could stickle it. Summer was cressing
> Her mats, an inch from reeds. The brooklet
> Ran clearly under bramble. Dressed
> In the newest of feathers, black, trimmed
> With white, a pair of waterhens dimmed
> Away from me, with just a dot
> Of red. Three visitors, one soul
> Among them or not. Know-all can tot it
> Up. Lesser bits of life console us:
> Nature at jest in light and shade,
> Though somewhat afraid.

Clarke pays tribute to it, to its freedom, clarity, organic health and life-enduring qualities, its harbouring of a pair of water-hens. Seeing them he observes in lightly dismissive mood that matches the carefree atmosphere of the setting:

> Three visitors, one soul
Among them or not. Know-all can tot it
Up

It is not an occasion for solemnity.

> Lesser bits of life console us:
> Nature at jest in light and shade,
> Though somewhat afraid.

The response to nature is not as exuberantly celebratory as it was at the end of 'Ancient Lights', nor as profound. He is consoled by particulars, not by a grand design. The limitation, however willingly accepted, is taken up in the following stanza. The past can be evoked:

> I climb among the hills no more
> To taste a last water, hide in cloud-mist
> From sheep and goat. The days are downpour.
> Cycle is gone, warm patch on trousers.
> All, all, drive faster, stink without,
> Spirit and spark within, no doubt.
> When hope was active, I stood taller
> Than my own sons. Beloved strength
> Springs past me, three to one. Halldoor
> Keeps open, estimates the length
> To which I go: a mile to tire-a.
> But I knew the stone beds of Ireland.

He voices his regret for lost horizons with dignity and simplicity: 'I climb among the hills no more/. . . To taste a last water, hide in cloud-mist'. Those enjoyments are gone; the bicycle has been replaced by faster, noisome cars. The mood of the stanza is warmly personal, expressing regret, remembering former hope and pride in his own power: 'When hope was active, I stood taller/Than my own sons'. Now the boys ('Beloved strength') have the energy he lacks. An old man grows tired easily; the 'mile to tire-a' has echoes of Tara and the tyre of his bicycle. The stanza's warmth of feeling and that image of age is abruptly checked by the counter-assertion of the last line: 'But I knew the stone beds of Ireland'. The mainly monosyllabic opening line ended with the sad 'no more' but the stanza has a strong ending, an almost entirely monosyllabic line. In fact the whole stanza is characterised by this simplicity of manner in which the language is plain, concrete, mainly monosyllabic and un-adorned. The assonantal music and fluency of which Clarke is capable have been replaced by the new mode, the words chiselled into place in the lines. In stanza after stanza he writes with mastery and ease. Having declared his acquaintance with the 'stone beds' of Ireland, a reference to the sleeping places of saints in the early Church, he moves in stanza four to a description of the journeys he made as a young man. That early self is recreated, his adventurous, optimistic quests re-enacted, with a slight touch of humorous self-mockery in the alliterations of the opening line and in the playful punning:

> Beclipped and confident of shank,
> I rode the plain with chain that freed me.
> On a rim akin to air, I cranked up . . .

The 'rim akin to air' combines the top of a hill with the rim and tube of the bicycle wheel. The freewheeling recalls the release of those journeys which were geographical and emotional. To go beyond the catechism, for Clarke, meant to gain personal liberation. His hope to find 'the very roc's nest', a huge legendary bird, is a measure of the idealistic nature of these journeys, their mythic quality, their fabulous associations.

For all that the journeys were important, a form of therapy, a mode of self-discovery away from the regulations of home, city, Church and school:

> The young must have a solitude
> To feel the strength in mind, restore
> Small world of liking.

In the solitude of remote places the young can discover their inner strength and replace their sense of alienation and restriction. The stanza opposes this secular, natural process of self-healing to clerical teachings: 'Saints have spewed/Too much', Clarke says in bluntly alliterative comment.

> I wanted test of stories
> Our poets had talked about, pinmeal
> To potboil long ago. Cloud-feelers
> Featherers, touched our restlessness.
> Lost prosody restrained us. Summit
> Showed valleys, reafforesting,
> The Fianna, leaf-veined, among them.
> Now only a wishing-cap could leave me
> On the top of Slieve Mish.

In this stanza Clarke explains and justifies his early career: his interest in mythological tales under the influence of Yeats, Ferguson and others, a healthier imaginative food ('pinmeal/To potboil'). His 'restlessness' was alleviated by the mythological, semi-divine characters. Cuchullin, for example, had the sun-god for a father; Conaire Mor's was a bird. The prosody of Irish poetry helped to discipline his work. The Fianna excited his imagination. He looked for traces of the mythical Curoi Mac Dara at Sliabh Mish, in Co Kerry. In that legendary past the sea-god, Manannan, visited Ireland: the 'three-legged Manannan rolled on his legs like a wheel'.[6] The supernatural appeared. Transformations now are destructive: 'engineering/Machinery destroys the weirs'. Where in legend the Shannon had been the source of magical changes made in the service of man, now it is the scene of man's capacity to limit and control. Clarke has in mind the hydro-electrical power station at Ardnachrusha on the Shannon, built in 1925, that reduced the current and spoiled the falls at Castleconnell downstream. As a result its famous spray is 'hidden in a tap'. The gapped line emphasises the loss. This stanza, number vi, juxtaposes the legendary and the ordinary, the exploits of the god of hilarity with the actions of the engineers, who 'monk-like', as Clarke remarks with doleful humour and a sexual pun, direct 'our natural flow'.

> Shannoning from the tide, a sea-god
> Became our servant once, demeaned
> Himself, a three-legged, slippery body:
> Uncatchable, being submarine,
> He spoked the hub. Now engineering
> Machinery destroys the weirs,
> Directs, monk-like, our natural flow:
> Yet it was pleasant at Castleconnell
> To watch the salmon brighten their raincoats.
> The reeds wade out for what is gone:
> That mile of spray faraway on the rapids
> Is hidden in a tap.

That sexual innuendo is taken up in stanza vii. The references to water, stream, sex, history, process, recur in the poem, helping to unify it and to make its theme of loss more inclusive. Sexual references in Clarke are often associated with nightmare: 'My childhood dreams were devildom'.

> My childish dreams were devildom.
> Sleep rose and sank: the Great Flood waked me.
> Reservoir at low level! Come,
> Dear rain and save our Roundwood lake!
> Should man complain of plans that curb
> Torrent in turbine? Great disturbance:

The hush of light. Why keep with Fintan
The Falls of Assaroe, trample
Of transmigration, void of man
In shape of salmon? Those currents were ample.
Voltage has turned them, riddle and all,
To a piddle and blank wall.

The Great Flood that waked him is the Deluge sent by God to punish the world; it is also sexual emissions magnified to convey the guilt associated with them. 'Reservoir at low level!': Clarke recalls his visits as a child to relations who lived beside the reservoir at Roundwood. Rain is invoked to 'save' the lake by raising the water-level. The allusions and exclamations in the first four lines are mock-heroic, indicating Clarke's maturer perspective on his sexually related dreams. The question in lines 4-5 is relevant to the lament in stanza vi for what the Shannon Scheme has done to the river: should man complain that engineering curbs the torrent? The internal and external rhymes 'curb'. . . 'turbine' . . . 'disturbance' both emphasise and mimic. What follows after 'turbine' is what has been taken away. The great disturbance is both the changes effected by the turbine and the great flow of the river that used to be visible and audible at the numerous falls at Castleconnell, where the river descended fifty feet in under three miles; the 'hush of light' refers to the mist above the falls. The question about Fintan, the falls of Assaroe and transmigration refers to a different change. Fintan, one of the early settlers in Ireland, as recorded in *Lebor Gabála*, lived before the Great Flood which he survived. He became a salmon and lived under the falls at Assaroe, at Ballyshannon, Co Donegal ('void of man/In shape of salmon'). 'Those currents', Clarke declares modestly, 'were ample', including both those at Ballyshannon and Assaroe.[7] The final couplet refers to their reduction by the electrical schemes: those at Assaroe suffered by the Erne hydro-electric scheme in which dams and power-houses were erected between Belleek and Ballyshannon. The word 'ample' includes all the rivers mentioned and the last couplet derides what man has done to them. The 'riddle' refers to the mystery of Fintan's metamorphosis and survival; the blank wall refers to the wall of the dam down which water, no longer ample, trickles in a man-made 'piddle'. The stanza has moved from images of mystery and magnificence to images of blankness and banality. The mythical connection between sexuality and the Deluge, between sexual emissions and the Roundwood reservoir are extended to considerations of contemporary restrictions.

Thousands ply the wonted scissors,
Cut up the immaterial, take

Our measure. When the soul is body-busy,
Rhyme interferes for its own sake
But gets no credit. Late in the day,
Then, coasting back from Milltown Malbay,
I saw before bell rang a warning,
Scattery Island and its round tower.
A child was scorching by that corner
To hurl me back, unknottable power,
Hell-fire in twist and turn, grotesque:
Now, Celtic-Romanesque.

The connections between man and the mysterious or mythological
which were present in the past — in Clarke's childhood experience of
sex, in Manannan in the story of Fintan, in the stories associated with particular places, in man's relationship with places of wonder and beauty —
have been weakened by change and progress. This is another theme that
develops through the poem: the bicycle, vehicle of escape to potential
discoveries gave way to the car; engineering skills have harnessed the
rivers but reduced their capacity to excite wonder. The process, according to stanza viii, goes on. The 'immaterial' is being cut-up to suit 'Our
measure'; the supernatural, the spiritual, the magical, are made habitual
and ordinary. The result for the imagination, when man's measure has
been treated mechanically, is similar to what has happened to rivers in
the preceding stanzas. When the 'soul' becomes a busybody, concerned
with the ordinary, 'rhyme' or poetry, tries to take its place, to articulate
the other dimension, the spiritual, but 'gets no credit' for doing so, no
recognition or appreciation for its important countering of diminishment.
Clarke's experience on the road from Milltown Malbay is an example of
the imagination discovering lessons of morality in the Celtic-Romanesque
period. When 'Thousands . . ./Cut up the immaterial' and 'take/Our
measure', the poet's task is to fill the void, to make up for that loss of
strength. He associates his discovery of the Celtic-Romanesque period
with asceticism. In the intricate designs of the illuminated manuscripts
and high crosses, he finds images of religious terror: 'Hell-fire in twist
and turn'. These recall his own efforts to wrestle with spiritual dread, as
'grotesque' as some of the art forms. By concluding with the positive
'Now, Celtic-Romanesque' Clarke is able to go on in stanza ix to describe
what he identified with in that world: its austere religion. The clergy are
'My companies' who gain access to 'Abraham's Bosom' through 'medi-
tation'. Their high crosses, bibles in stone, unfold stories from the
gospel: 'figured speech'. Traditionally the high crosses show scenes from
the Old Testament on one side and from the New Testament on the other;

the judgmental mode of the former gives way to the redemptive promise of the latter. The disciple, John, 'inspired' the Celtic church and was called 'John o' the Bosom' by some Irish religious poets, such as Donnchadh Mór Ó Dálaigh. At the Last Supper John placed his head on Christ's bosom and became a symbol of love and peace. The ideal of the all-male, childless monastic world is comically disturbed by the Devil.

The portrait is selective, but enables Clarke to make an easy transition to 'our' church, where celibacy is still the ideal. His attitude is subtly conveyed in the verbal adjustments between 'adherents' and 'Stuckhoney' by which the neutral observation that an increasing number of people support the idea of celibacy is judged in the statement that sexual frustration causes bitterness. The next stanza develops this further. Churchmen, reminiscent of some medieval 'schoolmen', condemn the 'senses' and, in Clarke's opinion, foolishly try to create fear in their hearers. He objects to a religion based on fear, having already showed his preference in stanza ix for one based on hope and love. Women may try to have a masculine appearance, to hide their sexuality, but 'Piety', Clarke declares, in harsh condemnation, 'hates their very guts', but will not comment on their sexual organs. The final couplet drily summarises a society in which celibacy gains increasing adherents and sexuality itself is under suspicion.

The poem moves to his former experience of involuntary exile and a different kind of 'vexation':

> Too long in London, I broke in exile
> Another bread. The nightingales
> Naturalised my own vexation:
> Yet, dearer on Inish Caltra, one boat-hail
> At dawn. There Cummin learned to hum
> Angelic breves and found the Thummim.
> Illuminative centre, arc
> By arc was circumscribed. A field
> Too small, perhaps, in truth: the skylark
> May hatch out cuckoo. Thought shielded
> Sunnier pen-stroke. No friend of Alcuin's
> I saw God's light through ruins.

The sobbing song of the nightingales echoed Clarke's loneliness. The rest of the stanza compresses some of the reasons why he preferred to be in Ireland. Inish Cealtra, or Holy Island, on Lough Derg in the Shannon, was in early christian times a famous centre of learning. There St Cummin 'learned to hum angelic breves/And found the Thummim', the former an indication of his personal sanctity, the latter of his knowledge of

Hebrew. 'Thummim' refers to one of two devices used to ascertain the divine will; it indicated affirmation; the other was called 'Urim'. Cummin's scholarly qualities were demonstrated in that his Psalter, as Archbishop Ussher observed, had a collation of the Hebrew text on the upper part of each page, with a brief scolia added on the outside margin.[8] One can live on a small, 'circumscribed', island and still radiate, 'arc by arc', poetic or scholarly power. When the centre is 'illuminative' the influence spreads outward. In truth the centre may be too small: 'the skylark/May hatch out cuckoo'. But Cummin transcended the limitations of place, soaring in song, his 'angelic breves', like the skylark, not confined like the cuckoo. His 'Thought shielded/Sunnier penstroke'. Through his writings Inish Cealtra became famous. Unlike Alcuin, Bishop of York, who wrote an elegy on the destruction of Lindisfarne by the Danes, Clarke 'saw God's light through ruins': he found the light of the imagination in Scattery and elsewhere in the landscape of the Celtic-Romanesque era.

Stanza xii begins as a tribute to that small dynamic centre from which sanctity and learning spread. The 'staves' are primarily those carried by the missionaries who went to Europe, but refer also to the wooden planks of their boats, and to the poetry that they wrote. In 'Isle of fair hills' Clarke uses the title of a poem about Ireland, written by Doncad MacConmara about 1736. He prays that his own 'ills' may be cured. The achievements of Celtic-Romanesque ecclesiastics included actions not approved by Rome: levitation, the tonsure across the forehead, and the ability to divert rivers. 'Clearly,' Clarke comments, in dry mockery, 'religion never hated/A better world'. Ostensibly opposed to the pleasures of this world, the saints enjoyed miraculous power over it.

Stanza xiii is packed with historical allusion. The poem has moved in large chronological steps from evocations of the mythological and early Irish literary past to the Celtic-Romanesque and its collapse. The only justification for their appearance in the poem is their relevance to the history of Clarke's imagination. These are the incidents in the Irish past that he found attractive; therefore they appear in the poem. His opinion that Ireland was overpowered by the continental monastic church and not by the Normans is debatable.

> Too great a vine, they say, can sour
> The best of clay. No pair of sinners
> But learned saints had overpowered
> Our country, Malachi the Thin
> And Bernard of Clairvaux. Prodigious
> In zeal, these cooled and burned our porridge.
> (Later came breakspear, strong bow backing)

The arch sprang wide for their Cistercians.
O bread was wersh and well was brack.
War rattled at us in hammered shirts:
An Englishman had been the Pontiff.
They marched to Mellifont.

Clarke argues that it was the Cistercian monks, Malachi of Bangor and Bernard of Clairvaux, who 'overpowered' Ireland by introducing the Cluniac reforms to the Irish Monasteries. The reference to 'our porridge' recalls the condemnation of the philosophy of Eriugena at the Synod of Valence as *'pultes Scotorum'*, that is, 'Irish porridge'. The Normans came later. The 'pair of sinners' are Dermot McMurrough and Dervorgilla whose elopement contributed to the Norman invasion: McMurrough invited them to help him to regain his throne from which he had been ousted by Tighearnan O Ruairc. Nicholas Breakspear, the English Pope Adrian IV, granted the lordship of Ireland to Henry II and authorised him to conquer Ireland in order to teach 'the truth of the Christian faith to the ignorant and rude'. Strongbow, Earl of Pembroke, was Henry's vassal; he arrived in 1170. 'Later came breakspear, strong bow backing'. The reference is also to the superior power of the Norman soldiers. Heavily mailed, 'in hammered shirts', carrying heavy battle axes, their cavalry protected by Welsh infantry with longbows, they overpowered the Irish who fought on foot and carried spears and light axes. But, Clarke argues, it was the reforming monks who had greater impact. It was they who 'marched' on Mellifont which they founded in 1142. From there their influence spread. Mellifont was the mother-house of twenty-five Cistercian abbeys; its architecture showed the soaring form of Gothic, the long tapering windows.

Three creative influences came to Ireland with the Cistercians: their new monastic order, Gothic architecture, and the friars. It was the beginning of the end of the Celtic-Romanesque style, as well as of the early Irish Church and when the Normans came the century went into turmoil. 'O bread was wersh,' Clarke exclaims in linguistic illustration of what happened, 'and well was brack'. 'Wersh' means lacking in salt, therefore tasteless, and 'brack' means too salty. Much history has been compressed in this stanza. Since the religious reforms replaced the Irish monastic system with the modern diocesan and parochial system, Clarke's argument that they were more important than the consequences of the Norman invasion is understandable. For him, too, the association with modern Ireland is important. 'Since the establishment of our republic', he wrote, 'many continental orders have spread again throughout our country.[9] 'Again' is the significant word.

But time goes back. Monks, whom we praise now,
Take down a castle, stone by stone,
To make an abbey, restore the chain-light
Of silence. Gelignite has blown up
Too much: yet on the Hill of Allen
The blasters are at work. Gallon
By gallon our roads go on. Stonecrushers
Must feed them. Fionn hunted here, Oisín
Complained of age. I think of rushed bones,
Bogland, in furnaces, grown greener,
The prophecy of Colmcille —
Car without horse — fulfilled.

The present consumes the past, indifferent to its associations, committed to progress. Even the Hill of Allen, headquarters of Fionn MacCumhaill is being destroyed. Clarke's tone is acerbic: we praise monks now even when they destroy a castle to build an abbey, we approve of road-making no matter what the consequences, we welcome the car. His few allusions recall, like the legendary Oisin's Colloquy with Saint Patrick, faint memories of the Fianna. The very quietness of the references following after nouns and verbs that are noisy and destructive accentuates the losses. The 'rushed bones' of the dead are consumed in furnaces to heat the living.

The poem's concluding stanzas sum up Clarke's time. Stanza xv deals with political changes: English rule replaced by Catholic power, the Easter Rising, the civil war, the treaty. Now the planes of the national airline are named after Irish saints, another commercial usage. 'Greeting/ To overheads!', Clarke punningly exclaims, adding a dry reflection on the price of freedom and an aside on his own loss of freedom. The image of the self begins with the eager schoolboy and ends with the frustrated old man. The freedom won is seen to be of dubious value: a scratch in empire, a prosperity gained at a high price and through a commercialised use of saints whose achievements Clarke has already commemorated. The theme of indifference to past values continues here. Rust and mould have removed Clarke's means of transport; even his St Christopher medal has succumbed. By putting these images of decay side by side with the high-flying planes, Clarke achieves a sardonic humour. The reference to 'Whitefriar Street', home of the Carmelites, connects with his other references to the Cluniac reforms. In a mischievous colloquialism, Clarke suggests that the planes' screws may be loose.

Stanza xvi takes up some of Clarke's dominant interests: the excessive influence of the Church, even in the area of medical science, and the pilgrimages to Lourdes. The tone is lightly mocking from the invitation to 'See' the strange reconciliation of faith and science, traditionally and inherently in conflict. In Ireland the medical 'specialist' is replaced by a faith in the spiritual; and credulous pilgrims, with the blessings of the Church, fly to Lourdes to be cured; the clouds shape themselves into grottoes in the foolish imaginations of the people. Again the injunction 'Let' and the mocking flashes from the light-houses mimic an approval of something that Clarke finds ridiculous. But he is more amused than angry. 'Loss', as he says in the next stanza, 'but repeats the startling legend/Of time'. In his state of reduced activity he takes comfort from that knowledge and views events with a realistic detachment.

> Loss but repeats the startling legend
> Of time. A poet wants no more
> To palliate his mind, edging
> Worn cards behind a shaky door
> Or tinting them until the puce
> Shuffle the purple. May the Deuce
> Take all of them and thought get better
> While faith and country play a far hand!
> Plod on, tired rhyme. The streams that wetted
> Forgotten wheels push past Rathfarnham,
> Half underground: slime steps on stone.
> I count them — not my own.

The poet's faith is in himself, in his own hand of cards, despite the frailty of his state. The 'shaky door' is literally the halldoor of Bridge House but also the door of life. The cards are well worn but may still be used to effect change. The lines illustrate one of the risks that Clarke takes and in this case not successfully. He is committed to the metaphor of the playing cards and he also has to find a rhyme for 'Deuce'. 'Puce' and 'shuffle' are therefore appropriate, but their meaning is not clear. The reference to tinting cards until one colour becomes another lacks precision, and the ecclesiastical association of 'purple' does not seem to work. The context is of diminished activity and of persistence and defiance. 'May the Deuce/Take all of them'. The 'them' are the opposing players, Church and state, who play 'a far hand'. He will continue to write, despite the loss of strength. 'Plod on, tired rhyme'. His attention is not on his own shaky progress but on the wheel of energy in the opening stanza. The poem concludes with an act of faith in the rational imagination. In circling back upon itself, it suggests that it is the best evidence of the truth affirmed in the last stanza.

The unspectacular ending of 'The Loss of Strength' is in keeping with Clarke's philosophy of quiet persistence, which also characterises the conclusion of 'The Hippophagi'. Much of the material in this poem of eighteen twelve-line stanzas, with a regular pattern of assonantal rhyme, relates to the first twenty years of Clarke's life, even though the events that occasioned it, the mistreatment of horses being shipped abroad to be used as meat, happened in the late Fifties, reaching a peak in December, 1959. The metaphor of destructive cruelty towards animals, known for their gentleness and willingness to serve man, is the unifying theme of the poem; it joins examples of ecclesiastical mistreatment of people with the inhuman treatment of horses and both with modern man's destructive capacity. Clarke denounces the failure of the Government and the people to protest against the suffering of the horses. The suggestion that instead of shipping them abroad on the hoof they should first be killed at home arouses his anger. 'Knacker Rhyme' is his initial sarcastic response; its tightly packed lines of echoing end-rhyme and internal rhyme highlight his rage.

> Don't ship, kill, can them
> First — abattoirs pay —
> Or chill the carcases
> For hook and tray:
> Packed, sacked, quay-stacked,
> The neighless all saved
> From wavetops, ill-treatment
> Abroad.

'The Hippophagi' is more thoughtful. We are the horse-eaters, noted for cruelty, insensitive to the pain we inflict on both horses and humans. The theme appears in many guises throughout Clarke's later poetry. Here it is concentrated on examples mainly from his boyhood years, as though the later evidence of cruelty and lack of compassion confirms, or even increases, his realisation of the nature of Irish life and character. The stanzas about those early years, i-x and xiv-xv, are details in the portrait of a life impinged upon by cruelties. Cruelty, wherever it takes place, puts man into the category of horse-eaters, kin to the monsters described by Othello: 'the Cannibals that each other eat,/The Anthropophagi, and men whose heads/Do grow beneath their shoulders'.

The mocking tone of the first stanza distances the speaker from past experience,

> Up-to-date infant, rubbered, wheeled out,
> I kicked up heels, soon took to them,
> Learned the first premise of a race
> Now lost in space. I was immortal,

Yea, so important that monks pursued me,
Similitudes of bygone ages.
Bodikin rages to be itself
When bookshelf fills with catechism.
The pubic schism makes Latin hoarser,
Scholastics coarsen the ignorants,
Sew up their pants. Single idea
Has circumscribed us, lyre'd Judea.

The encounter with reality is dynamic and fruitful, but not entirely free.
'I kicked up my heels, soon took to them' playfully carries the visual
image of the child; the stanza changes rapidly to the colloquial 'kick up
your heels' and the freedom of 'take to the hills'. The 'race' connects
with the idea of escape, with the human race, and with the space race.
The mocking tone of the opening lines is carried through in 'Yea, so important that monks pursued me'. The conflict, thus suggested, is developed
in the clash between the 'race' and the need to be left alone; between
clerical control, the filling up of space with the 'catechism', with the
regulations and the need for freedom. During puberty, when the voice
breaks, it is the schoolmen, who 'coarsen' the innocent, 'the ignorants',
making them conscious of sin, particularly sexual sin, and of the need
for restraint ('Sew up their pants'). The stanza concludes that one idea
has 'circumscribed us', its source 'lyre'd Judea', home of christianity,
much sung about but also liable to deceive. The stanza has moved from
images of joy, release, and discovery to images of division and restriction
and in that development introduces the theme of insensitivity and
cruelty: the innocent child becomes the victim of ancient prohibitions.

The following stanzas outline the effects of clerical pursuit. Even the
language of prayer contributes to the confusion of adolescence. Religion,
both alluring and authoritative, is sensually disturbing in its language.

Frankincense, flowers of speech,
Small gifts, beseech us to be good;
Premature swoon of sense, globe-spurning,
Cup-borne; gums burn us, celestial lilies
Vase mortal chill. Soul fades, love-sick,
In rhetoric. But oh! Those O's
And Ah's, glows, melts at me in sweet print.
I clasp my *Key of Heaven.* Cover
Be gold, let boy discover bine, grain,
Glues in that binding of desert tan
Mahommedan had palmed! A link went:
Beads, decades and all: self was delinquent.

Clarke sought refuge from such emotionalism in the classic discipline of early Irish poetry. Here he creates the hypnotic effect of the language, suggestively erotic but vaguely understood. Even his prayer book, with its Moroccan leather cover was touched with sensual association.[10] The Hopkinesque use of language records his embarrassment at the language of some prayers.

> . . . I was embarrassed by those exclamatory prayers, perfumed as incense, sharp as the red hot charcoals. My mother had been embarrassed by an angel's prayer; I was afflicted by the continual litanies in my teens: *O Most adorable, precious and infinitely tender Heart pierced for the love of me, pierce my heart with the love of Thee.* Such words drew me down to unknown depths. *Sacred Heart, I put my trust in Thee. Inflame my heart with Thy love. O Wisdom of the Sacred Heart! O light of the Sacred Countenance, shine upon us. O Love of the Sacred Heart, consume me in Thy fire.*[11]

Religion, like sex, was a 'swoon of sense'. The last line of the stanza ambiguously joins the feeling of release in religious fervour with sexual emissions. Confusingly, religion and sex were similar in feeling yet one was holy, the other sinful. His sense of 'moral degradation rapidly increased'[12]: he became a 'delinquent'.

Stanza three is a parable of moral degradation founded on the Old Testament, the source of much of Clarke's guilty discoveries. It represents his progression from cosy acceptance to guilty alienation.

> Fond ones dozed with the patriarchs.
> Afrits, darkening from Syria
> In later myriads, saw dust-men,
> Who rode in rust, guard wormwood, shoe-holes
> Mad for Jerusalem. Sin shrouded
> The plural couch, concubinage.
> There was new vinage awash in ships:
> Love without lips and night prolonged:
> Our pallid Song o' Songs — her Talmud
> In ghetto — rudded in slumber of don,
> Aye, demijohn. Shall no cruse aid her?
> Lickerish echo: 'no crusader.'

It also represents the deterioration of christianity, including its loss of authority. 'Fond ones dozed with the patriarchs' refers to those who trusted in Old Testament figures from Adam to Abraham. That dream turns to nightmare when demons of Arabian mythology descend upon Jerusalem. Images of doctored wine, sexual immorality and darkness suggest moral deterioration. The wine, associated with Christ, is impure, the message of God's love is stifled, darkness is 'prolonged'. The magnificent eroticism of the Song of Songs is diminished; the 'demijohn' is a pun on the reduced measure, connecting 'vinage' and 'don', meaning both drunken stupor and spiritual loss. The 'Talmud/In ghetto' adds to the idea of restriction in the operation of christianity. The canticles, once seen as an allegorical account of God's dealing with the Church, are 'pallid'; the code of Jewish civil and moral law is confined. By the end of the stanza the Church is helpless, with no hope of renewal: there will be no crusade and no curative oil.

Clarke's confused and sentimentalised notion of religion as a boy is the subject of stanza iv in which the miracles of a former period are 'domesticated'.

> Would Padua find, Xavier miss
> My prayer, Francis de Sales forget
> In elegant letters, silk-knots of Dijon?
> And, then, those seizures and that gasp:
> How often clasp was mortified;
> Gonzaga lying in boyish state
> That we might pray for happy death,
> Give say to Saith, watching the flames
> Roll by. All saints wore foreign disc.
> Astonished, asterisked from waist down,
> We starred and crowned lest we incite
> Their Europe with immodest sight.

These saints, Anthony of Padua, Francis Xavier, Francis de Sales, and Aloysius Gonzaga, were renowned as preachers, miracle workers, and devotees of austere codes of personal behaviour. But in Clarke's boyish imagination they were diminished, made available as helpers, turned into pious models.[13] The boy saint, Aloysius Gonzaga, was an image of a 'happy death', happy because sinless. As Clarke records: 'We prayed daily for a happy death and our thoughts were mortuary'.[14] The 'seizure and the 'gasp' in this context are primarily associated with death. At Belvedere College Clarke was told exemplary stories of sinners on their death beds surrounded by demons waiting to seize them; their 'enormous ... last breath' was a screech for a priest to save them.[15] He looks back in amusement at such inducements in the jocular 'Give say to Saith, watching the flames/Roll by'. The saints are 'foreign' in a literal sense of being non-Irish but also in wearing haloes. Clarke recalls encircling their heads with stars and prudently putting asterisks for genitalia in order to avoid sexual incitement.

But saints were not immune to 'immodest' temptations. St Alphonsus Liguori, 'sainted at thirty', was subjected to diabolical apparitions and temptations at the end of his life. Ironically, he was tormented by shameful language and visions of the sexual practices he had discussed in *Theologia Moralia*, a treatise on sexuality in marriage: 'turn, touch, hot stuff/Misspent', which quotes one of his questions: '*Quares an, et quanto liceant tactus, aspectus, et verbia turpia inter conjuges?*'

> Liguori, early or late. Alphonsus
> Carried the sconce, queried in Latin
> The secret matrimonial code
> Of laymen, showed their vice-in-virtue:
> Sainted at thirty — but at four-score
> And ten, the court held every night
> By his own writings. Verba Turpia,
> Mock-purple, judged base turn, touch, hot stuff
> Misspent; buff witnessing by proxy,
> Confession-boxed. How his stole fends
> For aureole! Doting on hymn,
> Hell snatched the stand from under him.

'Fearful temptations assailed him by day and night,' Clarke wrote in *Twice Round the Black Church*; 'the Devil conjured up unchaste sights before him'.[16] While the language of the poem is humorous, almost malicious in its picture of the devils pulling the stand from under him, the experience is frightening both for Liguori and for Clarke: 'he entered into the dark night of the soul which we knew already in our teens'.[17] The portrayal of the old saint, who had judged what others might or might not do, being himself subjected to a diabolical trial in which his writings are used in evidence against him, is both comic and terrifying. It confirms an already familiar personal experience.

The disappearance of the horse — 'The streets . . . suddenly horseless' — is associated with the destruction of Sodom and Gomorrah. The theme that develops through these stanzas is that of disappointment with christianity's failings. Initially, religion restricted childhood's freedom; it is seen then as an ambivalent mixture of eroticism and morality, as softly supportive, as unnervingly vulnerable to the Devil's power and therefore insufficiently protective, until finally, its terrifying punitive and judgmental power is associated with cruelty and the disappearance of the horse.[18] Clarke proceeds to develop the theme of unchristian destruction. It is not so much that the horse has disappeared, but that God's love and protection have disappeared, with the result that the boy feels threatened. There was 'terror' by day at the thought that he, made in God's image, 'A little likeness', could also be destroyed. Now, memories of 'Respectable People' bring him back to those fears and to the thought that God after all might destroy the world. The idea of the chaotic nature of childhood experience continues in stanza vii. Just as 'Cities remember ancient religion' in stanza vi, so here 'Tables were breaking the Commandments'. In the biblical account, Moses broke the tablets on which the Commandments were written, when he came down from the mountain and found the Israelites engaged in sinful practices. In the early twentieth century mathematical tables, scientific inventions and discoveries, were altering the world. The discoveries, such as electricity, steam-trams, and the phonograph, were however outdone, Clarke notes, by an eclipse of the sun.[19] Stanza viii comments on the destructive power of the modern age. 'No pore has pity'. Ecclesiastical justifications for war makes a hell on earth for its victims, the 'Burnt offerings'. Stanza ix returns to the theme of his escape from the constrictions of religion. He 'mitched from miracles', preferring 'Older/Legends'. The image of the boy in imaginative 'horse-play' leads to his discovery of poetry and the flights of Wright and Blériot, pioneers in aviation. Wrily, he records the innocent optimism of those years. He did not foresee that Pegasus would throw him or that the Parnassian 'fount', 'would be half mud'.

Abrupt shifts in perspectives, exaggerated recreation of experience, distorted sensory images and irrational transitions characterise the style of the poem. Through language, syntax and stanzaic structure it illustrates the confusions, exaggerated reactions and illogical associations of childhood. Chronology is speeded up, the sequence of events is fragmented, events themselves heightened as in the first films he saw in the Rotunda or the Volta.[20] The bioscope made reality seem crazy and those effects matched in some respects the sensations he struggled with. The style is less subject to such distortions when dealing with adult perceptions, such as those in stanza x, which outlines events. These include Ireland under colonial rule, the 1914-18 war, the Easter Rising, the cinema news reels, the civil war, the replacement of idealism by greed and apathy, and the emergence of a Catholic Church indifferent to the needs of the poor but expanding in prosperity.

The question that begins stanza xi brings the issue of cruelty to horses to the centre of attention: why should we 'think', why should we 'regard' the horse in such a personal way when horses can be sold as meat. The tenderness of 'Patting our dumb' friends and the familiar image of 'nose-bag in the dust' give way to the demeaned 'snout' and the aggressive demand of Europe 'thrusting its bloody face/In ours'.

Patting our dumb, why should we think,
To-day, of drinking-trough in streets
A-clatter with meat no butcher sold,
Regard that nose-bag in the dust,
When Europe, thrusting its bloody face,
In ours, will pay for every snout?
Horses, in thousands, are out of work.
But, must we burke their past? Breed them
For lesser needs: our word will carry.
They galloped with Sarsfield, after Aughrim,
Kept Ballinasloe in decent trade.
Off course, old bets are soon betrayed.

In this mechanised age horses, like people, are out of work, but Clarke objects to their contribution to Irish life being forgotten so callously. The analogy with the notorious William Burke (1792-1829) who murdered people and sold their bodies underlines the enormity of the trade in horse-meat. The reference to the dashing Irish leader, Patrick Sarsfield, represents their participation in past events; the reference to Ballinasloe is to a famous horse-fair that demonstrated the horse's importance. Of course, Clarke concludes bitterly, when the horse is no longer useful, he is quickly 'betrayed'.

But what can poetry do? 'Can jingle straighten the horse's mouth?' The jingle is the sound of the bit, but control has passed to mercenary dealers who forestall the market by buying the horses in advance in order to make a profit. Their squalid dealing is expressed in the ritual of private bargaining, 'hand-spit, chink/And rustle'; their debased opinion of the horse is heard in the terms they used — 'scruff', 'stuff', 'dollop', 'trolloped'. The horse is at the mercy of 'tinkers' and 'tanglers'. Government deputies support the trade. The 'Hurrah' for horse-eaters expresses this support, mockingly; it is mimicked in the cry of children that combines the sound of shipping with the idea of meat. The child's word 'gee-gee' at the end of xii links with the ride a cock-horse opening of xiii, as though the exports were merely rocking horses. 'St. George' recalls the legendary dragon-slayer and patron of England; but now mercenary, not chivalric, interests are uppermost. The pretence that St Audoen, patron saint of traders, approves of this trade is mocked, as was the notion in the previous stanza that there are acceptable nationalistic reasons for it. 'Cockhorse' and 'clothes-horse' are connected. 'Be my hurt', Clarke says. 'Rhyme is no comforter'. Jingle cannot straighten the horse's mouth.

Cockhorse is all aboard, child, with painter
And pulley, St. George has lost a stirrup;

> Paper knights galloped away with gold standard.
> St. Audeon stows the Channel, blesses,
> They say, our business deals. Go, peep
> Behind the clothes-horse, be my hurt.
> Rhyme is no comforter. Learn later
> How battened trade exposed by storm
> Proved Lowry Lorc had pinched the ear-flaps
> Of Tulyar. Mishap was ill-defended
> In stall and Senate. Weather reports
> Lay bare our soul in ancient ports.

A dishonest trade battened on horses, that is, throve at their expense and fastened the hatches on them. Lowry Lorc, a dishonest king, had horse's ears but hid his unworthiness to be king; that he should be disguised as the great Tulyar is a metaphor for the enormity of a trade that is indefensible in the equestrian or the political arenas. The storms that expose the plight of the horse, Clarke concludes, reveal the moral state of 'our soul'.

The reference in stanza xiv to Swift's Houyhnhnm fleetingly recalls Gulliver's instinctive affinity with the idealised horses as Clarke playfully matches its nasal sound with the rhyme 'Minim' and uses this musical reference to introduce his violin lessons, and to emphasise that man has lost his way. Childhood terms in the previous stanza and mention of his violin lessons here recall the first stanza. Man is, Clarke concludes, 'unsure in time'. The nature of his relationship with God is uncertain. So, too, is the scale of his position in time, as the contrast between 'moth' and 'behemoth', the colossal biblical beast, implies.

Stanza xv refers to the Irish Parliamentary, or Home Rule Party, their defence of Edward VII (1901-10), to Eamon de Valera's period as a teacher at Carysfort Training College (1906-10). It characterises the Edwardian era as weakly deferential and respectful. Even the bishops at St Patrick's College, Maynooth, in order to please their royal visitor, removed the symbols of death, a moral lesson, and replaced them with his racing colours. The 'truth' that their 'flattery' keeps hidden is the truth of their moral outlook, as well as the truth of the king's dissolute life. The stanza concludes with the idea that the 1914-18 war confused the effect of the Easter Rising and that injustice still exists in Ireland. The poem turns in conclusion through references to confusion and loss: man 'unsure in time', ecclesiastical subservience, political failure, injustice. The Edwardian era lacks moral principle. But modern Ireland is no better: 'equity is still unwon'.

Stanza xvi returns to the theme of hippophagy. The Government profits from horses, both through the national stud in Kildare and through the export of other horses, their 'blood relations', to be cut up abroad for food. 'Horse-eating helps this ill-fare state'. 'The worst abroad is now our best' refers to the export of both horses and people. The State is pleased that people who might otherwise cause 'social unrest' have to emigrate to find work, and care little about the injustice. They are the 'worst' in the sense of being worst-off; they are the best in the sense of being best for the country since by their leaving they remove the risk of social upheaval.

In a despairing apostrophe to the power that controls the modern world, Clarke invokes 'Hate', to 'civilise all' who are yet 'unatomised!'. 'Earth goes a mooning' seems to imply that the world has gone mad, 'shooting' objects through the vastness of space on great surges of energy. The 'vasty cod' is a mocking metaphor for the world as a scrotum. Machines are now given the affection once given to horses. Man's measure of achievement is in the skies, his new stage.

The final stanza is in effect a reaction to that bleak vision of a destructive, technological world. The child that sat and 'played in self' has grown up in a bewildering world of changed values, of cruelty and monstrous inventions. How then is the adult to cope? A statement and four questions make up the poem's conclusion.

> Bib shall obey the ever-known.
> Why keep the grape-stone, leave the vine stock,
> Sweet stain on frock? Could self have learned
> In woody, ferny glen to choose
> With Fionn the music of what happens,
> Found in some Clapham an honest sect
> Of intellect? Lastly a premise
> That wants much phlegm: can polyglot,
> Carried in snot so easily wiped
> Away, decide? What dare we call
> Our thought, Marcus Aurelius,
> Unwanted void or really us?

The adult, like the child, 'shall' respond to the familiar. Briefly Clarke mentions alternatives: an emotional harmony with the Fenian past; an intellectual identification with some 'sect'. But the two final questions go deeper, the one pointing to the sheer difficulty of reaching decisions, the other to the value of thought itself. The Aurelian argument was essentially positive, a finding of an harmonious oneness between man and nature. Aurelius saw man as a microcosm reflecting the vaster organism of the universe, his body made of the four elements and created from and controlled by a particle called Mind. Clarke raises the idea that thought itself may be a void. It may, as Aurelius argues, be 'really us', that which differentiates man from other creatures, but there is also the possibility that it may be nothing.

Aurelius struggled to reconcile science and faith; he thought that there might be a moral and benevolent power which can feel for humanity and concern itself with human problems. Clarke, as the poem makes clear, felt that the very sources of faith had been sullied, that man's capacity for self-reliance had been impaired. He may be a 'polyglot' but he is also inescapably mortal. The final questions are profound, involving human identity and value. They raise the issue of hippophagism to a different level, involving the nature of being, the purpose of existence, and the possibility of things, including thought, being meaningless. The pessimism inherent in these questions seem to have affected the mood of the poem which loses its liveliness of manner and descends occasionally into flat statement. Clarke's tenacious realism is expressed in the first line: 'Bib shall obey the ever-known'. That is the faith on which his later poetry rests.

Forget Me Not (1962) is an examination in another mood of material already recalled in 'The Hippophagi'. A long, flowing line and a loose syntax replaces the tight, four stressed, closely rhymed twelve-line stanza. The emotional low point on which 'The Hippophagi' ends is countered by the high spirits of the new poem. The lament for the disappearance of the horse is replaced by a celebration of the qualities he embodies.

The poem begins with playful identification — 'Trochaic, dimeter, amphimacer/And choriamb' — of the metres of its introductory jingle, the 'anonymous patter' of:

> Up the hill
> Hurry me not;
> Down the hill,
> Worry me not;
> On the level,
> Spare me not,
> In the stable,
> Forget me not.

The mood is light. Poetry, childhood and the sounds of the horse-drawn vehicles, the rhythms of life and the patterns of children's games, belong to a unified, harmonious, forget-me-not world; the flower itself is an 'emblem/Of love and friendship, delicate sentiments'. 'Verse came like that, simple/As join-hands'. Journeys by pony and trap to places near Dublin formed a 'consensus' of feeling, both shared and sensory.

> Place-names, full of Sunday,
> Stepaside, Pass-if-you-can Lane, Hole in the Wall.
> Such foliage in the Dargle hid Lovers Leap,
> We scarcely heard the waters fall-at all.
> Often the open road to Celbridge: we came back
> By Lucan Looks Lovely, pulled in at the Strawberry Beds,
> Walked up the steep of Knockmaroon.

The rhythms are relaxed and flexible, the rhymes playful and light, the lines packed with detail. The poem recalls the sights and sounds, the voices, the movements, the rhythms of days related to the movements of the horse-drawn vehicles: the race every evening to meet the express train from Galway, the return journey with the customers, his Uncle John 'coaxing by name his favourite mare'. The boy is conscious of the 'affectionate glance' he might receive from a horse at the kerb. In memory Clarke plays happily over those days when 'Champions went by . . ./ Their brasses clinked, yoke, collar shone at us:/Light music while they worked'. Other sounds were less pleasant: the crack of whip, the slapping of children, the taking away of prisoners in the Black Maria, the funerals. But the horses were beautiful and once, memorably, he saw a white horse in Phoenix Park that 'unfabled/The Unicorn'.

The arrival of 'Mechanised vehicles' destroyed that world. Uncle John lost his business, but kept his last mare. 'They aged/Together'. That image of sad companionship begins a lament for what has been lost, not just the animals but the values that were part of the relationship between man and horse: 'All the gentling, custom of mind/And instinct, close affection, done with'. The poem shifts directly to the export trade in horses. 'What are they now but hundred weights of meat?' Greed replaces gentleness. Once again Clarke rejects the argument that it is better to kill horses at home than subject them to the risks of a sea journey: 'Greed with a new gag of mercy/Grants happy release in our whited abbatoirs'.

'I've more to say', Clarke announces and outlines a series of facts: that Great Britain also exports horses, that classical authors, like Herodotus and Pliny condemned hippophagy, that besieged towns forbade it. 'Stare now at Pegasus. The blood/Of the Medusa weakens in him'. Even Pegasus sprang from violence, from the blood of the gorgon. That thought is quickly replaced by a section that recalls the glory of the horse.

> Yet all the world
> Was hackneyed once — those horses o' the sun,
> Apollo's cars, centaurs in Thessaly.
> Too many staves have splintered the toy
> That captured Troy. The Hippocrene is stale.

> Dark ages; Latin rotted, came up from night-soil,
> New rush of words; thought mounted them. Trappings
> Of palfrey, sword-kiss of chivalry, high song
> Of grammar. Men pick the ribs of Rosinante
> In restaurants now. Horse-shoe weighs in with saddle
> Of meat.
>
>   Horseman, the pass-word, courage shared
> With lace, steel, buff.

In classical mythology horses pulled the car of the god of music and poetry and fabulous creatures, half man half horse, roamed in Thessaly. But the imaginative force of such images has declined. Troy's horse has splintered, destroyed by over-use and familiarity. 'The Hippocrene is stale': classical sources have lost their power. The reference to the fountain on Mt Helicon, sacred to the Muses and to Apollo, connects with the reference to Pegasus, since it sprang from the ground where his hoof struck; the word hippocrene itself combines the Greek for horse and fountain. The dark ages obliterated the classical world which returned with the revival of learning and of Latin as the language of the schoolmen. Their adherence to rational discourse is present in the equestrian metaphor: 'New rush of words; thought mounted them'. The age of chivalry brought in an attractive code of conduct and of thought, but that has been lost. Now Don Quixote's horse means no more than food; the saddle once used on a lady's 'palfrey' refers to meat, a butcher's term. The word 'Horseman' once referred to individuality and courage. But horses were 'regimented' and replaced by motorised transport. In a final elegiac note Clarke images the neighing of horses and 'man's cry' in the noise of engines, as though the unhappiness of the 'draggers of artillery' has been prolonged. The union of horse and man in this lament is an appropriate conclusion to the general loss of feeling and contact between them.

The poem's concluding Irish section has the same theme: the decline in the force of mythological material. Recreating a moment of insight, during the moon's eclipse, when he saw the 'Sign of the Sagittary' in Cormac's Chapel in Cashel, he turns instead to earlier pagan material. The Sagitarry, a drawing of a centaur shooting a lion with a bow and arrow, represents the triumph of christianity over paganism, but Clarke turned his back 'On all that Celtic-Romanesque; thinking'

> Of older story and legend, how Cuchullain,
> Half man, half god-son, tamed the elemental
> Coursers: dear comrades: how at his death
> The Gray of Macha laid her mane upon his breast
> And wept.

This warmly humanised portrait of the relationship between man and horse replaces the moral allegory of the Sagitarry.

It is followed by an elegiac address to Ireland, the 'Too much historied/ Land', its politics, rebellions and hope in help from abroad, all ending in the poverty of the eighteenth century and an Irish poet's allegorical name for Ireland: 'The Slight Red Steed'. Clarke's conclusion is ironical; it seems to make a virtue of necessity — 'Word-loss is now our gain:/Put mare to stud' — but mocks the complacency of the time. That Ireland is no more destructive than countries that inflict appalling destruction on other countries is not something to be proud of; tipsters extol equestrian bloodlines, but for commercial ends. His advice to the 'Boys' to 'pack tradition in the meat-sack' also is sarcastic. The advice that they should 'Write off the epitaph of Yeats' is equally sarcastic, a reference not only to 'Horseman, pass by!', but to forgetting the poet's high achievements and the austere command 'Cast a cold eye/On life, on death'. Clarke turns again to rhyme, ending the poem as he began, in the same self-delighting manner. The lines are more than a jingle. They express a commitment to poetry, a philosophy of life, of self-reliance, of persistence. They are an epitaph disguised as anonymous patter.

Forget Me Not's relaxed, playful mode and easy assimilation of classical and historical material indicates Clarke's renewed confidence in his own imaginative and linguistic powers and foreshadows the remarkable work to follow.

Chapter 9: *Flight to Africa* (1963)

The sense of lightness that is established in *Forget Me Not* continues in *Flight to Africa* which is a large collection of poems almost all of which were written in a ten week period in 1962, when Clarke returned from a visit to Mount Parnassus. 'Shortly after my return', he wrote in a note, 'I experienced for ten weeks a continual, voluptuous state of mind during which the various pieces arrived with such joyful ease that I suspect some to be Greek gifts'.[1] Three of the poems, 'Flight to Africa', 'Stadium', and 'Forget Me Not', were written previously. This 'voluptuous state of mind' is reflected in the self-delighting quality of many of the poems, in the frequent use of rhyme, and in the virtual absence of the satirical tone found in the preceding collections.

Flight to Africa repeats some of the familiar themes of these collections: the cruel treatment of children, the casuistry of ecclesiastics, mariolatry, the treatment of sinners, political satire, social satire, eroticism, and new religious and political developments, such as the Second Vatican Council, Irish membership of the European Economic Community, and Ireland's recognition of new African states. But the most remarkable feature is its linguistic energy which may be examined in two representative examples: 'Abbey Theatre Fire' and 'Cypress Grove'. The former begins as follows:

> One of our verse-speakers, driving
> His car at dusk to Alexander
> Dock, saw a fine ship on fire, loitered
> Among the idlers, urchins, at the gateway,
> Came back by crane, warehouse, bollard,
> The Custom House, corniced with godlings —

184

Nilus, Euphrates, detected a smell
Of burning again and in alarm,
Jumped out, to poke the bonnet, turned, noticed
Smoke piling up near Liberty Hall,
Smoulder of clothes. Suddenly, ghosts
In homespun, peasants from the West,
Hurrying out of the past, went by unheard,
Pegeen, her playboy, tramps, cloaked women,
Young girls in nothing but their shifts.
Glimmerers stalked, tall, mournful eyed,
In robes, with playing instruments,
By shadowy waters of the Liffey.
He drove around the corner, guessing
That flames were busier than their smoke
In the Abbey Theatre. Civic Guards
Shouldered, broke down the door-glass, carried
Yeats, Lady Gregory, Synge, Máire
O'Neill, F.R. Higgins, blindly
Staring in disapproval.

Two qualities are dominant: the driving energy of the active verbs and the density of the lines. The narrative voice records events as they happened and dramatises their impact so that the verse-speaker's testimony seems to be immediate. It is not the language of reflection but of witnessing. The poet imagines the stages by which the verse-speaker perceived and understood what was happening. The essential ingredient of the interplay between observer and event is momentum; the rhythm of perception is illustrated in the run-on and fragmented syntax in which the individual subject is connected with the event through a sequence of active verbs: 'saw', 'loitered', 'Came', 'detected', 'Jumped out', 'turned', 'noticed'. The impression is enhanced by the density with which the setting is established — Alexander Dock and the Custom House with its riverine statuary and Liberty Hall — and by the specificity of concrete images, such as 'crane, warehouse, bollard'. Packed lines, vibrant with life, are the hallmarks of Clarke's later style. They also express a movement of thought: the verse-speaker mimics a sequence of responses in a theatre of gesture and sensation. The sudden appearance of 'ghosts/In homespun', like a visionary scene in a play, is both an evocation of Abbey Theatre plays and an expression of how his mind has worked. Already with the 'Smoulder of clothes' he has jumped to the right conclusion: that it is the theatre which is on fire. His action in driving around the corner confirms this. Again the scene he comes upon is theatrical. Life seems to imitate art as the Guards 'Shouldered, broke . . . carried'. In another act of mimesis the poem mirrors that theatrical ritual and in processional outlines a theatre's history: 'Yeats, Lady Gregory, Synge, Maire/O'Neill, F.R. Higgins'.

The poem's description of the fire maintains the linguistic energy of active verbs; in the theatrical metaphor flames take a bow, their personified 'flickers' unlock the bookcase in the greenroom, turn the pages of old scripts, cinder prompt copy. The sense of enactment and of re-enactment grows until the impersonal becomes personal when Clarke recalls his response to Abbey Theatre plays 'That turned my head at seventeen'. The style is less descriptive as he records the work of the Lyric theatre and lists the plays of Yeats that they performed. The passage ends with a simple statement: 'So, I forgot/His enmity'. Yeats omitted Clarke from the *Oxford Book of Modern Verse* (1936), but whether forgetting includes forgiveness is not clear.

In 'The Abbey Theatre Fire' the histrionic imagination has replaced the historical imagination. The language of the theatre compensates for the physical and imaginative losses outlined in 'The Loss of Strength' and *Forget Me Not*. Theatricality is the mode of several poems in this collection. Even in those which use it less explicitly the point of view is that of the spectator. The human figures, including the author, are seen as participants in an action. They are often treated in exaggerated fashion, in heightened language or gesture, and always from a distance.

'Cypress Grove' is another example of linguistic energy. Section I is written in one of Clarke's most effective styles: the long, run-on sentence, the densely packed line, the rhythmic variation from the uninterrupted line to the fragmented one, the structuring effect of active verbs and qualifying clauses, the situating of the action in specific places: Lough Bray, Kippure, Glencree, Bohernabreena, Seefin, Punchestown, Church Mountain, King's River, Annalecky, Slaney, Poulaphouca, all readily identifiable.

> 'Grob! Grob', goes the raven peering from his rift
> Above Lough Bray, glimmer on eyelid, feather —
> Shadow in water — sets out for Kippure
> By upper Glencree, at morning, devil-dot
> Above the last bog-cutting, hears the lark totting
> And dips along gullies by the twig-drip of heather
> Down to the pond-level, the steps of Bohernabreena,
> Then winging over Seefin, takes the pure
> Cold air — ravenous, searching — comes to that green
> Bowl set among hills, Punchestown, its race-course
> So often whiskeyed with the roar of crowd

Nearer, farther, as binoculars
Hastily swivel the Grand Stand, hoarser
Where black-red-violet-blue-white-yellow dots
Are hunched along the slope: backers from bars
And, shaded by huge umbrellas, bookmakers,
Are waving caps above the stalls. That hurly-burly
A mile away: he sees the pewter cloud
Above Church Mountain, past the double lake,
Flaps by the King's River, sandy spots:
Behind him the dairy farms — the acres tree'd,
Thin-streamed — then flies up where the gusts are blowing
Over the ceannavaun and nothing is showing,
Hidden awhile in vapouring of screes
'Ur! Ur', he croaks to himself, a flying speck
And turning northward over Annalecky
Where a man by the Slaney might stoop to hook a
Trout, play it, looks down into Poulaphouca.

The raven's croak announces his entrance onto the landscape of south Dublin, Wicklow, and Kildare. His flight is conveyed through a series of verbs and participles — 'goes', 'peering', 'sets out', 'hears', 'dips', 'winging', 'takes', 'searching' and 'comes'. These are attended by brief descriptive images, such as 'glimmer on eyelid, feather-/Shadow in water', or 'at morning, devil-dot/Above the last bog-cutting', or 'twig-drip of heather . . . pond-level . . . steps'. The flight, the bird, the landscape are brought together in a style that is responsive to movement, visual imagery, the vividness of things in nature. The syntax reflects this liveliness of perception in its onward momentum within which these are the pointed interruption that focus on particulars. The arrival at the racecourse at Punchestown results in an extended evocative description of a race meeting. Again the language is both animated and exact: binoculars swivel and what they focus are the jockeys in their identifying colours — 'black-red-violet-blue-white-yellow dots'. The raven flies on, his progress still realised in active verbs — 'sees,' 'flaps', 'flies', 'croaks', 'looks down'. As in 'The Abbey Theatre Fire' the purpose of the poem is to delight, to create a vivid portrait of a bird in flight within an identifiable landscape. Again the notion of being a spectator is central; the journey and its accompanying experiences are brought before us through the perspective of the bird, the protagonist in the drama of his flight. The technique is theatrical and cinematographic. Section II is written in the same manner, a delightfully exact account of the raven's return journey. Like 'The Abbey Theatre Fire' the poem ends by changing its perspective: the concluding lines describe not the bird's flight but the encroachment of Dublin suburbs onto the historical landscape, in particular the eighteenth-century aristocratic past. 'The sewered city with a rump of suburbs/Has reached the pillared gate in its expansion . . .' The imagery of defilement of profiteering builders, of concrete mixers that 'Vomit new villas' destroys the images of the pastoral. The elegiac tone grows, not from the raven but from the poet. He has imagined the raven's flight in terms of dynamic perception and sensation. Now all that is spoiled, replaced by unattractive sights and sounds:

> The shadow is going out from Cypress Grove,
> The solemn branches echoing our groan,
> Where open carriages, barouches, drove:
> Walnut, rare corktree, torn up by the machine.
> I hear the shrills of the electric saw
> Lopping the shelter, unsapping the winter-green
> For wood-yards, miss at breakfast time the cawing
> Of local rooks. Many have moved to Fortrose.
> They hear in my lifted hand a gun-report,
> Scatter their peace in another volley.
>   I stare:
> Elegant past blown out like a torchère.

The poem's rhythm has lost much of its liveliness and self-delighting quality. The relationship between the poet and nature, including the local rooks is also disrupted. The raven's flight is an imaginary one. In reality the rooks have left and are fearful of the poet. His 'stare' is an inanimate response, numbed by what has happened, incapable of the vivid variety of Section I. The past is blown away in an abrupt, stunning movement.

The world is active for Austin Clarke in this volume. Poem after poem is enlivened by a similar controlled energy. The sun in 'A Mile from Tallaght' brings the world to life; in 'Japanese Print' the near collision of a swallow and a heron is illuminated in the delicate pattern their movements inscribe in the sky:

> Both skyed
> In south-west wind beyond
> Poplar and fir-tree, swallow,
> Heron, almost collide,
> Swerve
> With a rapid
> Dip of wing, flap,
> Each in an opposite curve,

Fork-tail, long neck outstretched
And feet. All happened
Above my head. The pair
Was disappearing. Say I
Had seen, half hint, a sketch on
Rice-coloured air,
Sharako, Hokusai!

In 'A Strong Wind' a succession of active verbs captures the effects of the wind; the imagery, naturalistic and accurate, advances to its conclusion: 'All Ireland raced'. In the descriptive narrative, 'Beyond the Pale', the poet and his wife drive south, enjoying the sights that the poet selects and renders in concrete imagery. Landscape and history are of equal interest, both brought alive as part of a journey. The movement of energy lies at the heart of this poetry, the imaginative energy of the poet himself as it is revealed in the style and syntax. Clarke brings the external world to life through his own dramatic empathy. In 'Beyond the Pale' he shares his delight with his wife, Nora; shows his civilised, intelligent response to the countryside and to its historical past. The quality of companionship adds to the poem's pleasantness. And pleasure, delight in the observed details, places and people of the country are the primary intentions of the poem. As elsewhere in the book – in 'Looking Back' where he delights in the passing parade of 'Young girls, slim, rounded in slacks', or in 'Richmond Hill' where he records a love-scene with an English girl and makes it a fable of Anglo-Irish relationships, or 'Medical Missionary of Mary' where Sister Michael tumbles off her bicycle – Clarke records with delight in his own skill with language and rhythm, his ability to bring incident to accurate life. His more personal autobiographical poems, 'From a Diary of Dreams' and 'Guinness Was Bad For Me', are written in the same comic spirit of delight and occasional mockery. The world, as it were, is on display. In the pubs the men are actors in a familiar, delightful ritual; the language is jocoserious, both realistic and mocking:

Men elbow the counter in public-houses, drink
Their pints of plain, their chaser, large or small one,
Talk in the snug, the lounge, nod gravely, wink fun
In meanings, argue, treat one another, swallow
The fume, the ferment. Joyful, self-important,
Soon all are glorious, all are immortal
Beings of greater day, hierophants; . . .

The fact that he himself was unable to enter into such masculine rituals causes him to construct another, contrasting scenario, a solo performance

with nightmarish elements: 'I could not drink their fill.' 'I rode the
bolster, picturing wall/Filmed upward, upward, to the ceiling: spool-fall/
To nothingness'. The poem's real story is the account of John Power,
a 'fellow-exile' in England who became a legend in his own lifetime for
his drunken exploits. His progress from one disaster to another, each
rendered in images of the bizarre, climax in his atavistically motivated
sacrilege:

> A Chalice brimming with wine of Goodness
> Came down to take his thirst from him. Hatred
> Of Protestant service held him, splintering
> Reason. His parents, pinched by a bad winter
> Had been evicted. An urchin, near open fire,
> He heard the story blaze. The Royal Irish
> Constabulary had marched beyond the byre,
> With baton, carbine. Seven shots were fired
> At Heaven. Bailiffs with crowbar, battering ram,
> Broke down the clay wall, tin-mended door, the jamb:
> Unionist landlord watching from his lake-lodge.
> John saw through fog a gold-ringed finger podge
> A blessing. In his fury to break faith,
> Despoil, he grabbed the astonished Graal, emptied
> It: then, sack-clothed, devil-tailed, unkempt,
> Tried to escape . . .

Like a figure in one of Clarke's cycloramic plays he undergoes a rapid
series of adventures, an episodic decline into 'the big Asylum' in Wexford.
   'From A Diary of Dreams' also emphasises experiences that are irrational and abnormal. The dream world by its very nature disrupts time
and space; the dreamer undergoes experiences in unpredictable and illogical ways; the underside of the mind is revealed.

> Hurrying out of memory, impure things
> Come back, the past, the present, intermixed.
> I loiter in the now-and-then, am bi-located
> A saint, victim of diabolical tricks:
> Dublin is London, elbowing rossie, bloke,
> Chaff with me; the dead return, disturb my sleep,
> Seeing them again, what can I do but weep?

'The under-mind is our semi-private part.' Sexual desires lurk in the
unconscious, 'below in the pit of us', below being both genital and psychological. Clarke's emphasis is explicit; the image of the naked goddess,
satyr, Priapus, the processional dildo not only anticipate some of the

classical references in *Mnemosyne Lay in Dust*, in *Orphide*, and in *Tiresias*, but echo the sexual allusions in the early narrative poems. 'Loins are the ages/Unknown to us'. Sexuality is a persistent force throughout human history, suggested in cave drawings, in mythology, in prehistory. In 'lawless dream' his youth returns with its burden of sexual guilt and its fascination with literary accounts of 'the culprit below': 'Dreams of salt pillar, incest, pederasty'. Classical literature attracted him for its sexual content: 'All of Greece/Hid, feminine: I dream of the Golden Fleece'. The Clarke-Jason identification is pubic.

Clarke's 'Diary of Dreams' is in part the diary of a dirty old man except that, more importantly, it is a candid expression of the sexual responses of age: the scene with his Dolly bird is consciously pathetic; the scenes with the Bloomsbury prostitute, with Isolda and Avril have the vacuity of an interrupted dream. The poem is self-indulgent, a facile account of material already found in *A Penny in the Clouds*. But there is an element of preparation in these half-confessions, these admissions of private sexuality; they clear the way for the more explicit revelations of *Mnemosyne* and the more direct narratives in *Orphide*. 'Diary of Dreams' is more effective when it turns from naughtiness to reality, from the land of dream to the garden of Bridge House:

> Down below, my twenty bobbers
> Under the lauristinus. Blackbird hobnobs
> With starling, chaffinch, blue tit. All of them waiting.
> Then comes a young thrush, so virginal, she might
> Have hurried out of the honeysuckle light,
> Still variegated by the mottling shade,
> Could I but count each brindle, spice-brown spot,
> Or find, in cut-glass, the silver-topped pepper-pot,
> That speckled her and daintified such white,
> Castor of cinnamon.

The poem concludes as it began and this cyclical form, with slight variations, suggests the nature of dreams that 'Expose themselves, linger in Jesus Lane'; they come and go in accordance with some hidden force and poets can use their uncensored nature to reflect on issues normally kept from the light of day. In Clarke's poem the self is dramatically present as a participant in a succession of scenes, their focus. One may note, in passing, that the use of delirium in these dream poems and the device of hallucination foreshadows the methods used in *Mnemosyne* and are also present in 'Martha Blake at Fifty-One'.

Different kinds of drama are found in 'Burial of an Irish President' and 'Martha Blake at Fifty-One'. The former, occasional poem is based on an actual event when Dr Douglas Hyde, a former President of Ireland, died and his funeral service was held in St Patrick's Cathedral. Because he was a Protestant, Catholics with the exception of Austin Clarke and the French Ambassador, remained outside. In that pre-Vatican Two era Catholics were expected to get permission from their priests if they wished to attend a Protestant religious service. The poem is remarkable for its detachment and distancing. Clarke might justifiably have expressed anger or contempt at the dishonour shown to a President and to a man who had served the country well as founder of the Gaelic League, professor, scholar, historian, translator, folklorist, and at the craven behaviour of the VIPs who refused to enter the cathedral. Its silence on such matters makes their absence palpable. The poem's distancing effect is achieved in the careful provisions of the setting. The 'brangling' of the funeral bell indicates the poem's direction in its harsh sound and in its meaning — 'upraiding' — and in the use of the derisive pun 'pat tricks' to describe the behaviour of the Catholic members of Government and of the professors in cap and gown. Inside the Cathedral by contrast, the coffin rightly draped with the national flag and decorated with wreathes and flowers, testifies to the solemnity of the occasion: a country's President is being honoured and mourned 'in the gloom'. The sense of inadequate ceremonial grows in the poem in the references to the small number of mourners, to gloom, to the striking allusion to 'the desperate tomb of Swift', another Protestant and Irish patriot, and to the drooping flags of regiments who fought in famous battles in the Crimean and Boer Wars. The hollow connecting rhymes of 'room', 'Coombe', 'gloom', 'tomb', 'booming' and 'doom' mock the absence of appropriate honour.

The opening seventeen and a half lines describe the setting. Into it step the participants. The contrast in the alternating pattern of the poem is between 'Two Catholics' inside and the VIPs outside, ridiculed for their failure to respond to 'the simple word/From heaven'.

> The simple word
> From heaven was vaulted, stirred
> By candles. At the last bench
> Two Catholics, the French
> Ambassador and I, knelt down.
> The vergers waited. Outside:
> The hush of Dublin town,
> Professors of cap and gown,
> Costello, his Cabinet,
> In Government cars, hiding
> Around the corner, ready
> Tall hat in hand, dreading

> *Our Father* in English. Better
> Not hear that 'which' for 'who'
> And risk eternal doom.

The detachment that characterises 'Burial of an Irish President' is found also in 'Martha Blake at Fifty-One', a portrait poem of an ordinary woman who is both an individual, a type of pious Catholic, and the poet's sister. It is a lament for a way of life that brought little comfort and a protest against the life that it realises with accuracy and care. The poem is organised around a series of ironic contrasts of soul and body, piety and mysticism, dream and reality. The first seven stanzas introduce Martha Blake who feels at one with the Church and receives Communion every day.

> To her pure thought,
> Body was a distress
> And soul, a sigh. Behind her denture,
> Love lay, a helplessness.

Two stanzas provide the prosaic details of her life. Despite her apparent spirituality, she suffers severe physical discomfort: 'the bile/Tormented her'. Even the holy statues and pictures in her room seem to disapprove: the Virgin 'sadly smiled', 'The Saviour showed/His heart, daggered with flame', St Joseph is 'disapproving', the new Pope is 'frowning', and night and day she experiences 'dull pain'. The dichotomy of soul and body persists. Martha is fleshbound but has spiritual aspirations. She is so weighed down by the physical that she is 'soul-less' and in the end her body, 'ill-natured flesh', despises her soul and denies her the spiritual consolation of Christ's body in the sacrament of communion.

So far the contrast is between Martha's piety and her physical suffering. In the next seven stanzas the contrast is between her adolescent reveries about saints in Spain and Italy and the true nature of their religious experiences, between her bodily discomforts and their erotic mysticism, between physical pain bounded within the body and physical pain that is transcended and transmuted by religious energy. Martha's day-dreaming about the saints resembles the adolescent enthusiasm that Clarke describes in *Twice Round the Black Church*.

> High towns of Italy, the plain
> Of France, were known to Martha
> As she read in a holy book. The sky-blaze
> Nooned at Padua,
> Marble grotto of Bernadette.

> Rose-scatterers. New saints
> In tropical Africa where the tsetse
> Fly probes, the forest taints.

The equal value given to the details reduces all to the level of the nameless 'holy book'. No discrimination is made between degrees of religious experience; everything is made part of Martha's sentimental response. In an absurdly superficial manner she thinks of St Teresa suspended in levitation and fails to comprehend the saint's tormenting visions of the Devil who appeared as 'an abominable form' and as 'a most hideous little negro, snarling'. Martha thinks of 'small black boys in their skin'. Teresa's vision of hell is also blurred in Martha's account:

> a muddy passage
> That led to nothing, queer in shape,
> A cupboard closely fastened.

What Teresa related reads as follows:

> The entrance, I thought, resembled a very long, narrow pasage, like a furnace, very low, dark and closely confined; the ground seemed to be full of water which looked like filthy, evil-smelling mud, and in it were many wicked-looking reptiles. At the end there was a hollow place scooped out of a wall, like a cupboard, and it was here that I found myself in close confinement. But the sight of all this was pleasant by comparison with what I felt there. . . . this place that looked like a hole in the wall, and those very walls, so terrible to the sight, bore down upon me and completely stifled me. There was no light and everything was in the blackest darkness.[2]

Martha does not mention the suffocation and darkness. Clarke not only presents her sentimentalised picture but in his description of her physical distress and her experience of the separation of soul and body presents ironic parallels with Teresa's account of intense pain and her passionate sense of division between the physical and the spiritual. In the mystic's account the disharmony of soul and body is radiantly transformed in moments of ecstatic union with Christ. Martha has no knowledge of Teresa's ascetic and mystical works, the *Way of Perfection* and the *Interior Castle* which give positive instructions in the spiritual life. Her daydream transports her beyond 'the walls of the parlour' and beyond the contingent reality of Garville Road, Rathgar: 'Soul now gone abroad'. Her imagined journey recalls the journey made by St Thérèse of Lisieux to Italy where she found, as Martha recalls, that:

> Our Lady's Chapel was borne by seraphs,
> Three leagues beyond Ancona.

Both Ancona and Loreto were visited by St Thérèse who, like Teresa of Avilla, experienced visions. Clarke again makes an ironic contrast between the visions of a saint and the day-dreams of a pious woman. The places mentioned in Martha's 'visions' are not only stopping places on Thérèse's pilgrimage but places associated with many saints. By mentioning that Martha had read of them in 'a holy book' Clarke criticises the watered-down hagiography of popular texts and reveals Martha's notions of sanctity. The irony in the following stanza, which is balanced between Teresa and Martha, underlines the dichotomy between historical actuality and Martha's morality.

> Teresa had heard the Lutherans
>   Howling on red-hot spit,
> And grill, men who had searched for truth
>   Alone in Holy Writ.
> So Martha, fearful of flame lashing
> Those heretics, each instant,
> Never dealt in the haberdashery
>   Shop, owned by two Protestants.

Clarke's technique of alternating between versions of the experiences of the mystics and Martha's limited comprehension of them is present also in the two climactic stanzas that come at the centre of the twenty-four stanzas of the poem. The first refers to St Teresa's ecstatic union with Christ. By not trying to present Martha's perception of the transverberation of Teresa, Clarke indicates that it is beyond her capacity to understand.

> In ambush of night, an angel wounded
>   The Spaniard to the heart
> With iron tip on fire. Swooning
>   With pain and bliss as a dart
> Moved up and down within her bowels
>   Quicker, quicker, each cell
> Sweating as if rubbed up with towels,
>   Her spirit rose and fell.

Teresa describes the experience as follows:

> He was not tall, but short, and very beautiful, his face so aflame that he appeared to be one of the highest types of angel who seem to be all afire. . . . In his hands I saw a long golden spear and at the end of the iron tip I seemed to see a point of fire. With this he seemed to pierce my heart several times so that it penetrated to my entrails. When he drew it out, I thought he was drawing

them out with it and he left me completely afire with a great love
for God. The pain was so sharp that it made me utter several moans,
and so excessive was the sweetness caused me by this intense pain
that one can never wish to lose it, nor will one's soul be content
with anything less than God. It is not bodily pain, but spiritual,
though the body has a share in it — indeed, a great share.[3]

The next stanza describes the mystical union as related by St John of the
Cross, founder with St Teresa of the Order of the Discalced Carmelites.

> St. John of the Cross, her friend, in prison
>   Awaits the bridal night,
> Paler than lilies, his wizened skin
>   Flowers. In fifths of flight,
> Senses beyond seraphic thought,
>   In that divinest clasp,
> Enfolding of kisses that cauterize,
>   Yield to the soul-spasm.

St John's mystical poetry envisions the love of Christ for the individual
and the love of the individual for Christ in terms of the union of 'the
bridal night'. This stanza describes the physical transformations of the
mystic union: his wasted flesh 'Flowers', his senses soar beyond the
highest order of angels, the closest to God. St John's poem, 'The Living
Flame of Love' is the song of a soul that has reached a highly perfect
love; its four stanzas refer to transient, intense union experienced by
one advanced within the state of transformation. The union is expressed
in a metaphor of purifying flame.[4]

The very next stanza, returning to Martha, emphasises her inability
to relate to such intensity. She recoils from it, rejecting it. Instead of
the mystical union she experiences terror and palpitations of the heart;
instead of the musical ecstasy, 'the fifths of flight', her ears are 'full of
sound'; instead of ecstacy she is 'Half fainting'. 'Cunning in body had
come to hate all this'. Instead of a spiritual union with Christ achieved
by means of the body, her body 'stirred by mischief/Haled Martha from
heaven', away from God.

The themes of failure and disappointment exist throughout the poem
which declines now from its expressions of erotic-religious ecstasy.
Martha's body is afflicted by indigestion. 'Ill-natured flesh/Despised her
soul'. Her physical suffering does not bring her spiritual gains. She grows
'Tired' of her daily religious practices, even forgets the promise of
redemption made when Christ became man in Bethlehem. The banality
of her life is bleakly rendered:

Tired of the same faces, side-altars,
　　She went to the Carmelite Church
At Johnson's Court, confessed her faults,
　　There, once a week, purchased
Tea, butter in Chatham St. The pond
　　In St. Stephen's Green was grand.
She watched the seagulls, ducks, black swan,
　　Went home by the 15 tram.

Ironically, her religious apathy is associated with St Teresa's order, the Carmelites, and her final disappointment is also connected with the Carmelites, specifically with the Third Order. By becoming a member of this lay order Martha thinks she will be spared 'long purgatorial pain' and that in death she will be arrayed in 'Brown habit and white cord'. She prepares for death also by borrowing money for her grave. These fancies include the notion

　　. . . of a quiet sick-ward,
　　　　Nuns with delicious ways,
　　Consoling the miserable: quick
　　　　Tea, toast on trays.

The reality, as the last six stanzas calmly show, is medical neglect, noise, sleeplessness, anxiety, — 'O how could she be saved' - institutional regulations, a lack of compassion, further bodily discomforts, spiritual death. Ironically she is refused daily communion. In her last days she is distracted: 'How could she pray to God?' The nuns have allowed an Amusement Park to be set up in the field beside the hospice.

　　Unpitied, wasting with diarrhoea
　　　　And the constant strain,
　　Poor Child of Mary with one idea,
　　　　She ruptured a small vein,
　　Bled inwardly to jazz. No priest
　　　　Came. She had been anointed
　　Two days before, yet knew no peace:
　　　　Her last breath, disappointed.

That final word, understated and exact, sums up the poem. It is one of Clarke's best poems: sustained in manner, disciplined and exact in rhythm and language, controlled in its intelligent and telling contrasts.

　　Linguistic virtuosity also characterises Clarke's 'free variations' of Irish poems in section II of *Flight to Africa* which begins with 'Mabel Kelly' and ends with 'Song of the Books'. Turlough O Carolan's original poem, depending mainly on the assonance of stressed syllables, has lines of varying length, with end-rhyme, both assonantal and consonantal, and a varied four stress pattern.

> Ciabí a mbeith se (i) ndán dó
>   A lámh dheas fháil faoi n-a ceann,
> Is deimhin liom nárbh eagal bás dó,
>   Choidhche go bráth ná in a bheo bheith tinn.
> A chúl deas na mbachall fáinneach, fionn,
>   A chúm mar an 'ala is gile (a') snámh air a tuinn:
> Grádh agus spéis gach gasraidh Máible shéim Ní Cheallaigh,
>   Déad is deise leagadh i n-árus a cinn.[5]

The rhyming groups are disyllabic, with the first vowel long and stressed, and the second unstressed (ndán dó: lámh dheas; bás dó: bráth ná). He also uses assonance (bachall: ala) and consonantal rhyme (tuinn: cinn). In line seven each stressed vowel of the first half of the line assonates with the corresponding stressed vowel of the second half:

> Grád gus spéis gach gasraidh:
> Máible shéim Ní Cheallaigh,

And there are other vowels and consonants corresponding with one another throughout the stanza. The result is a fluid musical pattern that suits the poet's manner of eloquent compliments. The flow of sounds that carries his enthusiasm disguises the deficiencies of the descriptive details. This reliance on sound over sense is one of the main differences between Irish assonantal poetry and English translations. Since the sounds cannot be duplicated in English, one of the essential features of the poem's meaning cannot be realised by the same means.

> Whoever is fated
> to find his right hand under her head
> I am certain is in no fear of death
> or of ever in his lifetime being sick.
> Her lovely back has blond ringlet curls,
> her side is like the whitest swan swimming on the wave:
> Beautiful Mabel Kelly is the love and desire of every lad,
> most beautiful teeth lie in the house of her head.

The conventional imagery of these poems, seen here in the last four lines, sound affected in English, whereas in Irish the music of their saying hides their familiarity. The Irish habit of using two words of closely similar meaning and of building emphasis and nuance into the structure of the sentence, into the word order, increases the translator's difficulty. Clarke's nine line stanza, replete with imaginative energy and sensual delight, reflects the spirit of the original.

> Lucky the husband
> Who puts his hand beneath her head.
> They kiss without scandal
> Happiest two near feather-bed.
> He sees the tumble of brown hair
> Unplait, the breasts, pointed and bare
> When nightdress shows
> From dimple to toe-nail,
> All Mabel glowing in it, here, there, everywhere.

The lines vary in length from two to four stresses, the rhythm, supporting the meaning, sometimes interrupts the iambic pattern, to focus attention – 'the breasts, pointed, bare' – or to accentuate the enthusiastic praise – 'here, there, everywhere'. Assonance is not central to the poem's success, but the concrete imagery helps to compensate for the decrease in assonantal music.

Clarke's version of Aogán O Rathaille's 'Aisling Meabhuil' and 'An Aisling' also illustrate his ability to depart significantly from the original while retaining the spirit of the Irish poem.[6] The former, a typical vision of the Pretender, Prince Charles Stuart, as an avenger who will free the Irish from oppression, has a forceful rhythm and emphatically identifies the military prowess and destructive progress of the champion.

> Crithid flaithis, bailte, daingen, ranna, is compaoi a gcéin,
> D'fheartaibh arm-ghaisge an aicil gheallas ceart a tseanrigh phléidh.

'The heavens, towns, strongholds, continents, seas, and distant camps will tremble,/At the marvellous feats of arms undertaken by the hero who fights for the rights of the old king.' Clarke changes the imaginative resonance of the poem by giving it a European dimension with his imagery of 'great ships of the line', 'the earthworks at Namur', towns under siege, and 'our Catholic Majesty near Brest'. His 'Aisling' follows the structure of the original, absorbing some of the details of language and of place, to produce a poem different in mood and with its own distinctive assonance. An 'Aisling' has several of the conventions of the genre: the poet meets a host of fairy women in a magic mist; they light three candles as a sign of the return of the rightful king to the three kingdoms. That promise is made in symbolic terms, not in terms of the militaristic emphasis of 'Aisling Meabhuil'. The Irish poem has a dignified pace; its fluid five-stress lines complement the poet's mood of melancholy recall.

> Lasaid sin trí coinnle go solas nach luadhim
> Air mhullach Chnuic aoird Fhírinne Conallaigh ruaidh,

Leanas tar tuinn sgaoth na mban gcochaill go Tuamhuin,
Is fachtaim-se dhíobh díograis a n-oifige air cuaird.

They lighted three candles, their hands white to the thumbnail
And I followed that band to the Shannon through pollen of
    Thomond.
Quickly they climbed Knock Firinne. Rock shaled and summered
As I asked Queen Eeval what task had summoned them.

Clarke's version misses some of the magic and mystery of the original.
In this case assonantal requirements deflect him from the poem's simple
dignity which a more literal translation tends to reveal.

They light three candles with a brightness I cannot describe
On the top of the high hill of Firinne in red Conello
I follow the band of hooded women over waves to Thomond
I ask them about the devotion contained in their visit.

Of the two more lively poems that he translated, 'O Rourke's Feast'
and 'The Song of the Books', the former reflects the extravagant humour
and burlesque of the original. Carolan's 'Pleúraca na Ruarcach' has a
jaunty rhythm and an almost parodic use of assonance and alliteration
in its four stress line.

Pléaraca na Ruarcach do chuala gach duine
    Dá dtáinic a's dá dtiocfaidh a's da maireann riamh beo;
Bhí seacht bfichid muc, mart agus caora
    Dhá gcasgairt don ghasraidh gach aon lá.

Clarke imitates the emphatic exaggerative style but his longer, denser
line has difficulty in matching the rhythmic gusto of Carolan.

Let O'Rourke's great feast be remembered by those
Who were at it, are gone, or not yet begotten.
A hundred and forty hogs, heifers and ewes
Were basting each plentiful day and gallons of pot-still
Poured folderols into the mugs. Unmarried . . .

But his version of Tomás O'Sullivan's 'Amhrán na Leabhar', 'Song
of the Books', has the characteristic Clarke delight in the sounds, tex-
tures and rhythms of language and the characteristic density of the factual
and the literal. The original is about a poet-teacher's loss of books when
the ship that was transporting them from Derrynane to Portmagee foundered in the harbour of Derrynane. It is a simple *ambrán* in three-stress
metre and with an uncomplicated use of assonance. Clarke leaves out
much of the original, touching upon it occasionally for some details and

outlining the poet's career from the introduction to his *Songs*.[7] He transforms the poem into an evocative lament for cultural loss. There is more than ocean water broken in the storm that he mimics in the sounds and rhythms of the opening lines.

> South-westerly gale fiddled in rigging;
> Furled canvases in foam-clap, twigged
> The pulley-blocks. Billows were bigger.
>   The clouds fell out.
> In Madmen's Glen, snipe hit the grasses,
> Rains in Tralee had towned their phantoms
> While rocks were thrumming in the passes.
>   Below a shout
> Was whisper and among the boulders
>   The frightened trout
> Were hiding from the beaten coldness.
>   Soon every snout
> Was gone. The noises of new shingle
> Along the coast had swept the Kingdom
> Of Kerry, league by league, from Dingle
>   In whirlabout.

The stanza is complex in its patterns of sounds, its end-rhymes, its alternation between the dominant four stress lines to lines of two stresses (4,8,10,12,16). As in the original the end-rhymes are grouped in triplets with each fourth line having a different and recurrent rhyme. Clarke's technical skills are one feature of the poem's achievements, but it has a deeper and more comprehensive significance. His portrayal of O'Sullivan, a poet, a collector of books and manuscripts, as the 'Last of the race of the walking school-masters' is a portrait of the age. Clarke extends O'Sullivan's list of lost texts and thereby increases its significance.

> 'Macpherson, Voster's *Arithmetic*,
> Dowling's *Book-keeping*, Walter Binchie
> On Mensuration, Patrick Lynch's
>   *Geography*,
> Another by Deignam, Comerford,
> O'Halloran's *Ireland*, well-worded,
> Compass and scale, right angle, surd,
>   Every degree.
> Virgil and Homer long I kept,
>   *De Catone*,
> Sermons, *The Pentaglot, Preceptor*
>   Upon my knee,

With *Tristram Shandy* and *Don Quixote*,
Crook'd Aesop's *Fables*, *Reynard the Fox*.
Our Rapparees behind their rocks,
Drowned in the sea.'

'All's in my head', declared Tomás Ruadh O'Suilleabháin. He is the bearer of tradition, the educator of his people. His list of books reflects the range of the hedgeschool master's knowledge: Latin, Irish, English, Geography, History, Mathematics. Clarke's poem moves purposefully to outline seventeenth- and eighteenth-century intellectual, religious, cultural, literary and social history. It includes efforts on the continent to add a Gaelic voice to the Counter-Reformation and the role of the hedge-school in bringing classical and Irish learning to the people. Significantly the impressive and varied list of books above, ranging from MacPherson to Aesop ends with a reminder of the reality of political life in the reference to Rapparees, those outlawed soldiers, who stayed behind to carry on the fight after the Flight of the Wild Geese in 1691.

The intellectual and cultural activities could not hold back the inexorable decline of Gaelic Ireland. The defeat of Hugh O'Neill and Hugh O'Donnell at Kinsale, followed by the Flight of the Earls in 1607 signalled the collapse of the old order in the face of Tudor and Elizabethan aggression that included a determined assault on Catholicism. With the departure of the Gaelic chieftains, the people were deprived of leadership and the poets had lost both position and patronage. Many scholars also left for the continent, as Clarke's poem shows, in the references to the work of the Counter-Reformation in the third last stanza. There he draws a poignant contrast between scholars abroad — Florence Conry who edited *Sgathán an Crábbaidh* (1616), *The Mirror of Faith*, Luke Wadding who plotted successfully to get aid from Rome for the Catholic Confederation, Aodgh MacAingil, who wrote *Scathán Shacramuinte na hAithridhe* (1618), *The Mirror of the Sacrament of Penance* — between the conditions under which they worked and the much different conditions of scholars at home.

All Belgium shone on Gothic column
    Through leaded pane.
Monks laboured at printing press, selected
Type for a Gaelic or Latin text.
Our poets stumbled to the next
    Mud cabin through rain.

The religious works produced at Louvain, and other Irish colleges abroad, sought to strengthen Irish Catholic resistance to Protestantism by publishing literary, religious and historical material that emphasised the antiquity of Irish Catholicism. At home the poets continued to lament the loss of their Gaelic patrons and to rail against the upstart, boorish English, Protestant settlers. They gave political allegiance after the accession of James I in 1603 to the Stuart cause in the belief that a Catholic king would understand and redress the wrongs done to them by Elizabeth I. But the seventeenth century produced disaster after disaster, including Cromwell's destructive campaign and the massive confiscation of lands. In despair the poets could only hope in the possibility of a Stuart restoration with French help and divine assistance. Clarke's Irish translations — partly because of the influence of Daniel Corkery's *Hidden Ireland*, partly because of his interest in the *aisling* for its literary conventions and its revelation of the Irish reluctance to deal realistically, as opposed to allegorically, with female beauty — are predominantly drawn from this period of political and cultural collapse in which poets voiced the distresses of an afflicted people.

The 'Song of the Books' is particularly sensitive to these contexts. Its next three stanzas outline the lives of a number of seventeenth and eighteenth century poets — Donnchad Ruadh MacConmara, Piaras Fitz-Gerald, Eoghan Ruadh Ó Suilleabháin, Andrias MacCraith, and Seán Ó Coileán — with particular representative emphasis on MacConmara. Clarke draws upon incidents related by MacConmara in his long poem *Eachtra Giolla an Amaráin*, 'The Adventures of a Luckless Fellow', about a voyage to America, not Newfoundland, 'the Land of Fish', as Clarke says, although that is the title of another poem by MacConmara.[8] His 'best poem', reputedly written in 'Hamburgh', is the magnificent poem of exile, 'Bán Chnuic Éireann Oigh' — The Fair Hills of Holy Ireland'. The easy religious affiliations of several of these poets, to which Clarke refers, who became Protestants but then reverted to Catholicism, is part of their unhappy attempts to cope with the chaotic conditions. The stanza on Eoghan Ruadh O Suilleabháin that follows sums up the highlights of his rakish career; he was for a while a 'jolly jacktar', fought with Admiral Rodney in the West Indies, and celebrated victory with a poem in English called 'Rodney's Glory'. All the poets mentioned in this stanza, O Suilleabháin, MacCraith, O Coileáin, wrote aisling poems and Clarke's next two stanzas pays them the tribute of quiet, lyrical imitation.

> At dawn, in a wood of sorrel, branchy
> Dew-droppy, where sunlight gilded sapling
> And silvered holly, or by the bank
>   Of Brosna, Moy,
> Our poets saw a woman smiling.
> Her tresses, bright as celandine,
> Could not conceal her pure white side,

Was she from Troy?
Or was she Venus whose fondled breast
    Could never cloy?
Juno, half turning from her rest,
    To buss and toy?
That Queen of Carthage in hot haste —
Blue robe to her naked waist —
To make Aeneas in her embraces,
    Husband and roy?

Four stanzas outline the unpleasant realities of the lives of the hedge-school teachers — wandering scholars, tradition bearers, bilingual, Catholic, memorialists of their people. Some of the nicknames Clarke gives them have been taken from MacConmara. He notes the historical event that marked their lives: the departure of the 'first Earl of Lucan', Patrick Sarsfield, and his men to become 'soldiers of fortune' in the armies of Europe. Once again Clarke makes an effective contrast between lives lived abroad and those lived at home. These contrasts are additions to O Suilleabháin's poem. As often before Clarke finds parallels between eighteenth-century Ireland and his own time: 'We live again in a Penal Age'. The attention with which he has developed his picture of the age and of outcast poets demonstrates his sympathy with those whose experiences of hardship, and whose combination of poetry and scholarship together with their tenacious hold on tradition, resembles his own life and work.

Chapter 10: *Mnemosyne Lay in Dust* (1966)

In *Mnemosyne Lay in Dust* Maurice Devane enters a mental asylum, received treatment, and is released. He suffers severe depression and degradation, but is not totally lost. Mnemosyne, the goddess of Memory, may lie in dust, in a state of barren disconnection from existence, but she can be brought back to life again. The story of that recovery is the substance of the poem, but the process is obscure, its stages not clear to Devane himself; its origins and motivations lie below the level of consciousness. Most of the poem is taken up with descriptions of Devane's shocking encounters with a treatment that seems to be abnormally violent and yet is supposed to be therapeutic. Much of the poem, too, is devoted to dreams and hallucinations in which one may detect the underside of Devane's mind, the subconscious fears and desires, in which one may sense some of the hidden tensions that have caused his breakdown and whose resolution will lead to his recovery. Among the reasons for Devane's breakdown are sexual frustration, spiritual despair, and guilt.

The young, Clarke declared in 'The Loss of Strength', remembering his journeys through the countryside in search of a congenial imaginative landscape, must have solitude to feel the strength in mind. But in *Mnemosyne* 'Terror repeals the mind'. Unlike its more objective predecessors, such as 'The Loss of Strength' and 'The Hippophagi', the poem is a psychological narrative about curative trauma; its direction is inward, its purpose cathartic. Its progress may be interpreted from a variety of incidents, including shock therapy, drugs, dreams, hallucinations, enforced rest, and self analysis. In fact it is less concerned with recovery and more concerned with creating the experience of incarceration and institutionalised violence. It thrusts the experience in front of us without warning and with hardly any explanation. The reality was appalling and it is Devane's appalled encounter with mental breakdown and with cruel and degrading methods of treatment that the poem seeks to realise. Devane's recovery may have been helped by the treatment, but in Clarke's memory his restoration owes much more to his tenacity and creativity. The major sign of his recovery is the contrast between his withdrawal from reality in the opening section and his firmer grasp on reality at the end of the poem, but in terms of poetic energy and depth it is clear that the poem ends weakly, that the demonstration of normality is much less convincing than the evidence of abnormality. Memory, for Devane, is not totally inactive. He keeps contact with reality and with the past, and thereby with his own identity, through fleeting recollections of past experience and through reverie and dream. But the contact becomes more assured and positive by the end of the poem which moves away from Devane's distorted perceptions and terrors to a calmer, self-delighting appreciation of what he knows and sees.

In section I Maurice Devane is out of touch with the everyday world; places, people, and events do not impinge upon his consciousness. While Ireland commemorates the feast of St Patrick with 'unsaintly mirth', he is taken to St Patrick's Hospital and watches 'in vain/National stir and gaiety/Beyond himself'.

> For six weeks Maurice had not slept,
> Hours pillowed him from right to left side,
> Unconsciousness became the pit
> Of terror. Void would draw his spirit,
> Unself him. Sometimes he fancied that music,
> Soft lights from Surrey, Kent, could cure him,
> Hypnotic touch, until, one evening,
> The death-chill seemed to mount from feet
> To shin, to thigh. Life burning in groin
> And prostate ached for a distant joy,
> But nerves need solitary confinement.
> > Terror repeals the mind.

The immediate contexts are not propitious, as references to 'spike ends', to 'ribald gloom/Rag-shadowed by gaslight', and to harpies make clear. Devane, however, does not 'suspect' what lies ahead. The ominous signs are increased in the allusions to the hospitals: to Steevens Hospital, founded by Madame Steevens, who, as Clarke recalled in *Twice Round the Black Church*, was said to have been 'punished by Heaven for some grave offence' and to have 'given birth to a child with a pig's head'. Hence the reference to 'A monster with pig's snout, pot-head'; to St Patrick's Hospital, founded by Jonathan Swift, whose 'jest' refers to his well-known lines

He gave the little wealth he had
To build a house for fools and mad:
And show'd by one satiric touch
No nation wanted it so much . . .

In this 'Mansion of Forgetfulness', the self is disinherited and cut off from reality. *Mnemosyne* portrays the mental, spiritual and imaginative dimensions of that disruption; it is about loss of memory and what that involves and it is at the same time about the recovery of memory and what that means for sanity, for a viable relationship with reality.

On arrival at the asylum Devane is assailed, stripped of his clothes and plunged into a steaming bath in a sequence of events that resemble incidents in a 'Keystone' film. The very experience he most feared in section I, of being unselfed, is thrust upon him in a whirling, suffocating descent in Section II until 'All was void'. The transition from numbed withdrawal to helpless victim is abrupt and terrifying, the descent into nightmare instantaneous and overwhelming. His terror is rendered in the language of aggression: 'Sprang', 'shocked', 'flung', 'plunged'; and he is surrounded by other victims of similar outrage whose reactions he 'saw, heard, while he is 'Drugged in the dark, delirious'. Metaphors of colliding locomotives, noisy crowds, cries of 'Murder! Murder!' and images of monstrous births and police brutality illustrate his plight.

Maurice Devane is a victim; although withdrawn and passive he is handled with aggression. Clarke advances the ironic notion that terror is curative and seems to justify treatment that is seriously lacking in compassion and seriously indifferent to the possible consequences of such institutionalised violence on the minds and emotions of the patients. In other poems Clarke has exposed examples of cruelty and insensitivity; in *Mnemosyne* that concern turns with determination upon the humiliation and cruelty meted out to those unfortunates who were committed to the care of mental institutions and became victims of an inhumane system so that their private anguish was exacerbated by the ways in which they were treated; their inner derangement was matched, if not at times surpassed, by the unbalanced responses of those whose job it was to mind them and protect them, and if possible to cure them.

The first sections of the poem show Devane's discovery of what he has not suspected. He realises that he is being spied upon, discovers in dread that people die in this place, and becomes afraid of a particular madman who mutters curses as his hands make the motions of knitting, while others in bizarre pantomime 'gibboned his gestures'. It is an abnormal and degrading place. Unable to remember who he is, he is challenged by a nameless figure who urges him to think, to activate his memory and thereby overcome the anonymous blankness in which he exists.

> He wondered who
> He was, but memory had hidden
> All. Someone sat beside him, drew
>   Chair nearer, murmured: 'Think!'

Devane's dejection and anonymity, externalised in the imagery of the colourless dormitory, are poignantly realised when he looks 'in dread' at the empty ward and is then 'Saddened by the boughs' in the garden.

Later in the poem the garden becomes a potential source of growth, a mysterious place whose significance must be understood, if Devane is to rediscover his identity. But at this stage, in section III, when he is still involved in the process of discovery, still seeing and assessing the place into which he has been thrust, it is associated with his intense feeling of being alone. Within its distanced confines he sees other inmates, 'pallid dots' with 'faces gone blind', wandering aimlessly. Their mindless movements are mimicked in the recurrence of the same rhyme in the final word of each stanza and in the repetition of virtually the entire first stanza as the last. Like Devane, they are 'Lost to mind' and pitifully bereft.

> But all were looking up
>   At the sky
> As if they had lost something,
> They could not find.

Devane's inability to make contact with them adds to his feeling of abandonment.

It is one of the fundamental and frightening ironies of his situation that the medical attendants should be the source of terror. Dr Leeper is 'always ready to leap', Dr Rutherford is 'mad-eyed', Mr Rhys, the superintendent, is 'ready to pounce' with 'his band of seizers'. They drive him into paranoia, which is pathetically illustrated in his foolish preoccupation with the position of his soap-dish and in his references to 'spy', 'trap', 'foes' and 'suspicions'. He tries in vain to remember who he is.

> He seemed to know that bearded face
> In it, the young man, tired and pale,
> Half-smiling. Gold-capped tooth in front
> Vaguely reminded him of someone.
> Who was it? Nothing came to him.
> He saw that smile again. Gold dot
> Still gleamed. The bearded face was drawn
> With sufferings he had forgotten.

He cannot make sense out of what he observes: 'He seemed to know' . . . . 'Nothing came to him'; even the evidence of suffering fails to jog his memory. All he has is the present: 'Sunlight was time', in which he can 'in a dream' make uncertain, fleeting contact with his past. He can associate sounds from the laundry with similar sounds heard as a boy outside the wall and the 'enormous' gate of the Richmond Asylum in Grangegorman, now known as St Brendan's Hospital, but when, 'memory afoot', he tries to understand the connection, his mind produces a different memory:

> Out of the morning came the buzzing
> Of forest bees. The tiger muzzle
> Gnarled as myriads of them bumbled
> Heavily towards the jungle honey.
> A sound of oriental greeting;
> Ramàyana, Bhagavad-gita,
> Hymnal of Brahma, Siva, Vishnu.
> 'The temple is gone. Where is the pather?'
> A foolish voice in English said:
> 'He's praying to his little Father.'

Present and past are joined together by auditory and visual images. The references to the Sanskrit epic of Rama which tells of the incarnation of Vishnu, to the sacred writings of the Hindu, and to a triad of Hindu gods work both positively and negatively. The associations are religious, imaginative, and sensual but the sequence disintegrates into a nonsensical exchange about the 'temple' and the 'pather'. That the word for father in English, Sanskrit, and other languages, is etymologically the same provides a linguistic connection whose significance is not known to Devane. The tiger image for the bees associates them with Siva who sits on the skin of a tiger or panther; the missing 'n' in 'pather' strengthens the association and indicates the inadequacy of Devane's response. Hidden in the apparently meaningless exchange we may detect his anxiety about religious loss, sexual inadequacy, and the death of his father. The bees in their purposeful search for 'the jungle honey' and in their association with potent oriental literature and mythology embody an intellectual and imaginative openness and indicate Devane's unconscious need for such nourishment. His loss of appetite is a manifestation of the collapse of his will: 'Mind spewed,/Only in dreams was gluttonous'. The missed opportunity becomes more evident later when Devane dreams of the phallic columns; Siva, god of fertility and destruction, is symbolised by the lingam.

Section V continues the pattern of dreams and visions. The first dream corresponds to what Sigmund Freud called the brothel dream in which the dreamer passes from one gilded salon to another, mounts marble staircases and gazes down where billiard tables wait for him, but where a policeman watches. Devane sees himself in an opulent social setting in which there are 'fashionable women', but his enjoyment is spoiled by the presence of 'a silent form'; he goes up a marble stairs but is conscious of 'The Watcher' in 'uniform', 'a policeman' who is 'frowning'. In stanza two he again mounts the steps, 'alone', his movements reflected in mirrors, and looks down upon billiard tables, 'playerless', but sees 'the Watcher' frowning, 'Casting the shadow of a policeman'. The dream represents the possibility of sexual adventure but it also represents Devane's sense of exclusion and guilt. The second dream is more explicitly sexual. Devane sees 'Gigantic' phallic columns, 'Templed, conical, unbedecked', and recognises 'the holy ictyphalli' (sic). 'He worshipped, a tiny satyr,/ Mere prick beneath those vast erections'. This dream affirms the importance of sexuality; in classical literature and mythology the phallus is an object of religious worship, carried, for example, in processions in honour of Dionysus. Devane's dream reveals his need for sexual fulfilment, for unashamed openness about sex, his need for reassurance that his need is not evil. His vision of a cult of phallic worship validates the normality and naturalness of sexual desire. In his dream he worships the phallus, but experiences feelings of sexual inadequacy.

The dream of children running to Eden is also liberating. 'Love/ Fathered him with their happiness'. This dream also is oriental, or 'eastern', as Clarke called it when he described these 'visions'.[1] In their entry through the gate and into the garden the children affirm the positive force of these images for Devane. His dream of Mnemosyne in dust takes place in a context of terror and helplessness. Instead of the marble stairs and the sexual promise of the brothel dream, he is forced to climb 'spiral steps/Outside a building'. In 'a cobwebbed top-room', littered with 'bric-a-brac', and in a moment of heightened sensation he arrives 'stumbling/ Where Mnemosyne lay in dust'. It is a devastating discovery, a confirmation of the 'Olympic doom' that propelled him forward. The contexts are made of images of waste, abandonment, and disorder. This dream also externalises Devane's sense of deprivation and radical loss. Mnemosyne, goddess of Memory, is also the mother of the Muses and Jupiter's consort. Her significance is therefore comprehensive. When she lies in dust, the sources of creativity have dried up.

> Always in terror of Olympic doom,
> He climbed, despite his will, the spiral steps
> Outside a building to a cobwebbed top-room.

There bric-a-brac was in a jumble
His forehead was distending, ears were drumming
As in the gastric fever of his childhood.
Despite his will, he climbed the steps, stumbling
    Where Mnemosyne lay in dust.

The phantasy of being a Republican guerilla compensates for Devane's inactivity and asserts his nationalism in a way that compensates for his passivity. He can act out deeds of daring — 'darted', 'Unbarracked', 'relieved', 'fought to the last bullet', and then escaping easily. But the 'melancholy/Man', another reproachful figure, brings him back to his real predicament.

The other brooded: 'Think.' His gaze
Was so reproachful, what was his guilt?
Could it be parricide? The stranger
    Still murmured: 'Think . . . Think.'

The syntactical ambiguity between 'His gaze' and 'his guilt' raises the possibility that the stranger is a mirror image, but unrecognisable because representing suppressed anxieties. In Jungian terms he is the shadow, standing for unknown or little-known attributes and qualities of the self. He may be detected in several places: in the 'Someone' who sits beside him in section II and urges him to 'Think!' in order to remember who he is; in the unrecognisable 'someone' in the mirror in section IV; in the mirrored self, the reproachful policeman, and the stranger in section V who urges him to 'Think'; in the 'someone' being suffocated in section VII; even in the 'terrible Twangman' in section X, who is not merely insistent or reproachful but sternly judgmental and punitive — the 'he' here is also slightly ambivalent — and in 'Echo', his accomplice in search of Onan. To the other's insistent 'Think . . . Think' in section V Devane reluctantly wonders if he could be guilty of 'parricide'. In section IV there was no clear answer to the question, 'where is the pather?'. Self-confrontation is part of the process of renewal. Devane must use his mind, must activate his memory, in order to discover his identity, to recognise where he is, to face up to his inner fears and psychic needs in order to regain psychological balance. To kill your father is to experience a radical sense of alienation and loss, and to be confronted with the infertility of Mnemosyne. To be fatherless is to be cut off from the past, from the sources of creativity, and to be unable to discover one's personal identity. The Hindu deities are all male, all father figures, all sources of fertility. When Mnemosyne mates with Jupiter the Muses are born and it is the muse of Poetry who will eventually lead Devane out of the asylum.

There is a progression in section V from one exclusion to another, through an increasingly stronger sense of guilt to the final accusation of parricide. Even the happy vision of the Lebanese children dancing to an earthly paradise serves to underline Devane's remoteness from innocence. At first obliquely and then explicitly connected with sexuality, the dreams represent Devane's deep-seated feelings of sexual inadequacy and his powerful unconscious need for sexual fulfilment.

Section VI begins with a catastrophic sense of loss when he imagines that his mother and sisters die. It is a manifestation of his radical insecurity.

> One night he heard heart-breaking sound.
> It was a sigh unworlding its sorrow.
> Another followed. Slowly he counted
> Four different sighs, one after another.
> 'My mother,' he anguished, 'and my sisters
> Have passed away. I am alone, now,
> Lost in myself in a mysterious
> Darkness, the victim in a story.'
> Far whistle of a train, the voice of steam.
> Evil was peering through the peep-hole.

The 'heart-breaking sound' is his own heartbreak at the news of each death and the desolation of each of the dying, a whole world of sorrow released in a sigh. With the death of his father and now the removal of each member of his family he is totally bereft of familial support. The realisation is transfixing, registered in slow motion as he feels the shock of each individual death and experiences an even greater sense of aloneness. The references to the train's whistle, the sound of steam from the laundry, and the evil eye at the peep-hole of his cell surround the moment with the earlier portrayals of his observations on his surroundings. They, too, contribute once again to his feelings of being removed from human contact. 'I am', he concludes, 'alone, now.' To be lost in one's self is to be in a subjective maze, in a darkness that shows nothing outside the self. To be a victim in a story is to be a fiction and thereby placed beyond human contact. It is a form of death. Devane's panicked reaction only results in further violence as warders carry him to a padded cell.

He is moved from one kind of incarceration to another, from a cell in which his clamour for help finds a response, however unfeeling, to one where he cries in vain; from the heat of his palpitations to cold stillness; from a 'mysterious darkness' to an even more 'private darkness'.

> Lock turned. He cried out. All was still.
> He stood, limbs shivering in the chill.

In Clarke's poetry objects sometimes act independently: 'Key turned. . . . Lock turned'. It is an adult version of childhood fears in which solid objects cannot be trusted and may be frighteningly active. Their autonomy heightens the individual's feelings of vulnerability and terror. Devane's helplessness is seen in uncontrollable physical reactions – 'Suddenly heart began to beat/Too quickly'; in the activity of inanimate objects – 'key turned', and in the actions of nameless agents – 'Body was picked up'.

Devane fears he is dying, then mistakes the padded-cell for a grave. His cries are made in vain, but recovering he realises where he is: 'reason had returned to tell him'. He has been 'shocked back/To sanity'. In darkness, silence, and the horror of the padded-cell, when he seems not only to have lost all sense of place and time, and to have been thrust beyond human contact, to be most deprived of imaginative, spiritual and intellectual support, reason, sanity, and memory return.

> Lo! in memory yet,
> Margaret came in frail night-dress,
> Feet bare, her heavy plaits let down
> Between her knees, his pale protectress.
> Nightly restraint, unwanted semen
> Had ended their romantic dream.

This is not another hallucination, but a clear memory of a recent reality and a rational assessment of what happened to their love. The theme of sexual inadequacy and its opposite, sexual pleasure, is identified. While Devane's neuroses have other sources as well, the failure with 'Margaret' was the immediate cause of his breakdown.[2] By the end of section VI Devane had reached the pit of degradation, awakening to the 'greyness' of the leather walls and to the knowledge of his own incontinence.

> He turned, shivering, all shent.
> Wrapping himself in the filthied blankets,
> Fearful of dire punishment,
> He waited there until a blankness
> Enveloped him. . . When he raised his head up,
> Noon-light was gentle in the bedroom.

Since religion provides no comfort, only in sleep can Devane escape from the abject miseries of his condition, but nothing protects him when awake, nothing makes life worth living. He yearns for death as a release, 'but delicately clinging/To this and that, life drew him back'. His loss of appetite, a manifestation of this death wish, makes him weaker, causing attendants once again to act aggressively towards him. When they force-feed him, it is a terrifying ordeal: 'The noise and fear of death, the throttling./Soon he lost all consciousness'.

Section VII details the ignominies Devane suffers in his feeble state; each stanza is a precise account of what it feels like to want to die, to be forced to accept nourishment through 'a tube forced halfway down/ His throat', to struggle desperately against the attendants, to lose consciousness, to awake and be grateful to find 'The counterpane/Gentle with noon and rid of pain', but then to be subjected again to the violent administration of Dr Leeper who 'sprang, incensed', at him until he becomes dissociated from the experience, as though 'it was someone else/ The men were trying to suffocate'. Appropriately the section ends with ominous images of 'Midnight follies', mad shrieks, storm flashes, as Devane's memory produces the saving word 'Claustrophobia' and he is taken to the dormitory.

Originally published in *Night and Morning* as 'Summer Lightning', section VIII vividly exposes the state of the 'madmen', as the storm that flashes in the previous section lights up the dormitory.

> The heavens opened. With a scream
> The blackman at his night-prayers
> Had disappeared in blasphemy,
> And iron beds were bared;
> Day was unshuttered again,
> The elements had lied,
> Ashing the faces of madmen
> Until God's likeness died.

The experience is of blinding exposure — 'beds were bared', 'Day was unshuttered' -- and divine retribution. That the blackman should disappear 'in blasphemy' while saying his prayers suggests punishment. That fearful consequences may follow is also conveyed in that 'elements' lie. By its vividness the lightning changes night into day and by their state of mindlessness the madmen are excluded from divine grace; for them the elements of bread and wine are not changed into the body and blood of Christ. The storm for those in whom 'God's likeness' has died is a sign of His rejection. Excluded from His grace, they fear His wrath.

As though suddenly illuminated by the lightning the next two stanzas describe the delusions of several of the madmen. The clarity with which their distorted perceptions are described exposes and isolates their condition, but the cold objectivity of the language is alleviated in the final explanatory and appealing stanza:

> When sleep has shot the bolt and bar,
> And reason fails at midnight,

Dreading that every thought at last
Must stand in our own light
Forever, sinning without end:
O pity in their pride
And agony of wrong, the men
In whom God's image died.

The monosyllabic bluntness of the first lines restate the condition of the mad and recall Clarke's references to Piranesi's architectural fantasies as images of the lost state and spiritual despair of those for whom reason has failed:

> . . . when in a succession of delirious dreams, I hurried for months along grim corridors, up and down dark treacherous stairways, in and out of the wards and closets of great institutions, I was always trying to remember something that I had forgotten. As I rushed, in dreams, through those institutions, full of miserable and thwarted souls, all of us in frenzy trying to escape, yet imprisoned as if within the horrible architectural fantasies of Piranesi — in which ingenuity is bolted and barred by itself — there came at last that distant consolation:

> > Flight upon flight, new stories flashed
> > Or darkened with affliction
> > Until the sweet choir of Mount Argus
> > Was heard at every window,
> > Was seen in every wing . . .[3]

Clarke's cry — 'O pity in their pride/And agony of wrong, the men/In whom God's image died' — is deeply felt and emerges at a time in the poem when the horrors of the asylum and the dejection of the inmates have become compellingly clear. Section VIII, when the heavens open, bears witness to the price paid for intellectual independence, that 'pride' that places the men beyond redemption.

Section IX, at the centre of the poem, begins with a portrait of a particular madman, Mr Prunty, his fear of death, delusion of being a corpse, nightly defecation in bed. Devane, knowing that his own incontinence will produce a similar angry reaction, watches in fear. But now, in the depths of despair, when the warders christen him 'Dogsbody', in disgust, as though to mark his exclusion from participation in the communion of the faithful, Devane shows his connection with life itself: he hears the sounds of Dublin, the voices of the warders in conversation, the rustle of the familiar evening papers, and learns that Hawker has flown the Atlantic. This event which took place on May 18, 1919, is the first, and one of the few, events in the poem that can be dated. The passage has a positive, attractive tone: 'Dublin guff,/Warm glow', followed by a series of identifications, acts of recognition, not dependent exclusively on memory, but on the audible and the familiar: 'Stall-owners, bargains, in Thomas Street'. In this mood of calm attentiveness Devane is particularly drawn to, 'lulled' by, the tale 'Of the Gate, the Garden and the Fountain' that the warders repeat.

> The words became mysterious
> With balsam, fragrance, banyan trees,
> Forgetting the ancient law of tears,
> He dreamed in the desert, a league from Eden.
> How could he pass the Gate, the sworded
> Seraphim, find the primal Garden,
> The Fountain? He had but three words
> And all the summer maze was guarded.

In the Book of Genesis Eden's gate is guarded by a Seraphim. From a spring at the foot of the tree of life four rivers flow. To regain spiritual grace Devane must find the enclosure of the Garden, later identified as the Garden of Memory. The contexts which are soothing and hypnotic enable him to forget the miseries to which mankind is prone and to experience hope, to anticipate the possibility of gaining admission to Eden. He can dream of such renewal, but cannot find a way there, since 'all the summer maze was guarded'; but he knows the passwords.

His perceptions of others, as well as of the outside world, are significantly more rational. The warder, now seen in more normal circumstances, is equated with 'Reason, the master of ancient madness'. The warders have become the bearers of knowledge; they repeat the magic passwords, they have the keys by which Devane may be released. Section VIII gave a direct picture of the torments of the insane. Section X gives an oblique picture of people blissfully remote from actuality. Each of the first three stanzas evokes a state of security: the soldiers lie in the dark, contemporary events pass them by, they watch the high boots of the colonists. They are free because 'Justice cannot reach them'. The following lines specifically define justice:

> All the uproar of the senses,
> All the torment of conscience,
> All that twists and breaks.
> Without memory or insight,
> The soul is out of sight
> And all things are out of sight
> And being half gone they are happy.

They are not afflicted by spiritual crises or moral issues, they do not have to endure the torments of guilt, they exist in an unnatural state of detachment and fancy.

Devane, however, is subject to hallucination. One day 'his senses lied' and he imagined a man had been beheaded in the ward and thought it was John the Baptist. He is perplexed: 'no axe . . . no blood. How did it happen?' Accepting the evidence of his own eyes, he is baffled. The incident demonstrates that he is not fully recovered. 'Soon Mnemosyne made him smaller', taking him back to childhood, to his home, but the quiet, domestic scene is disturbed by the irruption of 'Madmen' crying 'Murder!' and a terrible 'Twangman' sits on his bed, muttering 'Hang him! Hang him!' These disturbing undercurrents of fear and guilt intrude upon the general calm of section X and Devane seeks solace in masturbation. His quest through shadowy, sinister streets, with Echo as a ghostly companion, prepares for the appearance of Onan.

> Often in priestly robe on a
> Night of full moon, out of the waste,
> A solitary figure, self-wasted,
> Stole from the encampments — Onan,
> Consoler of the young, the timid,
> The captive. Administering, he passed down,
> The ward. Balsam was in his hand.
> The self-sufficer, the anonym.

This solitary figure, rising from the waste on a night of full moon, is eerie and destructive. His is a perverse priesthood as he administers the 'balsam' of masturbation. Although he consoles, his relief is furtive, shameful, and associated with madness. That he 'stole from the encampments' connects him with the soldiers in the earlier stanzas and their state of numbed withdrawal.

Devane's recovery continues in the remaining sections (XI-XVIII). It is summer time. Tempted by a dish of strawberries sent by his mother, he 'Ate for the first time'. His physical recovery is accompanied by a gradual mental renewal, as he turns towards the magical Garden and Gate and dreams of the Fountain 'Glistening to the breeze, self-poised/ Lulled by sound'. Section XIII ends with the metaphor of unseaming a suture, which expresses Devane's release from the strait-jacket of the asylum, and with a promise of release: 'His soul' would be 'rapt'. His exercising with the 'imbeciles' in section XIV is also a form of release, since it is the first time he has been allowed to move freely; the jaunty rhythm and light-hearted mood, while part of a 'loony' world, cause Devane to forget 'his ancient sighs'; his ability to laugh is an indication of recovery. In the next section he sees the madmen objectively; they are his 'friends' who appear now in a congenial light. The behaviour of Dr Rutherford, the little Hindu, in section XVI is strange, but Devane knows how to deal with him. To his question, 'Do you believe in God?', Devane answers 'Yes', which suggests a confidence and composure previously absent. In relation to Devane's past despair it represents a major recovery of confidence. When asked if his Uncle George, who visits him, is wealthy, he lies and this too is evidence of his rationality, since he understands the reason for the question. He is now free to read, but cannot concentrate. Nevertheless, in section XVII, when he walks in Phoenix Park with one of the attendants, he has a firm grasp on the particulars of place and on external detail. He remembers where his family lives and recognises people that he meets. He is 'Behind invisible bars', since he has not been officially released, but his hold on reality and on his own past is sensible. When he walks up Steevens Lane back to the asylum his state of mind is notably different from what it was when he was taken there by taxi, when the same images and associations were present.

In section XVIII he is 'Rememorised' and has 'his future in every vein'. He is led forth, as Clarke writes in 'A Sermon on Swift', by Mnemosyne's daughter, Erato the muse of love poetry:

> Beyond the high-walled garden of Memory,
> The Fountain of Hope, the rewarding Gate,
> Reviled but no longer defiled by harpies.

His experiences in the asylum were a form of defilement. In his claustrophobic descent into the void of lost memory, lost identity, lost creativity, he suffered a defilement of body and spirit. Now 'goodness' is in the everyday, in contact with the ordinary; now he is part of what he merely observed in section I. He knows who he is and where he comes from. Natural objects — the garden, sunlight, the fountain, strawberries, flowers in Phoenix Park — have a positive, fertile force in the poem. They counter the negative elements: the ignominies of the asylum, the perceptual distortions, the mad terrors, the darkness, the images of dust and waste associated with Mnemosyne and Onan.

There is a pattern of contrasting images that relate to Devane's crippled sensibility. On the one hand are all the references to impeded movements that include not only the fact of his restriction within the asylum, but particular sensations of choking, throttling, suffocation, and sexual frustration. Closely associated with them are references to victimisation, aggression, the loss of consciousness, defilement, the loss of control over bodily movements, functions, and directions, perceptual distortions, the failure of memory, and the inability of the mind to function normally. On the other hand are all the references to unrestricted activity usually outside the asylum and in particular references to pleasing sounds, attractive smells, cleanliness, images of children running, peaceful settings, sleep, sunshine, all the references to the familiar and the ordinary in Dublin, and sexual allusions like the phallic columns and Margaret. What Devane suffers within the asylum is alleviated and eventually overcome by what he can recall, value, and anticipate. The contrasting qualities embody and contribute to the poem's emotional and moral significance and indicate what is involved in Devane's struggle to gain control.

At the heart of that struggle is the recovery of creative energy. *Mnemosyne* is a descent into the Underworld. The harpies together with images of darkness, descent and suffocation are at the entrance. Maurice Devane is involved in an archetypal journey of descent and return, an allegory of death and rebirth, the winter of loss followed by the summer of renewal, the disoriented imagination replaced by the rational imagination. The poem begins with references to the darkness wherein he was 'got' and comes to rest with references to the shining place in which his mother was 'born' and in that circle parallels the movement in 'Ancient Lights' from a 'darkness/. . . roomed with fears' to the effulgence of the sun's appearance in the conclusion. The pattern of contrasts outlined above supports this unifying shape. The creative force of sexuality is a central element in the replacement of barrenness. In the Dionysian procession it is the powers of creativity that are worshipped, not the phallus itself. Hinduism also had a phallic cult in which the ritual of sexual intercourse symbolised the creative bringing together of opposites. That love fathers Devane indicates that to be cured is to become capable of love. Mnemosyne is recovered in the single figure of her daughter, for it is love, sexuality, creativity, that have been absent and that now must enter Devane's life and transform his barrenness.

The resolution of his collapse returns him to what he knows, to what he can see and understand. In his recovered state his senses do not lie; he can experience through them what he acclaimed in 'A Sermon on Swift' in Aristotelian terms as 'Divine Abstraction'. No greater claims are made, but the serenity of his mood contrasts with the mad discordancy of the asylum. To walk calmly through the city is to experience life evenly and satisfactorily, away from the anxieties and trauma of the asylum. It is not an earthly paradise; the magic passwords turn out to be quite ordinary objects; even the Fountain fills into a 'horse-trough'. The significance of this definition needs to be understood. In a large sense Clarke's narrative of Devane's incarceration and recovery parallels the development in his poetic career from mythic narratives to realistic narratives, from the anguish of *Night and Morning* to the relaxations of *Flight to Africa*. 'Illusions had become a story'. *Mnemosyne Lay in Dust* is a major undertaking in Clarke's career, a determined reappraisal of past misery and shame. That its conclusion should be so literal and realistic is not surprising, but it is nevertheless a declaration of faith in the ordinary and an assertion of his preferred approach. His poetic career from 1955 to 1974 confirms its validity and integrity. That he would be 'reviled' was only to be expected, but while social alienation troubled Devane, it is not a major impediment for Clarke. In fact it was a bonus, a reason for persisting and he would do so on his own terms.

Chapter 11: Last Poems 1967-1974

The next two collections may be seen as transitional between the intensity of *Mnemosyne Lay in Dust* and the emphatic sexuality of the final collections from *A Sermon on Swift* (1968) to *Tiresias* (1971). The autobiographical emphasis of *Mnemosyne* continues in both, in *Old-Fashioned Pilgrimage* (1967), which is composed of material withheld from *Flight to Africa*, twenty-two poems in all, and *Echo at Coole* (1968) which has more than twice that number. They show a release of feeling that is unusual in the overall context of Clarke's work, as though the purgation of private pain in *Mnemosyne* enabled him to write more freely about himself, although not more profoundly or more searchingly, and to give freer rein to his opinions. The travel poems in *Old-Fashioned Pilgrimage*, 'Old-Fashioned Pilgrimage', 'Fiesta in Spain', 'The Paper Curtain', and 'More Extracts from a Diary of Dreams', express Clarke's delight in the sights and sounds of other countries. The title poem introduces the new persona of Clarke as elderly literary pilgrim, interested in the homes of nineteenth-century American writers. It has some autobiographical interest, such as the statement that Whitman and Emerson were liberating influences in Clarke's early years, or the association of Poe's 'pale consumptive girls' with Clarke's first wife. 'Fiesta in Spain' is a series of impressions of the cities, the religion, the customs, the food and the wine, which are written in a style of economical, unelaborated allusions. The style which takes pleasure in its descriptions of the passing scenes, is a measure of the poet's enjoyment. 'The Paper Curtain', an account of a visit to Yugoslavia, is similarly directed towards what was seen and heard along the way. 'More Extracts from a Diary of Dreams', which has the randomness of dreams, with rapidly shifting incident and bizarre detail, portrays Clarke as fearful traveller and aged lecher, but its mere listing of amorous adventures is dull.

Another aspect of the feeling of release is the readiness to express opinions, sometimes with insufficient thought, on a variety of topics: the war in Vietnam, Vatican Two, the EEC, Irish politics, social issues, sexuality, and other writers. The language can be vigorous, as when he writes about American bombings, or ironical, as when he writes about the Church's reinstatement of former heretics and freethinkers. 'A Statue for Dublin Bay' notes that dockers have collected £20,000 to erect a statue of the Virgin Mary at a time when the Church has begun to play down 'hyperdulia'. It is also ironical, Clarke notes, that workers have paid for the construction of a sky-scraper for their headquarters. 'New Liberty Hall' develops broad contrasts between rich and poor, capitalist and unemployed, the dedication of James Larkin and the luxuries enjoyed by his successors. 'Workers must scrape and skimp/To own so fine a skyscraper'. A number of poems focus on social issues. 'In O'Connell Street' places Clarke in close proximity to the event; we hear the gruff voice of a poet who comments on social injustice. The occasion is the 'procession' of 'poor people, shabby, ill-fed' who have been put out of their homes.

> They have been put out
> (But politicians are never put out)
> And housed in an old British barracks,
> Chill dormitory, one gas-stove, W.C.
> Men, women, apart.

Clarke's views on such matters never change; he always condemns injustice and cruelty, whether seen in the eviction of the poor, the discovery of an old woman suffering from hypothermia in 'Miss Rosanna Ford', or the consequences of clerical regulations, particularly in the area of contraception.

'The Pill' begins with the question — 'Must delicate women die in vain/ While age confabulates?' For Clarke this is the crux of the matter: the lack of urgency and compassion on the part of elderly, celibate clerics. It is, as 'The Redemptorist' bluntly makes clear, a matter of life and death. The shutter of his confessional becomes the lid of the penitent's coffin; her husband's act of love kills her. The true meaning of christianity is written in chalk on the streets of Dublin: 'Love, Joy, Peace', is a poem appropriately written to the rhythm of a Buddhist prayer-wheel.

Clarke finds greater freedom of expression in poems about sexual activity. A number of short lyrics, such as 'Song for Cecilia', 'Afterthought', and 'Nunc Dimittis', are light sketches of an old man's love for a young actress. They are 'serious trifles' in that they make his loss of potency into a verbal game. Their frivolity of manner, however, masks the seriousness of physical decline. 'Elderly men', Clarke says, remember:

> The faithless member
> And bless the naked,
> Adorable act,
> Sigh for lack of
> It.

The lyrics delight in word play, in puns, verbal ambivalence, unusual rhymes and homonyms. 'Our Love was Incorruptible' is an example.

> Women, avoid the bed advice
> Of priests, who tell you to add sum
> To monthly sum, avoid the foetus
> That shouts to everyone, 'Adsum!'.
> The rhythmic method can defeat us

The 'bed advice' that they should rely on the rhythm method of birth control is bad advice, as the arrival of the lively foetus makes clear. Clarke's delight in clever rhymes — 'foetus . . . defeat us' and 'add sum . . . 'Adsum!' — is another example of the emotional release of these poems.

> Hidden where not a soul can see, men
> Open with caution what is sent
> To lessen joy but keep back semen:
> Plain envelope without a letter.
> With careful fingers they unroll
> The treated, pearly, glistening letter:

While the lines convey the furtive nature of the transaction, the art seems to be wasted on a trivial matter. The rest of the poem, describing women's enjoyment of sex because the fear of pregnancy has been removed, shows a similar misuse of talent. The imagery of the battlefield is effective, as is the proverbial echo in 'give him an inch and he'll take an ell', where 'ell' means liberties, but the final couplet with its pun on 'yard' as both a measurement and a word for penis and its listing of methods of contraception is less effective.

> It's but a yard that they can capture,
> All pessaried, syringed, war-capped.

'Phallomeda', a Rabelaisian account of the attempted mating of the Irish god, Dagda, with the Grecian goddess, Phallomeda, ('laughter-loving') is a burlesque of Fenian stories in which a champion arrives from abroad to challenge the Irish heroes, and of Fenian romances in which a woman from the Land of Youth entices an Irishman to go with her. It is based on an Irish tale in which the Dagda tries to mate with the daughter of Indech but finds it difficult because his stomach is distended from too much food.[1] Clarke retains the incident of the gluttonous meal, changes the Irish girl to a Grecian goddess, and treats the incident in a broadly comic manner. 'Impotence', the final poem in *Echo at Coole* has many of the virtues of Clarke's lighter mode; the rhymes and puns are precise and witty and there is a complex of feelings, including frivolity, honesty and regret.

> Disarmed, I lie, a malcontent,
> Outside the white-and-crimson tent-flap
> Of idle love. I cannot tent
> That wound, for all is good intent
> And yet desire becomes more wanton
> With every failure.

Beginning with the disarmingly honest admission of being 'almost impotent', the poem proceeds to the verbal play of these lines, whose militaristic metaphor, reminiscent of Elizabethan word-play, describes the tension between sexual desire and the physical inability to engage in sexual intercourse, together with the paradox that failure induces greater desire. 'Must I want on?' He remembers former passion and the transitory nature of sexual pleasure. The poem combines romantic-erotic language with a no-nonsense imagery for the weakened penis — 'Enwrinkled', 'Booby' that 'can do no more than piddle'. The final couplet reiterates the theme of the opening lines. 'Regular verb' may be 'in the past tense', but Clarke persists, despite failure, as though his sexual predicament could be a metaphor for his dealing with life itself.

But the most serious poem about the value of sexual fulfilment is 'A Student in Paris', an updated, more mature handling of a theme previously deployed in 'The Straying Student' and a reaffirmation of *Mnemosyne*'s positive emphasis on sexuality. In this poem Maurice hurries to Paris with one specific intention: 'To rid himself of a celibate training'. The rhythm, the rhymes and the language bring a comic perspective on this serious young man who 'dreamed of pure romance' and whose devotion to female 'Dummies undressed in windows' is contrasted with the amorousness of Paris when he was deciding which of the three goddesses 'should have the Beauty Prize/For her white apples' and who hurries 'Faster than piston of mail-boat, night-train', a metaphor that both expresses and masks the sexual motivation of his profane quest. The long first sentence of ten lines articulates his romantic phantasies and finds them amusing. The reality is not the '*gested/D'amour*' that he has naïvely imagined but a financial transaction with a 'laughing and shameless', sexually experienced 'girl of seventeen' whom the 'patron' of 'a cheap wine-shop' provides, with some unconscious irony, 'behind a row/Of monastic bedrooms'. She serves his sexual needs with 'unexpected' speed and efficiency. Romance gives way to the realities of professionalism and Maurice becomes 'an earnest student/Of venery'.

The poem gives a comic account of his experiences with prostitutes in Paris. His phantasies become more practical as he lies 'expectant . . . dreaming of different ways'. He often ponders on Messalina and on other literary sources in Juvenal, who denounced her profligacy. Messalina becomes in his mind not only Empress of Rome, the third wife of Claudius, but a goddess of sexuality whose exploits he imagines in scenes that echo those in Juvenal's *Satires*.[2] The language of contest and of combat combine to render her sexual prowess.

> Knees up, she bore assault of privates,
> And, quickly, warrior-like, deprived them
> Of their advantage. Head down, gladdened
> In her arena, gladiator
> Would crouch: her legs went round his waist.

Puns, ambivalent terms and homonyms add to the image of Messalina's sexual relish. Her prayers to Jupiter for a divine lover heighten the portrait of her sexual appetite, as it invokes mythological accounts of Jupiter's metamorphoses 'as bull, swan, eagle' in his mating with humans.

Maurice's enthusiastic phantasies about Messalina give way to a calmer mood. 'The law of natural pleasure saned him'. The link with *Mnemosyne* is explicit. His joyful, relaxed mood as he searches for Erotica is a sign of that return to sanity in which sexual release has been an important contributing factor. The next lines refer to some of the most famous of French erotic writers, or their works, revealing Clarke's customary ability to suggest and evoke material that enriches the primary text. The 'Petit Trianon', built by Louis XV for his mistress, Madame du Barry, has obvious romantic-sexual associations. It was also much favoured as a place of retreat by Marie Antoinette. The literary allusions are a miniscule history of French erotica.

> Louys,
> Crebillon, the enchanted sofa
> That thrilled a Do-re-me-so-fa
> Under the farthingales of ladies
> Whose gallants whispered indecencies.
> Often he read Catulle Mendès:
> Impudent stories that shuttered day.

Pierre Louys' novel, *Aphrodite* (1896), is a vivid account of Alexandrian morals at the beginning of the Christian era; his *Chanson de Bilitis* (1894) glorifies sapphic love. Claude Crebillon wrote many erotic novels; Clarke slyly refers to *Le Sopha* (1740) which was so explicit that it may have caused Crebillon's imprisonment. Catulle Mendès also wrote many licentious stories; Clarke refers in particular to 'Roman d'une nuit' for which Mendès was fined and imprisoned.

Clarke's detached, amused view continues when he writes that Maurice 'worshipped, early and late/Imagining all to be priestesses'. This religion of love replaces the religious fervour of his clerical training. Amorous Roman, sophisticated French erotica, all are transformed in his imagination to priestesses of love. Like Lucullus who was famous for spending vast sums of money on a single meal, Maurice devotes himself exclusively to 'One dish'. Financially impoverished by that single-minded pursuit, he goes back to Ireland 'with only his return/Ticket, five francs, a Juvenal'. The tone becomes more judgmental: he is 'too young to weigh the medieval/Degrading of Phallomeda'. Her 'votaries' are prostitutes who degrade themselves in homage 'to what is called unholy', that is, to what is denounced by the Church, in a perverse ritual by which they make the 'street a temple, bidet a throne'. In this appraisal Clarke places Maurice's excited, romantic sexuality in more sober contexts.

'A Student in Paris' is less emblematic than 'The Straying Student'; it does not personify the liberating experiences in a single person, nor does it emphasise the guilt of the celibate, his 'dread' of clerical teaching. The judgment is in terms of his inexperience and youthfulness. The amused, self-mockery as the older poet looks back at his earlier self is quite different from the serious tone of 'The Straying Student'. It relates a young man's notion of sexuality in terms of sexual athleticism, phantasy and erotic readings. The poem keeps its air of detached enjoyment, reflecting it in the characteristics of the enthusiastic innocent, the rhythms and the rhymes. It is one of many portrait poems in these two collections.

The portrait poems include Irish poets, like Yeats, AE, Stephens, George Darley and F.R. Higgins, and foreign poets, like Pound, Frost, Neruda, Hopkins and Rousseau. Some identify the predicaments of particular figures: Robert Frost's age, George Darley's melancholy, Hopkins's neglect. Others are qualified tributes: Clarke appreciates Yeats's use of the philosophic system of *A Vision* but doubts the value of his 'rhetoric'; he enjoyed the lifestyle of Mayo in the company of F.R. Higgins but was frustrated by its sexual puritanism; he summarises his initial unfair opinion of Pound but admires his dedication and endurance. The tributes often imitate the style of particular poets. The poem on Lorca, written in a compact, formal style, evokes the poet's poetic and personal worlds. 'Pablo Neruda' creates the poet in the style and imagery of the poem: 'how could I know him, if not by song?'

> The ancient forests
> Of his metaphors,
> Creeping soap-tree,
> Honey palm,
> Swan with black poll,
> Dire anaconda
> In water-hole,
> Near Aconcagua,

The portrait of George Darley is worked out in greater detail and with sympathetic account of his temperament. The first eight lines outline his life: his appearance, career, and the impression he made on others; these are followed by some particulars: his weepy letters to Miss Mitford, his indulgent grandfather, and his shrinking from the earthier sides of life. Part II develops a portrait of a delicate recluse. Clarke had less rapport with W.B. Yeats. The portrait of Yeats in the Savile Club is wickedly comic. Yeats is magisterially confident, Clarke is unimpressed but civil. When the would-be critic asks about the reality behind Yeats's love poems, he is sternly rebuffed:

> 'Mr. Yeats,
> In order — as it were — to understand
> *The Wind Among the Reeds*, those exquisite
> Love lyrics, can I venture to ask what is —
> If I may say so — their actual basis in
> Reality?'
>   How could I know a married
> Woman had loosened her cadent hair, taken him,
> All candlestick, into her arms?
>   A stern
> Victorian replied:
>   'Sir, do you seek
> To pry into my private affairs?'
>   I paled.
> The poet returned. His smile kept at a distance.
> 'Of course you could suggest — without offence
> To any person living — that . . .'

Part of the pleasure of this poem is its ease and flexibility of development, its mocking tone, and subtle characterisations. It is one of three poems about Yeats. 'The Centenary Tribute' concentrates on Yeats's house, not the man, assembling images and allusions from the poet's early work. 'The Echo at Coole' reflects briefly on the uncertainties of the poetic career, on the importance of persistence, and on writing as a process of discovery. Yeats's echo poem, 'The Man and the Echo' also questions poetic endeavour and postulates persistence as a virtue. Clarke knows that he too, must 'still hope, still body on'; the only guarantee of the rightness of what he does is writing itself. The final 'Yew' alters the 'you' of the question. It is associated with graveyards and with sturdiness. Death, as Yeats's poem says more rhetorically, is inevitable, but the work, as Clarke also says, can be sturdy and enduring.

'Rousseau' is a more sophisticated portrait than the others; here image and allusion resonate with the fuller version of events found in his life and works. The poem's suggestive use of imagery outlines his progress from 'awkward boy' to romantic, as he escapes from the influence of 'the decrees of Calvin' and wanders through Savoy. His stay with Madame de Warren is lightly evoked. It was she who:

> taught him
> A measured prose, good manners,
> Correctness when he waited
> Upon her. Folios sought
> Him, music. Late on a November
> Night, Madame, lifting a skirt-hem,
> Smiled, beckoned him upstairs

The poem moves lightly and easily and has a more attractive manner than the denser style of his F.R. Higgins poem in which the narrative is weighed down with the sheer amount of material, much of it unnecessary.

> At darkfall, we dropped in
> To a clay cottage where an elderly couple,
> Poor, belaboured by a monthly rent, were raffling
> Their donkey, to talk a while and take a drop.

In between the literary allusiveness of 'Rousseau' and the lumpy emphasis of 'F.R. Higgins' is the judicious illustrative detail of 'Miss Rosanna Ford', that is both factual and evocative. 'Aisling' itself over-does its use of the conventional detailed descriptions of the genre.

Two of the most effective poems in these two collections express Clarke's delight in nature. 'The Last Ditch' is a lament for flowers that have been sacrificed to progress:

Mare's tail that must have pined
A million years to be pine
Or spruce, young reed and flag
That helped me when spirit flagged.

'On a Bright Morning' has the kind of clarity, precision and skill that Clarke is capable of even when he seems in danger of writing badly.

A blackbird sat on a sun-spot
Warming his wings. Down by the bridge,
Flying from our elm, fat pigeon
                Had slowly got
                Himself into hot
Water. Along the garden walk
The scattered crumbs still lay.
Up in a pine, magpie was talking
Too much. I whistled in vain, for the sparrows,
After a dust-bath under the rose-buds,
Had gone on a holiday
To the river bend. I saw them play
        A game of 'Shall we?'
        'Yes, Let's', beside the shallows,
Then feather the drops to spray.

'Letter to a Friend' is a personal response that brings together some of Clarke's interests and concerns in his final years. It has a tone of familiarity.

                What can I say?
Local affairs are much the same.
Swallows are railing and our robin
Thinks we'll have snow. Hotels still rob
Our visitors. Grave-diggers are
On strike. Death loses dignity . . .

The friend has the consolations of his changing views in Venice but Clarke too has his consolations. He is an Irish 'Carpaccio':

For something has happened to this eye,
Since it discovered homonyms.
All things shine now, all have nimbus,
Nature displays nimiety;
Though dampness lodge the grain,
Vague shadows move around in greyness,
A cloudy lid hide Ireland's eye.

Clarke's discovery of homonyms was a mixed blessing, resulting some-times in a delightful play of rhyme, but sometimes in a lapse of taste, or a willingness to sacrifice meaning for the sake of a rhyme. Yet it is the spirit of the statement that is important: despite the losses of age, the lack of money, the bad weather, the shoddy local affairs — the strikes, the unemployment, the destruction of Georgian houses — the poet finds satisfaction in his work. 'I am consoled despite old age/And pen in need of book-reviews'. The best evidence of that is the air of easy achievement in this poem, which is not just a matter of homonyms, of 'robin' . . . 'rob', of 'August' . . . 'august', of 'gondola posts' . . . 'postcard', but of measured fluency and control, the easy punning of 'Swallows are railing', meaning gathering on railings and complaining, the intimate fancy of 'Our robin/Thinks we'll have snow', and the apparent humour of the lines about the relatives having to bury their dead, in which the disjointed phrases break the flow of the description, cutting the humour short:

> relatives must scab,
> Pass picket, shovel in their dead
> With tears, pass picket again.

Even the packed lines are part of the poem's mode of familiar address: things do not have to be explained, since the friend can readily under-stand their meaning. They register events from a shared world of outlook and experience.

It is just that relaxed openness that produces both the best and the worst poems of these two collections. None of the poems convey a sense of commitment or of urgency, none search within the self for additional depths of insight. The travel poems, except for the impressionistic 'Fiesta in Spain', are often dull. The literary portraits sometimes imitate the style of other writers effectively, but sometimes the style is merely a pastiche. The amorous lyrics fleetingly capture aspects of an old man's love. The political and social satires are usually effective but do not extend Clarke's achievements in these areas beyond similar poetry in the Fifties. Faults appear throughout the collections: the pedantic list-ings, as of religions and sects in 'The New Tolerance' or of vegetables in 'Lactuca Prodigiosa', the jarring homonyms, the lapses in taste, the super-ficial comment. Too many poems are casual reflections on incidental and largely unimportant topics. The poems that stand out, such as 'A Student in Paris' or 'Rousseau' do so because of their relative greater depth and intellectual and imaginative sophistication; a few personal poems quietly dramatise the conditions of age; one comes across 'Impotence' with a renewed appreciation of Clarke's predicament and courage. The lively rhythms of 'On a Bright Morning' express a fine attentiveness. Even the rakish humour of 'In the Rocky Glen' attests to his imaginative vigour and readiness to speak frankly and amusingly of sexual matters. In fact, while the release of feeling and of opinions is the force most poems have in common, the emphasis on sexual freedom is dominant. It is the force within and behind a large proportion of the poems, both those that fail and those that succeed. It is derived from the opening of *Mnemosyne* to the expression of personal issues, is part of the confidence and relaxation that Clarke experienced in these years, and prepares for the concentration on sexuality itself which is the central issue of all the final collections.

It is almost true to say that Austin Clarke concludes his poetic career with a surge of creative energy. Six long poems — 'A Sermon on Swift' and 'The Disestablished Church' in *A Sermon on Swift* (1968), 'Orphide', 'The Dilemma of Iphis', and 'The Healing of Mis' in *Orphide* (1970), and *Tiresias* (1971) — indicate how active he was towards the end of his life. At the time of writing *Tiresias* he was also revising and adding to *The Sword of the West* and the other early narratives. His career comes full circle as he prepares his *Collected Poems* (1974) for publication. His last published poem, 'The Wooing of Becfola' (1974), salutes the freedom and delight of the imagination. Even the theme of sexuality in these long poems receives a refreshingly comic treatment. Clarke is mercifully free from the feelings of guilt and shame that clung to much of his earlier treatment of sexual matters.

The new outlook is invoked in 'A Sermon on Swift' which commemorates the scatalogical side of Swift's work.[3] That the poem should be called a 'sermon' is justified for several reasons. Clarke delivered a lecture during the Swift Tercentenary Conference, April 1971, from the pulpit of St Patrick's Cathedral. It is also a jest in that the theme of both the lecture and the poem is irreverent and therefore somewhat inappropriate to the ecclesiastical setting. The poem is also personal, in part a statement of identification with Swift, the 'chuckling rhymester', who observed reality closely, enjoyed 'a quip/Or rebus' with his friends, and suffered during the:

> Night-hours when wainscot, walls, were dizziness,
> Tympana, maddened by inner terror, celled
> A man who did not know himself from Cain.

It identifies, too, with a man who was sexually indiscreet, particularly in old age, was sometimes despondent, sometimes enraged, and carried on a war of words with Church and State. Clarke's lecture concludes with an assessment of the qualities he admired in Swift's poetry.

> Plain, direct, sensible, outspoken, and devoid of ornament, the
> verse of Swift has not lost its appeal for us. It gives us intimate

glimpses of his puzzling personality; it expresses instantly his likes and dislikes with a grace and vehemence which hold us to the page. . . . We must accept its contradictory moods and fits of honest rage. Juvenal, in his notorious Sixth Satire, denounced in wanton detail the profligacy of Roman ladies of fashion. Swift is sometimes as ferocious in his denunciations of the frivolity of Augustan fashion and, with an illogicality which is difficult to understand, he dashed down on the page, with exact quill, his remonstrations against female functions, mingling sheer disgust with, if I may say so, a comic relief . . .[4]

Clarke's poem brings the whole man into view and in particular those aspects of his life and character that the scholars tended to ignore.

> They spoke of the churchman who kept his solemn gown,
> Full-bottom, for Sunday and the Evening Lesson,
> But hid from lectern the chuckling rhymester who went,
> Bald-headed, into the night, when modesty
> Wantoned with beau and belle, his pen in hand.

It is this unbuttoned figure and what he represented that Clarke would commemorate. In his lecture Clarke points out that while Swift was writing 'his witty complimentary verses' to Stella and Vanessa, 'his subconscious was brooding on its own darkening depths'. The scatological poems, Clarke argues, are 'really tributes to the Goddess Cloacina . . . In them Swift expresses the centuries-old Augustinian tradition of earthy disgust'. In his poem Clarke mockingly invokes this goddess.

> Ascend,
> Our Lady of Filth, Cloacina, soiled goddess
> Of paven sewers. Let Roman fountains, a-spray
> With themselves, scatter again the imperious gift
> Of self-in-sight.

The 'imperious gift' is nakedness, with the genitalia frankly exposed. The vigorous tone dismisses prurience and recalls those scatological poems in which Swift imagines a young man's disgust at 'female functions'. Clarke also must take 'privy matters' for his 'text', but Swift's disgust expressed in poems about Celia, Corinna, Strephon and Chloe, is not his. He has always enjoyed the 'gay mockery', the 'satire', the 'impudence and scepticism', the humour and the irony of Swift's writings. 'Women', he admits, 'are unsweet at times', but who can 'resist/The pleasures of defaulting flesh?' The flesh which one might fault, because of its unsweet functions, also gives and receives pleasure, just as male flesh does. The references to Rabelais and to Clarke's ancestor, Archbishop George Browne serve as a transition in which Clarke reduces the element of disapproval from descriptions of earthy, sensual matters. Rabelais's 'plethora' encompassed coarseness and physicality. Archbishop Browne, fierce upholder of the Protestant Reformation, forgets the confiscation of abbeys when he and Bishop Bale, another uncompromising upholder of Reformation doctrines and a playwright, linger 'over the talk/And malmsey'. So Clarke moves on in a vigorous, plain style, similar to Swift's and in imitation of his octosyllabic line, but without the rhyme, to summarise some of the broader comic incidents in *Gulliver's Travels*: Gulliver's 'double pendulosity' seen by the 'crack regiments', his noisome extinguishing of the fire in the Queen's apartment, his sitting astride of maidenly paps in Brobdignab and his discomfiture when placed 'in the tangle below'.

The poem moves from these reminders of Swift's coarser interests to salute the Age of Reason, the time of Henry St John Bolingbroke who wrote on politics and moral principles, of David Hume, a philosopher, who wrote on moral and philosophical matters, and of Voltaire, historian and philosopher. Clarke commemorates the complex, ambiguous nature of the Age, knowing that Swift's depiction of so-called disgusting behaviour had a moral purpose. The passage in which he outlines the neo-classical age contrasts in style with the preceding passage about the incidents in *Gulliver's Travels*, the one written in forward-moving, run-on lines, the other in summarising, interrupted sentences.

> But who
> Could blame the Queen when that almighty
> Man hosed the private apartments of her palace,
> Hissed down the flames of carelessness, leaving
> The royal stables unfit for Houyhnhnms, or tell (in
> A coarse aside) what the gigantic maidens
> Of Brobdignab did . . .

Clarke gives equal weight in the following section to the evidence of the 'Reasonable century'.

> Satyr and nymph
> Disported in the bosk, prim avenues
> Let in the classical sky. The ancient temples
> Had been restored. Sculptures replaced the painted
> Images of the saints. Altars were fuming,
> And every capital was amaranthed.

As short-hand recreation of how the neo-classical age was expressed, this passage appeals to recognisable expressions of the revival of classical taste.

The poem changes then to incorporate other aspects of Swift: his charity to the Dublin poor, his exile after an active career in London, his consoling relationship with Vanessa. The language conveys the passion of his political pamphlets, as he relives his past political involvement:

> . . . with his pamphlets furrow the battle-fields
> Of Europe once more, tear up the blood-signed contracts
> Of Marlborough, Victualler of Victories . . .

The lines compress the past; again the method is to evoke a great deal of history within a few references before presenting contrasting images of Swift in decline, the Swift who willed 'a mansion of forgetfulness' to the Irish. Clarke recalls his own stay in St Patrick's and in a retrospective interpretation writes that he was led beyond the garden of Memory by the Muse of love poetry to where 'Divine Abstraction smiled'. The concluding paragraph brings Swift, Eriugena and Clarke together in an important philosophical statement.

> In his sudden poem *The Day of Judgment*
> Swift borrowed the allegoric bolt of Jove,
> Damned and forgave the human race, dismissed
> The jest of life. Here is his secret belief
> For sure: the doctrine of Eriugena,
> Scribing his way from West to East, from bang
> Of monastery door, click o' the latch,
> His sandals worn out, unsoled, a voice proclaiming
> The World's mad business — Eternal Absolution.

In Swift's poem when mankind stands before the throne of Jove, the judgment is one of universal forgiveness: 'The World's Mad Business now is o'er/And I resent these Pranks no more'. Similarly, Eriugena, in his *De Divisione Naturae*, formulated a non-judgmental, forgiving view of mankind which saw man as part of God from the beginning and destined to return to God at the end, no matter what they might have done. That position of moral detachment represents Clarke's own outlook. The issue of sin and damnation is no longer important. He does not entertain ideas of good and evil, as he writes poems of erotic liberation. He has become the 'chuckling rhymester' who views human affairs with Swift's detachment when, through Jove, he surveyed the 'Offending Race of Human Kind' and summed up its history in a dismissive phrase: the 'World's mad Business'. 'A Sermon on Swift' therefore provides a text for the final phase of Clarke's career.

Throughout his adult life Clarke tried to free himself from Victorian narrowness and Calvinistic Catholicism. In 'Ancient Lights' he absolved himself; in *Mnemosyne* he purged his mind: now he believes in 'Eternal Absolution' not just for himself, but for all. He is better able than ever before to affirm in joyous fashion the delights of the physical and to transcend the judgmental. The erotic poems form a happy conclusion to a life-time's engagement with repression and fear. Clarke writes approvingly but not always successfully, about sexual pleasure. But his deepest reservoirs of compassion are for those who have not achieved, or have been by others denied, a similar release. The story of Bernadette of Lourdes, as told in 'Orphide', is the major example from these late years. But first there is the joyful 'Healing of Mis', a pagan affirmation of sensual and mental recovery, and the well-intentioned but less successful classical narratives, 'The Dilemma of Iphis' and *Tiresias*, which have a similar purpose.

'The Healing of Mis' is based on the Fenian story, *The Romance of Mis and Dubb Ruis*, which Brian O Cuiv edited.[5] Mis goes mad when she sees her father's dead body and drinks his blood. Fleeing to Slieve Mish, a mountain near Tralee, Co Kerry, she terrorises the countryside round about. Fur and hair grow all over her body, her nails become claws, and she gains superhuman strength. Eventually, the harper, Duv Ruis, wins her back to sanity.

'The Healing of Mis' moves swiftly from an account of her initial madness, to her thirty-three years in the wilds, to Duv Ruis's acceptance of the challenge to cure her. Within six stanzas he is in the mountains where, exposing his genitals, he plays soothing music and entices Mis. The emphasis is not on the difficulty of winning her back but on the cure achieved by music and sex. Mis is surprisingly willing to participate in the feat of the wand. In accordance with the conventions of the romance the two figures are emblematical and one-dimensional. They participate in a ritual. The delights of sexual discovery, the energising properties of food, the re-use of a Fenian cooking-pit are part of a romance narrative. The washing of Mis is a natural baptism, a sluicing away of accumulated filth. It is reminiscent of the washing of Eithne in *The Bright Temptation* and of the natural baptism in 'Ancient Lights'. It is a preparation for the sacrament of sexual union by which Mis is restored.

> He sloshed
> Himself as he lathered her down, soaped the skin of her back
> With a lump of deer-fat, washed the crack between the slurried
> Cheeks, like a mother, turned her round, picked crabs from
> Her sporran, nit-nurseries hidden in tiny flurries

>   Through tangled tresses, then began
> All over again. He soaped her body, washed it down,
>   Drawing the wad of deer-skin to-and-fro
> Softly between her glossing thighs, . . .

After a brisk run to dry herself, she returns to his arms —

>   Then at the thrusting of the wand,
>   Her eyelids closed in bliss. The flowers of the quicken-tree
> Were poppies.

Once initiated, Mis is eager for further intercourse, reaches orgasm at the same time as Duv Ruis and sleeps peacefully with him afterwards 'in the deepening grass'. Their union is an idealised version of sexual intercourse. Clarke seizes upon the subject, reducing it to its essentials, purifying it of the irrelevant. Not concerned with verisimilitude, or psychological subtleties he elevates their union into a ceremony of sexual-medical miracle.

But Mis, as Duv Ruis notices, has 'curious dreams'. She tells him of memories of volcanic eruptions on Stromboli, of flight through 'labyrinthine corridors', of being lost in a dark 'subterranean/Maze', of a secret horror in the heart of this darkness.

>   'The unseen, the unheard-of, moved in self-horror
> Around me. Yielding to the force of writhesome limbs,
>   Unvirgined by the Minotaur —
>
> I knew my father.'

Sexual violation is at the heart of her nightmares. The imagery of a maze of corridors, of secret horror in the darkness make her situation resemble Clarke's versions of his own private nightmare. Mis's failure to recognise the 'wand' suggests that she has suppressed her memory of paternal violation. That is associated instead with secrecy, darkness, and terror, with what Clarke calls the 'Signs and symbols' that 'are underneath'. Duv Ruis's administrations transform Mis from sexual trauma to an ability to achieve a satisfying and fearless sexual relationship. Her scarred mind is healed, her filthy body is made beautiful. 'O she might have come from a Sidhe-mound for the gods/Had made her mortal.' In the medieval romance the beautiful woman often entices the mortal youth to the Land of the Ever Young; in this romance the mortal youth brings the demented woman back to the real world, back from her otherworld of insanity and isolation.

> Gaily she wore the blue gown,
> Shoes and Tyrian cloak he had brought her. A roan horse
> Waited, a servant at the bridle. Her arms were around him
> As he rode by ford, rath, to be invested.

The poem lifts in this conclusion into romance imagery. Duv Ruis has triumphed.

'The Dilemma of Iphis' and *Tiresias* also emphasise the normalcy and the religious dimension of sexual intercourse. Iphis, denied sexual fulfilment because she is of the same sex as her bethrothed, is changed into a man by the power of Io, the 'Blessed Lady' of classical mythology. The norm of heterosexual love is pointedly used in this story by contrast with the incestuous love of Biblis and her brother, Caumus in the preceding story. That the transformation of Iphis into a man is divinely sanctioned also gives approval to heterosexual love. Similarly, when Telethusa, the mother of Iphis, responds sexually to the sight of her 'son's' nakedness, she is 'ashamed of her momentary incestuous/Impulse'. In the pagan ritual of phallic power, however, all shame is swept aside. Iphis is moved to experience the joys of sexual intercourse when she responds to 'the sanctified image' carried in procession during the 'Feast of the Phallica'. Similarly, Tiresias who has been a woman for seven years, is called upon by Jupiter to say whether men or women experience the greater pleasure in sexual intercourse. In his years as the woman, Pyrrha, Tiresias learns the delights of womanhood and in particular the capacity to achieve multiple orgasm, 'a pleasure unknown to man'.

Prior to her achievement of full sexual satisfaction, Pyrrha appeals seductively to her husband

> '. . . carry your Pyrrha, flight
> After flight, carefully up the aspiring stone-steps
> Within the balistra-defying tower of Babylon to the top-most
> Storey lit by Chaldean lampads'.

The ascent is a sexual metaphor leading to the phallic tower and the illumination. It is reminiscent of the stone stairway that led to the discovery of Mnemosyne in dust. In one version the ascent leads to barrenness, in the other it is an affirmation of sexual satisfaction.

Even when Tiresias has been changed back into a man and even when he has been granted the gift of prophecy by which he can forsee, in a linguistic *tour de force*, the history of western civilisation from the Trojan War to the atomic age, he often remembers his years as a woman and the delights of feminine sexuality: 'desirous body so apt for hot pursuits'. Even his ability to call up spirits from the dead gives him little satisfaction. 'Such my happiness', he says wearily. 'Such my affliction./Such my vatic bondage'.

These classical narratives are among Clarke's weakest poems, not because they lack narrative power, but because they are not particularly interesting. Both are over-earnest in their emphasis on sexuality. In addition their descriptions of sexual pleasure are unconvincing. Iphis's sight of the 'sanctified image', for example, is at best clinically accurate:

> '. . . the delicate ivory-tinting,
> The great bluish vein, the little violet ones, the crimson
> Ring of flesh and above all the adorable ruby-like
> Heart-shaped sex-cap. How proudly it tilts above the masses
> Of people'.

and when Tiresias describes sexual intercourse as experienced by the woman the text-book is more in evidence than the imagination:

> Faster, yet faster, we sped, determined down-thrust rivalling
> Up-thrust — succus glissading us — exquisite spasm
> Contracting, dilating, changed into minute preparatory
> Orgasms, a pleasure unknown to man, that culminated
> Within their narrowing circles into the greater orgasmos.

In 'The Healing of Mis' sexual intercourse, being part of the romance genre, does not have to be realistic. Clarke is more successful in 'Orphide' in which Bernadette's encounter with the demon-goat is suggested through the metaphorical implications of rock, wind, bird-lime and slime:

> Gigantic rocks were bared. Mistral
> Blew. Beard divided, horns rafale'd it:
> Orphide pursued her along the trackless.
> Fallen on hands and knees in cave-slime,
> At Massabieille, she was limed in
>   The obliterating forest.

The language effectively realises the girl's fear. The association of cave-slime and bird-lime indicate her helplessness and degradation.

If 'The Healing of Mis' shows how one human being lovingly cures another, 'Orphide' shows how another human being, although granted miraculous contact with the divine, earns only suspicion, exploitation and deprivation. Bernadette's simple and homely account of her vision of the Blessed Virgin fires her mother with visions of earthly consequences: thousands in prayer at the grotto and her own reputation as the one who has 'borne a saint for France'. Bernadette dreams contentedly of minding sheep when she was a child, but her innocent days are over:

teachers question and rebuke her, companions tease her, the parish priest interrogates her. Over and over she has to repeat her simple story and does so with telling clarity and consistency. But the opposition and the popular hysteria increase. The Bishop condemns what is happening, the Lord Mayor erects barriers, horse-dragoons drive back the crowds, French newspapers report on the events. Finally, the Emperor commands the opposition to cease and modern Lourdes is born.

> On Easter Sunday pilgrims made
> Their way from townland, hillside hamlet,
> In France and Spain. Hucksters filled
> Tent, stall, with food and drink, salami,
> Roast chestnuts, farm-cakes, lucky dips, flasks.
> Wives smiled at the black caps of the Basque men,
> Sky-blue berets from Bearne. Beribboned
> Beauties from La Provence tripped by.
> > All hailed the Maid.

But the story of Bernadette goes on to suffering and loss. 'In her dark room/Bernadette coughed, cried.' When the first miracle occurs at the grotto, the Bishop decides that —

> '. . . this chosen girl must be sheltered
> By Holy Church, taken from her parents
> And humble home.'

Her objections are overruled; she becomes a novice against her will. The metaphor of the thrush pulling the snail from the shell is apt. Her alcoholic father understands.

> His child of fourteen was the future
> Of Lourdes. To her new hospices,
> Convents, shops, cafes, banks, offices,
> > Hotels were all beholden.

The supernatural event at Lourdes is subjected to vulgar and commercial exploitation. Ironically, Bernadette herself, the source of all this, has nothing to celebrate. She is 'no longer exalted/In soul'. Even the ceremony of her profession as a nun has no meaning for her.

> . . . Bride of Christ, unmoved,
> Indifferent to her own good,
> > Those nuptials unavailing.

She has become withdrawn, her eyes 'Raised/No more, voice scarcely heard'. Now when she remembers minding sheep as a child an evil memory, associated with an ugly smell that attends the 'demon-goat, Orphide' rises from her subconscious. She is obsessed with images of lascivious evil and of defilement.

> Feverish dreams gave her no rest.
> That local legend fled up mist
> With her into the alpine passes.
> Gigantic rocks were bared. Mistral
> Blew. Beard divided, horns rafale'd it:
> Orphide pursued her along the trackless.
> Fallen on hands and knees in cave-slime,
> At Massabieille, she was limed in
>   The obliterating forest.

Like Alphonsus Liguori she is tormented by evil. The experience that had brought Mis back to sanity and happiness, drives Bernadette into terror, back into the wildness where nature is harsh and frightening: 'Gigantic rocks were bared. Mistral/Blew'. The imagery suggests aggressive, male sexuality. Bernadette's final experience is of prolonged, incurable pain and delirium. Lourdes water, miraculous for others, is for her a 'galling sponge'. 'All that she once beheld' has been 'sullied' by the demon-goat. She dies of 'caries', that is, of decay and is 'irrelicable' which means that there is nothing that can be used as a relic. Her physical obliteration is total. And there is no memorial to her at Lourdes.

Hers is a grim story, told in a detached, realistic manner in which the cruel irony of her life is clearly revealed. Once again, as in 'Martha Blake' and *Mnemosyne*, to name only two major examples, Clarke voices his concern for the innocent victim. Once again he exposes the underside of the mind to show how even the innocent may be traumatised by evil. The goat-shaped embodiment of that evil has appeared elsewhere in his work — in *The Bright Temptation*, in the forked beards of frightening preachers and, more comically, in *The Sun Dances at Easter*. But in 'Orphide' it is deployed with particular compassion and detachment, in a story that is remarkably and consciously different from the popular notion of Bernadette's life.

'The Quarry', a short narrative poem about a counterfeit apparition of the Blessed Virgin in a quarry in Co Donegal, has an obvious thematic connection with 'Orphide'. A Government Deputy, his wife and a local poor man have joined together to defraud the people: the poor man charges admission to the quarry, Mrs Gallagher poses there as the Mother of God, and Michael Gallagher tries to secure the support of the Church in the person of Fr O'Donnell. The priest is the other quarry of the story. If his support can be obtained, the deception will be strengthened. The poem is not primarily about a shabby intrigue and superstition. It is a portrait of a gullible priest who understands why poor people are so ready to believe but who is also moved by their reports of what they have seen.

> Who could have foretold that, night after night,
>   Shy words would shuffle uncapped
> Or shawled, into the Presbytery
>   As if they had shared a rapture.
>
> Unknown to him?

Michael Gallagher's appeal to the priest is persuasive: the apparition, he says, resembles the statue of the Blessed Virgin in the church. His is a manipulative, political voice. When Fr O'Donnell goes to the quarry he is affected by its atmosphere of 'solemn hush' and yields to a 'luscious/ Feeling' —

>   for the quarry
> Seemed aswirl with soft vapour
> From which the form of a woman robed
> In shimmering white was shaping
>
> Itself.

But when he recognises the wife of Deputy Gallagher, smiling and lifting her night-dress, he feels 'half-damned'. Against his better judgment he has weakly yielded to superstition.

Religion itself comes more and more directly under scrutiny in Clarke's final phase. 'Orphide' and 'The Quarry' focus on the Catholic Church, on its unfeeling authoritarianism in one case, on its intellectual weakness in the other. Clarke's most sustained examination of religion in Ireland comes in 'The Disestablished Church' which must be considered on its own before any general conclusions can be drawn about Clarke's evaluation of religion within this final phase.

'The Disestablished Church' seems to be about the consequences of the disestablishment of the Protestant Church in Ireland, which took effect on January 1, 1871, since it refers to a number of churches which have fallen into disuse, have been sold, or used for non-ecclesiastical purposes.[6] But it is also about the ways in which religion, both Protestant and Catholic, has failed. The poem is a philosophical statement in which religion itself is disestablished, denied its authority. The evidence for and justification of that denial are central to the poem.

The theme is introduced in the first two stanzas between the imagery of St Mary's Church grown 'silent', unresponsive to the sunlight coming from Paradise Lane, and in the references to the cruel punishment of boys in the school by those named, ironically, Christian Brothers. The Good Shepherd is now a butcher, whose 'shepping', or shepherding, is a perversion for financial gain of the work of the Good Shepherd. The sun's rays do the redemptive work of the Holy Spirit.

The first four stanzas pursue the theme of cruelty, creating a context of fear, pain and furtive masturbation for the schoolboys. The reference to Mary Magdalene is a reminder of true love and service. Her comforting of Christ contrasts with their sexual longing. These contexts become Clarke's.

> The punishers in black robes only
> Beat harder. One afternoon a bolt
> Flooded the gutters. Mysteries
> Had fled. I sheltered at the bolted
> Protestant church-door; dire misbehaviour.
> No angel rolled back the faraway boulder
> A light shone out from misery.
> The hand that spared me was its own.

The stanza repeats the moment of personal redemption affirmed in 'Ancient Lights' and emphasises that it was not the result of divine intervention — 'No angel' — but of self-assertion. He escapes from restriction, cruelty and darkness, from the tomb that they have formed, by virtue of his own strength. That release and its philosophical basis is celebrated in stanza v.

> All human-beings will be redeemed.
> The clarabella, clavecin,
> Are not more sweet to hear in the bout
> Of melody when notes are single.
> Stuck in that pot of stirabout,
> My little spoon at last was singing —
> Impudent handle was unbowed,
> For consciousness is as we deem it.

'All human-beings will be redeemed'. That liberating philosophy underlies all of Clarke's final poems. 'Consciousness is as we deem it'. The references to 'spoon' and 'stirabout', or porridge, mockingly define the restrictive contexts from which Clarke struggles free. Just as the 'child of grace' in 'Ancient Lights', the ordinary individual, could frighten off the bronze bird, so here the 'little spoon' achieves its liberation; it is impudently 'unbowed' through the power of its own 'consciousness'. Stanza vi gives the historical association for this imagery of porridge and personal faith.

The Church Council at Valence declared that Eriugena's philosophy was *'pultes Scotorum'*, that is 'Irish porridge'. By calling it *'stultes/Scrotorum'* Clarke rudely and mischievously calls the philosophy 'foolish balls', an even more dismissive and explicitly sexual phrase which anticipates the reference to stultification two lines later and connects the ecclesiastical judgment with repressive teaching on sexuality, with excessive repressiveness in general and with the stultification of human minds that results from the beatings of the 'punishers in black robes'. At the same time he slyly argues that Eriugena had 'balls', had the courage of his convictions, and that his ideas were fertile. 'Spoon sang the Grace' — not just grace at meals, or Divine Grace, but the absolution achieved in the moment recalled and commemorated in 'Ancient Lights' the plenary indulgence for life, the 'Eternal Absolution' of Swift's 'Day of Judgment', the universal redemption of Eriugena's *De Divisione Naturae*. 'All Europe' may have assented to the Council's judgment on Eriugena but, Clarke insists, his 'holy saying' is superior to the teachings of any church Council. Those teachings have caused centuries of stultification, numbing the minds of the people in much the same way as corporal punishment dulled and impeded the development of the schoolboys: 'Doubt/And fear sit on the bench by numskull'. Once the individual's mind has been broken, Clarke declares, it is difficult to restore its confidence and the 'wayward soul', feeling itself to be out of touch with God's grace, 'can only stutter', its power inhibited. The connection with the sad, mindless figures in *Mnemosyne*, and elsewhere, is clear.

The poem moves then to other signs of religious decline. Stanza vii is a masterly social vignette of a former time, when Protestant ladies went to church.

> Bible accompanied elderly ladies
> In jetty bonnets, married women
> In veils with their alluring sun-spots,
> Lace gloves; straw-hatted girls, now dimming
> In photographic albums, once spotted
> By stare of lens, wore dimity.
> Dotage has hidden familiar spots
> They giggled to, memory mislaid.

By contrast the next stanza introduces and condemns sectarian conflict: the blowing-up of the equestrian statue of William of Orange in College Green and of Nelson's Pillar. 'Dismounted three times' refers to attempts made to destroy the royal statue. In March 1836 three attempts were made; in April of the same year it was successfully blown-up and when the pieces were reassembled the horse was 'ungainly', because it was estimated that if the left leg were straightened it would be eighteen inches longer than the right.[7] All that, Clarke points out, is over: 'William of Orange no longer attracts/A scowl or smile'. Sectarian conflict now takes place across the Border in Northern Ireland, but Clarke adds sarcastically, patriotism still exists, for Nelson's Pillar has been blown up (1966).

These signs of religious bigotry support the theme of religious loss. The rest of the poem (stanzas ix-xvi) is a catalogue of closures and of secularisation. At Newbridge, Co Kildare, the church has become a dance hall, as if the itch of mortification has been replaced by the modern itch for pleasure; where once bread and wine were changed into the body and blood of Christ, people now play cards. The 'Ancient Church at Clonfert', famous for its carven heads above the doorway and for its peaceful setting, has been invaded. Parish churches are stoned. Ardfert Abbey is desecrated. The church at Killester has become a factory. Stanza xv is a lament for churches that have disappeared: St Barnabas, Baggotsrath, Carysfort. That the 'Woman at Joppa . . . lays down her burden'[8] suggests the loss of faith that these closures indicate: when St Peter raised her from the dead, many people as a result believed in Christianity.

The remainder of the poem (stanzas xvi-xix) centres on the Church of St Catherine in Thomas Street, Dublin. Being Protestant it had a chilling, 'sunless' feeling for the Clarke family, associated with Tudor atrocities —

> the massive
> Walls, iron spikes, remembered the blood-drenched
> Block, Henry the Eighth and his six wives.

But it was sold. The itemising of its destruction focuses Clarke's outrage and regret.

> The Church Representative Body sold
> Furniture, fittings to save arrears.
> Methodist firm tramped in with hand-saw,
> Hammer, cold chisel, broke down the reredos,
> Altar, the gallery rails, the handsome
> Pews, eighteenth century organ. I saw from
> A ladder much anguish thrown in the rear,
> Knew Christ abandoned to the soldiery.

Robert Emmet, hanged in front of St Catherine's by order of the British authorities, died that Ireland might be free, might, in the words of his popular *Speech from the Dock*, take her place among the nations of the earth. Now, Clarke says, his 'blood will spurt' again, because British construction firms have 'enshrined' this part of the city with 'glass, cement, steel'. The blood of the patriot-martyr will, as it were, react to this fresh outrage on his native city. 'See Catherine staunch his wounded side', Clarke exclaims, recalling her capacity to nurse those in need of care and associating Emmet with Christ, another martyr whose side was wounded.

The final stanza is a vigorous condemnation of the Catholic Church for its association with the commercial despoliation of Dublin by which much of the eighteenth century city, including St Catherine's, was replaced by modern-style office blocks, banks and churches. Clarke pointedly juxtaposes the rise of the rich with the decline of the poor, the elegance of modern buildings with the dreary conditions of the poor. The Church's association with the new commercialism is emphasised in the appearance of the Archbishop of Dublin, blessing the foundation stone. Paradoxically, in this unchristian association of money and religion, 'Redemption' itself is ambivalent. In the metaphor of finance it 'banks on/Our credit' and the highest 'tender' is the one who succeeds, as though one could bid to be redeemed and not have to earn salvation by good works and the operation of Divine Grace. Catholicism has been drawn into the money market with the banks, the highrise office blocks, the British construction firms that destroy the city. The fate of St Catherine's is an example of what has been shown throughout the poem. The Protestant Church is in decline; the Catholic Church is the church of the wealthy.

What becomes clear in these final collections is that the poetry from 1955 to 1974 has its own unity of purpose, its integrating themes and responses. The declaration of release in 'Ancient Lights' functions for the whole period. The attack on prosperity of Church and State in 'Celebrations' continues. The concern for the hurt individual remains. What changes is the mood. As the subjects clarify themselves, as the style matures, as Clarke's confidence grows, the poetry becomes profounder and more complex. There is a growing realisation of the possibilities inherent in turning inward and backward to explore and express both the personal history and the racial conscience. The fullest flowering of these developments are found in *Flight to Africa* and *Mnemosyne*. Then comes the happier, uninhibited mood of the last books, from *Old-Fashioned Pilgrimage* to the end. For all their lapses in concentration they finalise what Clarke has been saying. There is both a gathering up of old themes and a return to earlier ones. Two related subjects dominate: sexuality and religion. There are three Churches, or three religions: Catholicism, Protestantism, and Paganism. The Protestant Church has been disestablished; its days of religious appeal and of social relevance have gone. The Catholic Church is still found wanting, still held to be joined with the wealthy, still inadequate to the needs of the individual, still aligned with wealth, still restrictive, still prone to superstition. If the last collections seem merely to repeat old positions, former attacks on the Church, former attacks on the State, it is not entirely Austin Clarke's fault. He notes once again that the poor are badly treated, that the Church causes suffering by its restrictive regulations, that it is visibly associated with the rich, that the workers are still exploited. Circumstances are much the same despite the apparent changes, such as Vatican Two or membership of the EEC. Paganism becomes a kind of alternative religion to the extent that the classical narratives, *Mnemosyne*, the amorous lyrics, some of the travel poems, celebrate sensuality, an unashamed, freely enjoyed eroticism. 'The Healing of Mis' is the Irish version of this advocacy of sexuality. The mood of these poems is part of the general mood of release, part of the emphasis on sexuality that pervades the whole period. It receives its philosophical justification in the references to Eriugena, Swift, and Clarke's own declaration of faith in a non-judgmental and merciful God.

Chapter 12: Conclusion

Had Austin Clarke ceased to write in 1936, when he was forty years of age and had published *Collected Poems*, his reputation would not have been secure. Instead of becoming a significant modern poet, he would have been remembered as a poet in whose work the aims and emphases of the Irish Literary Revival had been prolonged and extended; he would have been remembered for a few poems which are of interest for their use of assonance and for a couple of poems which have more than ordinary intensity and control. *The Bright Temptation* would be seen as an immature romance and his plays as moderately interesting examples of verse drama. On the whole the poetry of his early period is marked by an attachment to outmoded aesthetic and nationalistic aims, and by a lack of individuality. Even his ambition to create a new kind of Irish poetry, classical, casuistical, and based on a firsthand knowledge of Irish traditions, would not have contributed greatly to his reputation, since it never attracted enough response in his contemporaries and failed to be sustained in his own work. In 1936 his most recent collection was *Pilgrimage* (1929).

Two works changed all that: *The Singing Men at Cashel* (1936) and *Night and Morning* (1938), the former a work of intelligent conception and execution, but ultimately flawed. The significance of its failure, which must have been a serious blow to Clarke himself, is visible in the nervous breakdown that he experienced shortly afterwards, when he returned to Ireland. The strain of the time is expressed in the constricted space available to the self in *Night and Morning* and in the grim labyrinth of 'Return from England'. The judgmental voice of the narrator in *The Singing Men at Cashel* anticipates the conflict in *Night and Morning*, in which Gormlai's position is re-examined in personal terms. Already, in the novel, Clarke had begun to express the issues that make *Night and Morning* so compelling. 'Repentance', with its nostalgia for the innocence of former days, is one of Anier Mac Conglinne's poems.

> When I was younger than the soul
> That wakes me now at night, I saw
> The mortal mind in such a glory —
> All knowledge was in Connaught.

In the west, he felt 'Repentance gushing from the rock', but the poem concludes with the admission that neither the religion of Irish mythology nor intellectual strength can free him from the old fears. The poem ends with images of terror and oblivion that anticipate Anier's experiences in the Cave of Demons. Like Clarke, Anier has pursued the merry sins. Like Anier, Clarke faces the conflict between such pursuits and the Church's view of them. *The Singing Men at Cashel* is memorable for its story of Gormlai's predicament, caught between ecclesiastical rules and the needs of her own nature. The resolution in terms of simple, pre-Revelation, early Ireland, which is equated with man's essential goodness, and to which poetry can lead us, is only partially satisfactory. It has an essentially romantic, even fanciful aspect, and has little force in the everyday human world. 'Repentance' says as much. With remarkable determination Clarke turns in *Night and Morning* from virtually all that he had previously written and advocated. With one slim volume of thirteen poems, he wins a place for himself as a poet of the Irish Catholic conscience, an issue that indeed had not been addressed in the Irish Literary Revival.

Then came another silence, punctuated by his work in the Lyric Theatre, by the bread-and-butter activity of verse-speaking on radio and by book reviewing. But little in all of this prepared for the dramatic new voice in *Ancient Lights* and what followed, for the force of a poet who was almost sixty years of age, beginning all over again and advancing with growing strength and ability virtually until his death in 1974.

Before he died, he prepared *Collected Poems* (1974) for publication. The revisions of the early epic narratives, particularly *The Sword of the West*, are thorough and extensive. He rewrote five sections of 'Concobar', Parts II, III, V, VI, and VII, and two of 'The Music-Healers', Parts I and II. In a remarkable concentration of linguistic energy only a few lines of the 1921 text remained untouched. The rest are subjected to resolute reworking, in itself indicative of Clarke's strength of mind in his early seventies.

The most impressive examples of the changes he made are found in Part VI of 'Concobar' and Part I of 'The Music-Healers'. The first relates

the unarmed stranger's experiences in the past. Their compulsive, supernatural nature is emphasised in the added hypnotic repetitions, with
slight variations of 'Vision hurried me backward,/Vision hurried me
onward', in the procession of De Danann gods, and in the account of
the Battle of Moytura. Clarke's confidence and command of language
may be seen in the rigorous suppression, alteration and compression. He
is not just tightening up the loose rhythms of the original, not just trim-
ming its romantic diction or changing the melody, he is writing a new
kind of poetry. Whereas the original dealt with one of his main imaginative
obsessions, a visional encounter with a mythical world, the revised version makes a dramatic, personal engagement out of the confrontation
between the narrator and the mythic past. The lines not only describe
the experience, they illuminate it in their own texture and resonance.
The 1974 version is worth quoting at length, since it reveals the resources
of Clarke's later style and his ability to transform the language of his
youth.

'As a kittiwake
Driven, in sleet, from two thousand feet of cliff
With feeble screams, bewildered by a tumult
Of seaward mountains silent in the night,
I fled in a dream beyond the soundings, the forelands,
Into our forgetful past. There, King after King
With white-bronze-hammered shield that seemed to mourn
Their misery, despair, led the defeated
Fomorian hosts, mocked by iron harp-note,
By far-off laughter.
Vision hurried me backward,
Vision hurried me onward. I saw in confusion
The Battle of Moytura. I heard a clamour
Of shoring waters surge below me: a King
Passed, mantling the tide, tip of his spear,
A sea-green star. Within my vision, appeared
The demi-gods, Midir the Proud, Iuchar,
Bove Derg, clapped in thunder, Diancecht,
Erc, Len. I counted the assembly of those heroes
In wars, too terrible for the annals of men, as
Leaning on sword-hilts, their great paps dark as warts
Within the gleam of breast, their scrota bulged
In shadow.
Vision hurried me on, vision hurried me back.
Out of the tidal glimmer, Mannanan rose
Again from the shallows of bladder-weed, his cloak-hem

> Rolled slower than the lengthening billow lifting
> A curl of incoming spray on Carrig-na-rón.
> There I saw Losrem, fierce-born from the womb
> Upon a cold flagstone, among his attendants
> Greasing a targe of leather bull-hide, there,
> Balor — his baleful eye was fleshed with sleep,
> Cuoch, the harper, fretted by gull-cries, Tethra
> Whose nameless sea-children move in clumsy flight
> Slower than bull-seals carried on the billows.
> Dream within dream. . . .'

These descriptions of the De Danann leaders are succinct and colourful. The accounts of Gobain's work in the smithy, Brife's wail for the death of her son, Ruadan, the healing work of Diancecht, or the defeat and disarray of the Fomorians are all examples of Clarke's skill and success in the 1974 version.

Part I of 'The Music-Healers' has a similar energetic use of language. It is seen, for example, in Maeve's description of Cuchullin, which begins in outspoken sexual rebuke and proceeds by way of connecting circus metaphor:

> '. . . All's on the broil.
> Quick to the surrender, spurt, flow.
> Get me a hardier breed. Forget that our armies
> Were thrown about by their Laeg, trick-driver o'
> The North, when his eight spokes were shielded in speed
> That snaffled, lift, right, as he circused among
> Them — shank to leg — while that young acrobat,
> Cuchullin, changed into a juggler, encircled
> By swordlets. Ring-a-ruddy with their fresh
> Supply of crania, the bob-and-wheel
> Went widdershins.'

The transforming vigour and intensity of manner in these lines could only have been written by the later Clarke so different are they from the slow-moving, sluggish melody of 1921. But the most characteristic example of Clarke's later style is found in his compact narrative of the transmogrifications of a succession of creatures into the two bulls of the *Táin*. Whereas in 1921, and in 1936, he relied on objective description, now he releases what he describes directly within the words used; the language embodies the action. His delight in the possibilities of the language of metamorphosis may be seen in these concluding lines:

'I heard the tiny
Whimpering of the worm, then dipped a pitcher
Into the well, caught Timmius, saw him changing
In hue from green to purple, to black. The glug-glug
Was gone, the pitcher dry. The swineherds grew
From puny to huge again, tried on ill-fitting
Fantasies, pick-me-ups of air, new twists
Of anatomical variety,
Glottis, liver and lights, obscurer glands
Until they were completely bollocksed. At last
Their hate became prize-bulls, Findbenna, Pride
Of Connaught, roaming the plain, a might sire
Among my cows. His rival, the Brown Bull of Cooley,
Was haltered by my ranchers. They drove him by green road,
Blue road, brown road, after our army had crossed
The Border that I might graze him in my pastures.
So why should I fear now that get of a god
Skipping along a car-pole, showing off in
His trews the heavenly bulge of his father, pretending
To light o' loves the upshot is his own?'

The colloquialisms of 'bollocksed' and 'get' together with the explicit sexuality are in keeping with the coarser, earthier quality of this style. The inventive, creative use of language is particularly appropriate to Clarke's accounts of transformations and hallucinatory experiences in which physical details can be used, sometimes in a distorted way, to give a sensual feeling to bizarre experience. It is amusing to note that in his seventies Clarke can express at least some of the merry sins with appropriate gusto and panache.

The poetry that Clarke wrote between *Ancient Lights* (1955) and 'The Wooing of Becfola' (1974) is both public and private. It responds with vigour and anger, with sadness or humour to Irish life, and it returns, in more reflective mood, to autobiographical experience. It has something to say; it is realistic, expressing what it feels like to be part of Irish life and of modern experience. It is not concerned with remembered innocence, with the recovery of the past for its own sake, with the substitution of a religion of the imagination, with aesthetic lyricism. It is above all realistic, unimpressed with, not deceived by, the rhetoric of economic nationalism or of ecclesiastical texts. It is not a time for singing, when so much in the public arena is inhuman and when life is damaged by the controls and the inadequacies of Church and State. The loss of strength is both personal and historical, both private and public, a matter of aging for the poet, but the arteries of Church and State are also hardening into indifference and complacency. Celebrations are not in order. The rights of the poet need to be asserted. When hoardings proclaim our faith, that faith is unworthy of our devotion. At such a time, it falls to the poet, however isolated, however neglected, to articulate the morality of old-fashioned christianity, of love, of joy, love for those in need, joy in the presence of beauty, in women, in nature, in poetry. It falls to the poet to be the conscience of the time, to note publicly, in occasional poems, those events that signify the decline in public values, to define in terms of his own experience how the country and the Church have evolved. The most reliable evidence is to be found in personal experience, evidence of the devotional revolution and what it may do to the individual spirit, evidence of the collapse and disappearance of political and social ideals and of their replacement by commercialism and religiosity.

But one may exult in the freedom of the imagination and in one's technical powers. Clarke seems to be able to write poems on virtually any subject, to try out many styles and to succeed in most of them. He can be self-indulgent, can compensate for the encroachments of age by an over-worked delight in homonyms, by fake scholarship, by portraits that add little to his reputation, by tedious memories, by insignificant observations. He writes poems now as another man might write letters, sometimes with passion, direction, intelligence, and understanding, sometimes with an air of a man who has other things on his mind, sometimes in honest confession of amorous needs, sometimes with an unexpected delight in the everyday. He is honest, compassionate, ordinary, occasionally tetchy, sometimes angry, sometimes opinionated, often amused or delighted, at times seriously engaged, frequently surprising by the high standards of his work and by its sudden lapses of concentration.

His early work is both enriched and limited by its commitment to Irish sources. His later work is enriched and limited by its stubborn realism. It memorialises, records, actualises what is there in the external world and in his own life. Unlike some poets, Clarke does not fashion his own reality. He is tenaciously literal, as though he did not trust the power of imagination to construct a world that merely resembles the actual world. It may be that his imagination never fully recovered from its early trauma, as a number of his writings suggest. It is impossible to chart his progress from 1929, or even 1938. His imaginative development is not consistently worked out in a succession of poems, plays, and novels. Even the autobiographies conceal as much as they reveal. In his later phase, from 1955 to 1974, he pursues an ever deepening investigation of himself, reaches a high level of achievement, and is released thereafter into the cheerful manner of the last poems, but it is, ultimately, a limited development, narrowly focused.

Nevertheless, he is a significant presence in Irish literature; he revitalises different areas of the past, absorbs some of its technical achievements, and imitates its high standards of craftsmanship. At the same time his imagination is not profoundly engaged across the entire span of his work. His visionary states, of which he writes frequently as a young man, have not the mystical or metaphysical intensity of the saints' visions, nor do they reach areas beyond rational understanding. They are visions in the sense of being hallucinations and are even associated at times with mental disarray, with a sensibility broken on the rack of conflict between human desire and clerical rules. It is a measure of his growth as a writer that he can move from the unattached vision of the Battle of Moytura to the personal visions of Maurice Devane, from Dectora's wanderings and Grainne's glimmerings in a medieval landscape to Devane's trauma of loss. It is a measure of his development that he can change from the ornamental assonantal texture of *Pilgrimage* to the demanding metrical formalism of 'The Hippophagi', or from the unfocused account of Cuchullin's wrestling with the elemental chargers to the moral force of the metaphor for cruelty in 'The Hippophagi', or can turn that at once into the rhythmic delights of 'Forget-me-Not'. It is a measure of his achievement that he gave up imitating the wavering, meditative, suggestive rhythms of the Irish Literary Revival for the energetic, broken rhythms of his later engagement with real things. It is an indication of his growth in maturity that the phantasmagoria of the Suibhne legend should be altered into the sensual romance of Mis, or that the romance of the western land-scape should be replaced by a delight in the flight of a raven or the appearance of a blackbird. The man who found repentance gushing from a rock in Connaught now finds it revealed in Rutland Square. The man who once needed the religion of Irish mythology, passed on to him in his revered litany of names, Ferguson, Sigerson, Hyde, Trench, O'Grady, Larminie, AE, Yeats, now finds strength within himself, in the human littleness of 'Ancient Lights' that is paradoxically strong, in the puny spoon of 'The Hippophagi' that stirs for itself. The man who created an unbreakable moral frame for Gormlai in *The Singing Men at Cashel*, and for her associated figures of the plays, later found the relaxed absolution of 'A Sermon on Swift'. Abstraction itself becomes divine, not part of a tormenting struggle between soul and body. Sensuality becomes holy. There is no need to live in fear of an all-judging God, or to await the verdict recorded, as it was for Gormlai, in the Book of Life. Even the Young Woman of Beare, for all her delight in sexual pleasures, fears cen-sure of the clergy. The man who avoided the physical in the early nar-rative epics and in *The Bright Temptation* delights in his accounts of

amorous adventures, where he is needlessly explicit. The altar-boy hero
of the first novel is much different from the priapic student of 'Tiresias'.
In between, marking the way, is the lustful Malachi, the embodiment
of sexual sin in the dark imaginings of Clarke's second novel. Similarly
the spoiled priest fom Salamanca becomes the earnest student of venery.
When we move back and forth in Clarke's work we get a better sense of
what has taken place between the two parts of his career.

A sensibility sometimes divided could hardly make a unifying design
of his entire work. The self that stood its ground and faced the pertinent
issues in *Night and Morning* could in later life take on the known and the
visible and what memory could retrieve, not in terms of absorption and
recreation but in terms of straightforward, unambiguous representation.
The language may play with meanings but the material is inspected literally. As though feeling unsafe unless kept in close contact with the
specific, the imagination does not go beyond the evidence. The style of
active verbs, of histrionic enactment, of deleted articles, of the concrete
detail, is the style of a man in close touch with what can be verified by
the senses. He is a literalist of the imagination also in the structuring
methods of many of the poems which are pieced together stanza by
stanza, sometimes line by line, not by a fluid process of imaginal association. Sometimes a poem leaps into unexpected imaginative freedom
and usually the imagination binds the various parts together in an effective manner, but sometimes the poems are in danger of collapsing into
banality, when the language is not fresh and alive.

Although Clarke is a dramatist, he is not a dramatic poet in the sense
of creating characters different from himself. The figures, both historical
and contemporary, exist through experiences that are not greatly different from Clarke's own. The truth they reveal is the truth of his experience. He is not a symbol making poet in the usual meaning of that term.
He does not invest objects, events, or people with a significance based
on a sense of some ancestral power. He may recall moments of symbolic
significance, as when he sheltered at the door of the Black Church and
experienced an illuminating release from the cage of clerical control,
but it remains a specific event, metaphorically useful. He may recall
Douglas Hyde's funeral and make us quietly aware of its significance,
but there is no role-playing, no rhetorical flourishes. Similarly when he
uses himself in his work, there is no alteration of the social man into
something else. The man who reads a paper from the pulpit of St Patrick's
Cathedral is the poet who then writes his 'Sermon on Swift'. When he
writes about terror, we know that he has experienced it and wants to
recreate it as realistically as he can. There is no dichotomy between what
the self experiences and what the poetic self constructs. That is why the

autobiographies are helpful in understanding the long poems, that is why a knowledge of Irish history makes the work easier to understand. That is why, if we are to understand him and evaluate his work, we must accept him as he is, and as we find him in the work. The best of Clarke comes from the quotidian self, not from the singer of tales. When there is nothing left to sing, he finds his true voice, a voice for the ordinary, the everyday, the human. This voice speaks of and to men in the confusion and pain of living at a time when traditional certainties, of Church, of State, are no longer available. It is here that Clarke finds universality. When we follow him to the level on which he writes, we find ourselves.

NOTES

Introduction

1   Patrick J. Corish, *The Irish Catholic Experience, a historical survey*, Dublin: Gill and Macmillan 1985 p 211.
2   *Ibid.* p 210.
3   *Ibid.* p 232.
4   'The Dail and the Bishops', *The Bell*, 17, 3 (June 1951) p 10.
5   *First Visit to England*, Dublin: Bridge Press 1945 p 60.
6   *Ibid.* p 66.
7   *Twice Round the Black Church*, London: Routledge and Kegan Paul 1962 p 47.
8   'Irish Poetry To-day', *Dublin Magazine*, X, I, n.s. (January-March 1935) p 27.
9   *Ibid.* pp 26-32.
10 *Ibid.* p 15.
11 'Standish O'Grady', *Dublin Magazine*, XXII, I(January-March 1947) p 36.
12 *Ibid.* pp 36-40.
13 *The Flight of the Eagle*, London: Lawrence and Bullen 1897 pp 255-256.
14 *Poetry in Modern Ireland*, Dublin: Cultural Relations Committee 1951 p 11.
15 *Ibid.* p 8.
16 'Standish O'Grady', p 37.
17 *A Penny in the Clouds*, London: Routledge and Kegan Paul 1968 pp 84-85.
18 *Ibid.* p 128.
19 *Literature in Ireland. Studies Irish and Anglo-Irish*, Dublin: Talbot Press 1916 p 55.
20 *Bards of the Gael and Gall*, London: T.F. Unwin 1897 p 1.
21 *Ibid.* p 7.
22 *Ibid.* p 8.
23 *Pilgrimage*, London: Allen and Unwin 1929 p 43.
24 'Irish Poetry To-Day', p 32.
25 *Collected Poems*, London: Allen and Unwin 1936 p 309.
26 Pierre Bearn (ed.) *Paul Fort. Poetes d'aujourdhi*. Seghers 1960, 1970 p 62.
27 *Poetry in Modern Ireland*, p 42. Also *Irisleabhar Muighe Nuadhad* (A Cháisg, 1908.) Anier MacConglinne recites Clarke's translation in *The Son of Learning* (1927) which seems to have been written by 1922.

28 *Collected Poems*, Dublin: Dolmen 1974. *Poems 1917-1938*, p 195.
29 *Celtic Miscellany*, London: Routledge and Kegan Paul 1951 p 237.
30 'A Note on Austin Clarke', *Dublin Magazine*, IV, 2 (April-June 1930) pp 65-67.
31 *Medieval Irish Lyrics*, Dublin: Dolmen 1967 XI.
32 *Irish Syllabic Poetry*, Dublin: Institute for Advanced Studies 1974 p 1.
33 *Irish Classical Poetry*, Dublin: Sign of the Three Candles 1957 p 17.
34 *Literature in Ireland*, Dublin: Cultural Relations Committee p 25.
35 *Celtic Mythology*, p 65.
36 *Penny in the Clouds*, p 314.
37 *Poetry in Modern Ireland*, p 41.
38 'The Black Church', *Dublin Magazine*, n.s., 10, 1 (January-March) p 11.
39 *Early Christian Architecture*, London: George Bell 1878 pp 74-75.
40 *The Church in Early Irish Society*, London: Methuen 1966 p 108.
41 *Ibid.* p 154.
42 *Ibid.* p 166.
43 *Ireland and the Celtic Church*, London: Society for Promoting Knowledge 1907 p 114.
44 *Ibid.* p 339.
45 'The early Irish Church and the Western patriarchate', in Próinséas Ní Chatháin and Michael Richter, *Die Kirche im Frühmittelalter. Ireland and Europe. The Early Church*, Stuttgart: Klett Cota 1984 p 13.
46 'All through my early years, the word "Nationalism" shone in my mind, . . .', *Penny in the Clouds*, p 1.

Chapter 1 *Short Poems 1916-1925*

1 'The Seven Woods', *Nation and Athenaeum*, XXXVI, 11 (December 13 1924) p 411.
2 *Penny in the Clouds*, p 83.
3 'A Simple Folk. A Donegal Sketch', *New Statesman* (September 1923) p 673; Reprinted in *Penny in the Clouds*, p 137.
4 *Irish Statesman* (November 1, 8, 15, 1924) pp 237-301.
5 *T.P.'s Weekly*, VIII, 201, n.s. (September 31, 1927) p 585.
6 Clarke gives an amusing account of this meeting in his essay on Yeats in *The Yeats We Knew*, ed. Francis MacManus, Cork: Mercier 1965:

> His voice rose and fell in a lulling monotone, while secretly I cursed the fish. It might have come from the cauldron of the elder gods, might have held the very smelt of knowledge, for, despite my desperate efforts, it would not grow smaller, and its tiny stickles seemed to threaten my very existence.
> 'Verse should be ascetic, the beauty of bare words . . .'
> While he was speaking I seized the opportunity of pushing away the bewitched plate very gently.
> 'Master,' I said to myself in youthful enthusiasm, for I felt in happier mood, 'must not poetry sow its wild oats?'
> I could hear that inner voice, despite me, imitating his chanting tone. But aloud I asked some polite question, to which he replied:
> 'Poetry needs the symbolic, that which has been moulded by many minds . . .'
> 'I want,' he said later on, 'to see a neo-Catholic school of young poets in this country.' He spoke of Jammes, Peguy, Claudel, and said much

that I could not follow at the time, for I had been cast into a mild trance by the gleam of the great signet upon his waving hand. . . But even in that trance I was trying to defend myself from the religious novelty which he was evolving. . . .

'I have to catch a train at four o'clock,' exclaimed the poet, hastily rising from the sofa.

The sun was shining again, here and there, among the seven woods when we came to the door. As I stood with downcast head upon the threshold he must have noticed my depression, despite his short sight. For suddenly he cried above me in majestic tones:

'You must come and see me again, when I am in my castle!' (p 92).

7   'O'Donnell's Kern', *Silva Gadelica*, London: Edinburgh: Williams and Norgate 1892 pp 321-324.

8   Clarke makes these comments in a letter to Herbert Palmer, July 24, year unknown.

9   Conaire Mor is the primordial just king who unwittingly breaks his *geasa* and is hounded inexorably to his doom, as F.J. Byrne points out in *Kings and High Kings*, London: B.T. Batsford 1973 pp 59-64. Translations of *Togail Bruidhne Da Derga* may be read in T.P. Cross and C.H. Slover *Ancient Irish Tales*, London: George H. Harrap 1936 pp 93-126, or Jeffrey Gantz *Early Irish Myth and Legend*, Harmondsworth: Penguin 1981 pp 60-106. For a discussion of the story see Mairin O'Daly, 'Togail Bruidhne Da Derga', *Irish Sagas* ed. Myles Dillon, Dublin: Stationery Office 1959 pp 107-121. His *gessa* are listed in Alwyn and Brindley Rees *Celtic Heritage*, London: Thames and Hudson 1961 p 327.

10   'Mor's Sons and the Herder from Under the Sea', *Hero Tales of Ireland*. The literature about the goddess of sovereignty is extensive. See Proinsias MacCana, 'Aspects of the Theme of King and Goddess in Irish Literature', *Etudes Celtique*, VII (1955-1956) pp 76-114, pp 354-413 and VIII (1958-1959) pp 59-65. For the story of Niall of the Nine Hostages and the guardians of the sacred well described by Standish O'Grady, see Brian O Cuiv, 'A Poem Composed for Cathal Croibhdhearg O Connchubhair', *Eriu*, 34, 1984 pp 157-174. See also T.F. O'Rahilly, 'On the Origin of the names Erainn and Eriu', *Eriu*, XIV, 1943-1946 pp 7-28.

11   'The Poetry of Herbert Trench', *London Mercury*, X, 56 (June 1924) pp 157-166.

12   *Buile Shuibhne* (ed.) J.G. O'Keeffe, London: Irish Texts Society 1913. The Suibhne legend has attracted much critical attention. The story is summarised in Myles Dillon's *The Cycles of the Kings*, Cambridge: Cambridge University Press 1946 pp 68-74. See James Carney *Studies in Irish Literature and History*, Dublin: Institute for Advanced Studies 1955, chapter IV 'Suibhne Geilt' and 'The Children of Lir', and Robin Flower *The Irish Tradition* pp 63-64: 'If one part of their mind was dim from the quenched reason, another was illuminated by the divine light'.

13   The incident is found in 'The Destruction of Da Derga's Hostel'.

14   'Colloquy of the Old Men', *Silva Gadelica*, pp 142-144.

Chapter 2 *Epic Narratives 1916-1925*

1   'The Poetry of Herbert Trench', *London Mercury*, X, 56 (June 1924) pp 157-

166. Clarke also admits the immaturity of his response to Trench: 'Dynamic poems become to the young in mind an actual experience, an emotion, that makes the wisest criticism but an idle sound'. He points out that the style of *Silva Gadelica* and O'Grady's *Bardic History* is also flawed.

2   The *Times Literary Supplement* devoted two columns to it, summarising the poem carefully and quoting extensively. It noted that the metre is 'irregular but admirably responds to its various moods, smooth, agitated, wailful, or triumphant; the rhyme now absent, now barely perceptible, now coming out full and clear' (January 17, 1918). The *New Statesman* noted the 'eager, restless verse in which the rhyme appears and disappears without any of the uncomfortable effect which such a mixture usually produces. His descriptions of the mountain scenes . . . are extremely beautiful, and he reaches an excellent vigour in the beginning of the chase after the fugitives' (January 26, 1918). The *Irish Times* indulged in flowery tribute: 'Not since Mr. Yeats first put on his singing robes has any Irish poet appeared with such decisive claim to be in the bardic succession' (February 2, 1918) and there was more of the same. It almost comes as a relief to find Joseph Campbell in the *New Ireland* stating bluntly that it is 'a bad book' (March 2, 1918) even though the controversy that ensued boosted sales and led to a second impression. Stephen MacKenna's assessment in *Studies* is more balanced. Clarke, he wrote, 'has dramatic quality, very intense; he has passion; he has an almost incomparable wealth of rich words; he has a strange power over the line, the cadence, the pause, the weight of syllable' (7, 25, 1918 pp 179-180).

3   Some reviewers were surprised by the change of subject from Fionn to Moses; others rightly noted that it had been written at almost the same time as the *Vengeance of Fionn*. Some, remembering the promise of that poem, were reluctant to be harsh. The *Irish Independent*, among others, mentioned the influence of Milton and Keats and regarded *Fires of Baal* as 'a more finished and more classical poem' but qualified that opinion by judging it to be a poem of 'promise rather than achievement' (March 21, 1921). The *Dublin Evening Herald* thought it almost as good as the *Vengeance of Fionn* (March 26, 1921). The *Irish Monthly* noted the excess of 'gorgeous imagery' but the lack of human insight; 'we are told nothing of the things that Moses thought' (June 1921). The *Catholic World* had the same reaction (April, 1921). The *Freeman's Journal* praised the poem's epic force but regretted that the human interest was so slight (March 26, 1921). The *Irish Homestead*, AE's paper, praised the picturesque vocabulary but said the pictures often lacked precision. The *London Mercury* was also critical of the style: 'the epithets are at once too abundant and too strained' (April, 1921). The *Manchester Guardian* criticised the lavish style and could not resist the clever comment: 'you can't see Lebanon for the cedars' (May 19, 1921). The *Spectator* rather bluntly asserted that the poem 'neither rises to the sublime nor sinks to the incompetent' (May 28, 1921).

4   The reception of *Sword of the West* hurt. If the reviewers were restrained in writing about the *Fires of Baal* now at the end of 1921 they knew what Clarke's faults were. In fact the faults had also been present in the *Vengeance of Fionn* but in *Sword of the West*, which has little narrative clarity, characterisation, or verbal precision, they are all too visible. Even the *Dublin Evening Herald* called it 'morbid' (January 1, 1922) and the *Irish Times* said 'Nature, in fact, crowds out man . . . there is a serious lack of human incident

and almost no attempt at portrayal of character' (January 20, 1922). The reviewer went on to argue that a narrative poet must tell a story, must avoid excessive decoration of style and try for simplicity and directness in the narrative. The *Freeman's Journal* said that Clarke had become less disciplined (February 11, 1922). The *Times Literary Supplement*, taking up Clarke's comment that the poem is meant to be spoken, not read, that it is incantation, said 'This particular incantation is full of dripping swords, streaming hair, screaming eagles, thundering horses, and every other kind of heroic adjective' and 'it leads nowhere' (January 16, 1922). When Clarke went to visit Stephen MacKenna, the latter pushed the book aside with an impatient gesture and said he couldn't get through it (*Penny in the Clouds*, p 21). AE's review in the *Irish Homestead* was blunt and accurate. Clarke, he said, is not so much the master of his dreams as the slave of them.

> Mr Clarke's imagination is heavy with dream. His landscapes are the landscapes of dream. His characters speak in the same language as the poet. They are the spirits of the dream landscape made self-conscious and thinking of nothing but their own atmosphere, and are like figures on tapestry which do not emerge from their backgrounds. Mr. Clarke loads their speeches with his gorgeous adjectives and colours until they seem merely another mirror in which the landscape is seen. He has not yet learned that beauty made out of bare words to which Mr. Yeats came at last. The poems would impress us more if the characters had that simple beauty of bare words to lift them out of their setting. At present they talk about the scenery more than about their own hearts. (January 7, 1922).

5   For a discussion of the revisions see Maurice Harmon, '*The Sword of the West* (1921, 1936, 1974)', *Études Irlandaises*, 10, n.s. (December 1985) pp 93-104.

Chapter 3 *Pilgrimage (1929)*

1   *Collected Poems*, New York: Macmillan 1936 p 313.
2   These two, 'The Scholar' and 'The Cardplayer', which is about Manannan Mac Lir, have been reprinted from *The Son of Learning*. The Irish text for 'The Scholar' may be consulted in T.F. O'Rahilly, *Measgra Dánta. Miscellaneous Irish Poems*, Dublin, Cork: Cork University Press 1927 pp 16-17.
3   In *Penny in the Clouds* Clarke describes this storm. 'I found myself back in the seventeenth century'. The ship flaming in the sunlight is similar to the ship seen in 'The Itinerary of Ua Cleirigh'.
4   Clonmacnoise, a monastic city on the river Shannon, founded by St Ciaran, has hundreds of finely carved grave stones which show the technical and artistic skill of its craftsmen, about 1000 AD. The Nun's Chapel is a fine example of Celtic Romanesque architecture. The site also has the High Cross of the Scriptures, erected about 900 AD and two round towers. It is well known for its books, including *Leabbar na hUidhre*, *Chronicon Scotorum*, the *Annals of Clonmacnoise*, and the *Annals of Tigernach*. It produced the Cross of Cong, St Manchan's Shrine, and two famous croziers.
    Cashel was both a monastic site and a royal seat; at one time it was the ecclesiastical capital of Munster. Cormac's Chapel, built by Cormac MacCarthy in 1134, marks the high point of the Celtic-Romanesque; it has two towers.

The site also contains a High Cross and a round tower.

5   *T.P.'s Weekly*, XII, 301 (August 3, 1929) p 418.

6   Clarke commented later on what he wanted to achieve. 'The Celtic-Romanesque era with its intricate patterns in verse, in stone, metal and illumination, its conventionalised impersonal forms, attracted us as objective writers in an age of self-dramatisation and display'. *Poetry in Modern Ireland*, p 44.

7   A large and superb Cashel bell may be seen in the Hunt Museum, National Institute for Higher Education, Plessey House, Limerick, case 44; there are hand-bells in case 45. Cashel was traditionally called 'Cashel of the Bells'. In *Singing Men at Cashel* Clarke makes the point that Gospels were carried into battle, as the Ark of the Covenant was carried by the Israelites.

8   Ezekiel I,v 4 ff, Apocalypse IV, v 2 ff.

9   *The Irish Tradition*, Oxford: Clarendon Press 1947 p 53.

10   'The Black Church', p 13.

11   'Love in Irish Poetry and Drama', *Motley*, 1, 5 (October 1932) pp 3-4.

12   *Annals of Clonmacnoise* (ed.) Rev Denis Murphy, Dublin: University Press 1896 p 145. Eugene O'Curry *Lectures on the Manuscript Materials of Ancient Irish History*, Dublin: James Duffy 1861 pp 131-135. Douglas Hyde *A Literary History of Ireland*, London: T. Fisher Unwin 1899 p 421, pp 425-6. George Sigerson *Bards of the Gael and Gall*, London: T. Fisher Unwin 1897 pp 414-416.

13   For example, James Carney *Medieval Irish Lyrics*, Dublin: Dolmen 1967 XXVI. Anne Sullivan 'Triamhain Ghormlaithe' *Eriu*, 16, 1952 pp 189-199. John V. Kelleher 'On a Poem about Gormflaith' *Éigse*, XVI, part iv (1976) pp 251-54.

14   *Collected Poems*, 1936 p 312.

15   Edited by Osborn Bergin and Carl Marstrander, Halle: Max Niemeyer 1912 pp 346-369.

16   *Celtic Mythology*, London: Hamlyn 1970 p 95. James Carney, writing of the early christian poets, says that asceticism may have been the ideal, but they had a great love for what they poetically called 'the golden-cropped world'. As a result many fell for a time by the wayside and then wrote poems of penitence. Even while pursuing penance a poet may remember his sinful past with what seems to be a tender nostalgia. Sometimes the poet presents his thoughts dramatically through a famous character. The Old Woman of Beare contrasts the joys of youth with the lean old years of compulsory penitence. 'The Impact of Christianity', *Early Irish Society* (ed.) Myles Dillon, Dublin: Sign of the Three Candles 1954 pp 76-77.

17   *Irish Kings and High Kings*, London: B.T. Batsford 1973 p 167.

18   There are four or five categories of religious poems: the prayer, the eulogy of God or a saint, the *uirsgéal*, or story illustrative of some moral lesson, and the confession of sins. Introduction, X, L. McKenna (ed) *Dán Dé. The Poems of Donnchadh Mór O Dalaigh, and the Religious Poems of the Yellow Book of Lecan*, Dublin Educational Company of Ireland, no date.

19   'Love in Irish Poetry and Drama', pp 3-4.

20   Edited by James Clarence Mangan, 2nd ed. 1850 pp 189-191.

21   Published in 1932 at the beginning of Clarke's renewal of poetic activity.

22   Preface to *Three Middle-Irish Homilies on the Lives of Saints Patrick, Bridget, and Columba*, Calcutta 1877 VII.

23   *Collected Poems*, 1936 pp 312.

24   'Irish Poetry To-Day', p 32.
25   *Collected Poems* (1936) p 313.
26   'The Black Church', p 11.
27   'Irish Poetry To-Day', p 29.
28   *Ibid*. p 31.
29   *Ibid*. p 32.
30   'The Black Church', pp 30-31. In *Poetry in Modern Ireland* Clarke said he turned eventually to the study of Irish, p 55.
31   *Irish Times*, 5 November, 1941. Lambert McKenna *Aithdioghluim Dána; a miscellany of Irish bardic poetry*, Dublin: Irish Texts Society, vols. 37, 40, 1939. Donnchadh Ruadh Mac Conmara *Adventures of a Luckless Fellow, written by himself in verse*, translated by Standish H. O'Grady, Dublin 1853. Mrs Ellen Costello *Ambráin Mhuighe Seóla*, London: Journal of Irish Song Society, vol. 16, 1919. Clarke admired Padraic De Brun's translation of 'Anac Cuan'.
32   'Irish Poetry To-Day', p 26.
33   *Ibid*. p 27.
34   Letter to Seamus O'Sullivan, August 23 (?1935).

Chapter 4 *Night and Morning (1938)*

1   'There is no scripture of youth', Clarke wrote in the manuscript of *Twice Round the Black Church*, 'we are kept in ignorance and the imagination which might flower at puberty is corrupted by the doctrines of the middle aged celibates who educate us'.
2   'Irish Poetry To-Day', p 31.
3   *First Visit to England*, p 47; *Penny in the Clouds*, p 164.
4   *Twice Round the Black Church*, p 18.
5   Letter to Herbert Palmer, June 23, 1938. Clarke makes a similar point in a letter to Devin A. Garrity, about the function of the word 'satchels' in 'The Blackbird of Derrycairn': 'I use discords deliberately in the same way as a modern composer of music. In this case the blackbird is indicating his dislike of book learning. The poem is meant to convey something of the sound of Irish and so is full of sibilants and gutturals, sounds, too, which are to be found in the blackbird's song itself, and the harsh consonants of "satchel" is meant to be modulated by the liquid 'l' of the ending.' March 8, 1948.
6   'The Irish Abroad, 1534-1691', *New History of Ireland*, vol. III, eds. T.W. Moody, F.X. Martin, F.J. Byrne, Oxford: Clarendon Press 1976 p 619. Although Clarke says that the poem is 'after the Irish', there seems to be no Irish poem to which it particularly corresponds. There are many poems about the return of the spoiled priest from the seminary, such as 'An Caisdeach Ban', *Na Caisidigh agus a gCuid Filidheachta*, (ed.) Maighread Nic Philibin, Baile Atha Cliath: Oifig an tSolathair 1939 pp 53-55. Since 'The Straying Student' appeared in 1937 this is unlikely to be a source. There are many stories also about poets, such as Donnchadh Ruadh MacConmara, who returned from the seminary. James Carney sees a resemblance in the poem to Crinoc. Crinoc was a wise woman who counselled the student and slept with him when he was a boy of seven. In fact, Carney argues, she is a metaphor for the Book of Psalms. He has translated the poem in his *Medieval Irish Lyrics*, pp 74-78.
7   Letter to Herbert Palmer, June 23, 1938.

Chapter 5   *Three Prose Romances*

1   For a more detailed discussion see Roger McHugh and Maurice Harmon, *A Short History of Anglo-Irish Literature from its origins to the present day*, Dublin: Wolfhound Press 1982 chapters XI and XVII.

2   *Penny in the Clouds*, p 100.

3   All the references are to these editions: *The Bright Temptation*, Dublin: Dolmen 1965; *The Singing Men at Cashel*, London: Allen and Unwin 1936; *The Sun Dances at Easter*, London: Melrose 1952.

4   Material derived from 'The Intoxication of the Ulstermen' and 'Bricriu's Feast', Cross and Slover *Ancient Irish Tales*, pp 215-238, pp 256-280.

5   She has the same force as the woman in 'The Straying Student'.

6   Aidan also sees the figure of the knitting madman who turns up again in *Mnemosyne Lay in Dust*, as do the harpies.

7   See Gearóid Mac Eoin 'Gleann Bolcain agus Gleann na nGealt', *Bealoideas*, XXX, 1962 pp 105-120.

8   According to himself Bec-mac-De is St Ronan who cursed Suibhne.

9   Based on the desecration of Clonmacnoise in 840 when Ota, wife of Turgesius, was worshipped on the altar. G.T. Stokes *Ireland and the Celtic Church* pp 260-261. There are several other accounts also.

10   Clarke draws upon the description given by the poet, Aedh, in *Silva Gadelica*. 'Reciting of romances, of the Fian-lore, was there everyday, singing of poems, instrumental music, the mellow blasts of horns, and concerted minstrelsy', p 282.

11   It compares its ninth-century heroine with Fair Geraldine of the sixteenth century. If its accounts of the desecration of Cluanmore corresponds to the sack of Clonmacnoise, then other allusions are not dated correctly: Murtough of the Leathar Cloaks, son of Nial Glundubh, could not have made his famous circuit of Ireland, nor could the Cross of the Scriptures, built by Gormlai's father have been erected. Cluanmore would not have had its round tower.

12   Clarke expands an incident recorded in *Twice Round the Black Church*, p 74.

13   See Eleanor Knott *Irish Classical Poetry* p 74. The 'Contention' has been edited by the Rev L. MacKenna for the Irish Texts Society 1918.

14   In *The Singing Men at Cashel* Murtagh Mac Erca tells the story to Anier Mac Conglinne.

Chapter 6   *Plays*

1   The story is told in greater detail in Roger McHugh and Maurice Harmon *A Short History of Anglo-Irish Literature from its origins to the present day*, Dublin: Wolfhound Press 1982 chapter 15.

2   *The Irish Drama of Europe from Yeats to Beckett*, London: Athlone Press 1978 p 3.

3   *Penny in the Clouds*, p 4.

4   *Ibid.* p 7.

5   See Tina Hunt Mahony 'The Dublin Verse-Speaking Society and the Lyric Theatre', *Irish University Review*, 4, 1 (Spring 1974) pp 65-73.

6   'A Chronicle of Recent Books: Poetry', *Life and Letters* 1932 pp 488-489.

7   *New Statesman*, March 12, 1932.

8   *London Mercury*, XXXI, 184 (February 1935) pp 391-392.

9   *London Mercury*, XXXIV, 201 (July 1936) p 279.

10   'Gordon Bottomley', *London Mercury*, XXXIX, 234 (April 1939) p 658.

11   *Dublin Magazine*, XIV, 3, n.s. (July-September 1939) pp 85-87.

12   *Collected Plays*, Dublin: Dolmen 1963 p 398.

13   'The Plays of Austin Clarke', *Irish University Review*, p 63.

14   For a discussion of Anier and of *Aislinge Meic Con Glinne*, 'The Vision of MacConglinne', see Robin Flower *The Irish Tradition*, pp 75-77.

15   *Ireland and the Celtic Church*, pp 149-165. Bede's account is in Book III, chapter 25.

16   Vivian Mercier summarises the story in *The Irish Comic Tradition*, Oxford: Clarendon Press 1962 pp 25-26.

17   London: Macmillan 1866 pp 158-163. For a translation of the story which is found in *Lebor Gabála* and edited by Kuno Meyer in *Anecdota from Irish Manuscripts*, 1 24f, see Eleanor Hull 'The Hawk of Achill or the Legend of the Oldest Animals', *Folk-Lore*, XLIII (London 1932) pp 376-409. See Eleanor Knott's discussion of Fintan and the Crow in *Irish Classical Poetry*, pp 20-24.

18   The story may be read in Cross and Slover *Ancient Irish Tales*, pp 518-532.

19   For Clarke's source see Lilian Duncan's edited text, *Eriu*, XI, 1932, pp 184-225. See also Máire MacNéill 'The Legends of the False God's Daughter', JRSAI, 1949 and A.G. von Hamel 'The Celtic Grail', *Revue Celtique*, XLVII (1930) pp 340-381.

Chapter 8 *Poems and Satires 1955-1962*

1   The controversy is discussed by J.H. White in *Church and State in Modern Ireland 1923-1979* 2nd ed., Dublin: Gill and Macmillan; Totowa, New Jersey: Barnes and Noble 1980 chapters VII and VIII.

2   Douglas Hyde *Songs Ascribed to Raftery*, New York: Barnes and Noble 1973 pp 222-223.

3   *Irish Times*, February 26, 1943. For a more complete account of what happened see Mavis Arnold and Heather Laskey *Children of the Poor Clares. The Story of an Irish Orphanage*, Belfast: Appletree Press 1985.

4   *Collected Poems*, p 355.

5   Clarke, R. Dardis 'Austin Clarke at Templeogue', *Poetry Ireland Review*, 21 (Spring 1988) pp 41-46.

6   *Sanas Chormaic. Cormac's Glossary*. Translated by John O'Donovan, Editor Whitley Stokes, Calcutta: Irish Archaeological and Celtic Society 1968 p 114.

7   Of the falls at Assaroe Clarke wrote: 'stricken now because of the ugly dam built for the new hydro-electric schemes'. *Penny in the Clouds*, p 127.

8   Works, volume VI, p 544. The suspicion that Clarke may simply like the assonance of 'Cummin . . . hum/. . . Thummim' is somewhat allayed by this.

9   *Twice Round the Black Church*, p 14.

10   'My own particular joy and possession was a beautiful prayer book bound in Morocco leather and I clasped it to my breast, ignorant of the Mahommedan hands through which its fine mottling had passed'. *Twice Round the Black Church*, p 133.

11   *Twice Round the Black Church*, p 138.

12.   *Ibid*. p 139.

13.   *Ibid*. He writes: 'If a pin-cushion or a purse were mislaid, St. Anthony found it for us and it appeared mysteriously under the hand. The great centuries of

thaumaturgy had been domesticated for us ... We might be running down the hilly steps of Siena, following St. Francis de Sales around the narrow street corners of Dijon, or crossing a piazza in Padua' (p 20). That facile association characterised his adolescent piety; it had a bloodless and pallid quality. 'The sun was hotter in the sky, for we were no longer coming towards Camden Street, but were on the Continent. We were in the streets of Padua, where St. Anthony had prayed, or in the narrow by-ways of Dijon where Francis de Sales met Madame de Chalmey, at Charolles where Blessed Margaret Mary had her visions.' (p 50). In 'Martha Blake at Fifty One' he will deal more harshly with a religion based on such fancies.

14   *Ibid*. p 137.
15   *Ibid*. p 137.
16   *Ibid*. p 137.
17   *Ibid*. p 137.
18   *Ibid*. 137-138. These stanzas about the 'mixture of ferocity and fervour in religion' recall his boyish and adolescent trauma. At a time when he struggled against his 'base instincts' religion provided an ambiguous comfort. He was 'yielding to the voluptuous language of the Spanish and French mystics', but experiencing also in confession 'warnings against curiosity, body-blighting sins, voluntary emissions that would eventually bring on madness. The Devil was at my side, tempting with his sweets of darkness'.
19   *Ibid*. p 153. Clarke's Uncle Maurice delighted in the scientific achievements; he had, Clarke tells us, 'a mysterious contraption which emitted pin-and-needle shocks, and a phonograph with cylindrical records. Electricity was already home-made and I was always present when father renewed the sal ammoniac in the glass jar of the battery which was used for the hall-door bell. Soon we had electric fittings in the house but the switches, which were made of brass, could often be as painful to the touch as Uncle Maurice's energy giving machine.'
20   *Ibid*. p 155. 'In the darkness we watched the future age of speed in which all was quickened — men, women, darting down streets, through doorways, up and down steps, quicker than we could, wheels revolving, the globe itself turning . . . an express train hurtling through space at an absurd angle and then disappearing into the cracked smile of a pantomimic moon.'

Chapter 9   *Flight to Africa (1963)*

1   *Collected Poems* (1974), Poems 1955-1966, p 357.
2   E. Allison Peers (translator and ed.), *Complete Works of Saint Teresa of Jesus* vol. I, London: Sheed and Ward 1946 chapter XXXII pp 215-216.
3   *Ibid*. chapter XXIX, pp 192-193.
4   E. Allison Peers *Complete Works of Saint John of the Cross* vol. II, London: Burns, Oates and Washbourne 1934. Clarke's stanzas echo some of the imagery of St John's poem, 'The Dark Night': lilies, flowering breast, night of darkness; so do its references to flight beyond the highest order of saints, the Seraphim, and the description of the soul's union with God.
5   *The Poems of Carolan* (ed.) Tomás Ó Máille, London: Irish Texts Society 1916. 'Máible Shéim Ní Cheallaigh', pp 109-111; 'Pléaraca Na Ruarcach', pp 205-297.
6   *The Poems of Egan O'Rahilly* (ed.) Patrick S. Dinneen, London: Irish Texts

Society 1900. 'Aisling Meabhuil', pp 24-25; 'An Aisling', pp 22-23. Better editions now exist, but these ITS texts were those used by Clarke.

7   Edited by Tomás Dubh, Dublin: M.H. Gill 1914 pp 42-49.

8   'Donnchadh Ruadh i dTalamh na-n-Éisc'.

Chapter 10 *Mnemosyne Lay in Dust (1966)*

1   *Twice Round the Black Church*, p 8.

2   *Penny in the Clouds*, p 43.

3   *Twice Round the Black Church*, p 18.

Chapter 11 *Last Poems 1967-1974*

1   In *Revue Celtique*, XII (1891), 86n. Whitley Stokes omits the incident of the mating between the Dagda and the daughter of Indech, but Thurneysen includes it in 'Ceth Maige Turedh', *Zeitschriff für Celtische Philologie*, XII (1918) pp 401-2.

2   Books VI, pp 115-135; X, p 333 and XIV, p 331.

3   This has not been ignored by critics, but it did not feature in the Conference.

4   Roger McHugh and Philip Edwards (eds.) *Jonathan Swift — A Dublin Ter-Centenary Tribute, 1667-1967*, Dublin: Dolmen 1967 p 114.

5   *Celtica*, II, 1954 pp 325-333.

6   In *Twice Round the Black Church* Clarke wrote: 'many Protestant churches here, owing to the decline in the number of parishioners, have become dance-halls and there is merriment in those places where once the Son of Man was worshipped', p 130.

7   The statue's troubles increased in 1929 when it was again blown-up and this time when the pieces were collected the head was missing. Finally, in 1949, it was broken up for smelting.

8   Acts IX, vs 36-43.

SELECT BIBLIOGRAPHY

A. PRIMARY WORKS
1. Major and Individual Publications   2. Poems
3. Plays   4. Articles and Reviews

B. SECONDARY PUBLICATIONS
Books — Articles — Reviews

C. BACKGROUND

1. Major and Individual Publications

The Vengeance of Fionn. Dublin, London: Maunsel, 1917; repr. 1918.

The Fires of Baal. Dublin, London: Maunsel and Roberts, 1921.

The Sword of the West. Dublin, London: Maunsel and Roberts, 1921.

The Cattledrive in Connaught and other poems. London: Allen and Unwin, 1925.

The Son of Learning: a poetic comedy in three acts. London: Allen and Unwin, 1927; repr. Dublin: Dolmen, 1964.

Pilgrimage and other poems. London: Allen and Unwin, 1929; New York: Farrar and Rinehart, 1930.

The Flame: a play in one act. London: Allen and Unwin, 1930.

The Bright Temptation: a romance. London: Allen and Unwin, 1932; New York: William Morrow, 1932; repr. Dublin: Dolmen; Chester Springs, Pa: Dufour, 1965.

Collected Poems. London: Allen and Unwin; New York: Macmillan, 1936

The Singing-Men at Cashel. London: Allen and Unwin, 1936.

Night and Morning. Dublin: Orwell, 1938.

Sister Eucharia: a verse play in three scenes. London: Williams and Norgate; Dublin: Orwell, 1939.

Black Fast: a poetic farce in one act. Dublin: Orwell, 1941.

The Straying Student. Dublin: Gayfield, 1942.

'Foreword' to Mervyn Wall. *Alarm Among the Clerks.* Dublin: Richview, n.d.

As the Crow Flies: a lyric play for the air. Dublin: Bridge; London: Williams and Norgate, 1943.

The Viscount of Blarney and other plays. Dublin: Bridge; London: Williams and Norgate, 1944.

First Visit to England and other memories. Dublin: Bridge; London: Williams and Norgate, 1945.

The Second Kiss: a light comedy. Dublin: Bridge; London: Williams and Norgate, 1946.

The Plot Succeeds: a poetic pantomime. Dublin: Bridge; London: Williams and Norgate, 1950.

Poetry in Modern Ireland, with illustrations by Louis Le Brocquy. Dublin: Three Candles, 1951; repr. Cork: Mercier, 1967; repr. Folcroft, Pa.: Folcroft, 1974.

The Sun Dances at Easter. London: Andrew Melrose, 1952.

The Moment Next to Nothing: a play in three acts. Dublin: Bridge, 1953.

Ancient Lights: poems and satires. Dublin: Bridge, 1955.

Too Great a Vine: poems and satires. Dublin: Bridge, 1957.

The Horse-Eaters: poems and satires. Dublin: Bridge, 1960; Dolmen, 1961.

Later Poems. Dublin: Dolmen, 1961.

Forget-Me-Not. Dublin: Dolmen, 1962.

Twice Round the Black Church: early memories of England and Ireland. London: Routledge and Kegan Paul, 1962.

Collected Plays. Dublin: Dolmen, 1963.

Flight to Africa and other poems. Dublin: Dolmen, 1963.

Ed. with introduction. *The Poems of Joseph Campbell.* Dublin: Allen Figgis, 1963.

Poems, with Charles Tomlinson and Tony Connor. London: Oxford UP, 1964.

Mnemosyne Lay in Dust. Dublin: Dolmen; London: Oxford UP; Chester Springs, Pa.: Dufour, 1966

Introduction to *The Plays of George Fitzmaurice: dramatic fantasies* Dublin:

Dolmen, 1967.

Old-fashioned Pilgrimage and other poems. Dublin: Dolmen; Chester Springs, Pa.: Dufour, 1967.

The Echo at Coole and other poems. Dublin: Dolmen; Chester Springs, Pa.: Dufour, 1968.

A Penny in the Clouds: more memories of Ireland and England. London: Routledge and Kegan Paul, 1968.

A Sermon on Swift and other poems. Dublin: Bridge, 1968.

Two Interludes, adapted from Cervantes, 'The Student from Salamanca' and 'The Silent Lover', Dublin: Dolmen, 1968.

The Celtic Twilight and Nineties. Dublin: Dolmen, 1969.

Orphide and other poems. Dublin: Bridge, 1970.

Tiresias: a poem. Dublin, Bridge, 1971.

The Impuritans. Dublin: Dolmen, 1973.

Collected Poems. Dublin: Dolmen, 1974.

Selected Poems. ed. Thomas Kinsella. Dublin: Dolmen; Winston-Salem, Ill: Wake Forest UP, 1976.

The Third Kiss: a comedy in one act. Dublin: Dolmen, 1976.

Liberty Lane: a ballad play of Dublin in two acts with a prologue. Dublin: Dolmen, 1978.

2. Poems

A Reply to A.G.B. (with apologies to Byron's 'Isles of Greece'). *Irish Homestead,* January 31, 1914, 98. Signed A.C.(?)

The Isle – A Fantasy. *New Ireland,* July 8, 1916, 349.

Song. *New Ireland,* July 22, 1916, 381.

A Memory, *New Ireland,* August, 1916, 444.

A Cliff Song. *The Vengeance of Fionn,* 1917, 57.

In Doire Dha Bhoth. A Fragment. *New Ireland,* Feb. 17, 1917, 243; *The National Student,* no. 25, V, VII, 2 March 1917, 14.

To James Stephens. *The Shamrock and Irish Emerald,* Dec. 11, 1920.

Three Sentences. *Dublin Magazine,* I, 5 Dec. 1923, 372.

Silver and Gold. *Irish Statesman,* 1 1924, 650.

The Lost Heifer. *Irish Statesman,* 3 (1924), 138; *Nation and Athenaeum,* XXXVII, 13 (June 27, 1925), 400.

The Lad Made King. *Irish Statesman,* 3 (1924), 330.

The Son of Lir. *Irish Statesman,* 4 (1925), 555.

The House in the West. *Irish Statesman,* 5 (1925), 77.

The Son of Learning. *Irish Statesman,* 6 (1926), 121-122.

The Fair at Windgap, *T.P's Weekly,* VIII, 185, (May 14, 1927), 75.

Pilgrimage. *Dublin Magazine* II, n.s., 3 (July-Sept. 1927), 1-3.

The Confession of Queen Gormlai, *Dublin Magazine,* II, n.s. 3 (July-Sept., 1927), 4-9.

South-Westerly Gale. *Irish Statesman.* 11 (1928), 250.

Pilgrimage. *Spectator.* 140 (Feb. 11, 1928), 194.

Three Poems. The Planter's Daughter, The Marriage Night, Aisling. *Dublin Magazine* III, n.s., 3 (July-Sept., 1928), 1-4.

Vision. *Spectator,* 142 (March 9, 1929), 370.

Wandering Men. *Spectator,* 149 (Oct. 8, 1932), 446.

The Song of Repentance. *Dublin Magazine,* X, n.s., 1 (Jan.-March, 1935), 1-2.

Lost Heifer. *Saturday Review of Literature,* XIV (Aug. 15, 1936), 19.

Two Poems. The Lucky Coin, The Straying Student. *Dublin Magazine,* XII, n.s., 2 (April-June, 1937), 4-6.

Song in Lent. *London Mercury,* XXXV, 210 (April, 1937), 550.

Martha Blake. *London Mercury,* XXXVI, 212 (June, 1937), 119.

Night and Morning, *Dublin Magazine,* XII, n.s., 4 (Oct.-Dec., 1937), 1-2.

The Jewels. *Dublin Magazine,* XIII, n.s., 2 (April-June, 1938), 1-2.

The Lucky Coin. *The Bell,* X, 4 (July 1945), 290-291.

Mother and Child. *Irish Times,* June 12, 1954, 8.

An Early Start. *Irish Times,* Sept. 4, 1954.

Four Poems. Fashion, Return from England, An Early Start, The Envy of Poor Lovers. *Irish Writing,* 32 (Autumn, 1955), 14-15.

The Stadium. *Irish Times,* April 29, 1961, 6.

Forget-Me-Not. Poetry at the Mermaid. *London Poetry Book Society,* 1962, 29-34.

Song of the Books. *Poetry Ireland*. 1 (Autumn, 1962), 5-12.

Flight to Africa. *The Dubliner*, 6 (Jan.-Feb. 1963), 3-6; *Poetry C*, 2 (May 1962), 83-6.

Burial of an Irish President, *The Dubliner*, 2, 1 (Spring, 1963), 35.

I Saw from Cashel. *Poetry Ireland*, 2 (Spring, 1963), 55.

Two Poems. The Common Market, Ecumenical Council. *Arena*, 1 (Spring, 1963), 4.

Cypress Grove. *Arena*, 2 (Autumn, 1963), 3.

The Penitent, *The Dubliner*, 3, 1 (Spring, 1964), 3.

The Paper Curtain. *Dublin Magazine*, IV, n.s., 3 and 4 (Autumn-Winter 1965), 24-27.

The Loss of Memory. *Quarterly Review of Literature*, XIV, 1-2 (1966), 116-140.

Riversdale, 1965. A Centenary Tribute. *Kenyon Review*, XXVIII, 4 (Sept. 1966), 496-497.

Letter to a Friend. *Hibernia*, Oct. 10, 1966, 16.

Old-fashioned Pilgrimage. *Poetry*, CIX, 2 (Nov. 1966), 101-109.

Robert Frost at Newman House. Labours of Idleness. *University Review*, III, 10 (Winter, 1966), 31-33.

Extrivio. Black , White and Yellow. *University Review*, IV, 3 (Winter, 1967), 283-285.

Two Poems. A Sermon on Swift. Rose MacDowell. *Kilkenny Magazine*, 16-17 (Spring, 1969), 9-14.

A Sermon on Swift. *Massachusetts Review*, XI, 2 (Spring, 1970), 309-312.

The Trees of the Forest. *Ariel*, 1, 3 (July, 1970), 70-71.

The Wooing of Becfola. *Ireland of the Welcomes*, XXIII, 3 (1974), p. 19.

Tiresias. *The Malahide Review*, XXIII, July 1972, 8-28.

3. Plays

The Son of Learning: a poetic comedy in two acts: Act 1. *Dublin Magazine*, 1, n.s., 3 (July-Sept., 1926), 35-50.

The Flame: a play in one act. *Dublin Magazine*, IV, n.s., 4 (Oct.-Dec., 1929), 15-22; V, n.s., 1 (Jan.-March, 1930), 15-25.

Sister Eucharia: a play in three acts. *Dublin Magazine*, XIII, n.s., 3 (July-Sept., 1938), 1-26.

The Kiss: a light comedy in one act. *Dublin Magazine*, XVII, n.s., 3 (July-Sept., 1942), 5-18.

The Second Kiss: a light comedy in one act. *Dublin Magazine*, XXXI, n.s., 2 (April-June, 1946), 5-19.

The Student from Salamanca. *Poetry Ireland*, 5 (Spring, 1965), 25-38.

The Impuritans: a play in one act. *Irish University Review*, I, 1 (Autumn, 1970), 131-148.

Fragment of a Play. *Journal of the Butler Society*, 1, 5 (1973-74), 389-393.

The Visitation: a play. *Irish University Review*, IV, 1 (Spring, 1974), 74-50.

4. Articles, Reviews

'Joseph Mary Plunkett II. Poet'. *The Belvederean*, IV, 3 (1917), 5-7.

'Tory'. *The New Witness*. Sept. 29, 1922, 199.

'Tory. II'. *The New Witness*, Oct. 6, 1922, 218.

'Two novels', [Review]. *Nation and Athenaeum*, XXIV, 23 (March 8, 1923), 804.

'Adventure in Donegal'. *New Statesman*, Sept. 1, 1923.

'Simple Folk: a Donegal sketch'. *New Statesman*, Sept. 22, 1923.

'An Imp in Yorkshire: a woman Journalist's problems'. [Review]. *Daily News and Leader*, Oct. 3, 1923, 7.

[Review] of Padraic Colum's *Castle Conquer*. *Daily News and Leader*, Nov. 7, 1923, 9.

'Five Novels'. [Review]. *Nation and Athenaeum*, XXXIV, 8, Nov. 24, 1923.

'A Warning to Readers: four kinds of novelists'. [Review]. *Daily News and Leader*, Nov. 29, 1923, 9.

'Notable Novels'. [Review]. *Daily News and Leader*, Dec. 4, 1923, 8.

'America and Fiction'. [Review]. *Nation and Athenaeum*, XXXIV, 12 Dec. 22, 1923, 467-468.

'Art and Energy'. [Letters]. *Irish Statesman*, 3 (1924), 237-238, 270, 300-301.

'Ladies and Dishes: love in fiction'. [Review]. *Daily News and Leader*, Jan. 10, 1924, 7.

'Mr. Harris Talks'. [Review] of *Contemporary Portraits. Fourth Series* by Frank Harris. *Nation and Athenaeum*, XXXIV, 18 (Feb. 2, 1924).

'Stephen Dedalus: the author of Ulysses'. *New Statesman*, Feb. 23, 1924.

'Short Stories'. [Review]. *Nation and Athenaeum*, XXXV, 1 (April 5, 1924), 20 and 22.

'Russia and Rome'. [Review]. *Nation and Athenaeum*, XXXV, 5 (May 3, 1924), 150.

'Strong Drink and China Tea'. [Review] of *Miss Linn* by Douglas Golding and *The Black Soul* by Liam O'Flaherty. *Nation and Athenaeum*, XXXV, 8 (May 24, 1924).

'Two Novels'. [Review]. *Nation and Athenaeum*, XXXV, 9 (May 31, 1924), 297.

'The Poetry of Herbert Trench'. *London Mercury*, X, 56 (June, 1924), 157-166.

'Novels'. [Review]. *Nation and Athenaeum*, XXXV, 18 (August 2, 1924), 569-570.

'The Seven Woods'. *Nation and Athenaeum*, XXXVI, 11 (Dec. 13, 1924), 411.

'Story Teller'. *New Statesman*, April 11, 1925.

'The Plough and the Stars'. [Letter]. *Irish Statesman*, 5 (1926), 740.

'A Lost Province'. *New Statesman*, August 7, 1926.

'Fiction'. [Review]. *Nation and Athenaeum*, XL, 10 (Dec. 11, 1926).

'Art and Energy'. [Letters]. *Irish Statesman*, 8 (1927), 450-451.

'Fiction'. [Review]. *Nation and Athenaeum*, XL, 17 (Jan. 29, 1927), 598-599.

'Fiction'. [Review]. *Nation and Athenaeum*, XL, 26 (April 2, 1927), 930-931.

'How the Novel Grew: popular fiction through the ages'. [Review] of *The Light Reading of Our Ancestors* by Lord Ernle. *T. P's Weekly*, VIII, 187 (May 28, 1927), 156.

'Blake and His Sculptor: a centenary commingling of the arts'. *T. P's Weekly*, VIII, 198 (August 13, 1927), 491-492.

'A Connemara Poet: rapture of western sunlight and storm'. [Review] of *The Dark Breed* by F. R. Higgins. *T. P's Weekly*, VIII, 201 (Sept. 3, 1927), 585.

'A Parodist and His Victims'. *T. P's Weekly*, VIII, 203 (Sept. 17, 1927), 646.

'A Beloved Tyrant'. [Review] of *The Madonna of the Clutching Hands* by Christine Jope-Slade. *T. P's Weekly*, VIII, 207 (Oct. 15, 1927), 783.

'Antics of a Crazy Tsar. Paul I: a drama of conspiracy and crime'. [Review] of play at Court theatre *Paul I* by Merej-kovsky. *T. P's Weekly*, IX, 209 (Oct. 29, 1927), 8.

'A Classic that Paid the Rent. *The Vicar of Wakefield*: a home idyll by a homeless man'. [Review]. *T. P's Weekly*, IX, 200 (Nov. 5, 1927), 59 and 61.

'The Poet Who was too Ugly'. "Cyrano": heroic comedy of sword and song'. [Review] of *Cyrano de Bergerac* by Edmund Rostand, playing at the Apollo Theatre. *T. P's Weekly*, IX, 214 (Dec. 3, 1927), 183.

'A Pageant-Play on Villon'. [Review] of *The Judgment of François Villon: a pageant-episode play in five acts* by Herbert Edward Palmer. *Nation and Athenaeum* XLII, 10 (Dec. 10, 1927).

'The Feminine Riddle'. [Review] of *Something about Eve* by James Branch Cabell. *T. P's Weekly*, IX, 216 (Dec. 17, 1927), 287.

'Benn's Sixpenny Library'. [Review]. *T. P's Weekly*, IX, 217 (Dec. 24, 1927), 329.

'Art and Energy'. [Letters]. *Irish Statesman*, 10 (1928), 471.

'The Book that Freed English Prose: the unforgettable enchantment of Robinson Crusoe'. [Review]. *T. P's Weekly*, IX, 219 (Jan. 7, 1928), 399-400.

'Lyrics and Eclogues'. [Review]. *Spectator*, 140 (Feb. 18, 1928), 236.

'Limehouse Days'. [Review] of *East of Mansion House* by Thomas Burke. *T. P's Weekly*, IX, 227 (March 3, 1928), 653.

'The Homeless Novelist'. [Review] of *The Pilgrimage of Henry Days* by Van Wyck Brooks. *T. P's Weekly*, IX, 228 (March 10, 1928), 687.

'Golden March of the Conquistadors'. [Review] of *Discovery and Conquest of Mexico* by Bernard Diez del Castillo. *T. P's Weekly*, IX, 229 (March 17, 1928), 720.

'The Man Who Could Not Resign'. [Review] of *Etched in Moonlight* by James Stephens. *T. P's Weekly*, IX, 230 (March 24, 1928), 755.

'Poetry'. [Review of William Plomer, Cecil Day Lewis, Chand Powers, Margot Robert Adamson, Elizabeth Madox Roberts, R. C. Trevelyan]. *Nation and Athenaeum* XLII, (March 31, 1928), 976.

'From a Poet's Tower: stories from the Innisfree Country' [Review] of *The*

Tower by W. B. Yeats. *T. P's Weekly*, IX, 231 (March 31, 1928), 786.

'Satire and Song'. [Review]. *Spectator*, 140 (April 14, 1928), 572.

'Novel of Musical Critics'. [Review] of *Gemel in London* by James Agate. *T. P's Weekly*, IX, 234 [April 21, 1928), 901.

'Drum and Ukelele'. [Review] of *Jazz and Jaspar* by William Gerhardi. *T. P's Weekly*, X, 236 (May 5, 1928), 51.

'Modern Poets' Happier Quest: the rose and the rhyme'. [Review] of four books of poetry, including *Tristram* by Edwin Arlington Robinson. *T. P's Weekly*, X, 238 (May 19, 1928), 117.

'A Clydeside Comedy'. [Review] of *Paper Money* by George Blake. *T. P's Weekly*, X, 240 (June 2, 1928), 81.

'Masefield's New Lyrical Drama: the Whitsuntide play in Canterbury Cathedral'. [Review] of *The Coming of Christ*. *T. P's Weekly*, X, 240 (June 2, 1928), 171.

'Skyscraper Verses'. [Review] of *Toulemonde* by Christopher Morley. *T. P's Weekly*, X, 242 (June 16, 1928), 243.

'Poems of Green Fields'. [Review] of *Retreat: new sonnets and poems* by Edmund Blunden. *T. P's Weekly*, X, 243 (June 23, 1928), 277.

'A Light Woman'. [Review] of *Comfortless Memory* by Maurice Baring. *T. P's Weekly*, X, 246 [July 14, 1928), 371.

'The Daughter of Josephine: new light on Napoleon in long hidden memoirs'. [Review article of] *The Memoirs of Queen Hortense*. Ed. by Prince Napoleon. *T. P's Weekly*, X, 247 (July 21, 1928), 394.

'A Stoic Poet'. [Review] of *Goodwill* by Eden Phillpotts. *T. P's Weekly*, X, 254 (Sept. 1, 1928), 571.

'Blake Abroad'. [Review] of *William Blake* by Philippe Soupault. *T. P's Weekly*, X, 254 (Sept. 8, 1928), 599.

'Tales From an Ulster Shore: Donn Byrne's posthumous book'. [Review] of *Destiny Bay*. *T. P's Weekly*, X, 256 (Sept. 22, 1928), 655.

'King David'. [Review] of *The Promised Land* by Gilbert Parker. *T. P's Weekly*, X, 257 (Sept. 28, 1928), 683.

'Recent Poetry'. [Review]. *Spectator*, 141 (Oct. 20, 1928), 535.

'My Kingdom For an Opera'. [Review] of *The Man King Dies* by Sir Max

Pemberton. *T. P's Weekly*, XI, 261 (Oct. 20, 1928), 776.

'Last Poems of Thomas Hardy'. [Review] of *Winter Words*. *T. P's Weekly*, XI, 261 (Oct. 27, 1928), 74.

'The Round Table: Mr. Masefield's modern allegory of King Arthur'. [Review] of *Midsummer Night*. *T. P's Weekly*, XI, 263 (Nov. 10, 1928), 64.

'The Sphere of Poetry'. Includes a review of Noyes mentioned in *A Penny* (p. 189). *Spectator* 141 (Nov. 24, 1928), 783.

[Comment on censorship]. *T. P's Weekly*, XI, 265 (Nov. 24, 1928), 118.

'Ways and Means of Storytelling'. [Review] of *A Little Less Than Gods* by Ford Madox Ford [and 2 others]. *T. P's Weekly*, XI, 265 (Nov. 24, 1928), 130.

'Poetry of 1928: the new song-birds of the poetic bush'. [Review]. *T. P's Weekly*, XI, 266 (Dec. 1, 1928), 184.

'Pious and Immortal Memory: the early life of William III'. [Review] of *William, Prince of Orange* by Marjorie Bowen. *T. P's Weekly*, XI, 275 (Feb. 2, 1929), 451.

'Scotland's Poetry of Today'. [Review] of *Holyrood: a garland of modern Scots verse* chosen and edited by W. H. Hamilton. *T. P's Weekly*, XI, 279 (March 2, 1929), 562.

'Unconstitutional Poetry'. [Review of Pound and Sitwell]. *Spectator*, 142 (March 9, 1929), 377.

'Tennyson in Wales: as one that climbs to gaze o'er land and main'. [Review of essay by Herbert Wright in] *Essays and Studies* by Members of the English Association. *T. P's Weekly*, XI, 281 (March 16, 1929), 607.

'Realism in an Irish Village: Mr. Brinsley Macnamara's satiric humour'. [Review] of *The Various Lives of Marcus Igoe*. *T. P's Weekly*, XII, 288 (May 4, 1929), 43.

'The Island of Saints and Scholars'. [Review] of *Gaelic Literature Surveyed* by Aodh de Blacam. *T. P's Weekly*, XII, 301 (August 3, 1929), 418.

'The Den that Bernard Shaw Forgot'. [Review] of *Adventures with Bernard Shaw* by Dan Rider. *T. P's Weekly*, XII, 304 (August 24, 1929), 502.

'A Doctor's Case Book: husband and

wife's tropical thrills'. [Review] of *The Misadventures of a Tropical Medico* by Herbert Spencer Dickey. *T. P's Weekly*, XII, 312 (Oct. 19, 1929), 715.

'Poetry'. [Review of Dunsany, Day-Lewis, Jeffers, Cowley, Yeats]. *Spectator*, 143 (Dec. 28, 1929), 984.

[Review] of *The Renaissance of Irish Poetry 1880-1930* by David Morton. *Dublin Magazine* V, n.s., 1 (Jan.-March, 1930), 56-61.

'Shipwreck off Donegal'. *Spectator*, 145 (Sept. 20, 1930), 374-375.

'Thomas Chatterton'. [Review]. *Spectator*, 145 (Nov. 15, 1930), 733.

'Four Poets'. [Review] of Alan Porter, John Freeman, Lord Darling, Wilfred Gibson. *Nation and Athenaeum*, XLIII, (Dec. 20, 1930), 414.

'The Epic of Science'. [Review]. *News Chronicle*, (Dec. 22, 1930.)

'Poetry'. [Review] of Huxley and Sitwell. *Spectator*, 147 (August 1, 1931), 160.

'Three Poets'. [Review] of AE, Graves and Abercrombie. *Spectator*, 146 (April 25, 1931), 673.

'Prologue – for a Romance'. First chapter of *The Bright Temptation* (to be published shortly). *Dublin Magazine*, VI, n.s., 3 (July-Sept. 1931), 5-p14.

'Synge and Irish Life'. [Review] of *Synge and Anglo-Irish Literature* by Daniel Corkery. *Times Literary Supplement*, July 23, 1931, 578.

'Poems of John Skelton'. [Review] of *The Complete Poems of John Skelton* ed. by Philip Henderson. *Spectator*, 147 (Nov. 14, 1931), 648.

'Mr. Sturge Moore'. [Review] of *The Poems of T. Sturge Moore. Collected Edition Vol. I*. *New Statesman*, Dec. 12, 1931.

'Censor and Dramatist'. [Review] of *Bryan Cooper* by Lennox Robinson. *News Chronicle*, Jan. 13, 1932.

'The Age of "Sally in our Alley"'. [Review] of an anthology of Augustan Poetry. *News Chronicle*, Feb. 9, 1932.

'The Literary Mind'. [Review] of *The Literary Mind: its place in an age of science* by Max Eastman. *Spectator*, 148 (Feb. 27, 1932), 294.

'A Chronicle of Recent Books: poetry'. [Review article]. *Life and Letters*, VIII, 44 (March, 1932), 103, 228, 484.

'A Remarkable Woman'. [Review] of *Mary Everest Boole: Collected works* ed. by E. M. Cobham. 4 vols. *Observer*, March 6, 1932.

'Drama and Verse'. [Review] of 7 different books. *New Statesman*, March 13, 1932.

'Robert Emmet'. [Review] of *Robert Emmet* by Raymond W. Postgate. *Spectator*, 148 (April 9, 1932), 520.

'An Anthology of Love Stories'. [Review] of *Great Love Stories of All Nations* ed. by Robert Lynd. *Observer*, April 17, 1932.

'Cross Currents and Clear Streams'. [Review] of 5 books of poetry. *Observer*, April 24, 1932.

'Northern Ireland'. *Spectator*, 148 (April 30, 1932), 644.

'Skald!'. [Review] of *Heimskringla, or The Lives of the Norse Kings* by Snorre Sturlason, ed. with notes by Erling Monsen and translated into English with the assistance of A. R. Smith. *New Statesman*, May 7, 1932.

'Portrait of an Irishman'. [Review] of *An Incorruptible Irishman: being an account of the Chief Justice Charles Kendal Bushe and of his wife Nancy Crampton, and their times 1767-1843* by E. Oe. Somerville and Martin Ross. *Spectator*, 148 (May 14, 1932), 703.

'The Middle Ages'. [Review] of *The Inquisition* by Hoffman Nickerson [and 4 others]. *Observer*, June 12, 1932.

'John Redmond'. [Review] of *The Life of John Redmond* by Denis Gwynn. *Spectator* 149 (July 2, 1932), 18.

'The Muse's Task'. [Review] of *The Poems of T. Sturge Moore. Collected Edition. Second Volume*. *New Statesman*, July 16, 1932.

'Ireland and Other Lands'. [Review] of *Skerrett* by Liam O'Flaherty, [and 5 others]. *Observer*, July 17, 1932.

'A Poet Used to Slang'. [Review] of *John Clare: a life* by J. W. and Anne Tibble. *News Chronicle*, August 23, 1932.

'Some Poets'. [Unsighed review] of *Rimeless Numbers* by R. C. Trevelyan, [and 8 others]. *New Statesman*, Sept. 3, 1932.

'Su Tung P'o'. [Review] of *Selections from the Works of Su Tung P'o* translated by Cyril Drummond Le Gros Clark. *Spectator*, 149 (Sept. 3, 1932), 293.

'John Redmond'. [Review] of book of

Denis Gwynn. *Spectator*, 149 (Sept. 3, 1932), 149.

'Grand Tour of the Emotions'. [Review] of *Inflections, 1931* by James Cleugh, [and 6 others]. *Observer*, Oct. 16, 1932.

'The Stricken Lute'. [Review] of *The Stricken Lute: an account of the life of Peter Abelard* by Roger B. Lloyd. *Spectator*, 149 (Nov. 4, 1932), 638.

'Love in Irish Poetry and Drama'. *Motley*, 1, 5 (Oct., 1932), 3-4.

'Robert Browning'. [Review] of *Browning and the Twentieth Century: a study of Robert Browning's influence and reputation* by A. Allen Brockington. *Spectator*, 149 (Nov. 11, 1932), 670.

'A Chronicle of Recent Books. Poetry'. [Review] of *News from the Mountain* by Richard Church and *Lyric Plays* by Gordon Bottomley. *Life and Letters*, VIII, 47 (Dec. 1932), 484-491.

[Review] (unsigned) of *Death of Felicity Taverner* by Mary Butts. *Times literary Supplement*, Dec. 2, 1932, 988.

'Sherlock Holmes: man or myth?' [Review] (signed by W. R. Gordon) of *Sherlock Holmes: fact or fiction* by Thomas S. Blakeney; and *Sherlock Holmes and Doctor Watson: a chronology of their adventures* by H. W. Bell. *News Chronicle*, Dec. 9, 1932.

'Two Ways of Poetry'. [Review] (unsigned) of *A Face in Candlelight* by J. C. Squire; and *Halfway House* by Edmund Blunden. *New Statesman*, Dec. 24, 1932.

'The Passing of Beatrice'. [Review] of *The Passing of Beatrice: a study in the heterodoxy of Dante* by Gertrude Leigh. *Spectator*, 149 (Dec. 30, 1932), 927.

'Mr. Squire's New Anthology'. [Review] of *Younger Poets of To-day* selected by J. C. Squires. *Observer*, Jan. 15, 1933.

[Review] (unsigned) of *The Martyr* Liam O'Flaherty. *Times Literary Supplement*, Jan. 19, 1933, 38.

'Unfamiliar Poets'. [Review] of *Poems* by L. Aaronson; and *Poems* by Stephen Spender. *Observer*, Jan. 29, 1933.

[Review] of *The City Without Walls: an anthology setting forth the drama of human life* arranged by Margaret Cushing Osgood. *Observer*, Feb. 26, 1933.

'Great Man's Soul'. [Review] (unsigned) of *A Hillside Man* by Con O'Leary. *News Chronicle*, March 2, 1933.

'The "Scottish Chaucer"'. [Review] of *The Poems of William Dunbar* ed. by William Mackay Mackenzie. *Spectator*, 150 (March 24, 1933), 435.

'Travellers' Tales'. [Review]. *Spectator*, 150 (March 31, 1933), 470.

'Highland Songs'. [Review] (unsigned) of *Highland Songs of the Forty-Five* ed. and translated with glossary and notes by John Lorna Campbell, *New Statesman*, (April 15, 1933).

'Early Medieval French Lyrics'. [Review] *Early Medieval French Lyrics* by C. C. Abbott. *Spectator*, 150 (April 21, 1933), 577.

'Songs of Old France'. [Review] (unsigned) of *Early Medieval French Lyrics* by C. C. Abbott. *News Chronicle*, April 26, 1933.

'New Poems'. [Review] of *Flowering Reeds* by Roy Campbell, [and 4 others]. *Observer*, April 30, 1933.

'Refugees from Tsarist Russia'. [Review] (signed by W. R. Gordon) of *The Romantic Exiles* by Edward Hallett Carr. *News Chronicle*, May 12, 1933.

'New Novel'. [Review] (unsigned) of *Peter Abelard* by Helen Waddell. *Times Literary Supplement*, May 18, 1933, 346.

'Poet of the Commonplace'. [Review] (unsigned) of *Poems 1930-1933* by Robert Graves. *News Chronicle*, June 6, 1933.

'Poetic Contrast'. [Review] of *The Fleeting and other poems* by Walter De La Mare; and *Poems 1930-1933* by Robert Graves. *New Statesman*, June 10, 1933.

'The Vision of Sin'. [Review] of *Dante's Inferno: a version in the Spenserian stanza* by George Musgrave; and *Dante's Inferno, with a Translation into English Triple Rhyme* by Laurence Binyon. *Spectator*, 151 (July 28, 1933), 135.

[Review] of *The Celtic Peoples and Renaissance Europe* by David Mathew. *Observer*, August 20, 1933.

'Murderous Guests'. [Review] of *The Massacre of Glencoe* by John Buchan. *News Chronicle*, August 25, 1933.

'Rabelais'. [Review] of *Laughter for Pluto: a book about Rabelais* by Francis Watson. *New Statesman*, Sept. 16, 1933.

'Crime and Detection'.[Review]. *Spectator*, 151 (Oct. 6, 1933), 453.

[Review] of *Beauty Looks After Herself* by Eric Gill; and *The Hindu View of Art* by

Raj Anand. *Observer*, Oct. 8, 1933.

'A Nest of Simple Folk'. [Review] of *A Nest of Simple Folk* by Sean O'Faolain. *Times Literary Supplement*, Oct. 12, 1933, 688.

'Slang'. [Review] of *Slang. To-day and Yesterday* by Eric Partridge; and *Words, Words, Words* by Eric Partridge. *New Statesman*, Oct. 14, 1933.

[Review] of *The Curse of the Wise Woman* by Lord Dunsany. *Times Literary Supplement*, Nov. 2, 1933, 748.

'Poet's Fantasy of the Future'. [Review] (unsigned) of *The Avatars: a futurist fantasy by AE*. *News Chronicle*, Nov. 15, 1933.

[Review] of *Phantom Lobster: a true story* by Leo Walmsley. *Times Literary Supplement*, Nov. 16, 1933, 786.

'The Great Geraldine'. [Review of *Gerald Fitzgerald: the great Earl of Kildare* by Donough Bryan. *Spectator*, 151 (Nov. 17, 1933).

'The Golden Age'. [Review] of *Kenneth Grahame: life, letters and unpublished work* by Patrick Chalmers. *New Statesman*, Dec. 9, 1933.

'Poetic Prize Fights Among the Moderns'. [Review] of *One-Way Song* by Wyndham Lewis, [and 2 others], *News Chronicle*, Jan. 4, 1934.

'Mr. Sturge Moore'. [Review] of *The Poems of T. Sturge Moore, Collected Edition, Vol. IV. New Statesman*, Jan. 13, 1934.

'The Legend of Swift'. [Review] of *Swift or the Egoist* by Mario M. Rossi and J. M. Hone. *Spectator*, 152 (Jan. 26, 1934), 128.

'Literary Mysticism'. [Review] of *Reason and Beauty in the Poetic Mind* by Charles Williams. *New Statesman*, Jan. 27, 1934.

'Summit and Chasm'. [Review] of *Summit and Chasm* by Herbert Palmer. *New Statesman*, Feb. 17, 1934.

[Review] of *Magpie* by Lois Vidal; and *Interlude in Ecuador* by Janet Mackay. *News Chronicle*, Feb. 20, 1934.

'One Man's Road'. [Review] of *A Modern Prelude* by Hugh l'Anson Fausset. *Observer*, March 18, 1934.

[Review] (unsigned) of *Letters to the New Island* by W. B. Yeats. *Times Literary Supplement*, April 12, 1934, 259.

'Birds of a Feather'. [Review] of *Whether a Dove or a Seagull: poems* by Sylvia Townsend Warner and Valentin Ackland. *New Statesman*, April 21, 1934.

'Dublin in the Revolution'. [Review] of *Remembering Sion: a chronicle of storm and quiet* by Desmond Ryan. *Observer*, April 29, 1934.

'Poetic Drama'. [Review]. *Spectator*, 152 (June 6, 1934), 934.

'Pity's Kin'. [Review]. *Nation and Athenaeum*, XXXV, 12 (June 21, 1934), 384.

'Martin Luther: the man and his God'. [Review] of *Martin Luther: the man and his God* by Brian Lunn. *Spectator*, 152 (July 20, 1934).

'Florio's London'. [Review]. *Spectator*, 153 (August 3, 1934), 169.

'A White Woman in Mecca'. [Review] of *Pilgrimage to Mecca* by Lady Evelyn Cobbold. *News Chronicle*, August 27, 1934.

'Cannibal's Teeth.' [Review] of *Momo and I* by Frank Hives. *News Chronicle*, August 27, 1934.

'The French Foreign Legion'. [Review]. *Spectator*, 153 (Sept. 7, 1934), 334.

'The Lady With a Gun'. [Review] of *Constance Markievicz', or the Average Revolutionary: a biography* by Sean O'Faolain. *News Chronicle*, Sept. 10, 1934.

'Constance Markievicz'. [Review] (unsigned) of *Constance Markievicz, or the Average Revolutionary: a biography* by Sean O'Faolain. *Times Literary Supplement*, Sept. 20, 1934, 627.

'Poetry of the World We See'. [Review] of *Poems of Ten Years, 1924-1934* by Dorothy Wellesley; and *Selected Poems* by Charles King. *News Chronicle*, Oct. 26, 1934.

[Review] (unsigned) of *Man of Aran* by Pat Mullen. *Times Literary Supplement*, Nov. 15, 1934, 798.

'A Good Fighter'. [Review] of *Armour of Ballymoney* by W. S. Armour. *Observer*, Nov. 25, 1934.

'The Modern Essayist'. [Review] of *Both Sides of the Road* by Robert Lynd. *London Mercury*, XXXI, 182 (Dec. 1934), 187-188.

'Aran'. [Review] of *The Islandman* by Tomás O Cróhan; and *Man of Aran* by Pat Mullen. *New Statesman*, Dec. 8, 1934.

'Irish Poetry Today'. *Dublin Magazine*, X, n.s., 1 (Jan.-March, 1935), 26-34.

'A Poet and the Dark Lady'. [Review] of *The House of the Titans and other poems* by AE. *News Chronicle*, Jan. 8, 1935.

'Foreigners'. [Review] (unsigned) of *Foreigners* by Leo Walmsley. *Times Literary Supplement*, Jan. 24, 1935, 46.

'Experiment in Imagination: a silent Utopia'. [Review] of *Land under England* by Joseph O'Neill. With a Foreword by AE. *Observer*, Feb. 3, 1935.

'Poet on Holiday'. [Review] of *The Seals* by Monk Gibbon. *News Chronicle*, Feb. 12, 1935.

[Review] of *Wheels and Butterflies* by W. B. Yeats; and *The Collected Plays* of W. B. Yeats. *London Mercury*, XXXI, 184 (Feb. 1935), 391-392.

'The Desire and Pursuit of the Whole'. *London Mercury*, XXXI, 185 (March 1935).

[Review] of *A Dictionary of American Slang*. Compiled by Maurice H. Weseen. *London Mercury*, XXXI, 186 (April, 1935), 599.

'Henry James as Critic'. [Review] of *The Art of the Novel: critical prefaces* by Henry James. *London Mercury*, XXXII, 187 (May 1935), 77-78.

'New Poetry: six poets in search of their art'. [Review] of *Selected Poems* by Marianne Moore, [and 5 others]. *Observer*, June 23, 1935.

[Review] (unsigned) of *Printed Cotton* by Christine Longford. *Times Literary Supplement*, July 11, 1935, 449.

'Some Poets of Today'. [Review] of *Selected Poems* by Marianne Moore, [and 3 others]. *News Chronicle*, July 15, 1935.

'Irish Portraits'. [Review] of *Irish Literary Portraits* by John Eglinton; and *With Horace Plunkett in Ireland* by R. A. Anderson. *New Statesman*, July 20, 1935.

'The Abbey Theatre'. [Review] of *The Fays of the Abbey Theatre* by W. G. Fay and Catherine Carswell. *New Statesman*, Sept. 7, 1935.

[Review] of *The Miselto Kid: an autobiography of childhood* by Herbert Palmer. *Dublin Magazine*, X, n.s., 1 (Oct.-Dec. 1935), 7.

'Lord Dunsany's New Irish Novel: a witty fantasy'. [Review] (unsigned) of *Up in the Hills* by Lord Dunsany. *Times*, Oct. 15, 1935.

'The Problem of Verse Drama Today'. *London Mercury*, XXXIII, 193 (Nov. 1935), 34-38.

[Review] of *The Wind Blows Over* by Walter de la Mare. *Irish Times*, 1936.

'Mr. Yeats: contrasts in verse and prose'. [Review] of *A Full Moon in March* by W. B. Yeats. *London Mercury*, XXXIII, 195 (Jan. 1936), 341-342.

[Review] (unsigned) of *Somewhere to the Sea* by Kenneth Sarr. *Times Literary Supplement*, Feb. 22, 1936), 160.

'The Contemporary Scene'. [Review] (unsigned) of *Words for To-Night* by George Buchanan. *Times*, March 6, 1936.

'An Irish Education'. [Review] of *The Green Lion* by Francis Hackett. *Times Literary Supplement*, March 21, 1936, 241.

[Review] of *Jackets Green* by Patrick Mulloy. *Times Literary Supplement*, March 21, 1936, 242.

[Review] of *The Amaranthers* by Jack B. Yeats. *Times Literary Supplement*, April 4, 1936, 292.

'Two Irishmen'. [Review] of *The Silver Fleece: an autobiography* by Robert Collis; and *The Last Landfall* by Desmond Malone. *Observer*, April 5, 1936.

[Review] of *The Silver Fleece: an autobiography* by Robert Collis. *Times Literary Supplement*, April 9, 1936, 292.

'Modern Ireland'. [Review] of *The Spirit of Ireland* by Lynn Doyle, [and 2 others], *New Statesman*, April 18, 1936.

'Symbols of Defeat'. [Review] of *The Burning Cactus* by Stephen Spender. *Times Literary Supplement*, April 18, 1936, 333.

'Poet's Progress'. [Review] of *The Vampire* by Herbert E. Palmer. *News Chronicle*, May 1, 1936.

'Witch in Africa: a remarkable novel'. [Review] of *The African Witch* by Joyce Cary. *Observer*, May 3, 1936.

'Restorative Airs: Mr. Gwynn's study of Irish authors'. [Review] of *Irish Literature and Drama in the English Language: a short history* by Stephen Gwynn. *Observer*, May 10, 1936.

'Irish Literature and Drama: Mr.

Gwynn's survey'. [Review] (unsigned) of *Irish Literature and Drama in the English Language: a short history. Times*, May 15, 1936.

'A Century of Irish Literature: reminiscences of an historian'. [Review] (unsigned) of *Irish Literature and Drama in the English Language: a short history* by Stephen Gwynn. *Times Literary Supplement*, May 16, 1936, 415.

'Mr. Yeats's Reminiscences: years of peace and the age of disillusion'. [Review] (unsigned) of *Dramatis Personae, 1896-1902, and other papers* by W. B. Yeats. *Times Literary Supplement*, May 23, 1936, 434.

[Review] (unsigned) of *The Sounding Cataract* by J. S. Collis. *Times Literary Supplement*, May 23, 1936, 438.

[Review] (unsigned) of *They shall Inherit the Earth* by Morley Callaghan. *Times Literary Supplement*, May 30, 1936, 458.

'Mr. Yeats and His Contemporaries'. [Review] of *Dramatis Personae* by W. B. Yeats. *London Mercury*, XXXIV, 200 (June, 1936), 169-170.

'Poet in Prison'. [Review] of *Letters from Prison* by Ernst Toller. *News Chronicle*, June 17, 1936.

'Mr. O'Connor's Poems'. [Review] (unsigned) of *Three Old Brothers and other poems* by Frank O'Connor. *Times Literary Supplement*, June 20, 1936, 522.

[Review] (unsigned) of *Ballygullion Ballads and other verses* by Lynn Doyle. *Times Literary Supplement*, June 20, 1936, 526.

'Irish Literature'. [Review] of *Irish Literature and Drama in the English Language: a short history* by Stephen Gwynn. *New Statesman*, June 27, 1936.

[Review] (unsigned) of *Bird Alone* by Sean O'Faolain. *Times*, June 30, 1936.

'A Modern Verse Play'. [Review] of *Panic: a play in verse* by Archibald MacLeish. *London Mercury* XXXIV, 201 (July, 1936), 279.

'A Spiritual Rebel'. [Review] of *Bird Alone* by Sean O'Faolain. *Times Literary Supplement*, July 9, 1936, 561.

'Twilight Lovers'. [Review] (unsigned) of *The White Hare* by Francis Stuart. *Times Literary Supplement*, August 26, 1936, 679.

'Ireland's Chatterton'. [Review] of *Vagabond Minstrel: the adventures of Thomas Dermody* by Thomas Burke. *Times Literary Supplement*, Sept. 19, 1936, 745.

[Review] of *Collected Poems* by E. W. F. Tomlin. *The Criterion* XXV, LXII (Oct. 1936), 140.

'West Ireland Fantasy'. [Review] of *Rory and Bran* by Lord Dunsany. *Times Literary Supplement*, Oct. 17, 1936, 835.

'Christmas Books 2: books for boys'. [Review]. *London Mercury* XXXV, 206 (Dec. 1936), 234.

'Stephen MacKenna'. [Review] of *Journal and Letters of Stephen MacKenna. New Statesman*, Dec. 19, 1936.

'Two Novels'. [Review] of *Windless Sky* by Fritz Faulkner; and *Together and Apart* by Margaret Kennedy. *London Mercury*, XXXVI, 207 (Jan. 1937), 346.

'Modern Lyrics'. [Review] of *Straight or Curly?* by Clifford Dyment. *London Mercury*, XXXV, 209 (March 1937), 524-525.

'Northern Ireland'. *The Spectator*, 156 (April 1937), 644.

'R.L.S.' [Review] of *R. L. Stevenson* by Janet Adam Smith. *London Mercury*, XXXV, 210 (April, 1937), 642-643.

'Down Sackville Street'. [Review] (unsigned) of *As I Was Going Down Sackville Street* by Oliver St. J. Gogarty. *Times Literary Supplement*, April 10, 1937, 266.

'Dr. Gogarty and His Circle'. [Review] of *As I Was Going Down Sackville Street* by Oliver St. J. Gogarty. *London Mercury*, XXXVI, 211 (May 1937), 80-81.

[Review] of *A History of Ireland* by Edmund Curtis. *Observer*, June 6, 1937.

'A View of Michael Collins'. [Review] (unsigned) of *The Big Fellow: a life of Michael Collins* by Frank O'Connor. *Times Literary Supplement*, June 12, 1937, 437.

'Wolfe Tone'. [Review] of *The Autobiography of Theobald Wolfe Tone*. Abridged and edited by Sean O'Faolain. *New Statesman*, June 26, 1937.

'Four Stories'. [Review] of *Rainbow Fish* by Ralph Bates. *London Mercury*, XXXVI, 214 (August 1937), 397-398.

[Review] (unsigned) of *The New Ireland* by J. B. Morton. *New Statesman*, Sept. 17, 1937.

'Plot and Character'. [Review] of *Harvest*

Comedy by Frank Swinnerton. *London Mercury*, XXXVI, 216 (Oct. 1937), 597.

'Verse-Speaking and Verse Drama'. [Review article]. *Dublin Magazine*, XII, n.s., 4 (Oct.-Dec. 1937), 9-17.

[Review] of *A Key to Modern English Poetry* by Martin Gilkes. *Dublin Magazine*, XII, n.s., 4 (Oct.-Dec. 1937), 60-61.

[Review] of *The Works of Morris and Yeats in Relation to Early Saga Literature* by Dorothy M. Hoare. *Dublin Magazine*, XII, n.s., 4 (Oct.-Dec. 1937), 64-65.

[Review] of *Libraries and Literature from a Catholic Standpoint* by Stephen J. Brown. *Dublin Magazine*, XII, n.a., 4 (Oct.-Dec. 1937), 71-72.

[Review] of *The Silver Branch* by Sean O'Faolain. *New Statesman and Nation*, XV (Jan. 29, 1938), 178.

[Review] of *A Memoir of AE: George William Russell* by John Eglinton: and *The Living Torch* by AE., ed. by Monk Gibbon. *Dublin Magazine*, XIII, n.s., 1 (Jan.-March 1938), 61-63.

'Wistful Memories'. [Review] of *The Greenwood Hat: being a memoir of James Anon. 1885-1887* by J. M. Barrie. *London Mercury*, XXXVII, 219 (Jan. 1938), 351.

'A Stage Fantasy'. [Review] of *The Herne's Egg* by W. B. Yeats. *London Mercury*, XXXVII, 221 (March 1938), 551-552.

[Review] of *Spain* by W. H. Auden, [and 2 others]. *Dublin Magazine*, XIII, n.s., 2 (April-June, 1938), 77-79.

'Ireland and the Irish'. [Review] of *Mr. Ireland* by Lord Dunsany; and *The Face of Ireland* by Michael Floyd. *Observer*, May 8, 1938.

'After "Anthony Adverse"'. [Review] of *Action at Aquila* by Harvey Allen. *London Mercury*, XXXVIII, 223 (May 1938), 88.

'Poetry in This Century'. [Review] of *Post-Victorian Poetry* by Herbert Palmer. *London Mercury*, XXXVIII, 224 (June 1938), 182.

[Review] of *The Story of Lowry Maen* by P. Colum. *Dublin Magazine*, XIII, n.s., 3 (July-Sept. 1938), 83-85.

'Pursuit of a Saint'. [Review] of *I Follow St. Patrick* by Oliver St. J. Gogarty. *London Mercury*, XXXVIII, 225 (July 1938), 283-284.

'Gunmen and Blank Verse'. [Review] of *Winterset* by Maxwell Anderson. *London Mercury*, XXXVIII, 227 (Sept. 1938), 471.

[Review] (unsigned) of *Walt Whitman's Prose* by Esther Shephard. *New Statesman*, Sept. 10, 1938.

'A Precocious Poet'. [Review] of *Poems* by Helen Foley. *London Mercury*, XXXIX, 229 (Nov. 1938), 96.

[Review] of *Yeats's Inner Drama: a poet of two reputations*. *Times Literary Supplement*, Feb. 4, 1939, 72-74.

'Mr. Conrad Aiken'. [Review] of *A Heart of the Gods of Mexico* by Conrad Aiken. *London Mercury*, XXXIX, 232 (Feb. 1939), 461.

'A Story in Verse'. [Review] of *Penthesperon* by Christopher Hassall. *London Mercury*, XXXIX, 233 (March 1939), 562.

[Review] of *The Fountain of Magic* by Frank O'Connor. *Times Literary Supplement*, March 18, 1939.

'W. B. Yeats'. *Dublin Magazine*, XIV, n.s., 2 (April-June 1939), 6-10.

[Review] of *Tumbling in the Hay* by Oliver St. J. Gogarty; and *I Knock at the Door* by Sean O'Casey. *Dublin Magazine*, XIV, n.s., 2 (April-June 1939), 85-87.

'Gordon Bottomley'. [Review] of *Choric Plays* by Gordon Bottomley. *London Mercury*, XXXIX, 234 (April 1939), 658.

'Poet and Artist'. *Arrow*, W. B. Yeats Commemoration Number (Summer 1939), 8-9.

[Review] of *Finnegan's Wake* by James Joyce. *Dublin Magazine*, XIV, n.s., 3 (July-Sept. 1939), 71-74.

[Review] of *The Still Centre* by Stephen Spender; and *Autumn Journal* by Louis MacNeice. *Dublin Magazine*, XIV, n.s., 3 (July-Sept. 1939), 82-84.

[Review] of *The Family Reunion* by T. S. Eliot. *Dublin Magazine*, XIV, n.s., 3 (July-Sept. 1939), 85-87.

[Review] of *Jonathan Swift, Dean and Pastor* by Robert Wyse Jackson. *New Statesman*, Sept. 16, 1939.

'The Black Church'. *Dublin Magazine*, XIV, n.s., 4 (Oct.-Dec. 1939), 9-13.

[Review] of *Introduction to English Literature. ed. by Bonamy Dobree. Vol. V: The Present Age from 1914* by Edwin Muir. *Dublin Magazine*, XIV, n.s., 4 (Oct.-

Dec. 1939), 81-83.

[Review] of *The Welsh Review*, ed. Gwynn Jones, Vol. I, no. 1-6. Vol. II, no. 1. *Dublin Magazine*, XIV, n.s., 4 (Oct.-Dec. 1939), 103-104.

Foreword to *Alarm Among the Clerks* by Mervyn Wall. Richview Press, 1940.

[Review] of *Time's Wall Asunder* by Roibeárd Ó Faracháin. *Dublin Magazine*, XV, n.s., 1 (Jan.-Mar. 1940), 48-49.

'Ezra Pound's "Gigantic Poetic Notebook": more cantos'. [Review] *Irish Times*, March 30, 1940, 6.

'The Dramatic Fantasies of George Fitzmaurice'. *Dublin Magazine*, XV, n.s., 2 (April-June 1940), 9-14.

[Review] of *The Moore's of Moore Hall* by Joseph Hone. *Dublin Magazine*, XV, n.s., 2 (April-June 1940), 69-70.

[Review] of *The Irish Dramatic Movement* by Una Ellis-Fermor; and *Littérature Irlandaise Contemporaine* by A. Rivoallan. *Dublin Magazine*, XV, n.s., 2 (April-June, 1940), 70-71.

[Review] of *Poems Among Shapes and Shadows* by S. Oshima. *Dublin Magazine*, XV, n.s., 2 (April-June, 1940), 86.

[Review] of *An Irish Journey* by Sean O'Faolain; and *Where the River Shannon Flows* by Richard Hayward. *Observer*, July 21, 1940.

'Seumas O'Sullivan: poet of Dublin'. [Review] of *The Collected Poems of Seumas O'Sullivan*. *Irish Times*, Nov. 9, 1940, 5.

[Review] of *Aithdioghluim Dána: a miscellany of Irish bardic poetry* ed. by Lambert McKenna. *Dublin Magazine*, XVI, n.s., 1 (Jan.-March, 1941), 62-63.

[Review] of *If I Were Four & Twenty* by W. B. Yeats. *Dublin Magazine*, XVI, n.s., 1 (Jan.-March 1941), 64.

[Review] of *Collected Poems* by Seumas O'Sullivan. *Observer*, Jan. 19, 1941.

[Review] of *The Poetry of W. B. Yeats*. *Irish Times*, March 15, 1941, 5.

[Review] of *The Golden Treasury of Scottish Poetry* selected and ed. by Hugh MacDiarmid. *Dublin Magazine*, XVI, n.s., 2 (April-June 1941), 73-75.

[Review] of *The Poetry of W. B. Yeats* by Louis MacNeice. *Dublin Magazine*, XVI, n.s., 2 (April-June 1941), 75-76.

[Review] of *The Land of Spices* by Kate O'Brien. *The Bell*, II, 1 (April 1941), 93-95.

'Poetry and Contemporary Facts: Donagh MacDonagh's first book of poems'. [Review]. *Irish Times*, April 19, 1941, 3.

'The Contemporary Scene in Poetry'. [Review]. *Irish Times*, May 24, 1941, 5.

'Old-Fashioned Hymns of Hate'. [Review] of *War Poems* by Lord Dunsany. *Irish Times*, June 7, 1941, 5.

'Two New Books of Verse'. [Review] of *The Ship of Death and other poems* by D. H. Lawrence; and *New Year Letter* by W. H. Auden. *Irish Times*, June 21, 1941, 5.

'No Time to Stand and Stare'. [Review] of *Common Joys and other poems* by W. H. Davies; and *Later Poems* by T. S. Eliot. *Irish Times*, August 9, 1941, 5.

'The Poetry of Ulster'. [Review] of *Awake and other poems* by W. R. Rodgers, [and 3 others]. *Irish Times*, Oct. 4, 1941, 5.

'A Return to Light Verse'. [Review] of *Rackrent Hall and other poems* by M. J. MacManus; and *Willow Leaves* by John Irvine. *Irish Times*, Nov. 15, 1941, 5.

'The Age of Anthologies'. [Review] of *Look! the Sun: an anthology of poems*, ed. by Edith Sitwell, [and 2 others] *Irish Times*, Dec. 6, 1941, 7.

[Review] of *The Concise Cambridge History of English Literature* by George Sampson. *Dublin Magazine*, XVII, n.s., 1 (Jan.-March, 1942), 59-62.

'Some Recent Poetry'. [Review] of *The Buried Stream: collected poems, 1908-1940* by Geoffrey Faber, [and 3 others]. *Irish Times*, Jan. 17, 1942), 5.

'Coole Park'. (Unsigned article). *Irish Times*, Feb. 26, 1942), 2.

'New Verse'. [Review] of *The North Star and other poems* by Laurence Binyon, [and 2 others]. *Irish Times*, Feb. 28, 1942), 5.

[Review] of *Self-Portrait. Taken from the Letters and Journals of Charles Ricketts*, ed. by Cecil Lewis. *Dublin Magazine*, XVII, n.s., 2 (April-June, 1942), 51-52.

[Review] of *The Scene is Changed: a description of dramatic ventures by A. Dukes*. *Dublin Magazine*, XVII, n.s., 2 (April-June, 1942), 62-63.

'Three New Anthologies'. [Review] of *A New Anthology of Modern Verse, 1920-1940* chosen by C. Day Lewis and L. A. G.

Strong, [and 2 others]. *Irish Times*, May 9, 1942, 5.

'Timeless Verse'. [Review] of *Collected Poems* by Walter De La Mare; and *Natalie Maisie and Pavilastukay* by John Masefield. *Irish Times*, June 27, 1942, 5.

[Review] signed M.D. of *Horizon: a review of literature and art* ed. by Cyril Connolly. Vol. V, no. 25. *Dublin Magazine*, XVII, n.s., 3 (July-Sept., 1942), 66-67.

'Recent Poetry'. [Review] of *Wilderness Sings* by John Lyle Donaghy [and 2 others]. *Irish Times*, Sept. 5, 1942), 2.

'The Blue Monk and other memories'. *Dublin Magazine*, XVII, n.s., 4 (Oct.-Dec., 1942), 21-25.

'New Verse'. [Review] of *Poetry in Wartime: an anthology* ed. by M. J. Tambimuttu, [and 2 others]. *Irish Times*, Oct. 31, 1942, 2.

'The Poet in Debt'. *Irish Times*, Nov. 7, 1942, 2.

'Herbert Trench'. *Irish Times*, Nov. 14, 1942, 2.

'Militant Puritan'. *Irish Times*, Nov. 28, 1942, 2.

'First Visit to England'. *Irish Times*, Dec. 17, 1942, 3.

'Beyond the Catechism'. *Dublin Magazine*, XVIII, n.s., 1 (Jan.-March, 1943), 33-37.

[Review] of *Letters of George Moore* with an introduction by John Eglinton. *Dublin Magazine*, XVIII, n.s., 1 (Jan.-March, 1943), 60-61.

[Review] signed M.D. of *Gerard Manley Hopkins: priest & poet* by John Pick. *Dublin Magazine*, XVIII, n.s., 1 (Jan.-March, 1943), 63-64.

[Review] of *Strolling Players and Drama in the Provinces, 1660-1765* by Sybil Rosenfeld. *Dublin Magazine*, XVIII, n.s., 1 (Jan.-March, 1943), 67-68.

[Review] of *The Classics & Men of Letters* by T. S. Eliot. *Dublin Magazine*, XVIII, n.s., 1 (Jan.-March, 1943), 68-69.

[Review] of *The Time of Your Life and other plays* by William Saroyan. *Dublin Magazine*, XVIII, n.s., 1 (Jan.-March, 1943), 69-71.

'Go and Catch a Falling Star'. *Irish Times*, Jan. 9, 1943, 2.

'New Poetry and New Poets'. [Review] of *Little Gidding* by T. S. Eliot, [and 5 others]. *Irish Times*, Jan. 23, 1943, 2.

'The Hidden Poetry of Wales'. *Irish Times*, Feb. 6, 1943, 2.

'Two Women Poets'. [Review] of *A Democrat's Chapbook: a chronicle of the events of the present war, with reflections* by A Quiet Woman; and *Lost Planet and other poems* by Dorothy Wellesley. *Irish Times*, Feb. 20, 1943, 2.

'Conversation at Ebury Street'. *Irish Times*, March 3, 1943, 2.

'The Yeats Tradition'. [Review]. *Irish Times*, March 27, 1943, 2.

[Review] of *The Narrow Place* by Edwin Muir; [and 2 others]. *Irish Times*, March 27, 1943, 2.

[Review] signed M.D. of *William Butler Yeats, 1865-1939* by Joseph Hone. *Dublin Magazine*, XVIII, n.s., 2 (April-June, 1943), 60-63.

[Review] of *A Handbook of Irish Folklore* by Sean O Suilleabháin. *Dublin Magazine*, XVIII, n.s., 2 (April-June, 1943), 63-64.

[Review] signed M.D. of *The Romantics: an anthology* chosen by Geoffrey Grigson. *Dublin Magazine*, XVIII, n.s., 2 (April-June, 1943), 68-69.

[Review] signed M.D. of *Watergate* by Francis MacManus. *Dublin Magazine*, XVIII, n.s., 2 (April-June, 1943), 74-75.

'On Learning Irish'. *Irish Times*, April 10, 1943, 2.

'Nature Poetry in England'. *Irish Times*, April 24, 1943, 2.

'Popular Poetry'. *Irish Times*, May 8, 1943, 2.

'An Irish Poet in India'. [Review] of *The House of Uladh: two plays in verse* by James H. Cousins. *Irish Times*, May 22, 1943, 2.

'Spotting the Lady'. *Irish Digest*, XV, 4 (June, 1943), 26-27.

'Poetry and the Weather'. *Irish Times*, June 12, 1943, 2.

'Poetry and Clothes'. *Irish Times*, June 19, 1943, 2.

'A Penny in the Clouds'. *Irish Times*, July 10, 1943, 2.

'Anthology Overseas'. [Review]. *Irish Times*, July 24, 1943, 2.

'Repentant Puritan'. *Irish Times*, August 7, 1943, 2.

'Some American Poets'. [Review]. *Irish Times*, August 21, 1943, 2.

'The Poetry of Connacht'. [Review]. *Irish Times*, Sept. 4, 1943, 2.

'Books Beyond Reach'. [Review]. *Irish Times*, Sept. 18, 1943, 2.

[Review] of *The Development of W. B. Yeats* by V. K. Naroyana Menon. *Dublin Magazine* XVIII, n.s., 4 (Oct.-Dec., 1943), 59-60.

[Review] signed M.D. of *Intertraffic: studies in translation* by E. S. Bates. *Dublin Magazine*, XVIII, n.s., 4 (Oct.-Dec., 1943), 63-64.

[Review] of *The Honeysuckle Hedge* by Sheila Steen. *Dublin Magazine*, XVIII, n.s., 4 (Oct.-Dec., 1943), 65-67.

'Recent Poetry'. [Review]. *Irish Times*, Oct. 9, 1943, 2.

'Poet in the Shetlands'. [Review]. *Irish Times*, Oct. 23, 1943, 2.

'Sir Richard Whittington'. [Review]. *Irish Times*, Nov. 20, 1943, 2.

'Recent Poetry'. [Review]. *Irish Times*, Dec. 11, 1943, 2.

'In the Shadow of Folklore'. [Review] of Yeats' *Countess Cathleen* and George Fitzmaurice. *Irish Times*, Jan. 8, 1944, 2.

'Ulster Anthology'. [Review]. *Irish Times*, Jan. 29, 1944, 2.

'First Visit to the Abbey'. *Irish Times*, Feb. 19, 1944, 2.

'Scottish Verse'. [Review]. *Irish Times*, March 11, 1944, 2.

[Review] signed Maurice Devane of *Irish Folk Tales* by Jeremiah Curtin. *Dublin magazine*, XIX, n.s., 2 (April-June, 1944), 55.

[Review] signed Maurice Devane of *The Origin of the Grail Legend* by Arthur C. L. Brown. *Dublin Magazine*, XIX, n.s., 2 (April-June, 1944), 56.

[Review] of *The Secret Island: poems and plays in verse* by Mona Douglas. *Dublin Magazine*, XIX, n.s., 2 (April-June, 1944), 63-64.

[Review] of *Malachi Horan Remembers* by George A. Little. *Dublin Magazine*, XIX, n.s., 2 (April-June, 1944), 65-66.

[Review] of *Landmarks: a book of topographical verse from English and Welsh* chosen by C. R. Hamilton and John Arlott. *Dublin Magazine*, XIX, n.s., 2 (April-June, 1944), 66-67.

[Review] of *Mad Grandeur* by Oliver St. J. Gogarty. *Dublin Magazine*, XIX, n.s., 2 (April-June, 1944), 67-68.

'The Romance of Ruins'. *Irish Times*, April 8, 1944, 2.

'A New Irish Epic'. [Review] of Robert Farren's *The First Exile*. *Irish Times*, April 15, 1944, 2.

'Wanted: a tradition'. [Review]. *Irish Times*, May 13, 1944, 2.

'The Countess Cathleen'. Commemorates opening (June 7, 1944) of this play in the new Lyric Theatre. *Irish Times*, May 27, 1944, 2.

'Poets, American and English'. *Irish Times*, July 1, 1944, 2.

'Scotland and Wales'. *Irish Times*, July 22, 1944, 2.

'The Chesterton Legend'. *Irish Times*, August 12, 1944, 2.

'English Pilgrim's Progress'. *Irish Times*, Sept. 9, 1944, 2.

'Detective Stories'. *Irish Times*, Sept. 16, 1944, 2.

'Early Anglo-Irish Poetry'. *Irish Times*, Sept. 30, 1944, 2.

'New Verse'. *Irish Times*, Oct. 14, 1944, 2.

'A Fallen Giant'. *Irish Times*, Nov. 4, 1944, 2.

'New Verse'. [Review] of *Four Quartets* by T. S. Eliot, [and 2 others]. *Irish Times*, Nov. 25, 1944, 2.

[Review] signed M.D. of *The Linguistic and Historical Value of the Irish Law Tracts* by D. A. Binchy. *Dublin magazine*, XX, n.s., 1 (Jan.-March, 1945), 52-53.

[Review] signed M.D. of *Shakespeare & the Actors: the stage business in his plays* by Arthur Colley Sprague. *Dublin Magazine*, XX, n.s., 1 (Jan.-March, 1945), 52-53.

[Review] of *Edward Carpenter: an appreciation*. *Dublin Magazine*, XX, n.s., 1 (Jan.-March, 1945), 53-54.

'The Art of Translation'. *Irish Times*, Jan. 13, 1945, 2.

'The Poetry of Blunden'. *Irish Times*, Feb. 3, 1945, 2.

'Two Irish Books of Verse'. *Irish Times*, Feb. 24, 1945, 2.

'Modern Poet'. [Review] of Auden, MacNeice and others. *Irish Times*, March 17, 1945, 2.

[Review] of *Kate Kennedy: a comedy in 3 acts* by Gordon Bottomley. *Dublin Magazine*, XX, n.s., 2 (April-June, 1945), 48-49.

[Review] signed M.D. of *English, Scottish and Welsh Landscape 1700-c. 1800* by

John Betjeman & Geoffrey Taylor. *Dublin Magazine*, XX, n.s., 2 (April-June, 1945), 59-60.

'An Epic of Christ'. *Irish Times*, May 5, 1945, 2.

'Across the Atlantic'. *Irish Times*, May 26, 1945, 2.

'Poems of Our Times'. *Irish Times*, August 18, 1945, 2.

'The World's End'. *Irish Times*, Sept. 29, 1945, 2.

[Review] of *Voltaire: myth and reality* by Kathleen O'Flaherty. *Dublin Magazine*, XX, n.s., 4 (Oct.-Dec., 1945), 45-47.

[Review] by M.D. of *The Western Isle of the Great Blasket* by Robin Flower. *Dublin Magazine*, XX, n.s., 3 [sic] (Oct.-Dec., 1945), 47-48.

[Review] of *Poems* by Alfred O'Rahilly. *Catholic Standard*, Oct. 12, 1945, 2.

'The Spirit of the Shillelagh'. *Irish Times*, Oct. 20, 1945, 2.

'Genuflection'. *Irish Times*, Nov. 17, 1945, 2.

'New Poetry'. [Review] of *Farewell and Welcome* by Ronald Bottrall, [and 2 others]. *Irish Times*, Dec. 8, 1945, 4.

[Review] of *The Midnight Court: a rhythmical bacchanalia from the Irish of Bryan Merriman* translated by Frank O'Connor. *Dublin Magazine*, XXI, n.s., 1 (Jan.-March, 1946), 53-56.

[Review] of *Drums Under the Window* by Sean O'Casey. *Dublin Magazine*, XXI, n.s., 1 (Jan.-March, 1946), 56-58.

ELH: A journal of English Literary History. Sept. 1945, *Dublin Magazine*, XXI, n.s., 1 (Jan.-March, 1946), 72.

'Reflection and Genuflection'. *Irish Digest*, XXIII, 3 (Jan. 1946), 57-58.

'Lady Gregory and Folk Fantasy'. *Irish Times*, Jan. 12, 1946), 4.

'Recent Verse'. [Review] of *A Transitory House* by Freda Laughton, [and 4 others]. *Irish Times*, Jan. 19, 1946, 4.

'An Irish Singer'. *Observer*, Jan. 20, 1946, 12.

'Potted Biography'. [Review] of *Irish Literary Figures: biographies in miniature. Vol. 1* by William J. Maguire. *Irish Times*, Feb. 9, 1946, 4.

'The Commerce of Poetry'. [Review] of *Selected Letters of Rainer Maria Rilke 1902-1926* translated by R. F. C. Hull. *Irish Times*, Feb. 23, 1946, 4.

'Shipwreck off Donegal'. *Irish Digest*, XXIV, 1 (March 1946), 51-52.

'Pilgrims to Parnassus'. [Review]. *Irish Times*, March 16, 1946, 4.

'Appointment for Tuesday'. *Irish Times*, March 30, 1946, 4.

'A Vision of Glendalough'. *Irish Times*, April 19/20, 1946, 4.

'Private Lives and Public Men'. [Review] of *Shelley: a life story by Edmund Blunden. Irish Times*, May 18, 1946, 4.

'Recent Verse'. [Review] of *Peter Grimes and other poems* by Montague Slater [and 3 others]. *Irish Times*, June 1, 1946, 4.

'Recent Verse'. [Review] of *The Garden* by V. Sackville West, [and 2 others]. *Irish Times*, July 13, 1946, 4.

'Local Talent'. [Review]. *Irish Times*, August 17, 1946, 4.

'Private File'. [Review] of *Bernard Shaw and W. B. Yeats: letters to Florence Farr* ed. by Clifford Bax. *Irish Times*, Sept. 14, 1946, 4.

'Three Poet's. [Review]. *Irish Times*, Oct. 5, 1946, 6.

'Perspectives'. [Review] of *The Milk of Paradise: some thoughts on poetry* by Forrest Reid; and *Feet on the Ground: being an approach to modern verse* by Margaret J. O'Donnell. *Irish Times*, Oct. 12, 1946, 6.

'Poetry in Ireland To-Day'. *The Bell*, XIII, 2 (Nov. 1946), 155-161.

'The True Background'. Essay on *Where Man Belongs* by H. J. Massingham. *Irish Times*, Nov. 9, 1946, 6.

'Centenary of an Irish Poet': George Darley 1846-1946'. *Irish Press*, Nov. 21, 1946.

'Plays in Verse'. [Review] of *The Poet in the Theatre* by Ronald Peacock. *The Bell*, XIII, 3 (Dec. 1946), 75-81.

'Strange Enchantment'. [Review] of *The Unfortunate Fursey* by Mervyn Wall. *Irish Times*, Dec. 21, 1946, 6.

'Standish James O'Grady'. *Dublin Magazine*, XXII, n.s., 1 (Jan.-March, 1947), 36-40.

[Review] of Oliver Elton, 1891-1945 by L. C. Martin. *Dublin Magazine*, XXII, n.s., 1 (Jan.-March, 1947), 53-54.

[Review] of *The Cycles of the Kings* by Myles Dillon. *Dublin Magazine*, XXII, n.s., 1 (Jan.-March, 1947), 54-56.

'Shakespeare-Phobia'. *Irish Digest*, XXVI, 3 (Jan. 1947), 4-13.

'We're Still a Race of Poets'. *Irish Digest*, XXVI, 3 (Jan. 1947), 9-12.

'Lady Gregory's Journals'. [Review]. *Irish Times*, Jan. 4, 1947, 6.

'Singers and Their Songs'. [Review] of *The Traveller* by Walter De La Mare, [and 6 Others]. *Irish Times*, Jan. 18, 1947, 6.

[Review] of *The Earth Gives All and Takes All* by Caradoc Evans; and *Caradoc Evans* by Oliver Sandys. *Irish Times*, Jan. 27, 1947.

'Three Translations'. [Review] of *The Poems of François Villon* translated by H. B. McCaskie, [and 2 others]. *Irish Times*, Feb. 15, 1947, 6.

'Home Ground'. [Review] of *Curlews* by Temple Lane, [and 5 others]. *Irish Times*, Feb. 22, 1947, 6.

'Church Parade for Poets'. [Review]. *Irish Times*, March 15, 1947, 6.

'The Bitter Word'. [Review]. *Irish Times*, March 29, 1947, 6.

'A Bundle of Poets'. [Review]. *Irish Times*, April 19, 1947, 6.

'Prospects'. [Review]. *Irish Times*, May 17, 1947, 6.

'The Affairs of Verse'. [Review]. *Irish Times*, June 21, 1947, 6.

[Review] signed M.D. of *Lady Gregory's Journals 1916-1930* ed. by Lennox Robinson. *Dublin Magazine*, XXII, n.s., 3 (July-Sept. 1947), 61-63.

[Review] signed M.D. of *Ibsen: the intellectual background* by Brian W. Downs. *Dublin Magazine*, XXII, n.s., 3 (July-Sept. 1947), 63-64.

[Review] signed M.D. of *Poets & Pundits: essays & addresses* by Hugh l'Anson Fausset. *Dublin Magazine*, XXII, n.s., 3 (July-Sept. 1947), 64-66.

[Review] signed M.D. of *The Life of Llewelyn Powys* by Malcolm Elwen. *Dublin Magazine*, XXII, n.s., 3 (July-Sept. 1947), 66-67.

'Matters of Choice'. [Review]. *Irish Times*, August 16, 1947, 6.

'A Sheaf of Poets'. [Review] of *The Stones of the Field* by R. S. Thomas, [and 4 others]. *Irish Times*, Sept. 20, 1947, 6.

'The Crowded Hours'. [Review] of *Life and the Dream* by Mary Colum. *Irish Times*, Oct. 25, 1947, 6.

'The Private Heart'. [Review]. *Irish Times*, Nov. 8, 1947, 6.

'The Prose of a Painter'. [Review] of *The Careless Flower* by Jack B. Yeats. *Irish Times*, Nov. 29, 1947, 9.

'Verse Speaking'. *The Bell*, XV, 3 (Dec. 1947), 52-56.

'Garlands of Poets'. [Review]. *Irish Times*, Dec. 20, 1947, 6.

'Along the Trail'. [Review] of *The Kid* by Conrad Aiken, [and 4 others]. *Irish Times*, Jan. 10, 1948, 6.

'The Artist and the World'. [Review]. *Irish Times*, Feb. 21, 1948, 6.

'Poet and Priest'. [Review]. *Irish Times*, Feb. 28, 1948, 4.

'Gentlemen of Letters'. [Review]. *Irish Times*, March 20, 1948, 4.

[Review] of *The Irish Tradition* by Robin Flower. *Dublin Magazine*, XXIII, n.s., 2 (April-June, 1948), 54-55.

[Review] of *Delius: a critical biography* by Arthur Hutchings. *Dublin Magazine*, XXIII, n.s., 2 (April-June, 1948), 63-64.

'The Doctor's Dilemma'. [Review]. *Irish Times*, April 3, 1948, 4.

'A Handful of Verses'. [Review] of *Light-Keeper's Lyrics* by D. J. O'Sullivan, [and 4 others]. *Irish Times*, May 29, 1948, 6.

'Critics' Circle'. [Review] of *English Literature Between the Wars* by B. Ifor Evans, [and 3 others]. *Irish Times*, June 12, 1948, 6.

'The American Muses'. [Review] of *A Little Treasury of Modern Poetry: English and American* ed. by Oscar Williams, [and 2 others]. *Irish Times*, June 26, 1948, 6.

'Poet of the English Twilight'. [Review]. *Irish Times*, July 17, 1948, 6.

'Born of Fire'. [Review] of Poems of the War Years: an anthology compiled by Maurice Wollman. *Irish Times*, August 14, 1948, 4.

'The Poet's Stage'. [Review] of *On Hamlet* by Salvador de Madariaga; and *The Eagle Has Two Heads* by Jean Cocteau. *Irish Times*, Sept. 4, 1948, 4.

'Scotland's Own'. [Review]. *Irish Times*, Sept. 18, 1948, 6.

[Review] of *A Stage for Poetry* by Gordon Bottomley. *Dublin Magazine*, XXIII, n.s., 4 (Oct.-Dec. 1948), 53-55.

'Auden and Others'. [Review] of *The Age of Anxiety: a Baroque eclogue* by W. H. Auden, [and 4 others]. *Irish Times*, Oct. 9, 1948, 6.

'From the Russian'. [Review]. *Irish*

Times, Oct. 23, 1948, 6.
'The Eggman Cometh'. [Review]. *Irish Times*, Nov. 6, 1948, 6.
'For Art's Sake'. [Review]. *Irish Times*, Dec. 4, 1948, 9.
'Mr. Eliot's Notebook'. [Review] of *Definition of a Culture*. *Irish Times*, Dec. 11, 1948, 6.
'A New Poet?' [Review]. *Irish Times*, Dec. 18, 1948, 6.
'Obituary of Gordon Bottomley'. *Dublin Magazine*, XXIV, n.s., 1 (Jan.-March 1948), 71-72.
'Art and State'. [Review]. *Irish Times*, Jan. 8, 1949, 6.
'Och, Johnny, I Hardly Knew Ye'. [Review] of *Inishfallen, Fare Thee Well* by Sean O'Casey, *Irish Times*, Jan. 29, 1949, 6.
'The Burning Tiger'. [Review]. *Irish Times*, Feb. 5, 1949, 6.
'Nature and Art'. [Review]. *Irish Times*, Feb. 12, 1949, 6.
'Period and Place'. [Review]. *Irish Times*, Feb. 19, 1949, 6.
'Yeats and "The Salley Gardens"'. *Irish Book Lover*, XXXI (March 1949-Nov. 1951), 133-134.
'The Magical Art'. [Review] of *The White Goddess* by Robert Graves. *Irish Times*, March 12, 1949, 6.
'On the Stage'. [Review]. *Irish Times*, March 19, 1949, 6.
'Critical Approach'. [Review] of *Modern Poetry and the Tradition* by Cleanth Brooks, [and 3 others]. *Irish Times*, March 26, 1949, 6.
'Prologue for a Romance: Congal (after the Irish'. *Dublin Magazine*, XXIV, n.s., 2 (April-June, 1949), 7-13.
'The Roaring Boy'. [Review]. *Irish Times*, April 2, 1949, 6.
'Blake the Mystic'. [Review] of *Poems* by William Blake. *Spectator*, 182 (April 15, 1949), 520.
'The Riotous Are Bold'. [Review] of *Cock A Doodle Dandy* by Sean O'Casey. *Irish Times*, April 16, 1949, 6.
'Lives and Times'. [Review]. *Irish Times*, April 23, 1949, 6.
'The Good-Humoured Man'. [Review]. *Irish Times*, April 30, 1949, 6.
'A Poet's Progress'. [Review]. *Irish Times*, May 14, 1949, 6.
'Poets' Gallery'. [Review]. *Irish Times*, May 28, 1949, 6.

'As Others See Us'. [Review] of *Life and Letters: Irish writers (April 1949)* ed. by Robert Herring, [and 2 others]. *Irish Times*, June 11, 1949, 6.
'Scholarly Pursuits'. [Review]. *Irish Times*, July 2, 1949, 6.
'The Devil in the House'. [Review]. *Irish Times*, July 23, 1949, 4.
'A Company of Poets'. [Review]. *Irish Times*, August 27, 1949, 4.
'Irish Impressions'. [Review] of Ussher's *The Face and Mind of Ireland*. *Spectator*, 183 (Sept. 2, 1949), 302.
'Author of "The Beaux Stratagem"'. [Review]. *Spectator*, 183 (Sept. 2, 1949), 302.
'London Lights'. [Review]. *Irish Times*, Sept. 17, 1949, 6.
'Personal and Public'. [Review]. *Irish Times*, Sept. 24, 1949, 6.
'The Defeat of Don Juan'. [Review]. *Irish Times*, Oct. 1, 1949, 6.
'Three Victorians'. [Review]. *Irish Times*, Oct. 29, 1949, 6.
'The Last Ditch'. [Review] of Graham Hough's *The Last Romantics*. *Irish Times*, Nov. 12, 1949, 6.
'Mr. Blunden and Others'. [Review]. *Spectator*, 183 (Nov. 11, 1949), 704.
'Ladies' Day'. [Review]. *Irish Times*, Nov. 19, 1949, 6.
'Oedipus and Philomel'. [Review] of *Yeats: the man and the mask* by Richard Ellman; and *The Golden Nightingale: essays on some principles of poetry in the lyrics of William Butler Yeats* by Donald A. Stauffer. *Irish Times*, Dec. 10, 1949, 6.
'Sense and Satire'. [Review] of *Poetry Ireland: ed. by David Marcus; No. 6 – The Midnight Court; a new translation* by Lord Longford, [and 3 others]. *Irish Times*, Dec. 17, 1949, 6.
'Apollo's Hen'. [Review]. *Irish Times*, Dec. 24, 1949, 6.
[Review] signed M.D. of *A Commentary on the General Prologue to the Canterbury Tales* by Muriel Bowden. *Dublin Magazine*, XXV, n.s., 5 [sic] (Jan.-March 1950), 51-53.
'Vade Retro'. [Review]. *Irish Times*, Jan. 14, 1950, 6.
'After 50 Years'. [Review]. *Irish Times*, Jan. 21, 1950, 6.
'Patchwork Poet'. [Review]. *Irish Times*, Jan. 28, 1950, 6.

'Verse in Action'. [Review]. *Irish Times*, Feb. 11, 1950, 6.

'Critics' Circle'. [Review]. *Irish Times*, March 4, 1950, 6.

'The Muse as Mistress'. [Review]. *Irish Times*, March 25, 1950, 6.

[Review] signed M.D. of *The Archaism of Irish Tradition* by Myles Dillon. *Dublin Magazine*, XXV, n.s., 2 (April-June, 1950), 47-48.

[Review] of *The Classical Tradition: Greek and Roman influences on Western Literature* by Gilbert Highet. *Dublin Magazine*, XXV, n.s., 2 (April-June 1950), 44-46.

'The Room Upstairs'. *Dublin Magazine*, XXV, n.s., 2 (April-June 1950), 6-11.

[Review] of *Strindberg: an introduction to his life and work* by Brita M. E. Morlensen and Brian W. Downs. *Dublin Magazine*, XXV, n.s., 2 (April-June 1950), 42-43.

[Review] of 'Yeats and "The Salley Gardens"' by Canice Mooney. *The Irish Book Lover*, XXXI (April 1950), 86-87.

'The Crystal Screen'. [Review]. *Irish Times*, (April 22, 1950), 6.

'Beyond the Mulberries'. [Review] of *The Forsaken Garden: an anthology of poetry 1824-1909* ed. by John Heath-Stubbs and David Wright, [and 2 others]. *Irish Times*, May 6, 1950, 6.

'Muscae Volitantes'. [Review]. *Irish Times*, May 27, 1950, 6.

'A Poet Encounters the Tans'. *Irish Digest*, XXXVI, 4 (June 1950), 12-14.

'High Jinks'. [Review] of *The Cocktail Party: a comedy* by T. S. Eliot; and *Stratton: a play in verse* by Ronald Duncan. *Irish Times*, June 17, 1950, 6.

'The Star Gazers'. [Review]. *Irish Times*, July 1, 1950, 6.

'Ex Machina'. [Review] of *The Georgian Literary Scene, 1910-1935: a panorama* by Frank Swinnerton, [and 2 others]. *Irish Times*, July 22, 1950, 6.

'The Return of the Native'. [Review]. *Irish Times*, August 5, 1950, 6.

'The Age of Anxiety'. [Review]. *Irish Times*, Sept. 16, 1950, 6.

'Scalping the Muse'. [Review] of *Poems 1938-1949* by Robert Lowell, [and 2 others]. *Irish Times*, Sept. 30, 1950, 6.

'Deirdre and Her Rival'. [Review]. *Irish Times*, Oct. 14, 1950, 6.

'Austin Clarke Writes'. [Letter to the editor]. *The Standard*, Nov. 17, 1950, 6.

'Letting Off Steam'. [Review]. *Irish Times*, Nov. 18, 1950, 6.

'The Achievement of T. S. Eliot'. [Review]. *Irish Times*, Dec. 9, 1950, 6.

'Things of the Spirit'. [Review]. *Spectator*, 185 (Dec. 15, 1950), 708.

'Travelling Man'. [Review]. *Irish Times*, Dec. 30, 1950, 6.

'A Nature Poet'. [Review]. *Spectator*, 186 (Jan. 12, 1951), 52.

'A Clutch of Critics'. [Review] of *New Bearings in English Poetry: a study of the contemporary situation* by F. R. Leavis, [and 3 others]. *Irish Times*, Jan. 13, 1951, 6.

'The Mind's Eye'. [Review] of *Lonely Tower* by T. R. Henn. *Irish Times*, Jan. 27, 1951, 6.

'Lyrical Allsorts'. [Review]. *Irish Times*, Feb. 10, 1951, 6.

'The Melting Pot'. [Review]. *Irish Times*, Feb. 17, 1951, 6.

'Green Helicon'. [Review] of *Irish Poets of the Nineteenth Century* selected by Geoffrey Taylor. *Irish Times*, Feb. 24, 1951, 6.

'Religion and Poetry'. [Review]. *Irish Times*, March 3, 1951, 6.

'Down the Ages'. [Review]. *Irish Times*, March 10, 1951, 6.

'Bandwagon from Babel'. [Review] of *The American Genius: an anthology of poetry, with some prose* selected by Edith Sitwell, [and 3 others]. *Irish Times*, March 23 & 24, 1951, 6.

'Greek in Modern Dress'. [Review]. *Irish Times*, March 31, 1951, 6.

'Footlights for Poetry'. [Review]. *Irish Times*, April 7, 1951, 6.

'Every Man His Own Crusoe'. [Review] of *The Enchanted Flood, or the Romantic Iconography of the Sea* by W. H. Auden; and *A-B-C of Reading* by Ezra Pound. *Irish Times*, April 14, 1951, 6.

'Treasure Trove'. [Review]. *Irish Times*, April 21, 1951, 6.

'Torchlight for Processions'. [Review]. *Irish Times*, April 28, 1951, 6.

'Poet and Peasant'. [Review]. *Irish Times*, May 5, 1951, 6.

'The Fire-born Moods'. [Review] of *Last Poems* by W. B. Yeats. *Irish Times*, May 12, 1951, 6.

'Haste to the Heavens'. [Review]. *Irish Times*, May 19, 1951, 6.

'The Votive Flame'. [Review]. *Irish*

Times, May 28, 1951, 6.

'The Ailing Muise'. [Review]. *Irish Times*, June 2, 1951, 6.

'A Western Parnassus'. [Review] of *A Celtic Miscellany: translations from the Celtic literatures* by Kenneth Hurlstone Jackson. *Irish Times*, June 16, 1951, 6.

'Seasonal Changes'. [Review]. *Irish Times*, June 23, 1951, 6.

'Miltonic Mysteries'. [Review]. *Irish Times*, June 30, 1951, 6.

'A Poet Come to Judgment'. [Review]. *Irish Times*, July 7, 1951, 6.

'The Riddle of the Sands'. [Review]. *Irish Times*, July 21, 1951, 6.

'Greek Fire'. [Review]. *Irish Times*, August 11, 1951, 6.

'A Knight Errant Rides Out'. [Review]. *Irish Times*, Sept. 1, 1951, 6.

'The Leaning Tower'. [Review] of *The Poetry of Ezra Pound* by Hugh Kenner. *Irish Times*, Sept. 8, 1951, 6.

'Tinkers Galore'. [Review] of *Travelling Tinkers* by Sigerson Clifford; and *Elegy for a Lost Submarine* by Ewart Milne. *Irish Times*, Sept. 15, 1951, 6.

'The White Blackbird'. [Review]. *Irish Times*, Oct. 6, 1951, 6.

'Displaced Poet'. [Review] of *Auden: an introductory essay* by Richard Hoggart. *Irish Times*, Oct. 13, 1951, 6.

'Mr. Eliot on Mr. Eliot'. [Review]. *Irish Times*, Oct. 20, 1951, 6.

'Tramping to Heaven'. [Review]. *Irish Times*, Oct. 27, 1951, 6.

'Shelley and His Critics'. [Review]. *Irish Times*, Nov. 3, 1951, 6.

'The Zenith and the Rainbow'. [Review]. *Irish Times*, Nov. 10, 1951, 6.

'The Future Tense'. [Review]. *Irish Times*, Nov. 17, 1951, 6.

'Literature in Verse?' [Review]. *Spectator*, 187 (Nov. 23, 1951), 714.

[Reply] to 'Yeats and "The Salley Gardens"' by Fr. Canice Mooney, *Irish Book Lover*, XXXI 6 (Nov. 1951), 133-4.

'The Laurels of Yesterday'. [Review]. *Irish Times*, Dec. 8, 1951, 6.

'The Wooden Horse'. [Review]. *Irish Times*, Dec. 22, 1951, 6.

'Victorian Eminence'. [Review]. *Irish Times*, Dec. 29, 1951, 6.

'Tory Island'. *Irish Geography*, 2, 4 (1952), 184-190.

'Shadowing Skies'. [Review]. *Irish Times*,

Jan. 5, 1952, 6.

'Pieces of Eight'. [Review]. *Irish Times*, Jan. 19, 1952, 6.

'North and South'. [Review]. *Irish Times*, Feb. 2, 1952, 6.

'The Great Unreal'. [Review]. *Irish Times*, Feb. 9, 1952, 6.

'Leander II'. [Review]. *Irish Times*, Feb. 23, 1952, 6.

'Before the Ides'. [Review]. *Irish Times*, March 1, 1952, 6.

'Fire-New-Words'. [Review]. *Irish Times*, March 15, 1952, 6.

'The Stuff of Youth'. [Review]. *Irish Times*, March 29, 1952, 6.

'A Sop to Cerberus'. [Review] of *Robert Ross: friend of friends* ed. by Margery Ross. *Irish Times*, April 12, 1952, 8.

'Beauty and the Beast'. [Review] of *Europa and the Bull and other poems* by W. R. Rodgers. *Irish Times*, April 19, 1952, 8.

'Little Lights'. [Review]. *Irish Times*, May 10, 1952, 8.

'March of a Nation'. [Review]. *Irish Times*, May 17, 1952, 8.

'Museum Pieces'. [Review]. *Irish Times*, May 24, 1952, 8.

[Review] of *Letters of Ezra Pound, 1907-1941* ed. by D. D. Paige. *The Bell*, XVIII, 3 (June 1952), 189-191.

'Contrary John'. [Review] of *Confidential, or Take It or Leave It* by John Eglinton. *Irish Times*, June 21, 1952, 6.

[Review] of *Rose and Crown* by Sean O'Casey. *John O'London's Weekly*, July 18, 1952, 692.

'Irish Authoresses'. [Review]. *Spectator*, 189 (August 1, 1952), 168.

'Plays in Search of a Theatre'. [Review]. *Irish Times*, Oct. 8, 1952, 8.

'John Eglinton'. [Review article]. *Irish Writing*, 20-21 (Nov. 1952), 74-77.

'Poetry in the Parlour'. [Review] of *Emily Dickinson* by Richard Chase. *Irish Times*, Nov. 1, 1952, 6.

'Spiritual Affairs'. [Review]. *Irish Times*, Nov. 8, 1952, 6.

[Review] of *Robert Browning: a portrait* by Betty Miller; and *Robert Browning* by J. M. Cohen. *Irish Times*, Dec. 13, 1952, 6.

'The Arrows of Apollo'. [Review] of *Purity of Diction* by Donald Davie. *Irish Times*, Dec. 20, 1952, 6.

'The Spring Tide'. [Review]. *Irish Times*,

Dec. 27, 1952, 4.

'Ancient and Modern'. [Review]. *Irish Times,* Jan. 24, 1953, 6.

'Public Papers'. [Review]. *Irish Times,* Jan. 31, 1953, 6.

'Metaphors and Language'. [Review]. *Spectator,* 190 (Feb. 6, 1953), 160.

'Flight from Fog'. [Review]. *Irish Times,* Feb. 7, 1953, 6.

'Towards a Verse Theatre'. [Review]. *Irish Times,* Feb. 21, 1953, 6.

'Sky Shades and Lamp Shades'. [Review] of *Selected Poems* by Wallace Stevens. Chosen by Dennis Williamson. *Irish Times,* Feb. 14, 1953, 6.

'Ourselves and Others'. [Review] of *Leabhra ar Éirinn: books on Ireland: a list* compiled by the National Library of Ireland. *Irish Times,* Feb. 28, 1953, 6.

'The Cuckoo's Church'. [Review] of *An Introduction to Welsh Poetry from the beginnings to the sixteenth century* by Gwyn Williams. *Irish Times,* March 7, 1953, 6.

'The Colloquial Muse'. [Review]. *Irish Times,* March 21, 1953, 6.

'Critic At Ease'. [Review] of *Memories* by Desmond MacCarthy. *Irish Times,* March 28, 1953, 6.

'The Higher Gossip'. [Review] of *Shelley: the last phase* by Ivan Roe, [and 3 others]. *Irish Times,* April 4, 1953, 6.

'The Pierian Spring'. [Review] of *Divided Image: a study of William Blake and W. B. Yeats* by Margaret Rudd; and *Jerusalem* by William Blake. *Irish Times,* April 11, 1953, 6.

'Willow Pattern'. [Review] of *The Book of Cricket Verse: an anthology* ed. by Gerald Brodribb, [and 3 others]. *Irish Times,* April 18, 1953, 6.

'Another Opinion'. [Review] of *Shakespeare* by Henri Fluchère, translated by Guy Hamilton. *Irish Times,* April 25, 1953, 6.

'Critic in the Cathedral'. [Review] of *T. S. Eliot: selected prose* ed. by John Hayward. *Irish Times,* May 2, 1953, 6.

'The Poet's Wife'. [Review]. *Irish Times,* May 9, 1953, 6.

'On the Nursery Floor'. [Review]. *Spectator,* 190 (May 15, 1953), 6.

'City of Man'. [Review] of *Paterson* by William Carlos Williams, [and 3 others]. *Irish Times,* May 16, 1953, 6.

'Banned Books'. *New Statesman,* May 23, 1953, 6.

'The Eyes of Youth'. [Review] of *Springtime: an anthology of young poets and writers* ed. by G. S. Fraser and Iain Fletcher. *Irish Times,* May 23, 1953, 6.

'The Woman Who Did'. [Review] of *Lélia: the life of George Sand* by André Maurois. *Irish Times,* May 30, 1953, 6.

'Pastoral Poet'. [Review] of *William Barnes of Dorset* by Giles Dugdale. *Irish Times,* June 6, 1953, 6.

[Review] (unsigned) of *The Other Mind: a study of dance in south India* by Beryl de Zoete. *Irish Times,* June 6, 1953, 6.

'Tremors and Thrills'. [Review] of *Ideas and Places* by Cyril Connolly and; *The Doctor and the Devils* by Dylan Thomas. *Irish Times,* June 13, 1953, 6.

'Spirit of Laughter'. [Review]. *Irish Times,* June 27, 1953, 6.

'Between Friends'. [Review] of *Letters of W. B. Yeats to Katharine Tynan* ed. by Roger McHugh. *Irish Times,* July 11, 1953, 6.

'No Signature'. [Review] of *Private View* by Walter De La Mare. *Irish Times,* July 25, 1953, 6.

'You Never Can Tell'. [Review] of *Chronicle of a Life* by Siegfried Trebitsch. *Irish Times,* August 8, 1953, 6.

'No Pudding for Poets'. [Review] of *A Hopkins Reader* selected by John Pick. *Irish Times,* August 22, 1953, 6.

'The River and Its Sources'. [Review]. *Irish Times,* August 15, 1953, 6.

'The Middle of the Road'. [Review] of *The Modern Writer and His World* by G. S. Fraser. *Irish Times,* August 29, 1953, 6.

'What You Will'. [Review]. *Irish Times,* Sept. 12, 1953, 6.

'World Beyond Words'. [Review]. of *Poets and Mystics* by E. I. Watkin. *Irish Times,* Sept. 19, 1953, 6.

'Sing a Song o' Suburbs'. [Review]. *Irish Times,* Sept. 26, 1953, 6.

'Give and Take'. [Review] of *W. B. Yeats and T. Sturge Moore: their correspondence, 1901-1937* ed. by Ursula Bridge. *Irish Times,* Oct. 3, 1953, 6.

'The Happy Warrior'. [Review] of *A Handful of Authors: essays on books and writers* by G. K. Chesterton; and *Humanities* by Desmond MacCarthy. *Irish Times,* Oct. 17, 1953, 6.

'A Long Look Back'. [Review] of *Two Worlds for Memory* by Alfred Noyes. *Irish Times,* Oct. 24, 1953, 6.

'The American Way'. [Review] of *Journal of the Illinois State Historical Society, Volume XLV: Number Four*; and *Always the Young Strangers* by Carl Sandburg. *Irish Times*, Oct. 31, 1953, 10.

'Enigma at Amherst'. [Review] of *The Riddle of Emily Dickinson* by Rebecca Patterson. *Irish Times*, Nov. 7, 1953, 6.

'Recapitulation'. [Review]. *Irish Times*, Nov. 14, 1953, 6.

'Age and Youth'. [Review] of *O Lovely England and other poems* by Walter De La Mare, [and 2 others]. *Irish Times*, Nov. 21, 1953, 6.

'Poetry and Pomps'. [Review] of *Gardens and Astronomers* by Edith Sitwell; and *The Triad of Genius. Part I: Edith and Osbert Sitwell* by Max Wakes-Joyce. *Irish Times*, Dec. 12, 1953, 6.

'Family Album'. [Review]. *Irish Times*, Dec. 19, 1953, 6.

'The Riddle of Emily Dickinson'. [Review] *Spectator*, 192 (Jan. 1, 1954), 26.

'Dreams Lie Deep'. [Review] of *Collected Poems of Charlotte Mew* by Alida Monro. *Irish Times*, Jan. 2, 1954, 6.

'Remembered Fields'. [Review] of *The Collected Poems of Padraic Colum*. *Irish Times*, Jan. 9, 1954, 6.

'The Case of Mr. Keats'. [Review] of *John Keats: the living – 21st September, 1818, to 21st September 1819* by Robert Gittings. *Irish Times*, Jan. 16, 1954, 6.

'Venus and Her Prey'. [Review] of *Nana: a realistic novel* by Emile Zola. A new translation by Charles Duff. *Irish Times*, Jan. 23, 1954, 6.

'Man and Superwoman'. [Review] of *Emily Bronte: her life and work* by Muriel Spark and Derek Stanford; and *George Eliot* by Robert Speaight. *Irish Times*, Jan. 30, 1954, 6.

'Faith and Works'. [Review] of *The Egotistical Sublime: a history of Wordsworth's imagination* by John Jones. *Irish Times*, Feb. 6, 1954, 6.

'For Smaller Shelves'. [Review] of *A Selection of Poems* by Edmund Spenser with an introduction by Richard Church, [and 5 others]. *Irish Times*, Feb. 13, 1954, 6.

'Rabbie and Robert'. [Review] *Burns into English: renderings of selected dialect poems of Robert Burns* by William Kean Seymour. *Irish Times*, Feb. 20, 1954, 6.

'Surprise Attacks'. [Review] of *Literary Essays of Ezra Pound* ed. with an introduction by T. S. Eliot. *Irish Times*, Feb. 27, 1954, 6.

'Two on a Tower'. [Review] of *The Art of Paul Valery: a study in dramatic monologues* by Francis Scarfe; and *The Return of the Prodigal. Preceded by Five Other Treatises, with Saul, a Drama in Five Acts* by André Gide. *Irish Times*, March 6, 1954, 6.

'The New Collegians'. [Review] of *The Penguin Book of Modern American Verse* selected, with an introduction and notes, by Geoffrey Marne. *Irish Times*, March 13, 1954, 6.

'Family Disunion'. [Review] *The Confidential Clerk: a play* by T. S. Eliot. *Irish Times*, March 20, 1954, 6.

'Sporting the Leek'. [Review] of *Under Milk Wood: a play for voices* by Dylan Thomas. *Irish Times*, March 27, 1954, 6.

'Out of Office Hours'. [Review] of *The First Decadent: being the strange life of J. K. Huysmans* by James Laver. *Irish Times*, April 3, 1954, 6.

'The Third Woman'. [Review] of *Jonathan Swift: a critical biography* by John Middleton Murray. *Irish Times*, April 10, 1954, 6.

'The Fall of Leaves'. [Review] of *The Overreacher: a study of Christopher Marlowe* by Harry Levin, [and 2 others]. *Irish Times*, April 17, 1954, 6.

'The Hill of Vision'. [Review] of *Collected Poems* by James Stephens. *Irish Times*, April 24, 1954, 6.

'Wolf! Wolf!' [Review] of *Petrus Borel, the Lycanthrope: his life and times* by Enid Starkie. *Irish Times*, May 1, 1954, 6.

'The Gentleman's Not For Burning'.[Review] of *Don Juan* by Ronald Duncan. *Irish Times*, May 8, 1954, 8.

'Band of Hope'. [Review] of *The Death Bell: poems and ballads* by Vernon Watkins; and *The Pot Geranium* by Norman Nicholson. *Irish Times*, May 15, 1954, 6.

'No Silver Lining'. [Review] of *Brother to Dragons: a tale in verse and voices* by Robert Penn Warren. *Irish Times*, May 22, 1954, 6.

'The Man from Stratford'. [Review] of *The Poetry of Shakespeare's Plays by F. E. Halliday*. *Irish Times*, May 29, 1954, 6.

'Put Aside the Lute'.[Review] of *George

Herbert: his religion and art by Joseph H. Summers. *Irish Times*, June 12, 1954, 8.

'Ancient Enemies'. [Review]. *Irish Times*, June 19, 1954, 6.

'The Great Anon'. [Review] of *The Masks of Jonathan Swift* by William Bragg Ewald. *Irish Times*, June 26, 1954, 8.

'As in a Glass Darkly'. [Review] of *The Dark is Light Enough: a winter comedy* by Christopher Fry. *Irish Times*, July 3, 1954, 6.

'In Their Moods'. [Review] of *Poems 1939-1952* by Edward Shanks, [and 3 others]. *Irish Times*, July 10, 1954, 6.

'Themes and Theses'. [Review] of *The English Epic and its Background* by E. M. W. Tillyard. *Irish Times*, July 24, 1954, 6.

'Wind From the North'. [Review] of *John Gibson Lockhart* by Marion Lockhead. *Irish Times*, July 31, 1954, 6.

'Behind Lace Curtains. [Review] of *Elizabeth Barrett to Miss Mitford; the unpublished letlters of Elizabeth Barrett to Mary Russell Mitford* ed. and introduced by Betty Miller. *Irish Times*, August 7, 1954, 6.

'Around the Gates'. [Review] of *The Collected Poems of Mary Coleridge* ed. with an introduction by Theresa Whistler. *Irish Times*, August 14, 1954, 6.

'Bright Intervals'. [Review] of *A Charm Against the Toothache* by John Heath-Stubbs, [and 3 others]. *Irish Times*, August 21, 1954, 6.

'Magic of Europe'. [Review] of *Scenes and Portraits: memories of childhood and youth* by Van Wyck Brooks. *Irish Times*, August 28, 1954, 6.

'Second Thoughts'. [Review] of *The Identity of Yeats* by Richard Ellmann. *Irish Times*, Sept. 4, 1954, 8.

'Out of Breath'. [Review] of *Rainer Maria Rilke. Selected Works, vol. 1: Prose* translated by G. Craig Hanston; and *The Broken Cistern: the Clark Lectures, 1952-53* by Bonamy Dobree. *Irish Times*, Sept. 11, 1954, 8.

'Reforming Zeal'. [Review] of *William Poel and the Elizabethan Revival* by Robert Speaight. *Irish Times*, Sept. 18, 1954, 6.

'The Mighty Puzzle'. [Review] of *Shakespeare: the last phase* by Derek Travers. *Irish Times*, Oct. 2, 1954, 6.

'Gay Days'. [Review] of *It Isn't This Time of Year at All! an unpremeditated autobiography* by Oliver St. J. Gogarty. *Irish Times*, Oct. 9, 1954, 8.

'Father and Sons'. [Review] of *Son of Oscar Wilde* by Vyvyan Holland, [and 4 others]. *Irish Times*, Oct. 16, 1954, 6.

'The Poet as Playboy'. [Review] of *Apollinaire* by Marcel Adéma, translated from the French by Denise Folliot. *Irish Times*, Oct. 23, 1954, 8.

'Catching the Post'. [Review] of *The Letters of W. B. Yeats* ed. by Allan Wade. *Irish Times*, Oct. 30, 1954, 6.

'Cock-A-Doodle Dandy'. [Review] of *Sunset and Evening Star* by Sean O'Casey. *Irish Times*, Nov. 6, 1954, 6.

'Some Elizabethans'. [Review] of *Ben Jonson of Westminster* by Marchette Chute, [and 3 others]. *Irish Times*, Nov. 13, 1954, 6.

[Review] of *Sunset and Evening Star* by Sean O'Casey. *Time and Tide*, Nov. 13, 1954, 1524.

'The Incomplete Egotist'. [Review] of *Wordsworth: a re-interpretation* by F. W. Bateson. *Irish Times*, Nov. 20, 1954, 6.

'The Wearers of the Bays'. [Review] of *The Poets Laureate: a study of the office and its holders and a collection of the official writings of the Laureates* by Kenneth Hopkins. *Irish Times*, Dec. 11, 1954, 6.

'Down to Earth'. [Review] of *Flight of the Skylark: the development of Shelley's reputation* by Sylvia Norman. *Irish Times*, Dec. 18, 1954, 6.

'The Season's End'. [Review] of *Autumn Sequel: a rhetorical poem in XXVI cantos* by Louis MacNeice. *Irish Times*, Dec. 24, 1954.

'The Burns Dilemma'. [Review] of *Robert Burns: the man, his work, the legend* by Maurice Lindsay. *Irish Times*, Jan. 18, 1955, 6.

'The Cost of Freedom'. [Review] of *The Pen in Exile: an anthology* ed. by Paul Tehane; and *New Poems 1954: a P.E.N. anthology* ed. by Rex Warner. *Irish Times*, Jan. 22, 1955, 6.

'What You Will'. [Review] of *The First Night of "Twelfth Night"* by Leslie Hotson. *Irish Times*, Jan. 29, 1955, 6.

'From One Country: an anthology of Irish Writing'. [Review] of *Anthology of Irish Literature* ed. by David H. Greene. *Irish Times*, Feb. 5, 1955, 6.

'A Gathering of Poets'. [Review] of

Collected Poems by Frances Cornford, [and 3 others]. *Irish Times*, Feb. 12, 1955, 6.

'In Modern Dress'. [Review] of *Lysistrata. By Aristophanes. An English Version* by Dudley Fitts. *Irish Times*, Feb. 19, 1955, 6.

'Poet of Peace: a new study of Alexander Pope'. [Review] of *Laureate of Peace: on the genius of Alexander Pope* by G. Wilson Knight. *Irish Times*, Feb. 26, 1955, 6.

'The Master Builder: an interpretation and a study'. [Review] of *The Master Builder by Henrik Ibsen. A translation* by Eva Le Gallienne. *Irish Times*, Mar. 5, 1955, 6.

'Carriages at Nine: the theatre in Stuart Ireland'. [Review] of *The Early Irish Stage: the beginnings to 1720* by William Smith Clark. *Irish Times*, March 12, 1955, 6.

'Confucius Worse Confounded'. [Review] of *The Classic Anthology Defined by Confucius* by Ezra Pound; and *Ezra Pound's Mauberley: a study in composition* by John J. Esey. *Irish Times*, March 19, 1955, 8.

'The Amoralist'. [Review] of *Sex, Literature and Censorship: essays by D. H. Lawrence* ed. by Harry T. Moore; and *Lorenzo in Search of the Sun: D. H. Lawrence in Italy, Mexico and the American South-West* by Eliot Fay. *Irish Times*, March 26, 1955, 6.

'Cast a Cold Eye'. [Review] of *Autobiographies* by W. B. Yeats. *Irish Times*, April 2, 1955, 8.

[Reviews]. *Irish Times*
'Poems of Ireland', April 9, 1955, 8.
'The Dark Worlds', April 16, 1955, 8.
'Comrades-in-Arts', April 23, 1955, 8.
'Around Parnassus', April 30, 1955, 8.
'La Fontaine Revisited', May 7, 1955, 8.
'Gownsmen All'. *Interpretations: essays on twelve English poems* ed. by John Wain, Nov. 19, 1955, 6.
'Poems of Today and Yesterday', Dec. 10, 1955.
'Salve', Dec. 24, 1955, 6.
'The Voice of the Swami', May 14, 1955, 8.
'A Tribute to A.E.', May 28, 1955, 8.
'Wise Man from the West', June 4, 1955, 8.
'Don Screwtape', June 11, 1955, 8.

'Once Upon a Time', June 18, 1955, 8.
'The Narrow Screen', June 25, 1955, 8.
'Pierian Spring', July 2, 1955, 6.
'The Storyteller', July 9, 1955, 8.
'Looking Backwards', July 16, 1955, 8.
'The Lowland Muse', July 23, 1955, 8.
'The Prince of Darkness', July 30, 1955, 6.
'The Last Hours', August 6, 1955, 6.
'Fallen Woman', August 13, 1955, 6.
'For Jamie Joyce', August 20, 1955, 6.
'Stager in Sack-Cloth', August 27, 1955, 6.
'Poet of Meath', Sept. 3, 1955, 6.
'The New Discipline', Sept. 10, 1955, 6.
'Indian Summer', Sept. 17, 6.
'Poetry and Prejudice', Sept. 24, 1955, 6.
'Style and the Man', Oct. 1, 1955, 6.
'Women of Destiny', Oct. 8, 1955, 6.
'The Higher Criticism', *Articulate Energy* by Donald Davie, Oct. 15, 1955, 6.
'A Major Poet?', Oct. 22, 1955, 6.
'All for Hecuba', Nov. 29, 1955, 6.
'The Cryptic Key', Nov. 5, 1955, 6.
'Three Poets', Nov. 12, 1955, 8.

'Christina Rosetti'. [Review]. *Spectator*, 196 (Jan. 6, 1956), 27.
'The Age of Conformity'. [Review]. *Irish Times*, Jan. 7, 1956, 6.
'Mirth-Maker'. [Review]. *Spectator*, 196 (Jan. 13, 1956), 58.

[Reviews] *Irish Times*
'Blake and Yeats', Jan. 14, 1956, 6.
'Robert Wilson', Jan. 21, 1956, 6.
'The Dunce's Epic', Jan. 28, 1956, 8.
'The Cheerful Critic', Feb. 4, 1956, 6.
'Poems of Happiness', Feb. 11, 1956, 6.
'Bards in the Wood', Feb. 18, 1956, 6.
'From the Imagined Corners', Feb. 25, 1956, 6.
'A Citizen of the World', March 3, 1956, 8.
'Dead Men's Tales', Mar. 10, 1956, 8.
'Eminent Victorians', March 17, 1956, 6.
'A Poet of Faith', *One Foot in Eden* by Edwin Muir, March 24, 1956, 8.
'The Cactus Has Its Prickles', March 31, 1956, 8.

[Review] signed M.D. of *Young Samuel Johnson* by James L. Clifford. *Dublin Magazine*, XXXI, n.s., 2 (April-June, 1956), 39-42.

[Reviews]. *Irish Times*
'Critics Choice', April 7, 1956, 8.
'Mask and Motley', April 14, 1956, 8.

'Fine Banks', April 21, 1956, 8.
'Mirth for Millions', April 28, 1956, 8.
'The Land of Memory', May 5, 1956, 6.
'Welsh Concert', May 12, 1956, 6.
'Walter de la Mare', May 19, 1956, 6.
'Three Poets', May 26, 1956, 6.
'The Lost Disciple', June 2, 1956.
'Divers Hands', June 9, 1956, 6.
'No Prospect Pleases', June 16, 1956, 8.
'The Novelist's Eye', June 23, 1956, 6.
'Voices in the Fog', June 30, 1956, 6·
'American Witch-Hunt', July 7, 1956, 6.
'Modern Poetry', July 14, 1956, 6.
'The Last Aesthete', July 21, 1956, 6.
'East and West', August 4, 1956, 6.
'The Fallen Soldier', August 11, 1956, 6.
'The Wicked Lord', Sept. 29, 1956, 6.
'Memories of Moore', Oct. 6, 1956, 6.
'American Poetry', Oct. 13, 1956, 6.
'Out of School', Oct. 20, 1956, 6.
'Ten Years Old', Oct. 27, 1956, 6.
'Ariel Observed', Nov. 3, 1956, 6.
'The Spirit and the World', Nov. 10, 1956, 6.
'Victorian Poet', Nov. 17, 1956, 6.
'Poems from Wales', Dec. 12, 1956, 6.
'Hopkins' letters', Dec. 15, 1956, 6.
'An Irish Poet', Dec. 22, 1956, 6.
'Travelling Men', Dec. 29, 1956, 6.
'The Bloomsbury Set', Jan. 5, 1956, 6.
'Lawrence', Jan. 12, 1957, 6.
'Peguy as Poet', Jan. 19, 1957, 6.
'Poets Cannot Err', Jan. 26, 1957, 6.
'Poet of Auld Reikie', Feb. 9, 1957, 6.
'New Poems', Feb. 16, 1957, 6.
'Dear Edward', Feb. 23, 1957, 6.
'Man Uncertain', March 2, 1957, 6.
'On Translation', March 9, 1957, 6.
'A Writer Born', March 16, 1957, 6.
'Synge and the Irish', March 23, 1957, 6.
'Down Fleet St.', March 30, 1957, 6.
'Here Be Dragons', April 6, 1957, 6.
'New Poetry', April 13, 1957, 6.
'Tiddly-Winks and Toss Pats', April 20, 1957, 6.
'Enter Iago', April 27, 1957, 6.
'Poems by L. A. G. Strong', May 4, 1957, 6.
'The Late Romantic', May 11, 1957, 6.
'The Common Muse', May 18, 1957, 6.
'Signposts to Stratford', May 25, 1957, 6.
'Storm and Stress', June 1, 1957, 6.
'Thirty Years Back', June 8, 1957, 6.
'Ars Poetica', June 15, 1957, 6.
'The Poets Pass By', June 22, 1957, 6.
'Eternity observed', June 29, 1957, 6.

'The Yea-Sayers', July 13, 1957, 6.
'Irish Classical Poems', July 20, 1957, 6.
'The Open Mind', July 27, 1957, 6.
'Anatomy of Melancholy', August 10, 1957, 6.
'The Modern Sitwells', August 17, 1957, 6.
'Three Voices', August 24, 1957, 6.
'Fog and Sunday', August 31, 1957, 6.

'Capel Street: a chapter of autobiography'. *Irish Writing*, 37 (Autumn 1957), 5-16.

[Reviews]. *Irish Times*
'Why the 12.30 Was Late'. *All That Fall* by Samuel Beckett, Sept. 7, 1957, 6.
'The Western World', Sept. 14, 1957, 8.
'A Murmuring of Moderns', Sept. 21, 1957, 6.
'Tea-Time in Twickenham', Sept. 28, 1957, 6.
'Behind the Scenes', Oct. 5, 1957, 6.
'The Senior Revolutionary', Oct. 12, 1957, 6.
'In Quest of Shakespeare', Oct. 19, 1957, 6.
'A Dreamer's Child', Oct. 26, 1957, 6.
'Love and Magic', Nov. 2, 1957, 8.
'Whence the Green Man?', Nov. 9, 1957, 8.
'Oscar in Earnest', Nov. 16, 1957, 8.
'Poet Without His Legend', Nov. 23, 1957, 6.
'A Poet of Dissent', Dec. 14, 1957, 6.
'Forbidden Fruit', Dec. 21, 1957, 6.
'Poets of Silence', Dec. 28, 1957, 4.
'Virtue Triumphant', Jan. 4, 1958, 6.
'The Study of Blake', Jan. 11, 1958, 6.
'The Poems of Rilke', Jan. 18, 1958, 6.
'On the Track of W. B.', Jan. 25, 1958, 6.
'The Storm and the Calm', Feb. 1, 1958, 6.
'Studies in Evaluation', Feb. 8, 1958, 6.
'A Guide to Bardolatry', Feb. 15, 1958, 6.
'The Age of Reason', Feb. 22, 1958, 6.
'Neglected Poets', March 1, 1958, 6.
'Sing A Song of Silly South', March 8, 1958, 8.
'Andromeda Unrescued', March 15, 1958, 8.
'The Perfectionist', March 22, 1958, 6.
'Poor Noll', March 29, 1958, 8.
'The Scholar Poet', April 5, 1958, 6.
'East and West', April 12, 1958, 8.
'Family Reunion', April 19, 1958, 8.

'The Strindbergs', April 26, 1958, 6.
'Situation Vacant', May 3, 1958, 6.
'All Hail, Great Master', May 10, 1958, 8.
'Fellow of Infinite Jest', May 17, 1958, 8.
'The Poet of Reform', May 24, 1958, 8.
'Dear, Dirty Dublin', June 7, 1958, 8.
'Prophet on the Warpath', June 14, 1958, 6.
'A Discreet Victorian, June 21, 1958, 8.
'Sweeney on the Rack'. *The Sweeniad* by Myra Buttle, June 28, 1958, 8.
'The Last Hellenist', July 5, 1958, 6.
'Poets Young and Old', July 19, 1958, 6.
'Opinions and Reality', July 26, 1958, 6.
'Virginia Woolf the Critic', August 2, 1958, 6.
'Mon Cher Ami', August 9, 1958, 6.
'Heroes of History', August 16, 1958, 6.
'A New View of Swift', August 23, 1958, 6.
'Question and Answer', August 30, 1958, 6.
'Night Thoughts', Sept. 6, 1958, 6.
'Poor Theo', Sept. 13, 1958, 6.
'The Songs of Steam', Sept. 20, 1958, 6.
'A Quartet of Poets', Sept. 27, 1958, 6.
'A Colloquy of Critics', Oct. 4, 1958, 6.
'New England Century', Oct. 11, 1958, 6.
'Tragic Interlude', Oct. 18, 1958, 8.
'Daring Young Woman', Oct. 25, 1958, 6.
'Straight Elizabethan', Nov. 1, 1958, 6.
'Under Two Flags', Nov. 8, 1958, 6.
'Portrait of Mr. W. H.', Nov. 15, 1958, 6.
'Kings and Chronicles', Nov. 22, 1958, 6.
'Writers at Ease', Dec. 6, 1958, 4.
'Signals of Distress', Dec. 13, 1958, 6.
'On Boswell on Johnson', Dec. 20, 1958, 6.
'Two Modern Poets', Dec. 25-27, 1958, 4.
'Turgenev and Others', Jan 3, 1959, 6.
'Pedagogue on Parnassus'. *A Grammar of Metaphor* by Christine Brooke-Rose, Jan. 10, 1959, 6.
'Ben in His Humour', Jan. 17, 1959, 6.
'Soothsayers All', Jan. 24, 1959, 6.
'The Regent's Gadfly', Jan. 31, 1959, 6.
'For A' That', Feb. 7, 1959, 6.
'A "Makar" of the Scots Revival', Feb. 14, 1959, 6.
'Hither and Thither', Feb. 21, 1959, 6.
'Poets Three', March 7, 1959, 6.
'The Bard on One Wing', March 14, 1959, 6.
'Mood of Disillusion', March 28, 1959, 6.
'A Fading Art', April 18, 1959, 6.
'A New-Old Tristan', April 25, 1959, 8.

'Shelley's Wife', May 2, 1959, 6.
'The Muse and the Critics', May 9, 1959, 6.
'On the Brink', May 16, 1959, 10.
'Poets of Today', May 23, 1959, 6.
'The Real Anne (Bronte)', May 30, 1959, 6.
'Seumas Beg', June 6, 1959, 6.
'New Light on Synge', June 13, 1959, 6.
'Ring and Blasted Heath', June 20, 1959, 6.
'Rifles and Roses', June 27, 1959, 6.
'Critic and Artist', July 4, 1959, 6.
'Three Translation', July 11, 1959, 6.
'Job Uncomforted', July 18, 1959, 6.
'Wales in Verse', July 25, 1959, 6.
'A Matter of Symbols', August 1, 1959, 8.
'Three Women Poets', August 8, 1959, 6.
'Prince of Letter-Writers', August 15, 1959, 6.
'Poets with with Honour', August 22, 1959, 6.
'Irish Poems from Rome', August 29, 1959, 6.
'The Actor's Masks', Sept. 5, 1959, 6.
'Laureate of Canada', *The Collected Poems of E. J. Pratt* ed. by Northrop Frye, Sept. 12, 1959, 6.
'The Innocents Abroad', Sept. 19, 1959, 8.
'H. P. B. and the Colonel', Sept. 26, 1959, 6.
'A Publisher's Memoirs', Oct. 3, 1959, 10.
'The Tenth Muse', Oct. 10, 1959, 6.
'A Wicked Trade', Oct. 17, 1959, 6.
'The Augustan Age', Oct. 24, 1959, 6.
'A Scholar in Elfland', Oct. 31, 1959, 6.
'The Common Touch', Nov. 7, 1959, 6.
'A Neglected Poet', Nov. 14, 1959, 6.
'Testament of Beauty', Nov. 21, 1959, 6.
'The Augustan Muse', Nov. 28, 1959, 4.
'Mask for a Modern', Dec. 5, 1959, 8.
'Legion of the Lost', Dec. 12, 1959, 8.
'Poetry off Stage', Dec. 19, 1959, 8.
'Whack-Fol-the-Riddle-O', Jan. 2, 1960, 8.
'Decent Ornaments', Jan. 9, 1960, 6.
'The Last of the Georgians', Jan. 19, 1960, 8.
'The Amorous Gael', Jan. 23, 1960, 8.
'Nothing to Declare', Jan. 30, 1960, 8.
'Cries as Clues', Feb. 6, 1960, 6.
'Busy and Brisk', *Poetry of This Age 1908-1958* by A. J. Cohen, Feb. 13, 1960, 8.
'Technique and Poetry', Feb. 20, 1960, 6.

'Exhilarating Optimism', Feb. 27, 1960, 8.

'Business as Usual', March 5, 1960, 6.

'Grave and Gay', March 12, 1960, 8.

'Blithe Spirit', March 19, 1960, 8.

'Greek to Gothic', March 19, 1960, 8.

'Two Ulster Poets', April 2, 1960, 8.

'Another Round', *The Guinness Book of Poetry: 3* [and 3 others], April 9, 1960, 8.

'Publish and Be Damned'.April 16, 1960, 6.

'Wyndham Lewis', April 23, 1960, 8.

'Form and Informality', *Moralities* by Thomas Kinsella, April 30, 1960, 8.

'A Pound Sterling', May 7, 1960, 8.

'Playing Possum', May 14, 1960, 8.

'Poets Collective', May 21, 1960, 8.

'Never wrote a Book', May 28, 1960, 8.

'The Lonely Child', June 4, 1960, 6.

'Life Is Real', June 11, 1960, 8.

'The Buzz of Criticism', June 18, 1960, 8.

'Poems Pleasant and Unpleasant', June 25, 1960, 6.

'Cosmopolitan Interlude', July 2, 1960, 6.

'Books and the Man', July 9, 1960, 8.

'Hither and Thither', July 23, 1960, 6.

'A Silenced Poet', July 30, 1960, 6.

'College Interlude', August 6, 1960, 6.

'The Hidden Hand', August 13, 1960, 6.

'Odd Man Out', August 20, 1960, 6.

'A Restoration Poet', August 27, 1960, 6.

'A Life of Poetry', Sept. 3, 1960, 6.

'The Poet's Pilgrimage', Sept. 10, 1960, 6.

'A Goddess Not So White', Sept. 17, 1960, 6.

'Weighty Words', Sept. 24, 1960, 6.

'Victorian Rebel', Oct. 1, 1960, 6.

'The Lessening Temptation', Oct. 8, 1960, 6.

'What They Saw', Nov. 5, 1960, 8.

'Poet of War', Nov. 12, 1960, 6.

'Dish and Stage', Nov. 19, 1960, 8.

'Without His Cloak', Nov. 26, 1960, 6.

'Merit and Roses', Dec. 10, 1960, 6.

'Mistakes of Milton', Dec. 17, 1960, 6.

'Swan Songs', Dec. 24, 1960, 6.

'All Irish', Dec. 31, 1960, 6.

'Three Poets', Jan. 7, 1961, 6

'Through the Paper Hoop', Jan. 14, 1961, 6.

'The Lion's Share', Jan. 28, 1961, 8.

'Barque and Bight', Feb. 4, 1961, 8.

'Augusta', Feb. 11, 1961, 8.

'Family Likeness', Feb. 18, 1961, 8.

'The Prose of Yeats', Feb. 25, 1961, 8.

'The Turn of the Screw', March 4, 1961, 6.

'The Poet of Democracy, March 11, 1961, 8.

'Poet's Pie', March 18, 1961, 10.

'London Calling', March 25, 1961, 8.

'Modern Greek Poetry', April 8, 1961, 10.

'At Home and Abroad', April 15, 1961, 10.

'Lake and Fell', April 22, 1961, 8.

'The Romantic Books', May 6, 1961, 6.

'Master of Arts', May 13, 1961, 8.

'The Prodigal Father', May 20, 1961, 8.

'Sensitive Satirist', May 27, 1961, 8.

'A Francophilic Critic', June 3, 1961, 8.

'Beyond the Lyre', June 10, 1961, 8.

'Amaryllis and Amanda', June 17, 1961, 10.

'The Poet Laureate and Oisin', June 24, 1961, 8.

'Poet of Loneliness, July 1, 1961, 8.

'The Last Gleeman', July 15, 1961, 6.

'Beyond their Ken', July 22, 1961, 8.

'Here and There', July 29, 1961, 6.

'The Border Men', [Review] of *The Border Men* by John Comley. *Irish Democrat*, August 1961.

[Reviews]. *Irish Times*

'A Man of Prosperity', August 5, 1961, 6.

'Poet of India', August 12, 1961, 6.

'Dublin Days', August 19, 1961, 6.

'The Brother', August 26, 1961, 6.

'Stage Lovers', Sept. 2, 1961, 8.

'Resurrection', Sept. 16, 1961, 10.

'Edward Martyn', Sept. 23, 1961, 8.

'The Round Table', Sept. 30, 1961, 8.

'The Quality of Thought'. *Many Named Beloved: poems* by Samuel Menashe, [and 4 others], Oct. 7, 1961, 8.

'The Way of Words', Oct. 14, 1961, 8.

'The Leopard and the Ring', Oct. 21, 1961, 10.

'Frolic and Fan', Oct. 28, 1961, 8.

'The Sad Critics', Nov. 4, 1961, 10.

'Gloom and Glow', Nov. 11, 1961, 8.

'Among the Essayists', Nov. 18, 1961, 8.

'Among the Lassies', Nov. 25, 1961, 6.

'My First Visit to the Abbey Theatre'. *Irish Digest*, LXXIII, 2 (Dec. 1961), 59-61.

[Reviews]. *Irish Times*

'Voice of the Rebel', Dec. 2, 1961, 8.

'Flight of the Furies', Dec. 9, 1961, 8.

'The Irish Liberal'. *The Senate Speeches of W. B. Yeats.* ed. by Donald R. Pearce;

and *William Butler Yeats: the lyric of tragedy*, Dec. 16, 1961, 10.

'Cauliflower and Toothpaste', Dec. 23, 1961, 6.

'Chinese Crackers', Dec. 30, 1961, 6.

'Quip and Crack', Jan. 6, 1962, 6.

'Solanum Tuberosum', Jan. 13, 1962, 8.

'Synge and Style', Jan. 27, 1962, 8.

'Three Irish Poets', Feb. 3, 1962, 8.

'Players and the Painted Stage', Feb. 10, 1962, 8.

'The Spoken Word', Feb. 17, 1962, 8.

'Ad Parnassum', Feb. 24, 1962, 6.

'Dr. Faustus', March 3, 1962, 8.

'Things That Go Bump in the Night', March 10, 1962, 8.

'Arctic Night', March 17, 1962, 8.

'Rock of Ages', March 24, 1962, 8.

'Poems and Prizes, March 31, 1962, 6.

'At the Play', April 7, 1962, 6.

'In Memory of the Dead', May 12, 1962, 8.

'The Land of Snows', May 26, 1962, 7.

'Past and Present', June 2, 1962.

'In Green Recesses', June 9, 1962, 8.

'A Forgotten City', June 16, 1962, 8.

'The Sage of Ferney', June 30, 1962, 8.

'In Memoriam', July 7, 1962, 6.

'The Man from Stratford', July 14, 1962, 6.

'The Cave of Mammon', July 21, 1962, 6.

'Cap and Bells', July 28, 1962, 8.

'On Losing One's Head', August 11, 1962, 6.

'Sun Worshippers', August 25, 1962, 8.

'The Terrible Years', Sept. 1, 1962, 8.

'My First Visit to the Abbey Theatre'. *Irish Digest*, LXXV, 4 (Oct. 1962), 59-61.

'A Book I Read at Twenty'. *Irish Press*, Oct. 20, 1962.

'Surprises in Synge'. [Review] of *J. M. Synge: collected Works Vol. Poems* ed. Robin Skelton. *Irish Press*, Nov. 3, 1962.

'A Troubled Time'. [Review] of *English Literature in the Earlier Seventeenth Century, 1600-1660* by Douglas Bush. *Irish Press*, Nov. 17, 1962.

'Letter from Ireland'. *New York Times Book Review*, Nov. 18, 1962, 30, 32.

'Irish Humour Without the Shillelaghs'. [Review] of *The Irish Comic Tradition* by Vivian Mercier. *Irish Press*, Dec. 22, 1962.

'Poet in a Sombrero'. [Review] of *A Trip to Texas* by Kenneth Hopkins. *Irish Press*, Jan. 12, 1963.

'Savage the Poet: no foolish face'. [Review] of *The Political Works of Richard Savage* ed. by Clarence Tracy. *Irish Press*, Jan. 26, 1963.

'Robert Frost: a tribute'. *Irish Press*, Feb. 2, 1963.

'Verse from the Western World'. [Review] of *Sailing to an Island* by Richard Murphy. *Irish Press*, March 9, 1963.

'Picking the Best Sellers'. [Review] of *The House of Words* by Lovat Dickson. *Irish Press*, March 26, 1963.

'Yeats through the Magnifying Glass'. [Review] of *Between the Lines: poetry in the making* by Jon Stallworthy; and *Yeats the Playwright: a commentary on character and design in the major plays* by Peter Ure. *Irish Press*, April 12 and 13, 1963.

'Imagination and the Little Magazines'. [Review] of *The Dubliner*, Spring 1963, *Threshold* no. 18, and *The Kilkenny Magazine*, Spring 1963. *Irish Press*, April 20, 1963.

'Verse Ancient and Modern'. [Review] of *Lady and Gentleman* by Richard Weber; and *The Penguin Book of Religious Verse* ed. R. S. Thomas. *Irish Press*, May 11, 1963.

'To Kew in Lilac Time'. [Review] of *Collected Poems in One Volume* by Alfred Noyes. *Irish Press*, June 1, 1963.

'Poems from the Small Churches'. [Review] of *The Little Monasteries: poems translated from the Irish* by Frank O'Connor. *Irish Press*, June 15, 1963.

[Review] of *Contemporary American Poetry* selected by Donald Hall; and *Recent American Poetry* by Glauco Cambon. *Irish Press*, June 29, 1963.

'The Poetry of Darkness'. [Review] of *Modern Poetry from Africa* ed. by Gerald Moore and Ulli Beier, [and 2 others]. *Irish Press*, July 13, 1963.

'Poets in a Noisy Age'. [Review] of *Island Lyrics* by Kevin Faller; and *Bricks: poems 1958/60* by R. J. Wather. *Irish Press*, July 27, 1963.

'Oscar's Father'. [Review] of *Moytura: a play for dancers* by Padraic Colum. *Irish Press*, August 10, 1963.

'New England Frost'. [Review] of *Poetry of Robert Frost* by Reuben A. Brower, [and 2 others]. *Irish Press*, August 31, 1963.

'The Last Poems of Louis MacNeice'. [Review] of *The Burning Perch* by Louis MacNeice. *Irish Press*, Sept. 14, 1963.

'Poet in Outer Space'. [Review] of *Aniara: a review of man in time and space* by Harry Martinson, [and 2 others]. *Irish Press*, Sept. 28, 1963.

'Yeats and His Companions'. [Review] of *William Butler Yeats: a memoir* by Oliver St. J. Gogarty, [and 2 others]. *Irish Press*, Oct. 12, 1963.

'A Fiddler and His Marvellous Memory'. [Review] of *Scholars and Gypsies: an autobiography* by Walter Starkie. *Irish Press*, Oct. 26, 1963.

'Irish Poetry Today'. [Review] of *Six Irish Poets* ed. by R. Skelton. *The Dubliner*, 6 (Jan.-Feb. 1963), 64-68.

'A Book I Read at Twenty'. *Irish Digest*, LXXIX, 1 (Nov. 1963), 87-90.

'The Knight and the Glass'. [Review] of *Squire: most generous of men* by Patrick Howarth. *Irish Press*, Nov. 9, 1963.

'Dispersing the Poe Legend'. [Review] of *Poe: a biography* by William Bither; and *Edgar Allen Poe: the man behind the legend* by Edward Wazenthecht. *Irish Press*, Nov. 23, 1963.

'An Irish Chronicle'. [Review] of *The Irish Comic Tradition* by Vivian Mercier, [and 2 others]. *Poetry*, CIII, 3 (Dec. 1963), 185-187.

'Poems from Ireland'. [Review] of *Tongue Without Hands* by Pearse Hutchinson; and *An Irish Faustus: a morality in nine scenes* by Lawrence Durrell. *Irish Press*, Dec. 7, 1963.

'Poet of the Rebel Thirties'. [Review] of *The Poetry of W. H. Auden: the disenchanted island* by Monroe K. Spears. *Irish Press*, Dec. 21, 1963.

'Sharp Criticinto Poet'. [Review] of *The Collected Poems of Geoffrey Grigson 1924-1962*; and *Scrap Irony* by Felicia Lamport. *Irish Press*, Jan. 4, 1964.

'Poet as Patient'. [Review] of *The Penguin Book of Sick Verse* ed. by George MacBeth. *Irish Press*, Jan. 18, 1964.

'John Cowper & Jean Racine'. [Review] of *Confessio Amantis (The Lover's Shrift)* by John Cowper; and *Iphigenia, Phaedra, Athaliah* by Jean Racine. *Irish Press*, Feb. 15, 1964.

'Tragic Poet'. [Review] of *The Life of a Poet: a biographical sketch of William Collins* by P. L. Carver. *Irish Press*, Feb.

18, 1964.

'Once at Midnight a Dashing Cossack'. [Review] of *Pushkin: selected verse* translated by John Fennell; and *The Mentor Book of Major British Poets from William Blake to Dylan Thomas* ed. by Oscar Williams. *Irish Press*, Feb. 22, 1964.

'King Arthur and His Knights in Modern Dress'. [Review] of Sir Thomas Malory's *Le Mort d'Arthur*, trans. by Keith Barnes. [Review]. *Irish Press*, March 14, 1964.

'MacNeice's Last Plays'. [Review] of *The Mad Islands and the Administrator: two radio plays* by Louis MacNeice. *Irish Press*, April 18, 1964.

'White Muse and Black'. [Review] of *Modern European Poets* by Dannie Abse; and *Negro Verse* selected by Anselm Hollo. *Irish Press*, April 25, 1964.

'Pavement Poets'. [Review] of *Out She Goes: Dublin street rhymes* collected by Leslie Dalken. *Irish Press*, May 9, 1964.

'Verse & Honey at Grantchester'. [Review] of *Rupert Brooke: a biography* by Christopher Nassall. *Irish Press*, May 30, 1964.

'Voice from the County Asylum'. [Review] of *The Shepherd's Calendar* by John Clare. *Irish Press*, June 13, 1964.

'Unrecognized Irish Poetess'.[Review] of *The Leaves Darker* by Sheila Wingfield, [and 2 others]. *Irish Press*, June 20, 1964.

'Graves: the poet's poet'. [Review] of *Swifter than Reason: the poetry and criticism of Robert Graves* by Douglas Day. *Irish Press*, July 11, 1964.

'Victorian Classics'. [Review] of *The Oxford Book of Nineteenth Century English Verse* chosen by John Hayward. *Irish Press*, July 25, 1964.

'Sonnets in an Irish Jail'. [Review] of *An Irish Gathering* by Robin Skelton; and *In a Blue Smoke* by James Liddy. *Irish Press*, August 8, 1964.

'The Deceptively Simple Robert Frost'. [Review] of *Frost* by Elizabeth Jennings; and *Laforgue* by Michael Collie. *Irish Press*, August 22, 1964.

'Voice of the Black Man'. [Review] of *The Rhythm of Violence* by Lewis Nkosi, [and 2 others]. *Irish Press*, Sept. 5, 1964.

'A Centenary Celebration'. *Massachusetts Review*, V, 2 (Winter, 1964), 307-310.

Reprinted in *Irish Renaissance*, ed. Robin Skelton and David R. Clark, 90-93.

'A Poet's Story'. [Review] of *The Voyage Home* by Richard Church. *Irish Press*, Oct. 17, 1964.

'Spence's Anecdotes Re-examined'. [Review] of *Anecdotes, Observations & Characters of Books and Men* by Rev. Joseph Spence. *Irish Press*, Oct. 31, 1964.

'The Hewn Voice of Poetry'. [Review] of *Dylan Thomas: his life and work* by John Ackerman; and *Twenty Years A-Growing*. A filmscript from the story by Maurice O'Sullivan by Dylan Thomas. *Irish Press*, Nov. 14, 1964.

'Frank O'Connor'. [Review] of *Collection Two* by Frank O'Connor. *Irish Press*, Nov. 28, 1964.

'A Noble Failure'. [Review] of *The Rebel Passion* by Vera Brittain. *Irish Press*, Dec. 5, 1964.

'Unsocial and Socialist'. [Review] of *G.B.S. and the Lunatic: reminiscences of the long, lively and affectionate friendship between George Bernard Shaw and the author* by Lawrence Langner. *Irish Press*, Dec. 12, 1964.

'Glimpses of the Poet' in *The Yeats We Knew* ed. by Francis MacManus. Mercier, Cork, 1965.

'Denis Devlin's Poetry'. [Review] of *Collected Poems* by Denis Devlin. *Irish Press*, Jan. 9, 1965.

'Poet and Talker'. *of James Stephens: his work and an account of his life* by Hilary Pyle. *Irish Press*, Jan. 16, 1965.

'Ezra Pound – a Controversial Figure'. [Review] of *Ezra Pound's Kensington: an exploration 1885-1913* by Patricia Hutchins. *Irish Press*, Feb. 6, 1965.

'Poetry of the Age'. [Review] of *20th Century English Literature 1910-1960* by A. C. Ward, [and 2 others]. *Irish Press*, March 6, 1965.

'Eliot in the Theatre'. [Review] of *T. S. Eliot's Dramatic Theory and Practice: from Sweeney Agonistes to the Rider Statesman* by Carol H. Smyth [and 2 others]. *Irish Press*, March 13, 1965.

'Synge as a Young Man'. [Review] of *The Autobiography of J. M. Synge* by P. J. Pollock. *Irish Press*, March 27, 1965.

'Poet as Saint'. *Arena*, 4 (Spring, 1965), 17.

'An Unfinished Story'. [Review] of *Taken Care Of: an autobiography* by Edith Sitwell. *Irish Press*, April 10, 1965.

Picasso and His Friends'. [Review] of *Life With Picasso* by Francoise Gilot and Carlton Lake. *Irish Press*, April 24, 1965.

'Yeats the Poet and Patriot'. [Review] of *Yeats and the Easter Rising* by Edward Mallins, [and 2 others]. *Irish Press*, May 8, 1965.

'Sculptoresque Poet'. [Review] of *Ezra Pound: poet as sculptor* by Donald Davie. *Irish Press*, May 22, 1965.

'Glimpses of W. B. Yeats'. *Shenandoah: The Washington and Lee University Review*, XVI, 4 (Summer, 1965), 25-36.

'Yeats: a centenary tribute'. [Review] of *Centenary Tribute to W. B. Yeats 1865-1965* ed. by A. Norman Jeffares and K. G. W. Cross; and *The Lonely Tower: studies in the poetry of W. B. Yeats* by T. R. Henn. *Irish Press* (June 12, 1965).

'W. B. Yeats and Verse Drama'. *Threshold*, 19 (Autumn, 1965), 14-29.

[Review] of The Celtic Cross: studies in Irish culture and literature by R. B. Browne, W. J. Roscelli and R. J. Loftus. *Dublin Magazine*, IV, 3 and 4 (Autumn-Winter, 1965), 118.

'Poems of a Diplomat'. [Review] of *Collected Poems* by Denis Devlin. *Irish Democrat*, Sept. 1965.

'Centenary Books of Yeats'. [Review] of *The World of W. B. Yeats: essays in perspective* ed. by Robin Skelton and Ann Saddlemeyer, [and 5 others]. *Irish Press*, Sept. 25, 1965.

'Yeats and the Noh Plays'. [Review] of *W. B. Yeats & Japan* by Shotaro Oshima, [and 2 others]. *Irish Press*, Oct. 23, 1965.

'A Visit with George Moore'. *New York Times Book Review*, Nov. 20, 1965, 2.

'Evolution of the History Play'. [Review] of *The English History Play in the Age of Shakespeare* by Irving Ribner; and *Sir Philip Sidney: selected poetry & prose* ed. by T. W. Craik. *Irish Press*, Nov. 18, 1965.

'Spanish War Poets'. [Review] of *A Poet's War: British poets & the Spanish Civil War* by Hugh D. Ford; and *Grace to a Witty Sinner: a life of Donne* by Edward Le Comte. *Irish Press*, Nov. 20, 1965.

Discussion on *An Dá Litríocht Seo Againne*

by Diarmaid O hAlmhain. *Irish Press*, Jan. 15, 1966.

'The Not So Famous Fathers of the Famous'. *[Review] of A Galaxy of Fathers* by Frank Swinnerton. *Irish Press*, Jan. 22, 1966.

'Two Experimental Writers'. [Review] of *The Saturnian Quest: a chart of prose works of John Cowper Powys* by G. Wilson Knight; and *Virginia Woolf & Her Works* by Jean Guiget. *Irish Press*, Feb. 12, 1966.

'Ballad Singers'. [Review] of *Irish Street Ballads* collected by Colm O'Lochlainn. *Irish Press*, Feb. 26, 1966.

'Pope's Poems Reappear'. [Review] of *The Poems of Alexander Pope* ed. by John Butt, [and 2 others]. *Irish Press*, March 12, 1966.

'When Mr. Rolls Met Mr. Royce'. [Review] of *Assorted Prose* by John Updike; and *Exhumations: stories, articles, verses* by Christopher Isherwood. *Irish Press*, March 26, 1966.

'Yeats the Prophet'. [Review] of *Swan & Shadow: Yeats' dialogue with history* by Thomas R. Whitaker, [and 2 others]. *Irish Press*, April 16, 1966.

'Shakespeare's Images'. [Review] of *The Development of Shakespeare's Imagery* by W. H. Clemen, [and 2 others]. *Irish Press*, April 30, 1966.

'Poets With Something to Say'. [Review] of *New Poems 1965: a P.E.N. anthology of contemporary poetry* by C. V. Wedgwood, [and 3 others]. *Irish Press*, May 14, 1966.

'Cowper's Domestic Epic'. [Review] of *Cowper's Poems* ed. by Hugh L'Anson Fausset, [and 2 others]. *Irish Press*, June 4, 1966.

'The Shy Thomas Hardy'. [Review] of *Providence & Mr. Hardy* by Lois Deacon and Terry Coleman. *Irish Press*, July 23, 1966.

'British Ballads'. [Review] of *A Book of British Ballads* selected by R. Brimley Johnson; and *The English Language: essays by English & American men of letters 1490-1839* selected by W. F. Bolton. *Irish Press*, August 6, 1966.

'Out-of-Fashion Poet'. [Review] of *The Mistress of Vision* by Francis Thompson, [and 2 others]. *Irish Press*, August 20, 1966.

'Joyce – Cinema Pioneer'. [Review] of

James Joyce by Richard Ellmann, [and 3 others]. *Irish Press*, Sept. 3, 1966.

'Poet-Conscript'. [Review] of *The Terrible Rain: the war poets 1939-45* selected by Brian Gardner. *Irish Press*, Sept. 10, 1966.

'Two Young Poets'. [Review] of *Figures Out of Mist* by Timothy Brownlow and Rivers Carew; and *Poetry Ireland, no. 6* ed. by John Jordan. *Irish Press*, Sept. 24, 1966.

'The International Sonnet'. [Review] of *The Elizabethan Love Sonnet* by J. W. Lever; and *The Harvest of Tragedy* by T. R. Henn. *Irish Press*, Oct. 8, 1966.

'Voice of the New Africa'. [Review] of *Poems from Black Africa* ed. by Langston Hughes. *Irish Press*, Oct. 22, 1966.

'Tardy Tributes'. [Review] of *Yeats' Quest for Eden* by George Mills Harper, [and 2 others]. *Irish Press*, Nov. 12, 1966.

'Poets and Friends'. [Review] of *The Company I've Kept* by Hugh MacDiarmaid. *Irish Press*, Nov. 26, 1966.

'Old Steam Men'. [Review] of *The Poetry of Railways*. Anthology selected by Kenneth Hopkins. *Irish Press*, Dec. 3, 1966.

'Pacifist Poet in Arms'. [Review] of *Alun Lewis: selected poetry & prose* with introduction by Ian Hamilton, [and 3 others]. *Irish Press*, Dec. 17, 1966.

'The Poetry of Swift'. In *Jonathan Swift 1667-1967: a Dublin tercentenary tribute*. Dublin: Dolmen, 1967, 94-115.

'The Courageous Publisher'. [Review] of *The Ample Proposition: autobiography III* by John Lehmann, [and 2 others]. *Irish Press*, Jan. 7, 1967.

'Midnight Court Updated'. [Review] of *The Penguin Book of Modern Verse Translations* ed. by George Steiner, [and 2 others]. *Irish Press*, Jan. 21, 1967.

'Poet in Politics'. [Review] of *Patriotic Suite* by John Montague, [and 2 others]. *Irish Press*, Feb. 4, 1967.

'Green Branches'. [Review] of *A Garland for Dylan Thomas* gathered by George J. Firmage, [and 2 others]. *Irish Press*, March 11, 1967.

'Browning Revival'. [Review] of *Robert Browning: a study of his poetry* by Thomas Blackburn. *Irish Press*, March 24/25, 1967.

'Byron the Showman'. [Review] of

Byron: the years of fame by Peter Quennell; and *Against Interpretation & other essays* by Susan Sontag. *Irish Press*, April 8, 1967.

'Elusive Maid'. [Review] of *Coleridge and the Abyssinian Maid* by Geoffrey Yarlott; and *John Keats* by Walter Jackson Bate. *Irish Press*, May 27, 1967.

'A Garland for Dear Stella's Birthdays'. [Review] of *Stella's Birthdays: poems by Jonathan Swift* ed. by Sybil Le Brocquy. *Irish Press*, June 3, 1967.

'Novelist, Poet and Critic'. [Review] of *Poetic Craft & Principle* by Robert Graves. *Irish Press*, June 24, 1967.

'Early Memories of F. R. Higgins'. *Dublin Magazine*, VI, n.s., 2 (Summer, 1967), 68-73.

'Taking the Gloomy View'. [Review] of *The Dark Edge of Europe: poems* by Desmond O'Grady, [and 2 others]. *Irish Press*, Sept. 30, 1967.

'The Dark Edge of Europe: new Irish poems'. [Review] of *Time Stopped* by Ewart Milne; and *The Dark Edge of Europe* by Desmond O'Grady. *Irish Democrat*, Oct. 1967.

'The Young Willie Yeats'. [Review] of *Running to Paradise: poems by W. B. Yeats* selection by Kevin Crossley-Holland, [and 4 others]. *Irish Press*, Oct. 28, 1967.

'Exciting View of Shakespeare'. [Review] of *Shakespeare Our Contemporary* by Jan Kott; and *An Explosion of Limericks* by Vyvyan Holland. *Irish Press*, Nov. 11, 1967.

'New Version of the Rubaiyat'. [Review] of *The Rubaiyat of Omar Khayyam* a new translation by Robert Graves and Omar Ali-Shah. *Irish Press*, Nov. 25, 1967.

'Tercentenary Tributes'. [Review] of *The Best of Swift* ed. by Robert Wyse Jackson. *Irish Press*, Dec. 9, 1967.

[Reviews]. *Irish Times*
'Real and Absurd', Jan. 27, 1968, 10.
'American Pioneers', Feb. 10, 1968, 8.
'Church Militant', Feb. 24, 1968, 10.
'Lover of All Humanity', March 9, 1968, 10.
'More on Ariel', March 23, 1968, 10.
'The Higher Gossip', April 6, 1968, 8.
'A Victorian Diary', April 20, 1968, 10.
'Rulers of the Waves', May 4, 1968, 10.

'Modern Irish Playwrights', May 18, 1968, 8.
'Jail Journal', June 8, 1968, 10.
'Self-Portrait of the Artist', June 15, 1968, 8.
'The Lay Bible of Agnostics', July 20, 1968, 10.
'Guilty or Not Guilty', July 20, 1968, 10.
'The Artist as Hermit', August 3, 1968, 10.
'Happy Larry and Sad Sam', August 17, 1968, 10.
'Yeats Late and Early', Sept. 14, 1968, 8.
'The Art of Quotation', Sept. 21, 1968, 8.
'Ruskin on Tour', Oct. 5, 1968, 8.
'The Three Fathers', Oct. 12, 1968, 8.
'Goddess Excellently Bright', Oct. 26, 1968, 8.
'Adopty Duncle', Nov. 9, 1968, 10.
'The Dismal Nineties', Nov. 23, 1968, 10.
'Hidden Land', Nov. 30, 1968, 8.

Letter to the editor. *Times Literary Supplement*, Dec. 12, 1968, 1409.

[Reviews]. *Irish Times*
'Ave atque Vale', Dec. 14, 1968, 10.
'Gloom Galore', Dec. 28, 1968, 8.
'Mangan to Joyce', Jan. 11, 1969, 8.
'The Picturesque Mode', Jan. 25, 1969, 10.
'Saving the Sonnet', Feb. 8, 1969, 10.
'Outside the Garden Gate', Feb. 22, 1969, 10.
'The Last Essayist', March 8, 1969, 8.
'The Return of the Native', March 22, 1969, 8.

'Writer at Work', *St. Stephen's*, [16], series 11, no. 14 (Trinity Term, 1969).

[Reviews] *Irish Times*
'Destined Victims', April 19, 1969, 10.
'On Being Sponged', May 3, 1969, 8.
'Ancient Springs', May 17, 1969, 8.
'O Rare Amanda', May 31, 1969, 8.
'Meeting the Neighbors', June 14, 1969, 10.
'Travellers' Tales', June 28, 1969, 10.
'Joyce and O'Casey', July 12, 1969, 8.
'Heretics All', July 26, 1969, 8.
'Ez and Old Billyum', August 9, 1969, 8.
'Modern Welsh Poetry', August 23, 1969, 10.
'The Fear of Literature', Sept. 6, 1969, 8.
'Darwin and His Voyage', Sept. 27,

1969, 8.
'Letters and Tales', Oct. 4, 1969, 8.
'Man and Superman', Oct. 18, 1969, 8.
'John Synge Comes Next', Nov. 1, 1969, 10.
'Magician Without Wand', Nov. 15, 1969, 8.
'The Ruling Class', Dec. 6, 1969, 8.
'Victorian Rebels', Dec. 20, 1969, 8.

'Seamus Heaney'. In *Contemporary Poets of the English Language* ed. by Rosalie Murphy. Chicago: St. James Press, 1970, 487-488.

[Reviews]. *Irish Times*
'The Blossom Time', Jan. 10, 1970, 8.
'The Courts of Poetry', Jan. 17, 1970, 8.
'Count Your Syllables', Jan. 31, 1970, 10.
'A Voice From Beyond', Feb. 14, 1970, 8.
'Decadence and Uplift', Feb. 28, 1970, 8.
'Patchwork Poets', March 14, 1970, 10.
'The Monkey's Paw', March 28, 1970, 10.
'In English and Scots', April 11, 1970, 8.
'Thomas Love Peacock', April 25, 1970, 8.
'Defending the Truth'. *The Mind of Chesterton* by Christopher Hollis, May 9, 1970, 10.
'The Hollow Men', May 23, 1970, 8.
'Nineties' Period Pieces, June 6, 1970, 8.
'Words to Arrid', June 20, 1970, 8.
'The Good Apprentice', July 4, 1970, 10.
'Changing Times', July 18, 1970, 10.
'Kisses Galore', August 1, 1970, 10.
'Reviews Past and Present', August 15, 1970, 10.
'Unresolved Mysteries', August 29, 1970, 8.
'Every Man in His Humour', Sept. 12, 1970, 8.
'The Higher Gossip', Sept. 26, 1970, 10.
'Short-Cuts to Success', Oct. 10, 1970, 10.
'Call Me Circe', Oct. 24, 1970, 10.
'Turkish Delight', Nov. 7, 1970, 10.
'The Path to Rome', Nov. 21, 1970, 11.
'When Rome Burned', Dec. 5, 1970, 9.
'The Great Refusal, Dec. 19, 1970, 10.

'Anglo-Irish Poetry'. In *Literature in Celtic Countries: Taliesin Congress Lectures* ed. by J. E. Caerwyn Williams. Cardiff, 1971, 155-174.
'When He Was Free and Young and He Used to Wear silks: [excerpt]'. *Canadian Forum*, 51, 20-23 (1971), 580.

[Reviews]. *Irish Times*
'The Bad Fairy of Abbey Street', Jan. 2, 1971, 8.
'Devotio Moderna', Jan. 16, 1971, 10.
'Read On', Jan. 30, 1971, 10.
'Genius Loci', Feb. 13, 1971, 8.
'Eminent Georgians', Feb. 27, 1971, 10.
'The Rector of Diss', March 20, 1971, 10.
'Fetch and Carry', March 27, 1971, 8.
'A Case of Red Tape', April 17, 1971, 10.
'Death in Trieste', May 8, 1971, 10.
'The Great Tradition', May 29, 1971, 10.

'The Thirties'. *The Lace Curtain*, (Summer 1971), 87-92.
[Reviews]. *Irish Times*
'Gentlemen as Poets', June 12, 1971, 10.
'Plain Poetry', June 26, 1971, 10.
'A Rake's Progress', July 10, 1971, 10.
'A Priestess of Venus', July 24, 1971, 8.
'The Prussian Eagle', August 7, 1971, 10.
'Parisian Kisses', August 21, 1971, 10.
'Trials of a Convert', Sept. 4, 1971, 8.
'Life With Father', Sept. 25, 1971, 8.
'The Wreck of the Three-Decker', Oct. 4, 1971.
'Sentimental Journey', Oct. 23, 1971, 10.
'Would-Be-Celibate', Oct. 30, 1971, 10.
'Soup and Sex', Nov. 67, 1971, 8.
'Turn of the Screw', Nov. 20, 1971, 10.
'The Last Puritan', Dec. 4, 1971, 10.
'Burying the Hatchet', Dec. 18, 1971, 10.
'The Wicked Magician', Jan. 8, 1972, 10.
'Veteran Bookman', Jan. 22, 1971, 10.
'Literary Revivalists', Feb. 12, 1972, 8.
'Why Browne Was Nolan', Feb. 19, 1972, 10.
'Synge's Fiancée', March 4, 1972, 8.
'Welfare Statist', March 18, 1972, 10.
'French Views on Eng. Lit.' [sic], April 1, 1972, 10.
'A Spiritual Anthology', April 15, 1972, 10.
'Syngespiel', April 29, 1972, 10.
'The Absurd', May 13, 1972, 10.
'Deep Waters', May 27, 1972, 10.

'Dunsany: diehard of the Celtic Twilight'. *Hibernia*, June 9, 1972, 10.
'The Cardinal and the Countess'. *Ariel: a review of international English literature*, 3, 3 (July, 1972), 58-65.

[Reviews]. *Irish Times*
'Ruskin and e.e. cummings', July 15,

1972, 10.
'Tories Galore', August 12, 1972, 10.
'Looking Back', Nov. 4, 1972, 10.
'An Indoor Man', Dec. 2, 1972, 13.
'Musical Affairs', Dec. 16, 1972, 10.

'Gaelic Ireland Rediscovered'. In *Irish Poets in English* ed. by Sean Lucy, 1973.

[Reviews]. *Irish Times*
Husband and Wife', Jan. 27, 1973, 10.
'Cross and Crescent', Feb. 24, 1973, 12.
'Some Talk of Alexander', August 25, 1973, 10.
'End of a Big House', Nov. 3, 1973, 12.

'The Dublin of My Youth'. [Radio Talk]. *Sunday Miscellany* ed. by Ronnie Walsh. Dublin: Gill, 1975, 120-122.
'Glimpses of W. B. Yeats'. In *W. B. Yeats: interviews and recollections* ed. by E. H. Mikhail. London: Macmillan, 1977. Vol. 2, 349-352.
'The Yeats I Knew'. in *W. B. Yeats: interviews and recollections* ed. by E. H. Mikhail. London: Macmillan, 1977. Vol. 2, 381-386.
Radio Discussion on *W. B. Yeats: interviews and recollections* ed. by E. H. Mikhail. London: Macmillan, 1977. Vol. 2, 316-333. Reprinted from *Literary Portraits: W. R. Rodgers's broadcast conversations with those who knew them.* London: B.B.C., 1972, 1-21.

B. Secondary Publications:
Books, Articles, Reviews

Reviews of *The Vengeance of Fionn*
Maynard, Theodore. 'The Men that God Made Mad'. *New Witness*, Jan. 3, 1918.
Glasgow Herald, Jan. 3, 1918.
Irish Independent, Jan. 7, 1918.
Times Literary Supplement, Jan. 17, 1918, 30.
'The New Irish Poet'. *Freeman's Journal*, Jan. 18, 1918.
'A Young Irish Poet'. *Aberdeen Free Press*, Jan. 21, 1918.
'Recent Verse'. *New Statesman*, Jan. 26, 1918.
C., G. 'A New Irish Poet'. *Irish Times*, Feb. 2, 1918, 9.
'MacKenna, Stephen. 'Some Recent Irish Books'. *Studies*, VII, 25 (March 1918), 175-180.
Campbell, Joseph. 'The New Epic'. *New Ireland*, March 2, 1918.

MacKenna, Stephen. 'I, Said the Quarterly'. *New Ireland*, March 9, 1918.
Manchester Guardian, March 11, 1918.
Stephens, James. Letter to ed. *New Ireland*, March 16, 1918, 307-308.
Campbell, Joseph. 'An Open Letter to Stephen MacKenna'. *New Ireland*, March 16, 1918, 307.
Ni Shionnaigh, Noirin. *New Ireland*, March 23, 1918, 326.
MacKenna's reply. *New Ireland*, March 30, 1918, 340-341.
Pim, Herbert Moore. *New Ireland*, March 30, 1918, 341.
Gibbons, Patrick J. *Irish Monthly*, XLVI (Dec. 1918), 706-710.
The Scotsman, Dec. 31, 1918.

'Irish Poetry'. *Bookman*, LIV (1920), 109-115.

Reviews of *The Fires of Baal*:
'Review'. *Irish Homestead*, March 12, 1921.
Times Literary Supplement, March 17, 1921, 1832.
'Austin Clarke's New Poem: superb word painting'. *Irish Independent*, March 21, 1921.
The Scotsman, March 24, 1921.
B., M; H; J. 'The Fires of Baal'. *Dublin Evening Herald*, March 26, 1921.
'A Master Craftsman', *Freeman's Journal*, March 26, 1921.
Catholic Book World, April, 1921.
'Poetry'. *London Mercury*, III, 18 (April 1921), 671-672.
Jewish Guardian, April 1, 1921.
'Austin Clarke', *Expository Times*, May 1921.
Twitchett, E. G. 'Verse'. *Daily Herald*, May 11, 1921.
Manchester Guardian, May 19, 1921.
'Today's Quotation'. *Evening Herald*, May 25, 1921.
'Poems Worthy of Consideration'. *Spectator*, May 28, 1921.
S., R. *Irish Monthly*, June 1921, 264.
L., W. 'The Fires of Baal', *New Witness*, Oct. 7, 1921.

Eagle, Solomon. 'The Critics at Large: Irish literature to-day'. Review of *Irish Poets of To-day* ed. by L. D. O'Walters. London: Fisher Unwin, 1921.
The Outlook, July 16, 1921, 53.
Swann, John H. Letter to editor.

Manchester Guardian, Sept. 20, 1921.
'From Current Books'. *Dublin Evening Herald*, Dec. 24, 1921, four lines from *The Sword of the West*.

Reviews of *The Sword of the West*
The Scotsman, Jan. 3, 1922.
'Review'. *Irish Homestead*, Jan. 7, 1922.
'Books of the Week: The Sword of the West'. *Irish Times*, Jan. 20, 1922, 2.
Dublin Evening Herald, Jan. 21, 1922.
'Poets of Earnestness'. *Westminster Gazette*, Jan. 28, 1922.
O'H., P.S. 'Mr. Austin Clarke's New Poem'. *Freeman's Journal*, Feb. 11, 1922.
'Two Irish Poets'. *Glasgow News*, Feb. 16, 1922.
Lepper, John Heron. 'Recent Irish Books'. *New Witness*, Feb. 18, 1922.
Bloch, Regina Miriam. 'About Books and Their Writers'. *Birmingham Weekly Post*, March 4, 1922.
'A Contrast in Verse'. *Times Literary Supplement*, March 16, 1922, 168.
Catholic Book Notes, June 1922.
'Poetry'. *Times Literary Supplement*, Dec. 28, 1922, 168.
Portrait. From a drawing by E.F.S. *Dublin Magazine*, II, n.s., 1 (August 1924), frontispiece.

Reviews of *The Cattledrive in Connaught and other poems:*
AE. *Irish Statesman*, 5 (1925).
    Graves, Robert. *Nation and Athenaeum*, XXXVIII, 12 (Dec. 19, 1925).
Clarke, Austin. Letter to editor. *Irish Statesman*, 5 (1926), 740.
Dublin Magazine, I, n.s., 2 (April-June, 1926), 64-65.
Colum, Padraic. 'Dublin in Literature'. *Bookman*, LV (1926), 556-561.

Reviews of *The Son of Learning:*
Scribe, Oliver. 'The Poet Who Cured a King: Mr. Clarke's comedy of beggars and lovers'. *T.P's Weekly*, VIII, 194 (July 16, 1927), 391.
Colum, Padraic. 'Two Poets'. *Dublin Magazine*, II, n.s., 4 (Oct.-Dec. 1927), 29-44.
T.P's Weekly, IX, 213 (Nov. 26, 1927), 161.
C., T.P. *Irish Book lover*, XVII (Sept.-Oct., 1929), 113-114.

Reviews of *Pilgrimage and other poems*
Moult, Thomas. 'New Magic Out of Connaught'. Mr Austin Clarke's latest poem. *T.P's Weekly*, XI, 276 (Feb. 9, 1929), 479.
O., Y. *Irish Statesman*, 11 (1929), 437-8.
C., T.P. *Irish Book Lover*, XVII (May-June, 1929), 66.
C., C. *Dublin Magazine*, IV n.s., 3 (July-Sept., 1929), 70-73.
Little, Arthur. *Studies*, XVIII, 72 (Dec. 1929), 704-705. Review also of *Cattledrive in Connaught*.
Colum, Padraic. 'A Note on Austin Clarke'. *Dublin Magazine*, IV, n.s., 2 (April-June, 1930), 65-67.

Reviews of *The Flame*
Irish Book Lover, XIX (March-April, 1931), 65-67.
P., M.S. *Dublin Magazine*, VI, n.s., 2 (April-June, 1931), 70-71.

Reviews of *The Bright Temptation*
Philibin, An [i.e. John H. Pollock]. *Irish Book Lover*, XX (May-June, 1932), 70.
MacKenzie, Compton. *Daily Mail*, May 3, 1932.
Dublin Magazine, VII, n.s., 3 (July-Sept. 1932), 65.
Beckett, Samuel. 'Recent Irish Poetry'. *Bookman*, LXXVII (1934), 235-236.
Crone, J. S. 'Sgéala ó Cathair na gCeó'. *Irish Book Lover*, XXII (Nov.-Dec. 1934), 127.
'Arnold Bennett's Journals: damages to Irish poet for libel'. *Times*, Nov. 9, 1934.
MacManus, M. J. Bibliographies of Irish Writers no. 8 Austin Clarke. *Dublin Magazine*, X, n.s., 2 (April-June 1935), 41-43.
Review of *The Singing-Men at Cashel*. *Dublin Magazine*, XI, n.s., 2 (April-June 1936), 88-90.
MacG., P. Review of *The Singing-Men at Cashel*. *Irish Book Lover*, XXIV (May-June, 1936), 65.
Fausset, Hugh L'A. 'Mr. Austin Clarke's Poems'. *London Mercury*, XXXIV, 201 (July 1936), 267-277.
Sheridan, Niall. Review of *Collected Poems*. *Ireland To-day*, 1, 3 (August 1936), 75-76.
Benet, W. R. 'Phoenix Nest'. *Saturday*

Review of Literature, XIV (August 15, 1936), 19.

Review of *Collected Poems*. *Dublin Magazine*, XI, n.s., 4 (Oct.-Dec. 1936), 98-100.

Tomlin, E. W. F. Review of *Collected Poems*. *Criterion*, XVI, LXIII (Oct. 1936).

C., T.P. Review of *Collected Poems*. *Irish Book Lover*, XXIV (Nov.-Dec. 1936), 140.

Belitt, B. 'Gaelic Mode'. *Poetry*, XLIX (Feb. 1937), 288-291.

Griffin, Gerald. *The Wild Geese: pen portraits of famous Irish exiles*. London: Jarrolds, 1938, 186-190.

Palmer, Herbert. *Post-Victorian Poetry*. London: Dent, 1938, 96-122.

Byrne, J. Patrick. 'Assonance and Modern Irish Poetry'. *Dublin Magazine*, XIII, n.s., 3 (July-Sept. 1938), 52-62.

Bailey, Ruth. 'A Verse-Play' (Sister Eucharia). *London Mercury*, XXXIX, 234 (April 1939), 659.

Craig, Maurice. 'The Poetry of Austin Clarke'. *The Bell*, IV, 6 (Sept. 1942), 413-419.

Fallon, Padraic. Review of *As the Crow Flies*. *Dublin Magazine*, XIX, n.s., 1 (Jan.-March 1944), 45-47.

Mercier, Vivian H. S. 'The Verse Plays of Austin Clarke'. *Dublin Magazine*, XIX, n.s., 2 (April-June 1944), 39-47.

Fallon, Padraic. Review of *The Viscount of Blarney and other plays*. *Dublin Magazine*, XX, n.s., 1 (Jan.-March 1945), 57-58.

Donaghy, J. Lyle. 'A Modern Gaelic Poet. *Irish Times*, Dec. 29, 1945, 2.

L., A.J. Review of *First Visit to England and other memories*. *Dublin Magazine*, XXI, n.s., 3 (July-Sept. 1946), 52-53.

Mercier, Vivian. 'Austin Clarke – the poet in the theatre'. *Chimera*, V (Spring 1947), 23-36; *Life and Letters*, LIII (April 1947), 7-18; *Commonweal*, June 6, 1947, 183.

Fiacc, Padraic. 'Austin Clarke'. *Irish Bookman*, 11, 3 (Dec. 1947), 28-32.

Kavanagh, Patrick. 'Poetry in Ireland Today'. *The Bell*, XVI, 1 (April 1948), 36-43.

Farren, Robert. *The Courses of Irish Verse in English*. London: Sheed and Ward, 1949.

Review of *The Plot Succeeds*. *Christian Science Monitor Magazine*, March 1950, 5.

Reviews of *Poetry in Modern Ireland*:

M., W.P. *Dublin Magazine*, XXVI, n.s., 3 (July-Sept. 1951), 67.

Taylor, Geoffrey. *The Bell*, XVII, 4 (July 1951), 63-65.

M., D. *Poetry Ireland*, 14 (July 1951), 23-24.

Mulkerns, Val. Review of *The Sun Dances at Easter*. *The Bell*, XVIII, 6 (Nov. 1952), 380-382.

Interview. *Irish Times Pictorial*, Dec. 10, 1952.

Review of *The Sun Dances at Easter*. *Dublin Magazine*, XXVIII, n.s., 2 (April-June 1953), 61-62.

M., W.P. Review of *The Moment Next to Nothing*. *Dublin Magazine*, XXX, n.s., 2 (April-June 1954), 42-44.

Kelly, Rev. John C. Review of *Poetry in Modern Ireland*. *Studies*, XLIV (Spring 1955), 114-117.

Davie, Donald. Review of *Ancient Lights*. *Irish Writing*, 34 (Spring 1956), 57-58.

Fallon, Padraic. 'Current Poetry'. Review of *Ancient Lights*. *Dublin Magazine*, XXXI, n.s., 2 (April-June 1956), 18-23.

Kinsella, Thomas. 'Art of Austin Clarke'. *Irish Press*, June 16, 1956.

Montague, John. 'Letter from Dublin'. *Poetry*, XC, 5 (August 1957), 310-315.

Montague, John. 'Contemporary Verse: a short chronicle of poetry by six authors in 1958'. *Studies*, XLVII (Winter 1958), 441-449.

Mercier, Vivian. 'The Art of Exclusion'. *The Nation*, CLXXXVIII, 15 (April 11, 1959), 320-321.

Montague, John. 'Isolation and Cunning'. *Poetry*, XCIV, 4 (July 1959), 264-270.

Reviews of *Later Poems*:

H. J., *Threshold*, 5 (Autumn-Winter, 1961-1962), 75-81.

Leahy, Michael. *The Dubliner*, 1 (Nov.-Dec. 1961), 13.

Tomlinson, Charles. 'Poets and Mushrooms: a retrospect of British poetry in 1961'. *Poetry*, C, 2 (Sept. 1962), 113-115.

Martin, Augustine. *Studies*, LI, 202 (Spring 1962), 182-184.

Delehanty, James. *Kilkenny Magazine*, 6 (Spring 1962), 45-48.

Kennelly, Brendan. Review of *Twice*

Round the Black Church. The Dubliner, 3 (May-June 1962), 52-53.

Delehanty, James. Review of *Twice Round the Black Church. Kilkenny Magazine*, 4 (Autumn-Winter 1962), 52-55.

Lane, Temple. 'Austin Clarke'. *Books Abroad*, XXXVI (Spring 1962), 270-272.

Sealy, Douglas. 'Austin Clarke: a survey of his work'. *The Dubliner*, 6 (Jan.-Feb. 1963), 7-34.

Miller, Liam. 'The Books of Austin Clarke: a checklist'. *The Dubliner*, 6 (Jan.-Feb. 1963), 35-39.

S., D.H. Review of *Forget-Me-Not. The Dubliner*, 2, 1 (Spring 1963), 80-81.

Morse, Samuel French. 'Veterans and Recruits'. *Poetry*, CII, 5 (Aug. 1963), 330-334.

O hAodha, Michael. 'Austin Clarke's Witty Verse Plays'. Review of *Collected Plays. Irish Press*, August 17, 1963.

Delehanty, James. Review of *Collected Plays. Kilkenny Magazine*, 10 (August-Winter, 1963), 100-103.

Harmon, Maurice. 'The Later Poetry of Austin Clarke'. *The Celtic Cross: studies in Irish culture and literature* ed. by R. B. Browne et al. Purdue: Purdue U.P., 1964.

Loftus, Richard. *Nationalism in Modern Anglo-Irish Poetry*. Madison: Wisconsin U.P., 1964.

Roscelli, William John. 'The Private Pilgrimage of Austin Clarke'. *The Celtic Cross*, 1964.

Saul, George B. 'The Poetry of Austin Clarke'. *The Celtic Cross*, 1964.

Tomlinson, Charles. 'Poetry Today'. *The Modern Age. Vol. 7 Pelican Guide to English Literature* ed. by Boris Ford. Harmondsworth: Penguin, 1964.

Torchiana, Donald T. 'Contemporary Irish Poetry. *Chicago Review*, XVII, 2 and 3 (1964), 152-168.

Kinsella, Thomas. Review of *Flight to Africa. Irish Press*, Feb. 1, 1964.

Jordan, John. Editorial. *Poetry Ireland*, 3 (Spring 1964), 91-93.

Delehanty, James. Review of *Flight to Africa. Kilkenny Magazine*, 11 (Spring-Summer 1964), 113-116.

S., D.H. Review of *Flight to Africa. The Dubliner*, 3, 2 (Summer 1964), 75-78.

Fitzgerald, David. Review of *Poems, Austin Clarke, Tony Connor, Charles Tomlinson. The Dubliner*, 3, 4 (Winter 1964), 72-75.

Farrington, Brian. 'The Satire of Austin Clarke'. Review of *Flight to Africa. Irish Democrat*, Dec. 1964.

Burrows, E. G. 'Three from Overseas'. *Poetry*, CV, 3 (Dec. 1964), 207-210.

Martin, Augustine. 'The Rediscovery of Austin Clarke'. *Studies*, LIV, 216 (Winter 1965), 408-434.

White, Sean J. 'The Strayed Student'. Review of *The Bright Temptation. Irish Press*, May 1, 1965.

Torchiana, David. 'Some Dublin Afterthoughts'. *Tri-Quarterly Review*, IV (Autumn, 1965), 140-145.

Montague, John and Liam Miller, eds. *A Tribute to Austin Clarke on his Seventieth Birthday 9 May 1966*. Dublin: Dolmen, 1966.

Martin, Augustine. Review of *A Tribute to Austin Clarke on His 70th Birthday. Irish Press*, June 18, 1966.

Reviews of *Mnemosyne Lay in Dust*
Payne, Basil. 'Vigour and Technical Virtuosity'. *Hibernia*, June 6, 1966, 12.

Martin, Augustine. *Irish Press*, June 18, 1966.

Harmon, Maurice. *Studies*, LV, (Autumn 1966), 326-328.

Sealy, Douglas. *Dublin Magazine*, V, n.s., 3 (Autumn-Winter 1966), 94-96.

Delehanty, James. *Kilkenny Magazine*, 15 (Spring-Summer 1967), 141-147.

Harmon, Maurice. 'The Era of Inhibitions: Irish literature 1920-1960'. *Emory Quarterly Review*, XXII, 1 (Spring 1966).

Harmon, Maurice. 'Austin Clarke: poetry of rich variety and vigour'. *Hibernia*, June 6, 1966, 12.

Moore, John Rees. 'Now That Yeats Has Gone: three Irish poets'. *Hollins Critic*, 3, 2 (1966).

Reviews of *Old-Fashioned Pilgrimage and other poems:*
Hogan, Robert. *After the Irish Renaissance*. Minn: Minneapolis UP., 1967; London: Macmillan, 1968, 151-154.

Jordan, John. 'Luxuriant Discontent'. *Hibernia*, March 3, 1967, 22.

Martin, Augustine. *Irish Press*, March 4, 1967.

Cluysenaar, Anne. *Dublin Magazine*, VI, n.s., 3 and 4 (Autumn-Winter 1967),

84-85.

Kilroy, Thomas. *Arusiwa*, LVI, 224 (Winter 1967), 437-440.

'Poets of Today'. *Times Literary Supplement*, 1970, 150-152.

Oppel, H. 'Austin Clarke: three poems about children'. 111, *Die Moderne Englische Lyrik* ed. H. Oppel. Berlin: Erich Schmidt, 1967.

Rosenthal, M. L. 'Contemporary Irish Poetry'. *The New Poets: American and British poetry since World War II*. Oxford and New York: Oxford UP, 1967, 263-274.

Cooney, Seamus. 'Austin Clarke's "Celebrations": a commentary'. *Eire-Ireland*, II (Summer 1967), 16-26.

Hart, William. Review of *Plays of George Fitzmaurice* ed. Austin Clarke *Studies*, LVI, 224 (Winter 1967), 433-437.

Harmon, Maurice. 'The State of Irish Letters'. *Hibernia*, Dec. 12, 1967, 23.

Reviews of *A Penny in the Clouds:*

Ganly, Andrew. *Hibernia*, July 7, 1968, 20.

Hart, William. *Studies*, LVII (Autumn 1968), 338-339.

Tracy, Seamus. 'Poet, Humanist and Social Critic'. *Irish Democrat*, Nov. 1968.

Fanning, Stephen. *Kilkenny Magazine*, 16-17 (Spring 1969), 157-160.

Earls, Brian. Review of *Echo at Coole and other poems*. *St. Stephen's*, series 11, 15 (Michaelmas Term, 1968).

Ussher, Arland. 'Austin Clarke: a tribute'. *Hibernia*, Nov. 29-Dec. 12, 1968, 7.

Sullivan, Kevin. 'Literature in Modern Ireland'. *Conor Cruise O'Brien Introduces Ireland* ed. Owen Dudley Edwards. London: Andre Deutch, 1969, 135-147.

Carew, Rivers. 'Review of 1968 Poetry'. *Hibernia*, Jan. 17-30, 1969, 14.

Delehanty, James. Review of *Echo at Coole*. *Kilkenny Magazine*, 16-17 (Spring 1967), 153-157.

Jordan, John. 'Austin Clarke: profile'. *Hibernia*, July 18-Aug. 7, 1969, 6.

Weber, Richard. 'Austin Clarke: the arch poet of Dublin'. *Massachusetts Review*, XI, 2 (Spring 1970), 295-308.

Fauchereau, Serge. 'Tradition et Révolution dans la Poésie Irlandaise'. *Critique: Revue Générale des Publications Françaises et Étrangères*, 26, 276 (May 1970), 438-456.

Rodgers, W. R. *Irish Literary Portraits*. London: British Broadcasting Corporation, 1972, 19.

McGrory, Kathleen. 'Medieval Aspects of Modern Irish Writing: Austin Clarke'. *Modern Irish Literature* ed. Raymond J. Porter and James D. Brophy. New York: Twayne, 1972, 289-300.

Boxhill, Anthony. 'When He Was Free and Young and He Used to Wear Silks'. *Fiddlehead*, 95 (Fall 1972), 117-118.

Deane, Seamus. Review of *Tiresias*. *Times Literary Supplement*, Dec. 1, 1972, 1459-1460.

Lucy, Sean. *Irish Poets in English*. Cork: Mercier Press, 1973.

Rafroidi, Patrick. 'Austin Clarke'. *Littérature de Notre Temps: écrivains anglais et irlandais. Recueil 1* ed. Bernard Cassen. Paris: Casterman, 1973, 49-52.

Boland, Eavan. 'Austin Clarke: the artist in old age'. *Hibernia*, April 27, 1973, 13.

Gelderman, Carol. 'Austin Clarke and Yeats's Alleged Jealousy of George Fitzmaurice'. *Eire-Ireland*, 8, 2 (Summer 1973), 62-70.

Halpern, Susan. *Austin Clarke: his life and words*. Dublin: Dolmen, Dublin.

Murphy, D. J. *Patrick Kavanagh and Austin Clarke*. Cork and Dublin: Mercier, 1974.

Davie, Donald. 'Austin Clarke and Padraic Fallon'. *Poetry Nation*, 3 (1974), 80-101.

Harmon, Maurice. 'Austin Clarke Special Issue'. *Irish University Review*, IV, 1 (Spring 1974).

Harmon, Maurice. 'Notes Towards a Biography', 13-25.

Kennelly, Brendan. 'Austin Clarke and the Epic Poem', 26-40.

Welch, Robert. 'Austin Clarke and Gaelic Poetic Tradition', 41-51.

McHugh, Roger. 'The Plays of Austin Clarke', 52-64.

Mahony, Tina Hunt. 'The Dublin Verse-Speaking Society and the Lyric

Theatre Company', 65-73.

Mercier, Vivian. 'Mortal Anguish, Mortal Pride: Austin Clarke's religious lyrics', 91-99.

Dodsworth, Martin. 'Jingle-go-Jangle: feeling and expression in Austin Clarke's later poetry', 117-127.

Garratt, Robert. 'Austin Clarke in Transition', 100-116.

Kinsella, Thomas. 'The Poetic Career of Austin Clarke', 128-136.

Obituary. *Irish Times*, March 21, 1974, 11.

Harmon, Maurice. 'The Priest of the Muses: Austin Clarke'. *Ireland of the Welcomes*, XXIII, 3 (May-June 1974), 17-18.

Killeen, Terence. 'Poets and Poetry'. *Hibernia*, May 24-June 6, 1974, 19.

Hewitt, John. 'Austin Clarke 1896-1974'. *Threshold*, 25 (Summer 1974), 3-6.

Redshaw, T. D. 'His Works A Memorial: Austin Clarke 1896-1974'. *Eire-Ireland*, IX, 2 (Summer 1974), 107-115.

Donoghue, Denis. 'Austin Clarke'. *New Review*, August 1974; *We Irish*. Brighton: Harvester Press, 1986, 242-252.

Boland, John. 'Long and Leaden, Short and Slight: another look at Austin Clarke'. *Hibernia*, Oct. 11, 1974, 13.

Dodsworth, Martin. 'To Forge the Irish Conscience'. *Times Literary Supplement*, Dec. 13, 1974, 1406-1407.

Davie, Donald. 'Austin Clarke and Padraic Fallon'. *Two Decades of Irish Writing* ed. Douglas Dunn. Cheadle: Carcanet Press, 1975, 37-58.

Kersnowski, Frank. *The Outsiders*. Fort Worth, Texas: Texas Christian UP, 1975, 63-72.

Tapping, Craig. 'The Poetry of Austin Clarke'. *Lines Review*, 52/53 (May, 1975), 22-31.

Fitzgerald, David. 'From Fantasy to Reality: an aspect of the life of Austin Clarke'. *Irish Socialist Review*, 2 (1976), 15.

Davie, Donald. 'Austin Clarke'. *New York Times Book Review*, March 7, 1976, 30.

Harmon, Maurice. Review of *The Third Kiss: a comedy in one act* and *Selected Poems*. *Irish University Review*, VI, 2 (Autumn 1976), 262.

Garratt, Robert F. 'Aware of My Ancestors: Austin Clarke and the legacy of Swift'. *Eire-Ireland*, IX, 2 (Summer 1976), 92-103.

Rosenthal, M. L. *New York Times Book Review*, Sept. 19, 1976.

Harmon, Maurice. Introduction to *Irish Poetry after Yeats*. Dublin: Wolfhound Press, 1977.

Murphy, Daniel J. 'The Religious Lyrics and Satires of Austin Clarke'. *Hermathena*, CXXII (1977), 46-64.

Scupham, Peter. 'The Green and Gold Bow Tie'. *Agenda*, 14, 4-15, 1 (Winter-Spring, 1977), 147-152.

Kennelly, Brendan, 'The Battle of the Ballads'. Review of *Liberty Lane: a ballad play of Dublin*. *Irish Times*, June 3, 1978, 13.

Saul, George Brendan. Review of *Liberty Lane*. *Eire-Ireland*, XIV, 2 (Summer 1979), 157-158.

Frazier, Adrian. '"The God-Bewildered Schoolboy": Austin Clarke's later poetry'. *Eire-Ireland*, XIV, 2 (Summer 1979), 52-67.

Montague, John. 'Global Regionalism'. *Literary Review*, 22, 2 (Winter 1979).

Tapping, Craig. *Austin Clarke: a study of his writings*. Dublin: Academy Press, 1980.

Schirmer, Gregory A. '"A Mad Discordancy": Austin Clarke's early narrative poems'. *Eire-Ireland*, XVI, 2 (Summer 1981), 16-28.

Timson, Beth. 'Austin Clarke: the poet's image of frustrated love'. *Irish Renaissance Annual* 111. Newark: University of Delaware Press, 1982, 59-70.

Boland, Eavan. 'Poets at Loggerheads'. *Irish Times*, June 23, 1982, 8.

Clarke, Dardis. 'Half a Century of the Irish Academy of Letters'. *Irish Times*, Sept. 14, 1982, 8.

Schirmer, Gregory A. *The Poetry of Austin Clarke*. Notre Dame: University of Notre Dame Press; Dublin: Dolmen, 1983.

Meir, Colin. 'Narrative Techniques in Austin Clarke's *Mnemosyne Lay in Dust* and Thomas Kinsella's *Nightwalker*'. *Etudes Irlandaises*, 8, n.s. (Dec. 1983), 57-78.

Garratt, Robert F. 'The Importance of Being Austin'. *Eire-Ireland*, XIX, 2 (Summer 1984), 143-151.

Dillon, Johnston. *Irish Poetry after Joyce.* Notre Dame: University of Notre Dame Press, 1985.

Harmon, Maurice. '*The Sword of the West* (1921, 1936, 1974)'. *Etudes Irlandaises*, 10, n.s. (Dec. 1985), 93-104.

Garratt, Robert F. *Modern Irish Poetry: tradition and continuity from Yeats to Heaney.* Berkeley: University of California Press, 1986.

Murphy, Daniel. *Imagination and Religion in Anglo-Irish Literature 1930-1980.* Dublin: Irish Academic Press, 1987.

Clarke, R. Dardis. 'Austin Clarke at Templeogue'. *Poetry Ireland Review*, 21 (Spring 1988), 41-46.

C. Background

Anderson, Madge. *The Heroes of the Puppet Stage.* London: Jonathan Cape, 1924.

Archer, William. *Poets of the Younger Generation.* London: Lane, 1902.

Arnold, Mavis and Laskey, Heather, *Children of the Poor Clares: the story of an Irish orphanage.* Belfast: Appletree Press, 1985.

Béarn, Pierre. *Paul Fort.* Paris: Editions Pierre Seghers, 1960.

Beer, Gillian. *The Romance.* London: Methuen, 1970.

Bentley, Eric. *The Playwright as Thinker.* New York: Reynal and Hitchcock, 1946.

Bentley, Eric. *In Search of Theatre.* New York: Knopf, 1953.

Bergin, Osborn. 'Poems attributed to Gormlaith'. *Miscellany Presented to Kuno Meyer.* Ed. Osborn Bergin and Carl Mastrander. Halle: Max Niemayer, 1912, 343-369.

Bergin, Osborn and R. I. Best. 'Tochmarc Etaine'. *Eriú*, XII (1934-38), 137-193.

Berleth, Richard. *The Twilight Lords: the epic struggle of the last feudal lords of Ireland against the England of Elizabeth I.* London: Lane, 1978.

Binyon, Lawrence. *The Death of Adam and other poems.* London: Methuen, 1904.

Bottomley, Gordon. 'Poetry Seeks a New Home'. *Theatre Arts Monthly*, XIII (Dec. 1929), 924.

Bottomley, Gordon. *Essays and Studies.* Oxford: Oxford UP., 1934.

Breathnach, R. A. 'Tóraigheacht Dhiarmada agus Gráinne'. *Irish Sagas.* Ed. Myles Dillon. Dublin: Stationery Office, 1959.

Brown, E. K. *Rhythm in the Novel.* Toronto: University of Toronto Press, 1950.

Brown, Terence. *Ireland: a social and cultural history 1922-1979.* London: Fontana, 1981.

Byrne, Francis John. *Irish Kings and High-Kings.* London: Batsford, 1973.

Cambrensis, Giraldus. *The History and Topography of Ireland.* Translated by John J. O'Meara. Dublin: Dolmen, 1982.

Carney, James. *Studies in Irish Literature.* Dublin: Institute for Advanced Studies, 1955.

Carney, James, ed. *Early Irish Literature* by Eleanor Knott and Gerard Murphy. London: Routledge and Kegan Paul, 1966.

Carney, James. *Medieval Irish Lyrics.* Dublin: Dolmen, 1967.

Carney, James. 'Notes on the Irish War Goddess'. *Eigse*, XIX, 2 (1983), 263-275.

Clark, David R. *W. B. Yeats and the Theatre of Desolate Reality.* Dublin: Dolmen, 1965.

Cohen, David J. 'Suibhne Geilt'. *Celtica*, XII (1977), 113-124.

Cooney, John. *The Crozier and the Dail: Church and State 1922-1986.* Cork, Dublin: Mercier, 1986.

Corish, Patrick J. *The Irish Catholic Experience: a historical survey.* Dublin: Gill and Macmillan, 1985.

Corkery, Daniel. *The Hidden Ireland: a study of Gaelic Munster in the eighteenth century.* Dublin: Gill and Macmillan, 1924.

Costello, Ellen. *Amhráin Muighe Seóla.* London: Journal of Irish Folk Song Society, 16 (1919).

Craig, Maurice. *Dublin 1660-1860.* London: Cresset, 1952.

Cross, T. P. and C. H. Slover. *Ancient Irish Tales.* London: Harrap, 1935.

Curtin, Jeremiah. *Hero-Tales of Ireland.* London: Macmillan, 1894.

de Blacam, Aodh. *Gaelic Literature Surveyed.* Dublin: Talbot, 1929; repr.

1973.

de Bhaldraithe, Tomás. 'Mis agus Dubh Ruis'. *Scríobh* 4 (1979), 60-63.

Delargy, James H. 'The Gaelic Story-Teller'. *Proceedings of the British Academy*, XXXI, 1945. London: Geoffrey Cumberlege, 1945.

Dickens, A. G. *The Counter Reformation*. London: Thames and Hudson, 1968.

Dillon, Myles. *The Cycles of Kings*. London and New York: Oxford UP., 1946.

Dillon, Myles. 'The Archaism of Irish Tradition'. *Proceedings of the British Academy*, XXXIII. London: Geoffrey Cumberlege, 1947.

Dillon, Myles. *Early Irish Literature*. Chicago: University of Chicago, 1948.

Dillon, Myles. *Early Irish Society*. Dublin: Cultural Relations Committee, 1954.

Dillon, Myles, ed. *Irish Sagas*. Dublin: Cultural Relations Committee, 1959.

Dineen, Patrick S., ed. *The Poems of Egan O'Rahilly*. London: Irish Texts Society, 1900.

Donoghue, Denis. *The Third Voice: modern British and American verse drama*. Princeton: Princeton UP., 1959.

Donough, Bryan. *Gerald Fitzgerald: the great Earl of Kildare*. Dublin: Talbot, 1933.

Duncan, Lilian, ed. 'Altrama Tige Da Medár'. *Eriú*, XI (1932), 184-225.

Eliot, T. S. *Poetry and Drama*. Cambridge: Harvard UP., 1951.

Eriugena. *Periphyseon (division of nature)*. Translated by I. P. Sheldon-Williams. Revised by John O'Meara. Bellarmin: Dunbarton Oaks, Washington, 1987.

Fanning, Ronan. *Independent Ireland*. Dublin: Helicon, 1983.

Fergusson, Francis. *The Idea of a Theatre: a study of ten plays: the art of drama in changing perspective*. Princeton: Princeton UP., 1949.

Fitzgerald, Brian. *The Geraldines: an experiment in Irish Government 1169-1601*. London: Staples, 1951.

Flower, Robin. *The Irish Tradition*. Oxford: Clarendon, 1947.

Fort, Paul. *Ballades Francaises: choix 1897-1960*. Paris: Flammarion, 1963.

Fyfe, Hamilton. *T. P. O'Connor*. London: Allen, 1934.

Gantz, Jeffrey. *Early Irish Myths and Legends*. Harmondsworth: Penguin, 1981.

Gwynn, E. J. 'The Idea of Fate in Irish Literature'. *Journal of the Ivernian Society*, 11 (1909-10).

Gwynn, E. J. 'The Teaching of Mael-Ruain'. *Hermathena*, 2nd supplemental vol., Dublin, 1927, 1-63.

Hauptmann, Gerhard. *Hannele: a dream poem*. London: Secker, 1926.

Hennessy, W. M. 'The Ancient Irish Goddess of War'. *Revue Celtique*, 1 (1870-1872), 32-55.

Henry, Françoise. *Irish High Crosses*. Dublin: Cultural Relations committee, 1964.

Henry, Françoise. *Irish Art*. 3 vols. London: Methuen, 1965-1970.

Hughes, Kathleen. *The Church in Early Irish Society*. London: Methuen, 1966.

Hull, Eleanor, ed. *The Cuchullin Saga in Irish Literature*. London: Butt, 1898.

Hull, Eleanor. 'The Hawk of Achill or the Legend of the Oldest Animals'. *Folklore*, XLIII (1932), 376-409.

Hyde, Douglas. *Legends of Saints and Sinners*. Dublin: Talbot Press, n.d.

Hyde, Douglas. *A Literary History of Ireland*. London: Fisher Unwin, 1899.

Hyde, Douglas, ed. *Songs Ascribed to Raftery*. New York: Barnes and Noble, 1973.

Inglis, Tom. *Moral Monopoly: the Catholic Church in modern Irish society*. Dublin: Gill and Macmillan; New York: St. Martins Press, 1987.

Jackson, Holbrook. *The Eighteen Nineties: a review of art and ideas at the close of the nineteenth century*. London: Grant Richards, 1913, repr. 1976.

Jackson, Kenneth H. *A Celtic Miscellany*. London: Routledge and Kegan Paul, 1951.

Jung, Karl. *Man and his Symbols*. London: Aldus Books, 1964.

Kelleher, J. V. 'On a Poem about Gormlaith'. *Éigse*, XVI, 4 (1976), 251-254.

Kennedy, Patrick. *Legendary Fictions of the Irish Celts*. London: Macmillan, 1866.

Keogh, Dermot. *The Vatican, the Bishops and Irish Politics 1919-39*. Cambridge: Cambridge UP., 1986.

Knott, Eleanor, ed. *Poems of Tadhg Dall O hUiginn*. London: Irish Texts Society, 2 vols, 1922 and 1926.

Knott, Eleanor. *Irish Classical Poetry.* Dublin: Cultural Relations Committee, 1957.

Larminie, William. *Fand and other poems.* Dublin: Hodges Figgis, 1892.

Larminie, William, 'The Development of English Metres'. *Contemporary Review,* 66 (1894), 717-736.

Lee, Joseph. *The Modernisation of Irish Society, 1848-1918.* Dublin: Gill and Macmillan, 1973.

Lehmann, Ruth P. M. 'A Study of Buile Shuibhne'. *Etudes Celtiques,* VI (1954-55), 289-311; VII (1955-56), 115-138.

Lehmann, Ruth P. M., trans. and ed. *Early Irish Verse.* Austin: University of Texas, 1982.

MacCana, Proinsias. 'Aspects of the Theme of King and Goddess in Irish Literature'. *Etudes Celtiques,* VII (1955-56), 76-114; VIII (1958-59), 59-65.

MacCana, Proinsias. 'A Poem Attributed to Cormac Mac Cuileannáin (+908)'. *Celtica.* V (1960), 207-211.

MacCana, Proinsias. *Celtic Mythology.* London: Hamlyn, 1970.

MacCana, Proinsias. *Literature in Irish.* Dublin: Department of Foreign Affairs, 1980.

MacDonagh, Thomas. *Literature in Ireland: studies Irish and Anglo-Irish.* Dublin: Talbot Press, 1916.

Mac Eóin, Gearóid. 'Gleann Bolcain agus Gleann na nGeilt'. *Bealoideas,* XXX (1962), 105-120.

McHugh, Roger and Maurice Harmon. *A Short History of Anglo-Irish Literature from its Origins to the Present Day.* Dublin: Wolfhound, 1982.

McHugh, Roger and Philip Edwards, eds. *Jonathan Swift. A Dublin Centenary Tribute 1667-1967.* Dublin: Dolmen, 1967.

McKenna, Lambert, ed. *Dán Dé: the poems of Donnchadh Mór Ó Dálaigh, and the religious poems in the Dunaire of the Yellow Book of Lecan.* Dublin: Educational Company of Ireland, n.d.

McKenna, Lambert, trans. and ed. *Aithdíoghluim Dána: a miscellany of Irish bardic poetry.* Dublin: Irish Texts Society, 37, 40 (1939, 1940).

MacManus, Francis, ed. *The Yeats We Knew.* Cork: Mercier, 1965.

MacNéill, Máire. 'The Legend of the False God's Daughter'. *Journal of the Royal Society of Antiquaries,* 1949.

MacReamoinn, Seán, ed. *The Pleasures of Gaelic Poetry.* London: Allen Lane, 1982.

Mahony, Tina Hunt. 'The Dublin Verse-Speaking Society and the Lyric Theatre'. *Irish University Review,* IV, 1 (Spring 1974), 488-489.

Mayer, David. *Harlequin in his Element: the English pantomime, 1806-1836.* Cambridge: Harvard UP., 1969.

Mendilow, A. A. *Time and the Novel.* London: Peter Nevitt, 1952.

Mercier, Vivian. *Irish Comic Tradition.* Oxford: Clarendon, 1962.

Meyer, Kuno, ed. *Aislinge Meic Conglinne: the Vision of MacConglinne: a Middle Irish wonder tale.* London: Nutt: Nutt, 1892.

Meyer, Kuno, ed. *Anecdota from Irish Mss.* vol. 1. Dublin: Hodges Figgis, 1907.

Moody, T. W., F. X. Martin, F. J. Byrne, eds. *New History of Ireland,* III. Oxford: Oxford UP., 1976.

Moore, Patrick. *Watchers of the Stars: the scientific revolution.* London: Michael Joseph, 1974.

Murphy, Denis, ed. *Annals of Clonmacnoise.* Translator Conell Mageoghagan. Dublin: University Press, 1896.

Murphy, Gerard. 'The Lament of the Old Woman of Bear'. *Proceedings of the Royal Irish Academy,* LV (Feb. 1953), 83-109.

Murphy, Gerard. *The Ossianic Lore and Romantic Tales of Medieval Ireland.* Dublin: Cultural Relations Committee, 1955.

Murphy, Gerard. *Saga and Myth in Ancient Ireland.* Dublin: Sign of the Three Candles, 1961.

Nathan, Leonard E. *The Tragic Drama of W. B. Yeats.* New York: Columbia UP., 1965.

Nesbit, Edith. 'Whereyouwantogoto, or the bouncible ball'. *Strand Magazine,* XVIII (1899), 584-592.

Ní Chatháin, Proinseas und Michael Richter, eds. *Irland und Europa. Die Kirche im Frühmittelalter. [Ireland and Europe. The Early Church].* Stuttgart: Klett, Cotta, (1984).

Nic Philibin, Mairghréaid, ed. *Na Caisidigh agus a gcuid Filídheachta.* Baile Átha Cliath: Oifig an tSoláthair, 1938.

Nutt, Alfred. *The Celtic Doctrine of Rebirth.* London: David Nutt, 1897.

O'Brien, Henry. *The Round Towers of Ireland; or the Mysteries of Freemasonry, of Sabianism, and of Buddhism, for the first time unveiled.* London: Whittaker, 1834.

O'Brien, John A., ed. *The Vanishing Irish: the enigma of the modern world.* New York: McGraw Hill, 1953.

Ó Cathasaigh, Tomás. *The Heroic Biography of Cormac Mac Airt.* Dublin: Institute for Advanced Studies, 1977.

Ó Coileáin, Seán. 'The Structure of a Literary Cycle'. *Eriú,* XXV (1974), 88-125.

Ó Cuiv, Brian. 'The Romance of Mis and Dubh Ruis'. *Celtica,* 11 (1954), 325-333.

Ó Cuiv, Brian. 'Cath Maige Tuired'. *Irish Sagas,* ed. Myles Dillon. Dublin: Stationery Office, 1959, 24-50.

Ó Cuiv, Brian. 'A Poem Composed for Cathal Croibhdhearg O Conchubhair'. *Eriú,* XXXIV (1984), 157-174.

O'Curry, Eugene. *Lectures on the Manuscript Materials of Ancient Irish History.* Dublin: James Duffy, 1861.

O'Daly, John, ed. *Irish Language Miscellany: a selection of poems by the Munster bards of the last century.* Dublin: John O'Daly, 1896.

O'Daly, Mairín. 'Tógúil Bruidne Da Derga'. *Irish Sagas,* ed. Myles Dillon. Dublin: Stationery Office, 1959.

O Donnchadha, Tadhg. *Filidheacht Fiannaigheachta.* Baile Átha Cliath: Comhlucht Oideachais na hÉireann, 1933.

O'Dwyer, Peter. *The Spirituality of the Céli Dé Reform Movement in Ireland 750-900.* Dublin: Carmelite Publications, 1977.

O'Faolain, Sean. 'The Dáil and the Bishops'. *The Bell,* XVII, 3 (June 1951), 5-13.

O'Grady, Standish H., trans. Donnchadh Ruadh MacConmara *Adventures of a Luckless Fellow.* Dublin: n.p., 1853.

O'Grady, Standish H., ed. *Tóraigheacht Dhiarmada agus Gráinne: the pursuit of Diarmuid and Grainne. Transactions of the Ossianic Society,* III. Dublin: O'Daly, 1857.

O'Grady, Standish H., ed. *Silva Gadelica: a collection of tales in Irish.* London: Williams and Norgate, 1892.

O'Grady, Standish H. *The Flight of the Eagle.* London: Lawrence and Bullen, 1897.

O'Keeffe, J. G., ed. *Buile Shuibhne.* London: Irish Texts Society, 1913.

O'Máille, Tomás, ed. *The Poems of Carolan.* London: Irish Texts Society, 1916.

O'Meara, John. *Eriugena.* Cork: Mercier, 1969.

O'Rahilly, T. F., ed. *Measgra Dánta: miscellaneous Irish poems.* Dublin, Cork: Cork UP., 1927.

O'Rahilly, T. F. 'On the Origin of the Names Erainn and Eriú'. *Eriú,* XIV, 1943-1946 (1946), 7-28.

O'Rahilly, T. F. 'Lost Legends of Mis and Dubh Ruis'. *Celtica,* 1 (1950), 382-384.

Ó Súilleabháin, Tomás Ruadh. *Songs.* Dublin: Gill, 1914.

O'Sullivan, Anne. 'Triamhuin Ghormlaithe'. *Eriú,* XVI (1952), 189-199.

O'Sullivan, Donal. *Carolan: the life, times and music of an Irish harper.* 2 vols. London: Routledge and Kegan Paul, 1958.

Palmer, Herbert Edward. *Post-Victorian Poetry.* London: Dent, 1938.

Peers, E. Allison, ed. *Complete Works of Saint John of the Cross.* London: Burns, Oates and Washbourne, 1934.

Peers, E. Allison, ed. *Complete Works of Saint Teresa of Jesus.* London: Sheed and Ward, 1946.

Petrie, George. *The Ecclesiastical Architecture of Ireland anterior to the Anglo-Norman Invasion: comprising an essay on the origins and uses of the Round Towers of Ireland which obtained the gold medal and prize of the Royal Irish Academy.* Dublin: Hodges Figgis, 2nd ed., 1845.

Poulet, George. *Studies in Human Time.* Baltimore: John Hopkins UP., 1956.

Prior, Moody. *The Language of Tragedy.* New York: Columbia UP., 1947.

Rees, Alwyn and Brindley. *Celtic Heritage.* London: Thames and Hudson, 1961.

Robins, Joseph. *Fools and Mad: a history of the insane in Ireland.* Dublin: Institute of Public Administration, 1986.

Rodenbach, Georges R. C. *Oeuvres,* 2 vols. Paris: Mercure de France, 1923.

Rolleston, T. W. *Myths and Legends of the*

Celtic Race. London: Harrap, 1911.

Shearman, Hugh. *How the Church of Ireland was Disestablished*. Dublin: Church of Ireland Disestablishment Centenary Committee, 1970.

Sigerson, George, trans. and ed. *Bards of the Gael and Gall*. London: Unwin, 1897.

Silke, John J. 'The Irish Abroad, 1534-1691'. *New History of Ireland*, III. Eds. T. W. Moody, F. X. Martin, F. J. Byrne. Oxford: Clarendon, 1976.

Staniforth, Maxwell, translated by *Marcus Aurelius Meditations*. Harmondsworth: Penguin, 1964.

Stokes, George T. *Ireland and the Celtic Church*. London: Hodder and Stoughton, 1886.

Stokes, Margaret. *The Early Christian Architecture in Ireland*. London: George Bell, 1878.

Stokes, Whitley, ed. *Sanas Chormaic: Cormac's glossary*. Translated by John O'Donovan. Calcutta: Irish Archaeological and Celtic Society, 1868.

Stokes, Whitley, translated by 'Aided Conculaind'. *Revue Celtique*, 3 (1877), 175-185.

Stokes, Whitley. *Lives of the Saints from the Book of Lismore*. Oxford: Clarendon, 1890.

Stokes, Whitley, ed. *The Martyrology of Oengus*. London: Henry Bradshaw Society, 1905, repr. (1984).

Stone, J. M. *Reformation and Renaissance*. London: Duckworth, 1904.

Thurneysen, Rudolf. 'Ceth Maige Turedh'. *Zeitschrift für Celtische Philologie*, XII (1918), 401-402.

Todd, J. H., translated by *The War of the Gaedhil with the Gaill, or the Invasions by the Danes and other Norsemen*. London: Longmans, Green, 1867.

Trench, Herbert. *Deirdre Wedded*. London: Methuen, 1901.

Ussher, James. *Works*, ed. C. R. Erlington. Dublin: Hodges & Smith, 1857-1864, 17v. Vol. 4, 432-443.

Verhaeren, Emile. *The Plays of Emile Verhaeren*. Translated by Arthur Symons, *et al*. London: Constable, 1916.

Verhaeren, Emile. *Poèmes*. Paris: Mercure de France, 1917.

Verhaeren, Emile. *Choix de Poèmes*. Paris: Mercure de France, 1935.

Von Hamel, A. G. 'The Celtic Grail'. *Revue Celtique*, 47 (1930), 340-381.

Waddell, Helen. *The Wandering Scholars*. London: Constable, 1927.

Whyte, J. H. *Church and State in Ireland 1923-1970*. Dublin: Gill and Macmillan, 1971.

Williams, Raymond. *Drama from Ibsen to Eliot*. New York: Oxford UP., 1953.

INDEX

A

Abbey Theatre, 11, 115
'Abbey Theatre Fire, The', 150, 184, 184-6, 187-8
Abelard, Peter, 90
Acallamh na Senorach 30, 91
Adrian IV, Pope, 168
'*Adventures of Leithin, The*', *130*
'*Afterthought*', *222*
'*Aisling*', *60, 66, 72-3, 74, 199-200*
Aislinge Meic Conglinne, 118
'Aisling Meabhuil', 199
Albert, 90
Aloysius Gonzaga, St, 174
Alphonsus Liguori, St, 175, 240
Altram Tige da Medar, 108-9, 132
'Ancient Lights', 18, 155-9, 161, 253
  theme of deliverance in, 154, 155-9, 235, 242, 243, 245
Ancient Lights, 36, 138-47, 150, 152-3, 248, 251
Aongus, 50, 52,131
As the Crow Flies, 35, 130-2, 133, 134, 137
Audoen, St, 177-8
Augustine, St, 158
Aurelius, 179-80

B

Bale, Bishop, 233
Beckett, Samuel, 92
Beckett, Thomas, 68
Bede, Venerable, 119, 122
Belvedere College, 9, 16, 21, 174
'Bequests', 143
Bergin, Osborn, 67
Bernadette, St, 235, 230-40
Bernard, St, 34, 168
'Beyond the Pale', 189
Binyon, Laurence, 55
'Blackbird of Derrycairn, The', 143
Black Fast, 34, 118, 119-23, 137
'Blessing', 39
Bolingbroke, Henry St John, 233
Book of Durrow, 33
Book of Invasions, 28, 64, 164
Book of Kells, 33, 40, 64-5
Bottomley, Gordon, 116, 117

Bright Temptation, The, 28, 30-2, 91-9, 137, 235, 240, 247
  banned, 10
  comic spirit in, 38, 96
  sexuality in, 95, 135, 253
Brigid, St, 74-5
Browne, Archbishop George, 233
Browne, Dr Noel, 141-2, 145
Buile Shuibhne, 45
'Burial of an Irish President', 191-3
Burke, William, 177
Byrne, Francis John, 70

C

Calderon, 132
'Cardplayer, The', 60
Carmelites, 169, 196-7
Carney, James, 25
Cashel, 61, 63-5, 75, 99, 101-2, 182
Cathach, The, 64
Catholicism, 32-5
  influence of, 14-18, 37, 77-90
Catholic Truth Society, 15
Cattledrive in Connaught, The 10, 26, 29, 59, 135
Cearbhall, King of Leinster, 67, 104, 105
'Celebrations', 139-41, 245
'Celibacy', 35, 60, 65-6
censorship, 10, 14, 85-6
'Centenary Tribute, The', 228
Cervantes adaptations, 118, 127
'Choice, The', 147
'Christmas Eve', 150
Cistercians, 34, 168
civil war, 10, 91, 169, 176
Clarke, Austin
  life
    childhood, 9
    and Gaelic League, 21-7
    health, 10, 11, 28, 159
    influence of Catholicism, 9, 16-18, 37
    and Irish Literary Revival, 9-10, 18-21
    at UCD, 9-10, 18
  themes
    autobiography, 48, 139, 152-3, 154-83, 189-90, 221, 252